*ALGEBRA AND CALCULUS
FOR BUSINESS*

ALGEBRA AND CALCULUS
FOR BUSINESS

THOMAS R. DYCKMAN
Cornell University

L. JOSEPH THOMAS
Cornell University

Prentice-Hall, Inc., *Englewood Cliffs, New Jersey*

Library of Congress Cataloging in Publication Data

DYCKMAN, THOMAS R

  Algebra and calculus for business.

  1. Business mathematics. 2. Algebra. 3. Calculus.
I. Thomas, L. Joseph, 1942, joint author. II. Title.
HF5691.D95   510′ .2′4338   73-22413
ISBN 0-13-021758-1

Printed in the United States of America

10 9

PRENTICE-HALL INTERNATIONAL, INC., *London*
PRENTICE-HALL OF AUSTRALIA, PTY. LTD., *Sydney*
PRENTICE-HALL OF CANADA, LTD., *Toronto*
PRENTICE-HALL OF INDIA PRIVATE LIMITED, *New Delhi*
PRENTICE-HALL OF JAPAN, INC., *Tokyo*

Contents

v

Preface

This text is designed for either a one-semester or one-quarter review and introduction to the basic mathematical skills required for the study of managerial problems. It is intended for students needing a refresher course in basic mathematics for management before beginning other course work. The topics covered are:

    I.   Algebra
        A. Algebra: Chapters 1–6
        B. Matrix Algebra and Linear Programming: Chapters 7–8
  II. Calculus
        A. Differential Calculus: Chapters 9–12
        B. Integral Calculus: Chapters 13–15
 III. Introductory Set Theory: Chapter 16

Although we assume the reader has been exposed to basic algebra at some previous time, the discussion develops the necessary ideas afresh. No background in mathematics at the college level is required to master the materials covered. Indeed, this book is not written for the mathematician. We have attempted to use the reader's intuition wherever possible, even if at times it may violate precise mathematical rigor. We are concerned with communicating to an audience that does not consider itself mathematically sophisticated but still needs to understand and be able to apply some of the basic ideas.

Each chapter normally requires one week's work in a 3-hour, one-semester course. Since the amount of time available differs from school to school, it may be necessary to either omit or combine some of the materials. If after electing to omit certain chapters, the number of chapters exceeds the number of weeks available, we suggest combining some chapters until the course constraints are met. The following combinations are suggested in order:

1. Chapters 1 and 2
2. Chapters 7 and 8
3. Chapters 5 and 6
4. Chapters 10 and 11
5. Chapters 14 and 15

Certain sections are starred. These sections can be omitted without loss of continuity or ideas essential to understanding later material. The set material is placed in Chapter 16 since despite its importance we do not use it elsewhere in this book. The topic is commonly used in texts on statistics and probability.

Some of you may wish to use this book as a review or as a text for self-study. We have tried to design it so this can be done. At the end of each section a review problem is given and solved. Try to work it before checking the solution. This should help you decide whether to review the section or go on to the next one. A list of problems that cover the basic ideas of each chapter is given at the beginning of each chapter's problems for those interested in self-study. These problems should be attempted before you go ahead to the next chapter. Answers are provided at the end of the book.

For those following a self-study program we suggest that you allocate two hours of continuous reading at least every other day, three days a week. It is reasonable to expect to complete one chapter a week, including the review problem material, on this schedule.

We caution the student that mathematics has neither a plot nor a cast of characters that permit it to be read as a novel. The student should attempt quantitative materials only when he is alert. This is not bedtime reading.

Perhaps a few hints are in order on how to get the most from this book. We suggest a quick reading to get an overview of a chapter section. At this point do not stop to underline, work examples, or puzzle over difficult passages. Follow this quick reading immediately, if possible, with a slow and careful reading. Keep your pencil and a scratch pad close at hand to work out difficulties. We have provided a review problem with an answer at the end of each section. Work these problems during your second reading. Try to work the problem without referring to the solution. If you can do these review problems, you are ready to continue to the next section. If you have trouble with them, it suggests that a review of the section's central ideas is in order.

After completing all the sections of a chapter in this fashion, try to work the problems assigned by your instructor. Some problems have answers at the back of the book. Other problems, indicated by an asterisk, are provided without answers. We believe that some work without the possibility of referring to an answer is useful. You will probably find it necessary at times to return to the text material to work some of the assigned problems. This should be expected and should not cause you undue concern. Most ideas do not crystallize until one works with them awhile.

Even at this point some of the ideas may elude you. If this is the case, we suggest you set the text aside for a day or so and then try these difficult places again. If you still experience trouble, do not continue to spend exorbitant amounts of time trying to resolve your difficulties alone. Your problem may be cleared up in a class lecture. If not, it is time to see your class instructor. You should be prepared to ask about your difficulty with intelligence and be ready to profit from discussion. Often your instructor can quickly clear up points that, at this stage, would require more of your time than they are worth. In mathematics when you don't understand something you are usually aware of it. And, if you have given it a reasonable effort, it is easy to overcommit your time to this subject to the detriment of your other studies. That is why we urge you to seek help at this stage of your study.

Mathematics, once mastered, will return with use. But, as with all learned skills, lack of use causes the concepts and methods to become rusty. Hence, periodic review of your notes and of the text is advisable. We urge you not to attempt to memorize the rules and procedures discussed. Learn how they work and understand them. You can always refer to the text for rules as they are needed. If, by chance, you use a rule often, it will naturally become part of your memory, and that is as it should be.

Sometimes it is not clear just how different concepts fit together. Typically, you will have a substantial number of the important ideas in place, much like working a jigsaw puzzle, but the overall picture continues to be elusive. Failure to see the entire picture and comprehend its message can obscure the fact that many of the major ideas have been grasped. Hence, this failure can lead to despair. There is no easy solution to this common difficulty except to be forewarned. It is fortunately true that a single new insight will often supply the connective piece necessary to clarify at least a significant segment of the total picture.

One of the major difficulties experienced by many students of mathematics is in notation. Care has been taken in this book to specify the meaning of new symbols. A list of the symbols together with their English translations appears at the end of each chapter. Once mastered, mathematics offers an efficient means of expressing complex ideas in an unambiguous fashion, and in a way such that new insights can be more easily reached than if verbal reasoning were used alone.

We have had substantial success with these materials and owe a great deal to our former students who have helped refine them to their present status. We would like to acknowledge Professor Robert L. Childress, University of Southern California, Dr. John E. Freund, and Professor Jay E. Strum, New York University, for their help in reviewing the manuscript. We also wish to express our appreciation to Mr. Robert Magee who developed much of the problem material and to Mesdames O. Weeks, M. Lee, P. Lee, M. Snedden, L. King, and E. Lovell who contributed long hours of transcribing our illegible scrawls. Finally, our foremost debt is to our families, who tolerate these frivolous escapades that their husbands stubbornly refuse to abandon in hopes that sales will justify what promises cannot.

Comments from users will be most welcome.

THOMAS R. DYCKMAN
L. JOSEPH THOMAS

ALGEBRA AND CALCULUS
FOR BUSINESS

1

Introduction

About 400 A.D. Saint Augustine remarked: "The good Christian should beware of mathematicians and all those who make empty prophecies. The danger already exists that the mathematicians have made a covenant with the Devil to darken the spirit and to confine man in the bonds of Hell." Perhaps most of us would take a less extreme position, even admitting to certain practical uses to which this specialized activity of mathematics could be directed. Certainly mathematics is useful in the calculation of taxes (an activity closely associated with its origins), the determination of costs used to select among alternative courses of action, and in developing descriptive measures of objects or processes—to mention but a few of its uses. But most of us would reply that we are already quite well equipped to deal with such calculations and that to be further subjected to these technical matters is an inappropriate use of the limited time we have available to learn.

There are two possible justifications for further exposure to this black art. It may, in fact, be true that you have already mastered a sufficiency of mathematics (the discovered truths) to allow you success in your chosen pursuits. But you cannot be sure. The explosion in knowledge and its application to managerial problems will yield new and useful mathematical techniques. These techniques will be available to you only if you are sufficiently trained to read about them and understand their use. This does not mean reading scientific journals; it means reading periodicals such as the *Harvard Business Review* and the *Financial Analysts Journal*. These and other periodicals are written for the manager and include new developments and actual applications (of mathematics as well as other areas) in his field. A good example is the application of a technique known as linear programming. One use of this technique is to solve problems in which the manager wishes to make something (say

1

profits) as large as possible subject to restrictions (or constraints) on his actions. For example, he may be limited by the productive capacity of his plant or by the market demand for his product. This technique was developed in the late forties and early fifties by economists and mathematicians to solve resource-allocation problems. The applications of linear programming to managerial problems are now extensive and are being realized only as more managers understand the subject and its limitations. The basic ideas of linear programming are not difficult, but it remains true that managers with better skills in (and perhaps less fear of) mathematics are in a position to make earlier and more profitable use of the technique as well as understand its limitations. Indeed, we will introduce you later to the basic elements of linear programming.

Let us share with you another example, one from our personal experience. A recent graduate of one master's program in business was assigned a job in the area of planning and control for a large manufacturing firm. In the course of his work he concluded that the firm's inventory policy was costing more than it should. He developed some simple rules based on the inventory techniques he studied in his master's program, techniques that he estimated would produce a net saving of nearly $100,000 per year. In spite of the magnitude of the expected savings, he experienced great difficulty in convincing his superior of the advantages of his suggestions. The difficulty was due largely to the fact that his superior was not adequately trained to understand the elementary but nonintuitive results of inventory control theory. Hence he remained skeptical of his assistant's analysis. Fortunately the story has a happy ending. About a year after the assistant first proposed his inventory plan, the superior attended an extensive executive development program. Here he was exposed overtime and in a different environment to many new ideas, including an introduction to the basic concepts of inventory control. Returning to his firm, he was quick to put the assistant's plan in action. During the next two years, a slightly modified plan saved the company a total of $325,000.

A subsidiary question is suggested by this anecdote. Are your skills adequate to evaluate future proposals that may come to your attention? Perhaps it would be fairer to ask whether they are adequate to permit you to continue learning the requisite skills.

The second justification for further work concerns your skill with mathematics, that is, with the *methods* used to discover the truths we call Mathematics. In a very real sense, this is the more important issue. It is this skill that permits one to see commonalities across situations and hence bring his knowledge of one situation to bear on another. This skill is the one that also allows for the convenient handling of long and complicated chains of reasoning. The ability to abstract from the situational content of a particular problem will often lead to insights not otherwise available. For example, it might surprise you to learn that the determination of the best allocation of scarce production resources among several end products or services, the assignment of a pool of individuals to a set of jobs, and the optimal location of distribution outlets can all be dealt with using a particular mathematical approach: linear programming.

But the power of abstraction is even greater. The flexibility in mathematical concepts can be extended to new situations. The development of binary and hexadecimal number systems and their importance in electronic computation, a subject discussed briefly in Chapter 2, is an example. This example suggests that we may at times see familiar symbols used in unfamiliar ways when they are applied to managerial problems.

Consider the statement $8 + 9 = 5$. This may appear nonsensical at first until it is pointed out that, for his purposes, someone has numbered the months consecutively beginning with January. The statement implies that the ninth month after August is May. The assignment of numbers to months may be convenient for the resolution of a particular problem and yet quite confusing otherwise—unless care is taken to spell out the particular use being made of the symbols and what operations with them are valid. The question, as one author puts it, is: "Who is in charge, the symbols or the user?" The author answers that he is, and if he is careful in definition, he may go about his business using the convenience of this new numerical assignment. Many substantial advances in theory and practice have been made in this way. Yet it may often seem, as Bertrand Russell observed, that "mathematics may be defined as the subject in which we never know what we are talking about, nor whether what we are saying is true." Hopefully, for most of what we want to do this will not be the case.

A coincident advantage obtained by being able to conceptualize (some would say model) or think abstractly about a problem is that it may suggest sources of problem assistance. Experts in various mathematical methods can be hired or they may already be available. But it is the irritation of the manager which needs to be formed into a problem. The mathematician can help him if the manager can do two things. First the manager must be able to abstract enough to see if he has a potential problem amenable to mathematical analysis and, if so, what type of mathematical skills are required. Second, the manager must be able to communicate the essence of the problem to the expert and to assist him in evaluating the adequacy of any assumptions made in resolving the problem. The inventory-control case discussed earlier represents a situation in which the manager was unable even to begin this important process. We do not imply that all or even most problems yield to mathematical analysis, but we do say that the more perspectives one can obtain on a problem, the more likely it is that a satisfactory solution will be found. The manager is well advised to adopt the practice of many expert golfers—who warily circle the green, pausing, and even crouching down at times to examine a bump here and an undulation there before stroking a critical putt.

The notion of communication is essential to our discussion so far. The communication of thoughts and ideas is ordinarily associated with the concept of language. It thus may come as no surprise that, for our purposes, it is very useful to consider mathematics as a language.

1-1 MATHEMATICS AS A LANGUAGE

As a noted mathematician has said: "One of the indisputable characteristics of mathematics is that it is a rigorous language with practically no synonyms." This permits us to be precise about what we communicate. But this very precision causes difficulties for some students. Charlie Brown of *Peanuts* put it this way: "My trouble with mathematics is that I'm at my best in something where the answers are mostly a matter of opinion."

We seldom stop to consider the fact that language and mathematics both rely heavily on symbols. For example, in the English language words are constructed from a set of 26 letters. These 26 letters are in turn merely symbols. When properly combined under an appropriate set of rules, words or groups of words convey an idea. Similarly with mathematics: symbols, alone or combined in accordance with the rules of the mathematics in use, also convey ideas.

The English language uses symbols other than letters to assist in the communication process. Periods, parentheses, question marks, exclamation points, commas, and so on are common. Many of these symbols (for example, parentheses) and a host of other symbols are used in mathematics. Examples of these include $\sqrt{\ }, \pi, =$, and $+$. In addition, mathematics occasionally uses a symbol or word from the English (or some other) language to represent an entire idea. The letter e, for example, stands for the number 2.71828 . . .(where the dots indicate that the decimal continues without any regularity). The number e is (as we shall see) very common in mathematics.

Anything that can be stated mathematically can be written out fully in English. The familiar $2 + 2 = 4$ becomes: two plus two is (or equals) four. But mathematicians are basically lazy (some more charitable observers would say efficient) and resort to symbols for words or groups of words to ease the expositional task. In this approach they mirror the secretary's use of shorthand to take dictation. Symbolic notation has still another advantage: it permits one to apply the rules of mathematics to the symbols in order to obtain new results. Using $2 + 2 = 4$ we recall, perhaps from our distant past, that the rules of mathematics permit us to add any quantity to the left-hand side of this equality as long as we add the same quantity to the right-hand side. Using the equation $2 + 2 = 4$ as an example, we may write $3 + 2 + 2 = 3 + 4$, or $7 = 7$. Again we could have said this in English: adding three to two plus two yields three plus four. But once the reader becomes familiar with the mathematical shorthand, its convenience and efficiency is compelling.

Many students are uneasy with those symbols that are new to them. This unfamiliarity leads to both frustration and a desire not to have anything to do with the subject. This understandable feeling can be allayed somewhat if the student will write out the unfamiliar mathematical symbol or statement in English until he becomes accustomed mentally to making the translation. To assist in this process, all symbols used are given word equivalents, and a summary list of these appears at the end of each chapter.

Many other parallels could be drawn between the language of English and the language of Mathematics. However, additional examples are unnecessary. If you will keep in mind the following basic thought, the subject matter of this book should be much easier for you.

Mathematical symbols are a special kind of shorthand. Any set of mathematical symbols can be expressed as an English word, phrase, or sentence, and it is usually helpful to do so, at least mentally.

Let's show our mastery over the concept of a symbol by inventing one of our own that will serve a very special purpose in this book. We are, quite often, going to ask you to become an active participant in the learning process. This we plan to do by asking that you solve problems and answer questions as we go along. If you are able to solve these problems and answer the questions correctly, you should continue your study with a feeling of confidence that you have understood what has transpired so far. If you have trouble with the question, it suggests that you have not completely mastered the related material and that a review may prove useful. In many books these types of exercises are informal and are suggested by a sentence beginning with the phrase "the student should." Shorthand for this expression is ⚲ . Combining these symbols, we generate the symbol ⚲ , which will signal that it is time for you to get your pencil ready. Let's try a couple.

⚲ : Complete the sentence, giving words to the following English and mathematical symbols.

In English

1. Dear Bill:
   The symbol: means _____.
2. Look out!
   The symbol ! indicates _____.

In Mathematics

    1. <
       The symbol < stands for_____.

    2. X^2
       The number 2 says_____.

Answers. The colon indicates a pause in the exposition. The symbol ! indicates surprise or exclamation. In mathematics the symbol < denotes "is less than" (for example, $2 < 4$). The number 2 as a *superscript* to X says multiply X by itself: $(X)(X)$. Did you recall these ideas? If not, don't worry. You will see them again.

1-2 SYMBOLS AND THEIR USES IN MATHEMATICS

Symbols have three separate uses in mathematics. These are (1) to represent constants, (2) to represent variables, and (3) to represent operations. Let's consider each of these uses separately.

Constants

Constants in mathematics are the equivalent of proper nouns in English. They stand for a specific thing. The numeral 3 stands for the number concept 3. (Note that the number is a concept, an abstract idea, whereas the numeral is a concrete symbol that stands for or represents the concept.) Other examples include 10^{100} (given the name googool by a very small boy, it represents a "large" number); π (the circumference of a circle with a diameter of one unit); $\sqrt{4}$; 0; and $(3 + 5)^2$, or 64.

It is sometimes necessary to specify a certain number that is a constant but that is unknown at the moment. For example, suppose that an individual wishes to know how much tax he will pay on a potential salary increase of \$1,000. He needs to know the appropriate tax rate given his new income level. This is a unique number, a constant, although it may be unknown to him. If he knew it, he would simply multiply the \$1,000 salary increase by this tax rate to determine that portion of the \$1,000 that would be surrendered in tax. Mathematically, if the tax rate is represented by the letter b, the tax on his salary increase is \$1,000b.

When it is desired to specify that a particular value is a constant but we either don't want to specify it or don't know its value, the constant is denoted by a letter typically taken from the early part of our alphabet: a, b, c, and so on. Sometimes, however, other letters are used when the appeal is natural, such as t for time or r for rate. And it is not uncommon for mathematicians to borrow from other languages (in particular from the Greek) for such purposes. Contrary to popular belief, this is not done merely to protect the priestly secrets, but because our own alphabet is not adequately rich in symbols to satisfy all the demands placed on it. Furthermore, tradition limits change; for example, the use of the Greek lowercase π (pi) to represent the constant 3.141592 . . . has been with us since first used by Greek mathematicians.

A very special constant in mathematics is zero, 0. The discovery of the number zero is a relatively recent event in the history of mathematics. Indeed, its invention preceded by several centuries its discovery as a concept.

Operations with zero are important and some of them are not obvious. A brief review is in order. Consider the following operations which involve zero and the number 8.

(1) $0 + 8 = 8$ (4) $0 \div 8 = 0$

(2) $0 - 8 = -8$ (5) $8 \div 0$ is impossible

(3) $0 \cdot 8 = 0$ (6) $0 \div 0$ is undefined (or indeterminant)

The first point to be made is that any nonzero constant could be used in place of 8 without changing the results indicated. The unusual situations are represented by cases (5) and (6). Case (5) is explained as follows. If eight divided by four has an answer, two, then four multiplied by this answer must be eight. Similarly, if eight divided by zero has an answer, then zero multiplied by this answer must be eight. But zero multiplied by anything is still zero. Thus, there is no answer to this problem; it is impossible. Similarly for case (6), if zero divided by zero gives an answer, then zero times this answer again gives zero. But any number multiplied by zero is zero. Hence any number satisfies the division required in case (6), and we say that no unique answer is specified; the answer is undefined.

The discussion so far has dealt with whole numbers and in particular what mathematicians call the counting numbers (the positive integers): 1, 2, 3, ... To these we have just added in our discussion the special constant zero. Other sets of numbers include the negative integers (as early as the twelfth century the Italian mathematician Fibonacci observed that a business loss could be viewed as a negative profit, although the negative integers were not discovered until the seventeenth century), the fractions, and the irrational numbers (those that cannot be expressed as fractions). These number sets combine to form the real number system, a representation of which is given in Figure 1–1. There are other numbers, with the intriguing name "imaginary numbers," but in this text we shall have use for the real numbers only.

$\sim\!\!\sqrt{}$: Circle the number where constants are defined.

1. Today's prime interest rate.

2. The average wage rate in the United States.

3. The variable cost of an electric motor during the last production period.

4. The proportion of defective parts produced by a given process.

FIGURE 1–1

The Real Number System

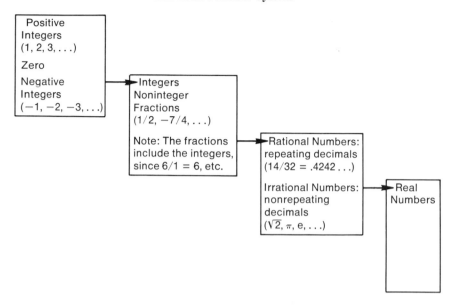

Answers.   Although it could be argued, items 1 and 3 are constants. If we modified item 2 to read last year's average wage rate, then we could consider it a constant even though we might not know its value. If we changed item 4 to read, in part, produced yesterday, then we could regard it as a constant, although its value may not yet be known until yesterday's production is fully inspected.

Variables

Variables in mathematics are the equivalent of common nouns in English. They stand for unspecified elements in a general class or set rather than for a specific member of the set. The words "congressmen" and "student" are common nouns. In mathematics, variables act as place holders for unknowns. The most common and familiar example is the use of the letter x to stand for the unknown in an equation. Another example is suggested by the phrase "let (the variable) Y represent the level of gross national product next year if the dollar is devalued."

In English the choice of article is helpful in specifying whether a specific or general object is being considered. *The* Senator refers to a particular individual, while *a* student refers to an unidentified member in the set of students. In mathematics we do not have symbols for the articles in English and must find other ways to denote variables. We shall adopt the generally accepted procedure of using letters near the end of the alphabet, such as x, y, and z, to represent variables.

$\sim\!\!\checkmark$: Circle the numbers where a letter is used as a variable.

1. x is an integer between 1 and 9 inclusive.
2. x marks the spot.
3. z is the last letter of the alphabet.
4. $3t = 18$.

Answers. In statements 1 and 4, the letter is used as a variable. In the other two cases, specific objects are implied. Case 4 is particularly important for two reasons. First, a letter other than x, y, and z is used as a variable. Second, any real number may be substituted for t even though only the substitution of 6 seems to make sense. The place holder t does not lose the characteristic of a variable just because it seems desirable to fill it with a particular real number.

1-3 OPERATIONS AND RELATIONSHIPS

The symbols that cause the most difficulty for students are those that direct him to perform an operation on or to interpret a relationship among a set of numbers. These symbols are often unfamiliar at first. The student may not even know their name, let along what, if anything, they demand of him. Several symbols of this kind will be introduced in this book and we must be careful to define each carefully. For the moment we hope to list and review a few symbols which are probably familiar to you.

Relationships

First there are several relationships of interest, the most important of which is given by the *equality symbol* $=$.

Symbol	*English Translation*
$=$	equals; is equal to

We have already used this symbol since we believe it is familiar to you. What appears on the left of the symbol must be numerically equal to what is on the right. It is like a balance. We may carry out any legitimate mathematical operation on the left-hand side as long as the same operation is repeated on the right-hand side. A simple extension of the equality relationship is its negation, or the *inequality relationship*.

Symbol	English Translation
$\neq$	does not equal; is not equal to

For example, $6 \neq 8$ states that the quantities separated by the symbol are not equal.

Occasionally, we may wish to *define* two quantities as being identical. The symbol $\equiv$ is used.

Symbol	English Translation
$\equiv$	is identical to; is defined to be

An example would be the mathematical expression for "let m be defined as the current borrowing rate." Then, $m \equiv$ current borrowing rate.

Sometimes it is useful to specify the ordered relationship between two mathematical expressions. For example, the amount of preservative to be used per 10-ounce loaf of bread, call it z, must be less than the federal limit, which we shall assume is 0.1 ounce. This is written using the order symbol, $<$, as $z < 0.1$. Other order relationships are written using the following symbols:

Symbol	English Translation
$<$	is less than
$\leq$	is at most; is less than or equal to
$>$	is greater than
$\geq$	is at least; is greater than or equal to

It is easy to remember which symbol to use if you remember that the closed end or point of the symbol always points to the smaller quantity.

As with the equality sign, the student may add and subtract the quantity on one side of an order symbol as long as the same operation is performed on the other side. This is also true of multiplication and division, with two exceptions. First, multiplying or dividing by a negative number changes the direction of the order relationship. Given $6 < 8$, then multiplying each side by negative two gives $-2(6) > -2(8)$ since $-12 > -16$. Second, division by zero is not allowed.

$\diagdown\!\diagup$: A drug company has 100 cc (cc stands for cubic centimeters, a volume measure in the metric system) of a special chemical which takes a month to be produced. No more of the chemical is available for another month. The chemical is used in the production of a drug called AKE; 3 cc of the chemical is required in 10 cc of AKE. There are 10 cc in one bottle of AKE. Circle the constraint below that indicates the limitation of the month's production due to the limited chemical supply.

1. $10x = 100$, where x is the number of bottles
2. $10x < 100$, where x is the number of bottles
3. $3x < 100$, where x is the number of bottles
4. $3x \leq 100$, where x is the number of bottles
5. $3x > 100$, where x is the number of bottles

Answer. Each bottle requires 3 cc of the chemical. If x is the number of bottles produced, then $3x$ is the amount of chemical used. This amount must be at most 100 cc. Thus answer 4 is correct. Such expressions are in common use in the mathematical technique called *linear programming*, which has many practical uses in management. (This technique is discussed in Chapter 8.)

Operations

The operation symbols are the most demanding. One with which you are already familiar from high school mathematics is the *square-root symbol*, $\sqrt{}$, which directs you to find a number (or expression) which when multiplied by itself gives the number (or expression) appearing under the root symbol. Thus $\sqrt{4}$ is 2 since $2 \cdot 2 = 4$. The root symbol can be extended to give the third root, $\sqrt[3]{}$, or the general nth root, $\sqrt[n]{}$, of the number under the root symbol. Thus the third root of 125, written $\sqrt[3]{125}$, is 5 since $5 \cdot 5 \cdot 5 = 125$.

The preceding paragraph illustrates another familiar operation symbol, which you probably didn't even notice. The dots between the 2s and between the 5s directs you to multiply the numbers together. We suspect that you are familiar with this symbol and so it caused you no difficulty. If we are careful with symbols we have not seen before, the same can be true for them.

Perhaps a new symbol to you is the *absolute-value symbol*. This symbol is represented by two vertical lines surrounding a mathematical expression, $|\ |$. The symbol directs the reader to perform all operations within the lines and then give a positive sign to the result. Thus $|-2 \cdot 3| = |-6| = 6$; the absolute-value signs require that the negative sign be dropped.

Symbol	*English Translation*
$|\ \ |$	Perform all operations within these lines and give the final result a positive sign.

A common task in business or administration is the summation of a series of quantities. The manager may wish to add up the sales for several months or for several salesmen. The treasurer may wish to sum the earnings from a set of securities, such as shares of stock. A health administrator may need to know the total patient hours requiring a certain treatment type; and so on. Consider, for example, the treasurer's problem. Suppose the organization holds stock in seven different firms. We can denote the earnings of security

1 in symbolic form by s_1, where the subscript 1 refers to the first security. Extending this approach, the organization's earnings for the seven securities can be written as

$$s_1 + s_2 + s_3 + s_4 + s_5 + s_6 + s_7.$$

Now, the mathematician, desiring simplicity and economy of expression, does not wish to write out such long sequences, particularly as the number of elements in the series gets quite large. So he borrows the symbol Σ, the Greek capital letter sigma, to designate a sum. If there is no possibility of confusion as to exactly what is to be summed, total security earnings might be written simply as

$$\sum s.$$

But to avoid confusion it is often useful to be more precise in specifying the exact operation to be performed. To this purpose the symbol is expanded to indicate how many items are to be summed. Rewriting the basic problem in more general mathematical form may help the reader to understand the symbol for summation. Total security earnings can be written as

$$s_1 + s_2 + \ldots + s_i + \ldots + s_7,$$

where the dots represent the terms not explicitly written but nevertheless belonging to the series. This method alone saves quite a bit of writing for a long series. Now using the subscript index i and the summation symbol, total security earnings are

$$\sum_{i=1}^{7} s_i.$$

Symbol	*English Translation*
$\sum_{i=1}^{n} x_i$	Add together the n values given to x.

Occasionally it may be necessary to multiply the terms together rather than to add them. Suppose that $1 is invested today in a savings account that pays compound interest each year. Suppose, further, that the rate of interest may change from year to year. How much is in the account in five years? Using subscript notation we let r_1 be the interest rate paid the first year. If this rate were 6 percent, the amount at the end of the first year would be $1.06. This can also be written $(1 + 0.06)$, or, in general, as $(1 + r_1)$. If the second year's rate were 0.05, then after 2 years of compounding the account would show $1.06 (1 + 0.05)$ dollars. In general terms, the amount at the end of the second year is $(1 + r_1) \cdot (1 + r_2)$. We may write the following general expression for the total value of the savings account in 5 years:

$$(1 + r_1) \cdot (1 + r_2) \cdot (1 + r_3) \cdot (1 + r_4) \cdot (1 + r_5).$$

Once again the mathematician has developed a shorthand symbol to represent the succession of similar multiplications. The symbol is the capital Greek letter pi, Π (not to be confused with the lowercase Greek letter pi, π, used to represent the constant $3.14\ldots$). If there is no possibility of confusion in the multiplication task, we may write simply

$$\Pi\,(1\,+\,r).$$

But it is also possible, as with summing, to be more explicit about the task. To do so for the current example we write

$$\prod_{i=1}^{5}\,(1\,+\,r_i).$$

Symbol	English Translation
$\displaystyle\prod_{i=1}^{n}\,x_i$	Multiply together the n values of x.

A useful fact to know about the sum (but not the product) symbol is that a term that is precisely the same in each of the elements to be summed can be brought (factored) outside the symbol. For example, given s_i as the dollar return on a single share of stock and an equal investment of 100 shares in each stock, total security returns on the seven-security portfolio would be

$$100s_1 + 100s_2 + \ldots + 100s_i + \ldots + 100s_7 = \sum_{i=1}^{7} 100s_i = 100 \sum_{i=1}^{7} s_i.$$

If different amounts, denoted by m_i for stock i, were invested in each stock, this factoring could not be done.

$$m_1s_1 + m_2s_2 + \ldots + m_is_i + \ldots + m_7s_7 = \sum_{i=1}^{7} m_is_i.$$

$\sim\!\!\checkmark$: A firm has 20 divisions with different assets. Each division earns a different rate of return on its total assets. Using A for assets and r for annual return, write an expression in the space below for the total annual dollar return to the firm.

Total return =

Answer. If we use the index i to represent the different divisions, the return for the general division is written r_iA_i. Either of the expressions below is correct, but the second is the more compact expression.

(1) $\quad r_1A_1 + r_2A_2 + \ldots + r_iA_i + \ldots + r_{20}A_{20}$

(2) $\quad \displaystyle\sum_{i=1}^{20} r_iA_i$

1-4 PARENTHESES

Mathematical expressions are often complex. Frequently several operations are required before a problem solution is obtained. Parentheses are used to indicate which operations are to be performed first. The general rule is always to begin within parentheses and work out. Thus the parentheses in the expression $9 - (8 - 3)$ direct us to consider the term $(8 - 3)$ first. After performing the subtraction and obtaining the result 5, the second subtraction, outside the parentheses, is performed, yielding $9 - (5)$, or 4.

It is possible to remove the parentheses as a first step, but care must be taken not to alter the meaning of the expression. The term $-(8 - 3)$ is identical to $-1(8 - 3)$ and states that all terms within are to be multiplied by -1. Hence $9 - 1(8 - 3)$ becomes $9 - 1(8) - 1(-3) = 9 - 8 + 3 = 4$. Sometimes it is necessary to remove parentheses in this way. (See case 2 in the ⌒⌒ below.) Still another use of parentheses is suggested here. They can be substituted for the dot multiplication symbol. Thus $5 \cdot 5$ can be written $5(5)$. Where confusion will not occur, even the parentheses are often omitted. For example, $6 \cdot s = 6(s) = 6s$.

⌒⌒ : Write answers to the following in the spaces provided.

  1. $-6 \div (2 - 5)$ Ans: _____
  2. $16 - 2(3y + 4)$ Ans: _____
  3. $6x(2y + 3(8 \div 2))$ Ans: _____
  4. $(2x - 3)(y + 7)$ Ans: _____

Answers

  1. $-6 \div (2 - 5) = -6 \div -3 = +2$
  2. $16 - 2(3y + 4) = 16 - 6y - 8 = 8 - 6y$
  3. $6x(2y + 3(8 \div 2)) = 6x(2y + 3(4))$
  $\qquad\qquad\qquad = 6x(2y + 12) = 12xy + 72x$
  4. $(2x - 3)(y + 7) = 2xy + 14x - 3y - 21$

The fourth case is the most difficult and may be clearer if you substitute some numbers into the expression and see that it works. In essence each term within the second parentheses must be multiplied by each term in the first parentheses.

Parentheses are also important in factoring. If a factor is removed from one term within a parentheses, it must be removed from all terms. Thus $9 - (8 - 4) = 9 - 4(2 - 1)$, where the factor 4 has been taken outside the parentheses by removing it from both terms within the parentheses.

1-5 SUMMARY

Symbolic notation may be efficient in that it permits one to perform known operations more easily in quest of new insights, but it also is what creates problems for the uninitiated reader. More than any other single factor, the use of symbols produces misgivings in students new to the subject.

The most important point in this chapter is that mathematical symbols are simply a shorthand. Each has its English translation, and the student should refer to the translation and even write it down when he is having difficulty. Several symbols in common use have been reviewed and some simple examples of their use have been given. In future chapters, additional symbols are introduced and their uses illustrated. Some of these symbols will refer to operations that are new to you. These symbols make it easier to obtain problem solutions once their meaning and use are mastered. Without these new symbols, problem solutions are much more difficult and time consuming to find, if they are obtainable at all.

Managerial problems do not arrive neatly wrapped and tied ready for routine solution. Actual problems are fraught with complexity. Often it is not easy even to establish clearly what the problem is, yet action is required. Some simplification must necessarily take place in the face of the complexity of the "real" world. To succeed the manager must be able to recognize a problem in an involved environment and abstract it, omitting noncritical elements without simultaneously losing the problem's essence. The ability to abstract is useful not only in finding commonalities among problems but in suggesting the type of expert assistance to be obtained. The successful manager knows when to seek the help of technical experts, how to communicate with them, and how to evaluate the results they produce. One of the most able managers we have known had little formal education but knew how to ask the right questions of the experts working on a problem.

We should point out, however, that abstraction can be dangerous. The noted economist John Maynard Keynes once said: "Confusion of thought is not always best avoided by technical and unaccustomed expressions, to which the mind has no immediate reaction of understanding; it is possible, under cover of a careful formalism, to make statements which, if expressed in plain language, the mind would immediately repudiate."

NEW SYMBOLS

Symbol	English Translation
$=$	equals; is equal to
$\neq$	does not equal; is not equal to
$\equiv$	is identical to; is defined to be
$<$	is less than
$\leq$	is less than or equal to; is at most
$>$	is greater than
$\geq$	is greater than or equal to; is at least

| | Perform all operations within these
                                   lines and give the final result a
                                   positive sign.

$$\sum_{i=1}^{n} x_i$$ Add together the n values given to x.

$$\prod_{i=1}^{n} x_i$$ Multiply together the n values given
                                   to x.

PROBLEMS

Problems for Self-Study: 5, 7, 9, 10, 17

1-1. For which of the following situations would you believe that mathematics could have importance?

a. Deciding whether or not to grant a loan.

b. Deciding on a new plant location.

c. Determining the yearly depreciation expense on an asset.

d. Investigating the allocation of sales effort to various products.

e. Choosing the number of staff needed in a hospital emergency room.

1-2. Pick the best answer.

a. A (variable, constant, symbol) may be defined as an unspecified number.

b. A (variable, constant, symbol) may be defined as a specific value.

1-3.* Are constants or variables being defined?

a. Highway deaths next Memorial Day.

b. Estimated life of a firm's office building used in computing tax liabilities.

c. Amount of stock presently outstanding for a given company.

d. State sales tax rate in Illinois on a given day.

e. Number of patients contracting Asian flu in any month.

f. Number of defective items produced by a mechanical process during any hour.

1-4.* Indicate whether y is a variable or a constant.

a. Sales were y dollars last month.

b. We do not know how much we will produce from month to month but assume it will be y units.

c. If we can estimate monthly use, we can estimate the monthly benefits y for any month.

    d. Cost, y, will be determined by patient usage.

    e. The level of the monthly welfare payment, y, needed for a given family of four in poverty is a matter of debate.

    f. The increase in Social Security benefits suggested by the Congress is y.

1–5.   *a.* Arrange each of the following by separating them with the symbol $>$: $\frac{2}{3}$, $-\frac{3}{4}$, $\frac{7}{8}$, -2, $\frac{4}{5}$, 0, $-\frac{1}{4}$.

    b. Arrange each of the following by separating them with the symbols $\leq$ and $<$: $\frac{4}{3}$, $\sqrt{1}$, $\frac{7}{8}$, $-\frac{1}{2}$, $-\frac{2}{3}$, $\frac{8}{6}$, $-\frac{3}{5}$, 1.

    c. Determine the larger value.

        (1) $|2 + (-2)|$ and $|2| + |-2|$

        (2) $|2 - (-2)|$ and $|2| - |-2|$

        (3) $|2 - (\ 2)|$ and $|2| - |\ 2|$

1–6.*   Perform the indicated operations.

    a. $(-3)(2)(-7)$

    b. $3(-2)(2) - 3(-1)(5)$

    c. $2(0)(1) - 3(2)(-2)$

    d. $3 \div (2 - 2)$

    e. $(3(+2) - 6) \div 4(-3)$

    f. $(3(+2) - 6) \div 2(0)(1.5)$

    g. $6\sqrt{9} - 2\sqrt{2.25}$

    h. $2\sqrt[3]{216} - 2\sqrt[5]{32}$

    i. $(1 + \sqrt{2})(1 - \sqrt{2})$

1–7.   Perform the following operations (remove parentheses).

    a. $3x(y + 2)$

    b. $(3x + 1)(4z)$

    c. $(y - 1)(x + 1)$

    d. $(y - 1)(y + 1)$

    e. $(x + y)(z - xy)$

    f. $(x - 2z)(y + 1)(a)$

1–8.*   Evaluate, leaving nonwhole roots under the radical.

    a. $\sqrt{162}$

    b. $\sqrt{0.09}$

    c. $\sqrt[3]{64}$

d. $(2\sqrt{24} + \sqrt{96}) \div \sqrt{3}$

e. $\sqrt{27x} + 3\sqrt{12x}$

f. $\sqrt{5}(2\sqrt{5} - 3\sqrt{20})$

1-9. Find answers to the following. (Be careful to note how the summing is defined here. It is slightly different from the text.)

a. $\displaystyle\sum_{x=1}^{4} x$

b. $\displaystyle\prod_{x=1}^{4} x$

c. $\displaystyle\sum_{y=2}^{4} 3y$

d. $\displaystyle\prod_{y=2}^{4} 3y$

e. $\displaystyle\sum_{x=0}^{5} 2(1 + x)$

f. $\displaystyle\prod_{x=0}^{5} 2(1 + x)$

1-10. Express the following statements algebraically.

a. The price, p, to be charged the buyer should be \$10 over the cost, c.

b. The price, p, to be charged the buyer should represent a markup of 20 percent on cost, c.

c. The leasing contract calls for a monthly fee, f, of \$200 plus \$20 per service call, s.

d. The amount of gypsum, g, used must not exceed the amount available: 1000 lb.

e. The temperature, t, of the mixture must be kept above 80 degrees centigrade.

f. We spend s, which is more than our income, I.

1-11.* Represent the unknown by a letter and set up an algebraic statement to represent each question.

a. A man worked for 5 hours and earned \$8.75. What was his hourly wage?

b. A company made four times as much this year as it did last year. If it made \$2000 this year, how much did it make last year?

c. If the current price is \$15 and it exceeds the previous price by 10 percent of the previous price, what was the previous price?

d. Fringe benefits account for 20 percent of our labor bill. If our fringe-benefit payments went up \$1000 this period, how much was our labor up?

e. Gold reserves dropped to 20 percent of the legal minimum from 25 percent last month. If the legal limit was \$25 million, what was the dollar decline?

1–12. The symbol $\forall$ is often used in more advanced mathematics. Its English translation is "for all." Using this symbol, write the following statement mathematically: Revenue from sales at 10 cents per unit exceeds total yearly fixed costs of 500,000 plus variable costs of 5 cents per unit, for all yearly sales levels, x, greater than 1,000,000 units.

1–13. In mathematics the symbol ! is used to signify a particular operation. When the exclamation point follows an integer it means multiply together all positive integers equal to or less than the one shown. Thus $3! = 3 \cdot 2 \cdot 1 = 6$. Evaluate

a. 1!

b. 2!

c. 5!

d. $\sqrt{4!}$

e. $\displaystyle\sum_{x=1}^{3} x!$

1–14.* Another example of mathematical symbolism is $\binom{m}{n}$, which is not "m divided by n" but is defined as

$$\binom{m}{n} \equiv \frac{m!}{(m-n)\,!n!} \quad \text{for } m > n.$$

Therefore,

$$\binom{3}{2} \equiv \frac{3!}{(3-2)\,!2!} = \frac{3 \cdot 2 \cdot 1}{(1)\,! \cdot 2 \cdot 1} = 3$$

(See Problem 1-13 for definition of $m!$.) Evaluate.

a. $\binom{4}{2}$

b. $\binom{5}{2}$

$$c. \begin{pmatrix} 5 \\ 3 \end{pmatrix}$$

$$d. \begin{pmatrix} 6 \\ 3 \end{pmatrix}$$

1-15. The following data represent the change in dividends this year for the firms specified, on a dollars per share basis.

Acme Company: $-\frac{1}{2}$,

Revelex: 0,

Ezygo: 1,

Bettergas: $|x + 1| \div 2$,   where x is profits in dollars per share.

a. For which firm did dividends remain unchanged?

b. Did Acme raise dividends more than Revelex?

c. If profits per share were $3 for Bettergas, what relation does their dividend change have to Ezygo?

d. If Bettergas lost $3 per share, what relation does their dividend change have to Revelex? To Ezygo?

1-16.* A chemical developing process requires 10 steps. At each step the chemical shrinks. The shrinkage at each step is always a constant percentage of what is left after the last stage, but the percentage changes from step to step. Using p_i for the percentage shrinkage at each stage, write an expression that would tell how much chemical was left after 10 steps if 100 gallons were used to start step 1.

1-17. The level of sales of a certain product is expected to increase by 10 percent next year, by 15 percent of next year's figure in year two, by 20 percent of year two's figure in year three, and so on for the next 15 years. If present sales are at a level of 75 units, write an expression for sales 15 years hence.

1-18.* The Peter Principle states that a man secures advancement in an organization to the position immediately above the one he is able to fill competently. If jobs in an organization are numbered consecutively, using one for the lowest job, and if $J_c \equiv$ highest job for which the individual is competent, and $J_f \equiv$ job which he finally fills, write an equation to express the Peter Principle.

1-19.* Express the following algebraically.

a. A worker's take-home pay, b, which increased by half his raise, d. His take-home pay last year was c.

      b. The average wage rate paid if a worker's time is divided into 80 percent regular time, at rate r_1, and 20 percent overtime, at rate r_2.

      c. The ratio of sales orders, s, to number of calls, n.

      d. The margin on sales, s, made at a sales price y dollars per unit and which cost x dollars per unit to make.

      e. The level of gross national product next year, if it increases r percent per year from its present level g_0.

      f. The level of gross national product in n years if it increases at a constant rate r each year from its previous year's level. It is at level g now.

1–20. Express the relations given for each problem as one relation.

      a. $x \geq 1000,\ x < 2000$

      b. $x \geq 1000,\ x \leq 1000$

      c. $x \geq 1000,\ x < 1050,\ x > 1042$

      d. $x > 1000,\ x < 1050,\ x \leq 1000$

1–21.* If, for any constants b and d and variable x, it can be said that $b \leq x \leq d$, then the constants b and d may be thought of as the lower limit and upper limit, respectively, of the values that x may have. Suppose that a manager thinks that sales, S, will be between \$100 and \$125 and that his costs, C, will be between \$80 and \$105. Express these estimates in the form of $b \leq x \leq d$ for

      a. Sales, S

      b. Cost, C

1–22. Four marketing experts were asked to make an estimate of the expected yearly sales level, S, of a new product. Express each of their estimates in mathematical form.

      a. "At least 50,000 units."

      b. "No more than 65,000 units."

      c. "At least 53,000 units, but less than 70,000."

      d. "More than 50,000 units, but less than 68,000."

      e. What range of sales is consistent with all the estimates made?

1–23.* The executives of FBN Corporation wish to estimate their company's profits for the coming year. The demand for their product is highly seasonal, and, in fact, FBN's executives believe that sales growth, as well as the level of sales, will vary from month to month. There is also a yearly fixed cost of operation plus a variable cost required to produce each unit.

Find an expression for FBN's profits next year. Use the following definitions.

$x_i \equiv$ sales in month i, last year,

$g_i \equiv$ expected sales growth rate for month i [for example, sales in month 3 of this year will be $x_3(1 + g_3)$],

$F \equiv$ yearly fixed cost of operation,

$c \equiv$ variable cost/unit (the cost of the labor and materials needed to make each unit); this cost is assumed constant over the year,

$P \equiv$ selling price/unit (assumed constant over the year).

1–24. The manager in charge of a warehouse must store three products in the area available to him. The products have the following characteristics:

Product	Weight/Unit (lb)	Area Required/ Unit (ft²)	Cost of Storage/ Unit ($)
1	20	6	0.50
2	30	8	0.65
3	40	4	0.60

Define x_i to be the number of units of product i stored in the warehouse. Express each of the following statements mathematically as it relates to the warehouse manager's job.

a. The total area taken up by the inventory assuming that no items are stacked.

b. The total weight of the inventory may not exceed the weight capacity of the warehouse floor, which is 15 tons.

c. The total cost of storage of the inventory.

1–25. For each of the next 10 years, the ABC Company will introduce a new product, x_i ($i = 1, \ldots, 10$). When a product is introduced, its initial sales are S_i, and these sales are expected to grow at r percent per year. Express the ABC Company's sales in the tenth year from now in mathematical form.

1–26.* If $Y = \prod_{i=1}^{n} ax^i$, where a is a constant, which of the following holds?

a. $Y = a^n \prod_{i=1}^{n} x^i$

b. $Y = a \prod_{i=1}^{n} x^i$

c. $Y = x^n \prod_{i=1}^{n} a$

d. $Y = x \prod_{i=1}^{n} a$

e. $Y = ax^n$

2

Exponents and Their Uses

The month was September. The place, the board room of the Hobart Sporting Goods Corporation. The directors of the Hobart Corporation were heatedly debating the advisability of refunding an outstanding bond issue this coming January. A corporate bond is essentially an interest-bearing loan to the firm by the holder of the bond. Refunding involves buying the old bonds and issuing new ones. The old issue is in the amount of $50,000,000 of 6 percent bonds (interest of $1,500,000 is paid semiannually). These bonds had been issued January 1 nine and three-quarter years ago. The bonds were originally issued for a 25-year period and management has agreed to keep the outstanding debt level at $50,000,000 over the next 15 years.

The purpose of reissuing the bonds is to take advantage of the current available market interest rate of 5 percent. This rate is expected to be available in the market until January 1. Refunding, then, would save the firm (0.06 − 0.05) (50,000,000) or $500,000 per year over the next 15 years. However, because the old bonds have only been outstanding a short time, a refunding penalty of 2 percent on the outstanding principal must be paid by the corporation to the present bond holders. This amounts to $1,000,000. Administrative and other expenses associated with refunding amount to $3,000,000. The question at issue is whether the interest saving from refunding over the next 15 years covers the total refunding expenses, estimated at $4,000,000.

An immediate response of "yes" might be given because the $500,000 yearly ($250,000 semiannual) saving on interest payments is available for the remaining 15 years of the bonds' life. Thus the total saving appears to be ($500,000) (15), or $7,500,000. This saving exceeds the necessary expenses of

$4,000,000. But this is not a valid analysis. The $4,000,000 must all be spent on or about this January while the interest savings are realized in equal $250,000 chunks, twice a year, for 15 years. As we all know, a dollar today is worth more than a dollar a year from now since, if we had the dollar today, we could at least put it in the bank and obtain a year's interest. For example, if yearly interest at 4 percent is available, then $1.04 a year from now is worth only $1.00 today because $1.00 invested today at 4 percent grows to $1.04 in a year.

We must then find a way of valuing a stream of savings of $250,000 every half-year (such a stream is called an *annuity*) over the next 15 years. Before we can solve this problem, however, it will be necessary to learn how funds invested at compound interest, where the interest rate applies to the previous interest earned as well as to the principal, change over time. The compounding process leads directly into the subject of exponents. We will digress to review the laws of exponents before returning to a solution to the Hobart Corporation's bond-refunding problem. (It is worth noting that actual refunding decisions are more complex than the issue at hand. We are only concerned here with one aspect of the total refunding problem.)

2–1 THE LAWS OF EXPONENTS

In discussing the Hobart Corporation's problem, we showed that at a yearly interest rate of 4 percent, $1.00 today becomes $1.04 a year from now:

$$
\begin{aligned}
\text{principal} + \text{interest} &= \$1.00 + \$1.00(0.04) \\
&= \$1.00(1 + 0.04) \\
&= (1 + 0.04) \text{ dollars} \\
&= (1.04) \text{ dollars.}
\end{aligned}
$$

This new value, $1.04, now becomes the principal for the second year. Interest at 4 percent is paid on $1.04. Interest is received on the previous interest as well as on the original principal. Thus after 2 years we have

$$
\begin{aligned}
\text{principal} + \text{interest} &= \$1.04 + \$1.04(0.04) \\
&= \$1.04(1 + 0.04) \\
&= (1.04)(1.04) \text{ dollars.}
\end{aligned}
$$

The compounding process leads to a result that could be phrased "multiply 1.04 by itself." Using $(1.04)(1.04)$ as the new principal, compounding 3 years gives

$$[(1.04)(1.04)] + [(1.04)(1.04)](0.04) = (1.04)(1.04)(1.04) \text{ dollars.}$$

The compounding process results in multiplying 1.04 by itself and by itself again for a 3-year period. The process is generalizable for any number of years. Hence after 4 years we have

$$(1.04)(1.04)(1.04)(1.04) \text{ dollars,}$$

and so on for any number of years. Writing this expression becomes very cumbersome for long periods. Hence it is not surprising to find that mathematicians have found a simpler way to denote such products. Mathematicians use *superscripts*, which are also called *exponents*, to denote repeated multiplication of identical quantities. The numerical value of the exponent indicates the number of repeated multiplications. We may write the amount of $1.00 invested at a compound interest rate of 4 percent for 2 years as $(1.04)^2$ dollars, the amount after 3 years as $(1.04)^3$ dollars, and the amount after t years as $(1.04)^t$ dollars. (Note that (1.04) written without an exponent is identical to $(1.04)^1$; the 1 is omitted.)

Symbol	*English Translation*
superscript or exponent t such as $(1.04)^t$	Form the product of t expressions like that to which the superscript or exponent attaches.

Some simple examples are:

$$3^2 = 3 \cdot 3 = 9,$$
$$(a + 2)^2 = (a + 2)(a + 2) = a^2 + 4a + 4.$$

The extensions of the use of exponent notation can be grasped by continually referring to the symbol translation just given. For example, where b is any constant,

$$(b^2)(b^3) = (b \cdot b)(b \cdot b \cdot b) = b \cdot b \cdot b \cdot b \cdot b = b^5 = b^{2+3}.$$

And if $b = 2$, then

$$(2^2)(2^3) = (2 \cdot 2)(2 \cdot 2 \cdot 2) = 4(8) = 32 = 2 \cdot 2 \cdot 2 \cdot 2 \cdot 2 = 2^5 = 2^{2+3}.$$

This example suggests the first rule for exponents.

Rule 1 for Exponents: PRODUCTS

The product of a set of identical terms each raised to an exponent (power) is given by the term raised to the sum of those exponents. If the different constant exponents are given by c_i, then, in symbolic form:

$$b^{c_1} \cdot b^{c_2} \cdot \ldots \cdot b^{c_i} \cdot \ldots \cdot b^{c_n} = b^{c_1 + c_2 + \ldots + c_i + \ldots + c_n} = b^{\sum_{i=1}^{n} c_i}$$

The terms raised to the powers must be the same before the powers can be added. Thus the rule cannot be applied to problems such as $(3)^2(2)^3$:

$$(3)^2(2)^3 = (3 \cdot 3)(2 \cdot 2 \cdot 2) = 9 \cdot 8 = 72.$$

This is not equal to 3^5 or to 2^5, which are 243 and 32 respectively.

An extension of rule 1 for exponents allows us to evaluate the expression

$$(b^2)^3.$$

The exponent 3 directs us to multiply b^2 by itself three times. Thus we have

$$(b^2)^3 = b^2 \cdot b^2 \cdot b^2 = b^6 = b^{2 \cdot 3}$$

by rule 1. This is the same result we would have obtained if we had multiplied the two exponents together. Using $b = 2$ again as an example:

$$(2^2)^3 = (4)^3 = 4 \cdot 4 \cdot 4 = 64 = 2 \cdot 2 \cdot 2 \cdot 2 \cdot 2 \cdot 2 = 2^6 = 2^{2 \cdot 3}.$$

This example leads us to the second rule for exponents.

Rule 2 for Exponents: POWERS

The result of raising a term with an exponent to a power is the original term with a new exponent. The new exponent is equal to the product of the original exponent and the power. In symbolic form:

$$(b^c)^d = b^{cd}.$$

The next several rules relate to quotients of identical terms raised to powers. Rule 1 allows us to put such quotients in a form whereby the result is intuitive. Before working with a general constant, b, consider, as an example, the ratio $32/8 = 4 = 2^2$. We have just seen that $32 = 2^5$, and we know that $2 \cdot 2 \cdot 2 = 2^3 = 8$. Hence

$$\frac{32}{8} = \frac{2^5}{2^3} = \frac{2 \cdot 2 \cdot 2 \cdot 2 \cdot 2}{2 \cdot 2 \cdot 2}.$$

Canceling we write

$$\frac{2 \cdot 2 \cdot \cancel{2} \cdot \cancel{2} \cdot \cancel{2}}{\cancel{2} \cdot \cancel{2} \cdot \cancel{2}} = 2 \cdot 2 = 2^2 = 2^{5-3}.$$

Note that the exponent of 2 in the answer could have been obtained if the exponent of 2 in the denominator of the fraction had been subtracted from the exponent of 2 in the numerator of the original fraction. This yields $5 - 3 = 2$.

The procedure works as long as the expressions are given as powers of the same thing, 2 here. Canceling gives the same result as subtracting exponents; that is, crossing out one 2 from both the numerator and denominator is the same as subtracting 1 from both exponents. We continue subtracting (canceling) until we run out of terms in the numerator or denominator or both. We can, of course, perform the same "sleight of hand" with letters. Thus

$$\frac{b^5}{b^3} = \frac{b \cdot b \cdot \not{b} \cdot \not{b} \cdot \not{b}}{\not{b} \cdot \not{b} \cdot \not{b}} = b^2 = b^{5-3}.$$

The discussion leads to the third rule of exponents.

Rule 3 for Exponents: QUOTIENTS

The quotient of two identical terms raised to powers is obtained by subtracting the exponent of the denominator from the exponent of the numerator. In symbolic form:

$$\frac{b^c}{b^d} = b^{c-d}.$$

This rule works for any real-numbered values for c and d.

Rule 3 is particularly powerful in that it helps us handle some difficult cases. Consider first the ratio

$$\frac{2^3}{2^3} = \frac{8}{8} = 1.$$

Using rule 3 we obtain

$$\frac{2^3}{2^3} = 2^{3-3} = 2^0.$$

But we already know that this result must be 1. The conclusion is that the expression 2 raised to the zero power is 1. This is also true for any other expression. We summarize this result in rule 4.

Rule 4 for Exponents: ZERO POWER

Any expression raised to the zero power is 1. In symbolic form:

$$b^0 = 1,$$

where b is any expression.

As a further application of rule 3, consider the ratio

$$\frac{2^3}{2^4} = \frac{8}{16} = \frac{1}{2}.$$

Using rule 3 we obtain

$$\frac{2^3}{2^4} = 2^{3-4} = 2^{-1}.$$

But we know that this result must be $1/2$. We conclude that the negative sign attaching to the exponent directs us to take the reciprocal (one over) of the expression raised to the exponent without the minus sign. Thus $2^{-1} = 1/2$ and $2^{-2} = 1/2^2$. This example leads us to the fifth rule for exponents.

Rule 5 for Exponents: NEGATIVE EXPONENT

An expression raised to a negative power is the reciprocal of that expression raised to the same power without a negative sign. In symbolic form:

$$b^{-c} = \frac{1}{b^c}.$$

- Perhaps these first five rules are familiar to you from previous work. The next extension may be new. The extension is that roots can be expressed as exponents. This is important since exponents are easier to manipulate mathematically than are roots. Consider as an introductory example the square root of 4. The square root of any expression, as we learned in Section 1-3, is a term which when multiplied by itself yields the original expression. Thus $\sqrt{4} = 2$ since $2 \cdot 2 = 4$. Using the first rule for exponents, $2^1 \cdot 2^1 = 2^2 = 4$. Now consider $\sqrt{2}$. The square root of 2 is a number, call it d, such that $d \cdot d = 2$. Now using what we know, let's try a sneaky trick, one you would not ordinarily think to do. Suppose there is an exponent, c, such that $d = 2^c$. Then substituting 2^c for d we can write

$$2^c \cdot 2^c = 2.$$

Using rule 1 for exponents this becomes

$$2^{c+c} = 2^1$$

and since the expression raised to the exponent is the same, the exponents must be equal. Therefore,

$$c + c = 1.$$

But this implies that $c = 1/2$. Thus $\sqrt{2} = 2^{1/2}$ since $2^{1/2} \cdot 2^{1/2} = 2^{1/2+1/2} = 2^1 = 2$. Hence the square root of $2 = 2^{1/2}$.

As a more general example, $\sqrt{b} = b^{1/2}$ since $b^{1/2} \cdot b^{1/2} = b$. The procedure can be extended to more complex problems. Thus $\sqrt[3]{2^3} = (2^3)^{1/3} = 2$ by rule 2; and $\sqrt[3]{2} = 2^{1/3}$ since $2^{1/3} \cdot 2^{1/3} \cdot 2^{1/3} = 2$ again by the first rule of exponents. This leads us to the sixth rule for exponents.

Rule 6 for Exponents: ROOTS

The nth root of an expression is equal to the expression raised to the 1-over-nth power. In symbolic form:

$$\sqrt[n]{b} = b^{1/n}.$$

These six rules provide all the procedures we need in order to use exponents. Indeed we have been slightly generous since rule 4, for example, is a special case of rule 3. It is important in applying these rules to observe that nothing restricts the expression or the exponent to which the expression is raised to be a constant. Although many of the examples presented so far involve constants, the rules, carefully applied, are also appropriate to expressions involving variables. The examples in "the student shoulds" will test your ability to apply the rules for exponents to some new situations.

$\sim\!\!\swarrow$: Simplify the following expressions, writing them in exponent terms.

Result

1. $2^2 \cdot 3^2 \cdot 2^3 \cdot 3^{-3}$ _____
2. $(a^x \cdot y^3) \div (a^{2x} \cdot y^r \cdot z)^2$ _____
3. $[(b^{-y})^0 (x^{-2})^{-3}] \div (a^{2x+y} \cdot a^{2x-z})^2$ _____
4. $(b^{1/2})^{2x+2} (c^{-1/3})^{-3} (b^2)^x$ _____

Answers

1. $2^5 \div 3$ or $2^5 \cdot 3^{-1}$
2. $(y^{3-2r}) \div (a^{3x} z^2)$
3. $x^6 \div (a^{8x+2y-2z})$
4. cb^{3x+1}

2-2 THE MATHEMATICS OF COMPOUND INTEREST

At this point the reader will wonder whether we ever intend to return to the Hobart Sporting Goods Corporation problem. We do intend to resolve the bond-refunding issues posed by Hobart's directors in this section. And we intend to do more. We intend to extend our discussion to other problems associated with compound interest. The reader may be relieved to learn that we will need only the straightforward applications of the rules for exponents which we have just studied.

In the introduction to this chapter we studied the effect of compound interest paid periodically at a rate of 4 percent on an initial investment of $1. The result for t periods was $(1.04)^t$. If $3 is invested, the result is the same for each dollar invested, yielding a total of

$$(1.04)^t + (1.04)^t + (1.04)^t = 3(1.04)^t.$$

In general, a single investment of an amount P invested for t periods at an interest rate of r yields a sum A of

$$A = P(1 + r)^t.$$

This equation is sometimes called the formula for the *future value of a present amount*. Fortunately, tables of $(1 + r)^t$ exist and can be used to obtain A. Using the equation above, we can also, with the help of tables, determine the present value (the value today) of an amount A to be received t periods from now. This requires solving the above equation for P. To solve for P, we use the rules for exponents. Multiplying both sides of the last equation by $(1 + r)^{-t}$ gives

$$A(1 + r)^{-t} = P(1 + r)^t(1 + r)^{-t} = P(1 + r)^{t-t} = P(1 + r)^0 = P$$

or

$$P = A(1 + r)^{-t}.$$

This equation is called the *formula for the present value of a future sum*. Given values for A and r and a table of values for $(1 + r)^t$ or $(1 + r)^{-t}$, the value of P can be found. The value of P in this equation is also called the *discounted value* of the amount A, to be received t periods from now.

Usually the compounding period is a year but this need not be the case. To attract more customers and larger deposits in recent years, most savings banks have adopted a policy of compounding quarterly or even more often. Our analysis is general enough to incorporate this complexity. For example, if a yearly rate of r percent is appropriate but compounding is done quarterly, then after t years an initial single investment of P dollars will have grown to

$$A = P\left(1 + \frac{r}{4}\right)^{4t}.$$

The yearly rate is divided by 4 since the appropriate rate is the rate for one-fourth of a year. The number of periods involved is multiplied by 4 since the compounding now takes place four times each year rather than once each year.

The Hobart Corporation situation, however, does not involve a single payment but rather a series of semiannual payments of equal amount. This type of payment is called a *level annuity* or simply an *annuity*. Annuities are very common in managerial situations, and it is therefore useful to develop the formula for an annuity.

The Hobart Corporation presently pays $50,000,000(0.06)($\frac{1}{2}$), or $1,500,000, every half-year on the 6 percent bonds outstanding. If it refunds the present issue and issues a 5 percent bond, it will pay $50,000,000(0.05) ($\frac{1}{2}$), or $1,250,000, every half-year. This constitutes a semiannual saving of $250,000. This saving is obtained every 6 months for the 15 years of life remaining to the outstanding issue. It therefore represents an annuity in the amount of $250,000 for the next 30 (semiannually for 15 years) periods.

The present value of this annuity is to be compared with the refunding expenses, which total $4,000,000. To do so we must discount each of the semiannual payments of $250,000 to the present using an appropriate discount rate. If the appropriate yearly discounting rate is r, we can use successive applications of the discounting formula to obtain the present value, P.V., of this annuity:

$$P.V. = 250,000\left(1 + \frac{r}{2}\right)^{-1} + 250,000\left(1 + \frac{r}{2}\right)^{-2} + \ldots$$

$$+ 250,000\left(1 + \frac{r}{2}\right)^{-30}.$$

We have adjusted the yearly discount rate and the periods involved to reflect the semiannual nature of the annuity.

Experts in the area of finance do not yet agree on just what rate of discount should be used. Since you will probably hear the alternative views of these financial wizards at another time, we will not attempt to give you an answer here. But, to emphasize that the discount rate may be different from the interest rates available in the market (and not because it is the correct rate), a yearly discount rate of 10 percent is used for illustrative purposes. Substituting the semiannual equivalent rate of 0.05 gives

$$P.V. = 250,000(1.05)^{-1} + 250,000(1.05)^{-2} + \ldots + 250,000(1.05)^{-30}.$$

With the help of compound interest tables and a desk calculator, the present value is $3,843,113. But the mathematician (as you might expect) is not satisfied with this lengthy method of calculation, and so he has devised a simpler one. Because the method he used is clever, yet simple, we will show

how mathematical legerdemain (or trickery, if you prefer) can be used to advantage. Most of us would not think of the particular trick used here. That is not important. What we want to show is that often a simple idea underlies formulas that seem to have little intuitive appeal of their own. (It is also a good exercise in algebra.)

To derive the formula for the present value of an annuity, we recall that we can operate mathematically on one side of an equation if we perform the same operation on the other side. The particular operation that works here is to multiply the basic equation by the factor $(1 + r)$. (The choice of this operation is not an obvious one.) The equation for the present value of an amount A deposited each of t periods and discounted at a rate r is

$$\text{P.V.} = A(1 + r)^{-1} + A(1 + r)^{-2} + \ldots + A(1 + r)^{-t+1} + A(1 + r)^{-t}.$$

Multiplying both sides by $(1 + r)$ and using rules 1 and 4 for exponents yields

$$(1 + r)\text{P.V.} = A(1 + r)^{-1+1} + A(1 + r)^{-2+1} + \ldots$$
$$+ A(1 + r)^{-t+2} + A(1 + r)^{-t+1}$$

or

$$(1 + r)\text{P.V.} = A + A(1 + r)^{-1} + \ldots + A(1 + r)^{-t+2} + A(1 + r)^{-t+1}.$$

Now subtracting this last expression from the original equation,

$$\text{P.V.} - (1 + r)\text{P.V.} = -A + A(1 + r)^{-t}.$$

Simplifying gives

$$\text{P.V.}(-r) = A[(1 + r)^{-t} - 1].$$

Multiplying both sides by $-1/r$ yields

$$\text{P.V.} = A\left[\frac{1 - (1 + r)^{-t}}{r}\right].$$

This equation gives the *present value of an annuity* of an amount A each period. The term in brackets has been calculated using computers and is tabulated in annuity tables. Given the number of periods and the appropriate period's interest rate, we simply obtain this value from a table and multiply by A to obtain the discounted value of an annuity of amount A. Indeed this is the way we determined the present value of Hobart's interest savings rather than the long series of calculations suggested earlier.

We now are finally ready to answer the question raised by Hobart's directors: Are the interest savings sufficient to justify total immediate refunding expenditures of $4,000,000? Since the present value of the interest savings amount to slightly over 3.8 million, the answer is no. We hasten to add that this does not resolve the refunding question. We have omitted taxes, consideration of future expected interest rates, and other factors that may influence the decision. Nevertheless, the interest savings are an important element in a final solution. It is also worth noting that the decision is sensitive to the discount rate that is used. For example, if an 8 percent rate rather than a 10 percent rate were used, the interest savings are about 4.3 million. The manager may wish to consider this sensitivity in a real case since there is usually some arbitrariness in the selection of this rate.

Although discounting calculations, particularly of annuities, are common in managerial problems, managers at times also need the future, rather than the present, value of an annuity. To develop the formula for the future value of an annuity, we could proceed as we did to develop the formula for the present value of an annuity. Instead, let us exercise our newly acquired algebraic muscles. We will use the formula for the present value of an annuity and some algebra to obtain the formula for the future value of an annuity.

In Figure 2–1 the present value of the annuity is indicated by P.V. at time "now." To find the value of this immediate amount t years away, we have merely to multiply P.V. by $(1 + r)^t$. It is once again a sly move, but it works. First we get an equivalent present value of the annuity. Then we act as though we put this single amount in the bank ar rate r for t periods. Algebraically, the future value, F.V., is then

$$\text{F.V.} = \text{P.V.}(1 + r)^t$$

and using the present-value formula for an annuity, this is

$$\text{F.V.} = A \left[\frac{1 - (1 + r)^{-t}}{r} \right] (1 + r)^t.$$

FIGURE 2–1

**Annuities: Present and Future Values
A Diagram**

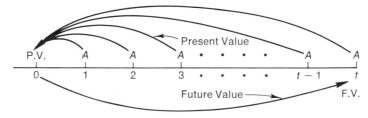

Using rules 1 and 4 for exponents,

$$\text{F.V.} = A \left[\frac{(1 + r)^t - 1}{r} \right].$$

Again the value in the brackets is tabulated in most finance or mathematics of finance texts. (Note that in these examples the first of the t payments is made one period hence.)

↗ : An organization wishes to accumulate sufficient funds in a bank account to allow it to replace certain equipment. The equipment will cost $10,000 and is to be replaced and paid for precisely 10 years from the present date. The bank pays interest at 4 percent compounded quarterly. How much must be deposited under each of the following plans?

1. A single immediate deposit? _____

2. An identical deposit made each quarter with the first of the 40 quarterly deposits made 3 months from the present date? _____

3. An identical deposit made each quarter with the first of 20 quarterly deposits made 5 years and 3 months from the present date? _____

4. Same as plan 2 with the first of 41 quarterly deposits made immediately? _____

Write your answer (in the space provided) in terms of the payment, A, equated to an expression using numbers which, if solved, would give a value equal to A. Do not attempt to obtain a numerical result. For example, $A = (1.04)^{10}$ is the form in which the answers are given.

Answers

1. $10,000 = A(1.01)^{40}$; hence $A = 10,000(1.01)^{-40}$.

2. $10,000 = A \left[\dfrac{(1.01)^{40} - 1}{0.01} \right]$; hence $A = \dfrac{100}{(1.01)^{40} - 1}$.

3. $10,000 = A \left[\dfrac{(1.01)^{20} - 1}{0.01} \right]$; hence $A = \dfrac{100}{(1.01)^{20} - 1}$.

4. $10,000 = A \left[\dfrac{(1.01)^{41} - 1}{0.01} \right]$; hence $A = \dfrac{100}{(1.01)^{41} - 1}$.

*2-3 BINARY AND HEXADECIMAL NOTATION

Modern mathematics is basically a decimal system based on the unit 10. Historically this is probably due to the fact that we have 10 fingers. Whatever the reason, it has proved to be a useful and easily understood system. But there is no fundamental law restricting us to a base 10 system. As the celebrated Harvard mathematician Tom Lehrer has said in song: "base 8 is just like base 10, if you have only eight fingers." Well, not exactly, perhaps, but you

* This section may be omitted without loss of continuity.

begin to get the idea that other bases are possible. Indeed if we are willing to use our toes, the base 20 suggests itself. Such a system was used long ago. The Babylonians were even more inventive using a system with 60 as a base. Vestiges of the Babylonian system still remain in counting time (60 seconds in a minute and 60 minutes in an hour).

Other systems turn out to have substantial practical value in the area of electronic computers. In particular, a base of 2 (count with your two ears or two eyes if you wish) turns out to be of particular interest. A system using a base of 2 is called a *binary* system. In the binary system only the digits 0 and 1 are used. Numbers in the binary system are represented by powers of 2. This is illustrated in Table 2–1.

TABLE 2–1

Some Binary Numbers

Binary Representation	*Conversion to Powers of 2*	*Decimal Representation*
0	$0 \cdot 2^0$	0
1	$1 \cdot 2^0$	1
10	$1 \cdot 2^1 + 0 \cdot 2^0$	2
11	$1 \cdot 2^1 + 1 \cdot 2^0$	3
100	$1 \cdot 2^2 + 0 \cdot 2^1 + 0 \cdot 2^0$	4
.	.	.
.	.	.
.	.	.
1001	$1 \cdot 2^3 + 0 \cdot 2^2 + 0 \cdot 2^1 + 1 \cdot 2^0$	9
1010	$1 \cdot 2^3 + 0 \cdot 2^2 + 1 \cdot 2^1 + 0 \cdot 2^0$	10
1011	$1 \cdot 2^3 + 0 \cdot 2^2 + 1 \cdot 2^1 + 1 \cdot 2^0$	11
1100	$1 \cdot 2^3 + 1 \cdot 2^2 + 0 \cdot 2^1 + 0 \cdot 2^0$	12
1101	$1 \cdot 2^3 + 1 \cdot 2^2 + 0 \cdot 2^1 + 1 \cdot 2^0$	13
.	.	.
.	.	.
.	.	.
0.1	$0 \cdot 2^0 + 1 \cdot 2^{-1}$	$\frac{1}{2}$
0.01	$0 \cdot 2^0 + 0 \cdot 2^{-1} + 1 \cdot 2^{-2}$	$\frac{1}{4}$

If the first column to the left of the decimal point is denoted as the zero column, 2^0, the second as the ones column, 2^1, the third as the twos column, 2^2, etc., then any binary representation can be converted into the base 10 number by raising the base 2 to each exponent given by the column number in which a 1 appears and adding the results. Hence 101.1 states, reading from left to right, that there is one 2 raised to the second power, no 2 raised to the first power, one 2 raised to the zero power, and one 2 raised to the negative 1 power. This yields

$$1 \cdot 2^2 + 0 \cdot 2^1 + 1 \cdot 2^0 + 1 \cdot 2^{-1} = 4 + 0 + 1 + \tfrac{1}{2} = 5\tfrac{1}{2}.$$

The system is based on powers of 2 rather than the powers of 10 that are used in the decimal system. The conversion of numbers in the base 10 to their binary equivalent can be tedious, but the binary system has advantages for use in electronic computers. Also arithmetic in a binary base is easier to perform since only 1s and 0s are used. Two examples of binary math are:

```
Add:   1.0     Binary:     1
      13.0                1101
       9.0                1001
       5.5                101.1
      ----                ------
      28.5              11100.1
```

The first binary column, counting from the right, adds to one. Since the second binary column adds to 4, two 2s, or 4, are carried to the next column by adding 2 to the next column. A zero is written below the line. Observe that in the binary scale 2s are carried. The sum of the third column is 2, so a zero is written below the line and a 1 (since there is one 2) is carried to the fourth column. The sum of the fourth column is 3. A 1 is written below the line and 1 is added to the fifth column to represent the 2 carried. The fifth column also adds to three so a 1 is written below the line and a 1 is carried to the sixth column. Since there are no further numbers, the 1 is written below the line. Checking the binary result gives

$$1 \cdot 2^4 + 1 \cdot 2^3 + 1 \cdot 2^2 + 0 \cdot 2^1 + 0 \cdot 2^0 + 1 \cdot 2^{-1},$$

which equals

$$16 + 8 + 4 + \tfrac{1}{2} = 28.5.$$

For a second example, consider the product of 27 by 13.

```
Multiply:   27     Binary:    11011
          × 13              ×  1101
          ----             --------
            81                11011
            27               110110
          ----              11011
           351            ---------
                          101011111
```

Checking the binary result gives

$$1\cdot 2^8 + 0\cdot 2^7 + 1\cdot 2^6 + 0\cdot 2^5 + 1\cdot 2^4 + 1\cdot 2^3 + 1\cdot 2^2 + 1\cdot 2^1 + 1\cdot 2^0,$$

which equals

$$256 + 0 + 64 + 0 + 16 + 8 + 4 + 2 + 1 = 351.$$

Although numbers are longer, the advantages of working with only the digits 0 and 1 overcome this minor difficulty. The advantages for electronic computer computation arise from the fact that 0 and 1 can stand for the presence or absence of an electronic or magnetic charge, an open or closed circuit, a lit or unlit tube. Hence binary notation simplifies the circuitry required to perform arithmetic operations.

Although the binary system facilitates the use of electronic mathematical operations, the longer numerical representations make the recording and storage of the data quite expensive. Since even electronic computers have limited capacities, the binary system also affects the size of problems that can be treated. These comments suggest that for storage purposes, we might return to the decimal system. Current practice, however, is to use bases greater than 10. A current favorite is the base 16, or hexadecimal system. In large part this is because conversion from binary to hexadecimal notation is facilitated by the relationship between their bases, namely $16 = 2^4$.

The hexadecimal system uses the digits 0 through 9, plus the letters A through F for the digits 10 through 15, respectively. Some examples of hexadecimal notation are given in Table 2–2.

Conversion of hexadecimal notation to binary (and vice versa) is relatively easy. For example, 4D in hexadecimal, where 4 is written as 0100 in binary, and D = 13 is written as 1101 in binary, becomes 01001101 in binary. The two binary numbers are simply attached. This is the number 77 in either system, as is easily verified:

$$4D = 4\cdot 16^1 + 13\cdot 16^0 = 77,$$

$$01001101 = 1\cdot 2^6 + 1\cdot 2^3 + 1\cdot 2^2 + 1 = 64 + 8 + 4 + 1 = 77.$$

TABLE 2–2

Some Hexadecimal Numbers

Hexadecimal Representation	*Conversion to Powers of 16*	*Decimal Representation*
0	$0\cdot 16^0$	0
1	$1\cdot 16^0$	1
F	$15\cdot 16^0$	15
1F	$1\cdot 16^1 + 15\cdot 16^0$	31
2A3	$2\cdot 16^2 + 10\cdot 16^1 + 3\cdot 16^0$	675
C5.4	$12\cdot 16^1 + 5\cdot 16^0 + 4\cdot 16^{-1}$	197.25

The economy of the hexadecimal system is evident in the example. One warning: when converting from hexadecimal notation to binary notation, all numbers should be written using four places before combining them. For example, the number 41 is written as 29 in hexidecimal notation. Now, using powers of two, 2 is written as 0010 in binary and 9 is written as 0101. Combining gives 00100101, or simply 100101 in binary. The use of different mathematical bases illustrates the power of creative thinking and the use of exponents to economize in a real situation.

⌇ : Write the number 8 in the following bases.

1. Base 2 _____

2. Base 4 _____

3. Base 8 _____

4. Base 16 _____

5. Base 37 _____

Answers

1. 1,000

2. 20

3. 10

4. 8

5. 8

2-4 SUMMARY

The exponent finds numerous applications in managerial problems. These include, but are not limited to, the examples discussed in this chapter: interest calculations and electronic computing procedures. Exponents will be lurking about many of the problems discussed in future chapters. Thus it is necessary to understand what they mean and how to work with them. The first task of the present chapter is to refresh our understanding of the algebraic rules for manipulating exponents. Six rules are discussed and illustrated.

The remainder of the chapter reviews the mathematics of compound-interest calculations. This is an important subject to students of management and economics and is included here because it is a practical example of the presence of exponents in managerial decisions.

Finally, a brief introduction is given to mathematical bases other than the familiar decimal system. This discussion illustrates an imaginative use with great practical significance to management of the power and value of exponents. The section also gives the reader insight into how electronic computers function.

NEW SYMBOLS

Symbol	*English Translation*
superscript n (or other letter)	Form the product of n expressions like that to which the superscript attaches.

RULES FOR EXPONENTS

Rule 1: Product

$$b^{c_1} \cdot b^{c_2} \cdot \ldots \cdot b^{c_i} \cdot \ldots \cdot b^{c_n} = b^{c_1 + c_2 + \ldots + c_i + \ldots + c_n} = b^{\Sigma c_i}.$$

Rule 2: Powers

$$(b^c)^d = b^{cd}.$$

Rule 3: Quotients

$$\frac{b^c}{b^d} = b^{c-d}.$$

Rule 4: Zero Power

$$b^0 = 1.$$

Rule 5: Negative Exponent

$$b^{-c} = \frac{1}{b^c}.$$

Rule 6: Roots

$$\sqrt[n]{b} = b^{1/n}.$$

Here b, c, d, and n are any real valued expressions, $n \neq 0$.

PROBLEMS

Problems for Self-Study: 4, 5, 8, 10

2–1. Compute the following.

  a. 3^3

  b. 4^4

  c. 2^6

  d. 8^{-4}

  e. $(-4)^5$

  f. $(-2)^6$

2–2.*   Compute the following.

  a. $(1.05)^3$

  b. $(1.21)^{1/2}$

  c. $(2.7)^2$

  d. $(-6.1)^4$

  e. $(43.6)^2$

  f. $-(4.1)^2$

2–3.*   Simplify each of the following expressions.

  a. $2^6/2^4$

  b. $2^4/2^{-2}$

  c. $2^2 + 2^{-2}$

  d. $3^{-2}/3^{-5}$

  e. $\left(\dfrac{4}{5}\right)^2 \left(\dfrac{3}{2}\right)^3$

  f. $12^3 \cdot 3^{-3} \cdot 2^{-5}$

2–4.   Simplify the following expressions.

  a. $\left(\dfrac{x}{y}\right)^3 \left(\dfrac{x}{z}\right)^{-2}$

  b. $\dfrac{x^3 \cdot y^2}{x^5 \cdot y^{-2}}$

  c. $\dfrac{(3x)^2}{6y}$

  d. $\dfrac{x^6 \cdot x^3}{(xy)^4}$

  e. $\dfrac{(x/z)^3 \cdot y^4}{(x/y)^2}$

2–5.   Evaluate each of the following expressions.

  a. $(9)^{3/2}$

  b. $(8)^{4/3}$

  c. $\left(\dfrac{1}{4}\right)^{5/2}$

  d. $27^{-2/3}$

  e. $\left(\dfrac{9}{16}\right)^{-1/2} \cdot \left(\dfrac{125}{64}\right)^{1/3}$

2–6.*   Simplify each of the following expressions.

     a. $(a^2 \cdot a^2)^3$

     b. $(a^2 + a^2)^3$

     c. $(a^2 + a^3)^2$

     d. $(a^2 + a^{-2})^2$

2–7.   Let x, y, and z represent the two sides and the hypotenuse, respectively, of a right triangle. The Pythagorean theorem states that the square of the hypotenuse length is equal to the sum of the squares of the side lengths.

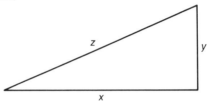

     a. Express the theorem mathematically.

     b. Find an expression for the hypotenuse, z, in terms of the two sides.

     c. Find an expression for a side, x, in terms of the hypotenuse and the other side.

2–8.   If the annual discount rate is 10 percent, find the present value of a cash-flow stream that yields $1100 at the end of the first year, $2420 at the end of the second year, and $3993 at the end of the third year.

2–9.*   The double-declining balance method of asset depreciation allows a firm to depreciate an asset by $(2/N) \cdot B_i$ each year, where N is the expected life of the asset and B_i is the current book value.

     a. Express the book value of an asset n years after it was purchased at a cost of B_0.

     b. An asset with an expected life of 10 years is purchased for $1000. Using the double-declining balance method of depreciation, calculate the asset's book value at the end of the third year.

2–10.   Find the future values of the following amounts. (Leave answers in exponent form.)

     a. $2000 at 5 percent interest after 10 years.

     b. $1,500,000 at 7 percent interest compounded semiannually for 6 years.

     c. $1000 deposited every quarter at 6 percent compounded quarterly for 5 years. The first deposit is made one quarter from now and the last deposit is made at the end of the fifth year.

2–11. The Abbott Construction Company is considering purchasing a new piece of equipment for $15,850. The net cash flows from the equipment over its lifetime appear below. The rate of discount is 6 percent per year.

Year	Net Cash Flow
1	$3000
2	$4000
3	$5000
4	$4000
5	$3000

Give an expression for the present value. The present value of the net cash flows exceeds the purchase price.

2–12.* Suppose that the cash flows for the investment in Problem 2–11 were

Year	Net Cash Flow
1	$3000
2	$3000
3	$4000
4	$5000
5	$4000

Give an expression for the present value. In this case the present value does not justify the purchase price of $15,850 if a 6 percent discount rate is appropriate. (Compare the answer to Problem 2–11.)

2–13. Sweepstakes prizes very often are awarded either as a lump sum or in payments over time. For instance, suppose that a sweepstakes winner has a choice between $100,000 now or $1000 per month for 100 months. Assuming a positive discount rate, which alternative has a higher present value?

2–14.* A man wishes to have $10,000 in his savings 10 years from now. The bank pays 5 percent interest, compounded annually. How much must a man deposit

a. If he wishes to deposit a lump sum now?

b. If he wishes to deposit equal amounts yearly for the 10 years?

c. If he wishes to deposit equal amounts yearly for the first 5 years and nothing thereafter?

Leave your answers in exponent form.

2–15.   How much money would be received from the sale of a bond if the current discount rate were 5 percent and the bond repayment would take the form of a 20-year annuity of $500 per year plus $10,000 in the twentieth year? Assume that the money received will be the bond's present value.

2–16.* A hospital is considering two plans for expansion. The first plan calls for an immediate expenditure of $5 million, although some of the facilities will remain idle for a few years. The second plan calls for a smaller expansion now (costing $3 million) and then a further expenditure of $3 million when it becomes necessary. This is expected in about 4 years. Suppose that the hospital's discount rate is 10 percent. Which alternative gives a lower present value of expenditures?

2–17.   A consumer wants to borrow $1200 at an annual interest rate of 6 percent and repay the loan in 12 equal monthly installments. How much will the installments be? Leave your answer in exponent form.

2–18.* For the XYZ Company, the cost of producing x units can be expressed as $100 + 3x + 2x^{1/2}$. Find the costs of production for

   a. $x = 100$
   b. $x = 400$
   c. $x = 900$
   d. $x = 225$

2–19.* In equipment-investment decisions, one common means of selecting among projects is to rank each alternative way of doing a given task by the time it takes the cost savings of the method to return the investment. This method is called the payback method.

   For example, consider the following alternative billing machines designed to replace hand operations over the next 5 years.

	Cost of	Savings by Year ($)				
	Machine ($)	1	2	3	4	5
Machine 1	12,000	6,000	4,000	2,000	1,000	—
Machine 2	12,000	3,500	3,500	3,500	3,500	3,500
Machine 3	12,000	2,000	4,000	6,000	—	—

   a. Which machine would be purchased using the payback method?
   b. Which machine would you recommend given that money has some time value?

2–20.   Express the following decimal numbers as binary numbers.
   a. 21

     b. 7

     c. 89

     d. 112

     e. 129

2–21.* Perform the indicated operations on the following binary numbers. Check your work by converting to decimals.

     a. $1111 + 1$

     b. $101 + 1101$

     c. $101 \cdot 1110$

     d. $100011 - 11001$

     e. $100011 \div 111$

2–22. Perform the indicated operations on the following hexadecimal numbers. Check by converting to decimals.

     a. $9 + 8$

     b. $21 - 12$

     c. $B \cdot 12$

     d. $23 \div 7$

2–23.* A binary coding system (one consisting solely of 0s and 1s) is required to represent product types. The product types are currently coded as a combination of a single letter (*A* to *Z*) followed by a single digit (0 to 9).

     a. What is the minimum number of binary digits necessary to represent this code?

     b. How many hexadecimal digits would be required?

2–24. Express the following as decimal numbers.

     a. 11010   given in base 2

     b. 735   given in base 8

     c. 4210   given in base 5

     d. 12121   given in base 3

2–25.* Convert the following numbers to decimal numbers.

     a. 101.11   given in base 2

     b. 32.3   given in base 4

     c. 7.23   given in base 8

     d. 444.44 given in base 5

3

Functions

A mail-order house is interested in knowing the response it could expect from a mailing of 10,000 circulars. A manufacturing organization wishes to estimate the expected variable unit cost for changes in the volume of productive activity. A public administrator wants to judge the benefits resulting from the expenditure of $1,000,000 on low-cost housing in New York City. The local director of a charity wants to know how much more could be collected if 100 additional door-to-door volunteers are obtained. A hospital administrator wishes to predict the impact on his emergency-room staffing needs as the local population continues to grow. All these and many more activities suggest an interest by the manager in the relationships between two (and sometimes more) variables. These relationships are known as functions. If the manager knows the functional relationship between two variables, then given the values of one of them he can determine the other without ambiguity. It is the purpose of this chapter to offer some insight into the use of functions in solving problems such as these.

The notion of a function is a central concept to mathematics, and its mastery is essential.

3-1 A FUNCTION MACHINE

Suppose the manager interested in describing cost behavior has established the relationship between cost and productive activity given in Table 3–1. The possible production levels in units per hour are limited in this example to the interval 100 to 125 inclusive and to increases by steps of 5. For now, the listed levels are the only ones to be considered. Table 3–1 gives the elements in a function.

46

TABLE 3–1

Expected Cost at Several Production Levels

Possible Levels of Production Activity (*units per hour*)	*Expected Variable Unit Cost* (*dollars*)
100	600
105	610
110	620
115	630
120	640
125	650

Function

Suppose two sets of elements are given. Call them sets 1 and 2. Then a function is specified *from* set 1 *to* set 2 by a rule that associates every element in set 1 with one and only one element in set 2.

In the cost–productive-activity example, set 1 is the set of activity levels. Set 2 is the set of cost elements, and the rule is the matching suggested by the table itself.

It is useful to think about a function in terms of an analogue: in this case a machine, a function machine (see Figure 3–1). The possible inputs to the

FIGURE 3–1

A Function Machine

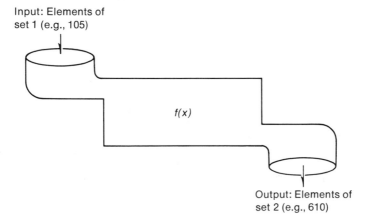

Input: Elements of set 1 (e.g., 105)

$f(x)$

Output: Elements of set 2 (e.g., 610)

function machine are the elements in set 1 (productive-activity levels in the example), and the outputs of the function machine are the elements in set 2 (expected costs in the example). In the example, if 105 is put into the machine, 610 comes out. We have given the name (the label) $f(x)$ to the function machine, for reasons that will become clear later. Using this notion, we can write $f(105) = 610, f(100) = 600$, and so on.

One convenient and common system for writing a function is simply to list the pairs of elements involved, always listing first the input element from set 1. For the cost–productive-activity example the following set of pairs represents the function in Table 3–1:

$$\{(100, 600), (105, 610), (110, 620), (115, 630), (120, 640), (125, 650)\}.$$

The names of the two sets may be omitted as long as the context is clear and no confusion is possible.

The reader may wonder how functions are represented when there are a great many, perhaps even infinitely many, elements in set 1. Certainly we would not write them out in pairs as was done above. More efficient notation is needed, and, fortunately, it is available.

〰️ : Which of the following represent functions from the set of positive integers less than 5 to the set of positive integers less than 10? See if you can explain why, if no function is specified.

		Yes	*No*
1.	$\{(1, 2), (2, 4), (3, 6), (4, 8)\}$	———	———
2.	$\{(1, 7), (2, 7), (3, 7), (4, 7)\}$	———	———
3.	$\{(1, 3), (1, 4), (2, 5), (3, 2), (4, 9)\}$	———	———
4.	$\{(1, 1), (2, 2), (3, 3)\}$	———	———

Reasons

1.

2.

3.

4.

Answer. Cases 1 and 2 are functions. Case 3 is not a function because the number 1 in the first set is associated with both the numbers 3 and 4 from the second set. This is not allowed by the phrase "one and only one" in the definition of a function. Case 4 is not a function because the number 4 in the first set is not associated with any number in the second set. The definition requires every element in the first set to be used in the association. Note the reliance in each case upon the definition to answer the question. (Relying on definitions is a common trick of mathematicians.) Note also that not all of set 2 need be used, and some elements in set 2 may be used more than once. All of set 1 must be used.

3-2 THE GRAPH

The cost versus productive-activity function is graphed in Figure 3–2, where the values on the horizontal scale, usually denoted by the variable x, are the levels of productive activity in set 1. The values on the vertical scale, usually denoted by the variable y or by $f(x)$, are the estimated costs. It is important to observe that only the six labeled points on the graph belong to the function. The dashed line is included only to assist in reading the graph. Also, because of the magnitude of the numbers involved, the lower portions of both scales have been omitted.

The graph tells us everything about the function we need to know. The points are the function and the graph in this case is the rule that permits the association to be made between the elements of the two sets.

FIGURE 3–2

Expected Cost Versus Productive Activity Graph

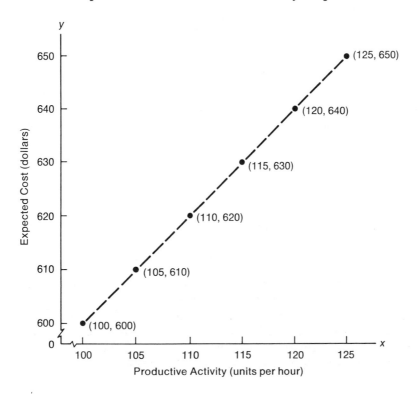

The graphical method of specifying a function also provides a means of dealing with infinitely large sets of numbers. Suppose that the possible levels of productive activity could be any number between 100 and 125 inclusive. The graph in Figure 3–2, using the points and the dashed line, allows us to determine (at least approximately) the expected cost associated with any activity level in the interval from 100 to 125. For example, an activity level of 112 leads to an expected cost of 624.

$\sim\!\!\sqrt{}$:   Circle the numbers of the statements below which are valid.

1. Using Table 3–1, the expected cost for an activity level of 112 is 624.
2. Using the expanded problem formulation, the expected cost for an activity level of 130 is 660.

Answer.   Neither statement is true. Table 3–1 does not include the activity level 112 in set 1. Hence it is not a part of the function and no expected cost for it is defined, no matter how logical the interpolation appears. The expanded example does not define a function for activity levels below 100 or above 125. Hence no expected cost is defined for 130, no matter how reasonable the extrapolation may seem. An entirely different relationship might hold for activity levels above 125.

3-3 THE EQUATION

The efficient mathematician is loath to draw a graph every time he wishes to specify a function. He prefers a more convenient means of specifying the rule for a function. Such a method is provided by the use of equations. Continuing the expanded example in which productive activity can be anywhere between 100 and 125, the equation rule for this function is

$$\text{expected cost} = 400 + 2 \text{ (productive activity)}$$

or, more conveniently,

$$y = 400 + 2x, \quad 100 \leq x \leq 125,$$

where $y \equiv$ expected cost and $x \equiv$ productive activity.

Several observations concerning the use of an equation as the rule for a function are in order. First, the equation is only the rule that associates an expected cost with an activity level. In other words, give us an activity level and we can give back an expected cost. The equation does the job of the function machine. The value of x (the activity level from set 1) is the input, and the value of y (the expected cost in set 2) is the output.

But suppose you supplied the activity level of 150 for x. The equation rule would suggest an expected cost of $400 + 2(150)$ equals \$700. But the value $x = 150$ is not included in the set of values for which the function is defined. The expanded function in question was specified only for activity levels between 100 and 125 inclusive. We are not permitted to use it for values above 125. This example emphasizes the fact that the equation is just the pairing rule, and it is necessary to be careful in specifying the precise sets of values in the sets for which the pairing rule holds. The set of activity levels for which the pairing rule holds is called the *domain* of the function.

You are probably familiar with equations from previous schoolwork and have been used to calling them functions. Is it incorrect to call an equation a function? In precise mathematical use, it is incorrect. But suppose that the parties to the communication process agree on the sets involved in the matching. Then the equation, the rule, tells everything of interest about the function. It is an efficient and convenient means of conveying the information in a function. Indeed this is the primary reason (not laziness) the mathematician uses equations so extensively. We shall follow the practice of using the terms "function" and "equation" (or "rule for the function") interchangeably as long as the sets involved are understood. Since, in general, we are concerned with functions that apply to all the real numbers, we will assume that the sets involved in the matching are both the real numbers unless otherwise specified. Hence, where no confusion concerning the function in question should arise, the symbol $f(x)$ will be used to denote the function.

A second point about using equations is that they usually provide more precision as well as more efficiency. It is much easier to determine the expected cost, in the extended example, from the equation than it is using the graph. Many functions are not linear, and in such cases graphs are even less precise.

A third point involves notation. The x term in the equation is called the *independent variable* since it is selected without regard for the value of y. Thus y becomes the *dependent variable* because, given the equation (rule), its value is uniquely determined once the value of x is specified. We might say that y is a function of x and write $f(x)$ for the words "is a function of x." Using this notation the expected-cost equation is rewritten

$$y \equiv f(x) = 400 + 2x$$

or simply

$$f(x) = 400 + 2x.$$

Symbol	*English Translation*
$f(x)$	The value of the function at x (also used to represent the function when the sets involved are clear).

This is common notation for the value of a function when the rule is given in equation form. The symbol is useful as well. For example, if we desire the expected cost for an activity level of 122.67 units, we know the value of x and seek the value of y or $f(x)$ for the known value of x. This is written, using the $f(x)$ form, as

$$f(x = 122.67) = 400 + 2(122.67)$$
$$= 645.34.$$

Once again the notation is simplified, however, to read

$$f(122.67) = 400 + 2(122.67).$$

This is the reason we gave the label $f(x)$ to our function machine. If 122.67 is input as x, the value of 645.34 is the output for y or $f(x)$. Notation of the form $f(122.67)$ will be used extensively in this book. In general, for an arbitrary constant, $a, f(a)$ simply means to evaluate $f(x)$ by putting a in each place that is occupied by x in the equation.

One final point. The equation $y \equiv f(x) = 400 + 2x$ is the equation of a straight line (see Figure 3–2). The number 400 is the value of $y \equiv f(x)$ when x is set equal to zero. It is called the y *intercept*. The number 2 is the amount $y \equiv f(x)$ increases when x increases by one unit. It is called the *slope* of the equation. If productive activity, x, is increased by one unit from 100 to 101 expected cost, $y \equiv f(x)$, increases two units from $f(100) = 400 + 2(100) = 600$ to $f(101) = 400 + 2(101) = 602$. In other words, the function experiences a rise of two units for a run of one unit. The slope is the *ratio of the rise to the run:* slope = rise ÷ run.

~~ : Using the sets of real numbers, find the value of the function for each of the following cases:

1. $y = 2 + 3x$ for $x = 2$	$y =$ _____
2. $f(x) = 2 + 3x$ for $x = 2$	$f(2) =$ _____
3. $f(p) = 400 + 2p$ for $p = 100$	$f(100) =$ _____
4. $f(x) = 200 \div (4 - 2x)$ for $x = 2$	$f(2) =$ _____

Answer. The first two problems have the same answer: y or $f(x) = 8$. [This could be written $f(2) = 8$.] Case 3 indicates that letters other than x and y can be used: $f(100) = 600$. The last case is a little tricky. In this case the denominator is equal to zero, and division of a positive integer by zero is an impossible operation, as we learned in Chapter 1. Hence $f(2)$ is impossible. No number can be matched to $x = 2$, and hence no function is defined unless the set of x values for the function is redefined to exclude the number 2.

3-4 EXAMPLES OF SEVERAL SIMPLE FUNCTIONS

Equations and their use will be studied in greater depth in Chapter 5. At this point we wish only to extend the discussion briefly to show the flexibility of the function concept and the use of equations.

Perhaps you are familiar with such expressions as the following:

1. "The average number of orders I obtain from one of my salesmen is not affected by his monthly salary."
2. "The demands on our facilities grow exponentially with increases in population."
3. "Certainly advertising expenditure increases the income of our firm up to a point, but eventually the increased cost is not recovered."

Each of these statements implies a functional relationship (although it may require further specification before it is very useful to us) between two sets of values. We have written an appropriate equation and graphed each of the three statements. It would be good practice if you tried to do this on a piece of scratch paper before you peek at our solutions.

Statement One

$$M \equiv f(s) = c,$$

where M stands for average (monthly) orders, s stands for the monthly salary level, and c is a constant.

The equation expresses mathematically the fact that no matter what value is substituted for s, average monthly orders, $f(s)$, remain equal to the constant level c. It is sometimes said in such cases that the variables are independent. We also need to state that this function only holds for the nonnegative real numbers, although this may be obvious. (Whoever heard of a negative salary?) A function of this type is called a *constant function* (see Figure 3–3).

Statement Two

$$D \equiv f(p) = h^p$$

where D stands for demand, h is a constant (assume that $h > 1$), and p is population (measured in appropriate units).

As long as h exceeds 1, Figure 3–4 illustrates the type of function implied by this statement. The constant h merely places the height of the line for each value of p. Since it is silly to talk about demand when there are no people, $p = 0$, the value of h is meaningless by itself, even though it is necessary to the calculation of D for any value of p.

FIGURE 3–3

Average Orders as a Function of Monthly Salary: $s \geq 0$

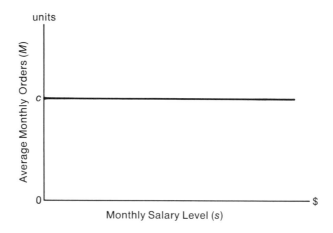

FIGURE 3–4

Demand as a Function of Population

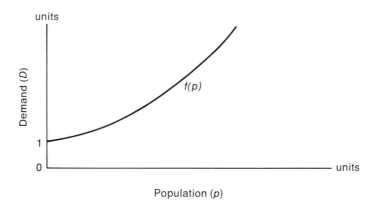

We have left h unspecified here since the statement does not make clear just what value is appropriate. The graph with h greater than 1 does seem, however, to represent what was meant by the statement. The curve can be made steeper by making h larger. (If we allow h to be less than 1 but greater than zero, a substantially different picture is obtained. The curve decreases for increasing values of p.) Population is treated as an exponent of h. You should have been able to guess the general shape of the curve in Figure 3–4 even if you were not able to obtain its equation.

Statement Three

$$I \equiv f(z) = -z^2 + az - b,$$

where *I* stands for income, *z* stands for advertising expenditure, and *a* and *b* are nonnegative constants.

The statement suggests that income first rises with increased expenditures on advertising, reaches a maximum, and then declines. In this case we have assumed an exponent of 2 for the first term on the right of the equality. This gives a curve called a *parabola*. The example is graphed in Figure 3–5. Such a curve is among those that satisfy the requirements of the statement, but it is not the only possibility, merely a convenient one. The reader should be able to guess the general shape of the curve in Figure 3–5, even though we would not expect him to know its equation or the fact that a parabola satisfies the statement's requirements.

FIGURE 3–5

Income as a Function of Advertising Expenditures: General Example

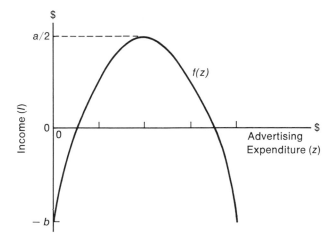

A function that yields such a curve is given by

$$I \equiv f(z) = -z^2 + 4z - 2,$$

where *y* is in units of $1,000 each and *z* is in units of $100 each.

This example, graphed in Figure 3–6, suggests that income (revenues less expenses) is negative if nothing is expended on advertising. This may not be realistic. If not, the value of *b*, equal to −2 here, could be increased to a positive value, indicating some income even with zero advertising expenditures. The effect of changing the last term from -2 to, say, $+5$ merely shifts each point on the curve up by the same amount, namely 7 units. If the type of curve is not changed, sufficiently large advertising expenditures will still cause income to become negative. For the original example, with the last term equal to -2, this occurs for a z value between 3 and 4. If the last term is increased to $+5$, then income is negative if advertising exceeds 5 units. [At $z = 5$, $-z^2 + 4z + 5 = -(5)^2 + 4(5) + 5 = 0$, and, from the graph, we see that larger values of z are associated with negative values of I.]

FIGURE 3–6

Income as a Function of Advertising Expenditures: Specific Example

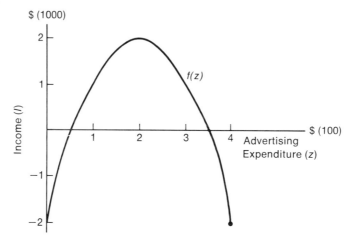

Again it is necessary (at least formally) to specify that the function holds only for nonnegative values of z. It does not seem sensible to talk about negative advertising.

One of the interesting points about this example is that there is a best (or optimal) level of expenditure for advertising. In this example income is highest when advertising expenditures are given by $z = 2$. This can be seen in the graph. The equation, or graph, also tells us what this best (maximum) income will be. Using the equation and substituting $z = 2$ gives the answer. It is also 2 (by coincidence) in this example. This checks using the graph. Later we will find more efficient means of finding the best or optimal level for the independent variable of interest. For now it is important to realize that careful graphing can give a good idea of where such optimal points may occur.

The use of the graph to specify a function illustrates the notation method in Section 3–1 to denote a function—namely, the set of pairs written within parentheses. Points on a graph are also usually denoted by pairs (x, y), where the first element is the x coordinate and the second is the y coordinate. For example, the leftmost point on the graph in Figure 3–6 is denoted by the pair $(0, -2)$. Thus a *partial* listing of the function implied by the equation

$$f(z) = -z^2 + 4z - 2$$

is

$$\{(0, -2), (\tfrac{1}{2}, -\tfrac{1}{4}), (1, 1), (2, 2), (3, 1), \ldots\}.$$

$\sqrt{}$: Circle the equation below which most reasonably reflects the following function. "We can't reduce the average number of defects in our assemblies to zero, but, by increasing the level of inspection effort, we can reduce it to as low a level as the government may require." (It may help if you graph these equations using specific numbers for a, b, and c. For this purpose, let $a = b = 2$ and $c = 6$.)

$$d \equiv \text{average number of defects per assembly}$$
$$x \equiv \text{level of inspection effort in units}$$
$$a, b, c \equiv \text{constants greater than 1}$$

1. $d \equiv f(x) = c - bx$ $x \geq 1$
2. $d \equiv f(x) = -x^a + abx - b$ $x \geq 1$
3. $d \equiv f(x) = bx^{-a}$ $x \geq 1$
4. $d \equiv f(x) = x - b$ $x \geq 1$
5. $d \equiv f(x) = ab$ $x \geq 1$

Answer. Using the suggested numerical values and the accompanying graph (Figure 3–7) may help you see that only equation 3 makes sense. In cases 1 and 2 the average number of defects can be reduced below zero. This is, of course, nonsense for this example. (Sometimes equations that give "nonsense" results for extreme values are used, but they are considered valid only "through a relevant range" over which the results are reasonable.) In case 4 the average number of defects increases for all x. Only in case 3 does it continue to decline, never quite reaching zero. Case 5 represents a horizontal line where the number of defects is not influenced by inspection effort.

3-5 ESTIMATING FUNCTIONS GRAPHICALLY

Graphing functions is a useful way to visualize functional relationships. As we have seen, the method can also be used to approximate important facts about such relationships, such as the best level of advertising expenditure to use. (We hasten to point out that other possibly important variables affecting income, for example product quality, have been ignored.)

FIGURE 3–7

Defects Related to Inspection Effort:
Four Examples

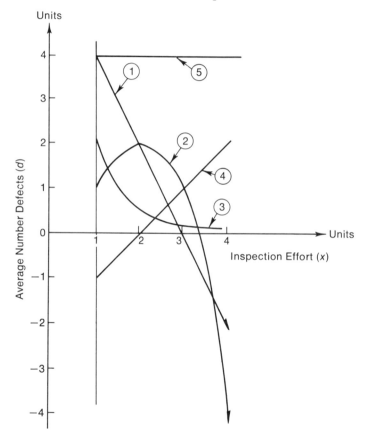

Sometimes a manager may have available substantial data concerning a functional relationship between two variables. The data, however, may not suggest a particular single functional relationship. For example, consider the data in Table 3–2, relating the number of defects in an assembly to the amount of time the assembler has been working. The manager believes that these historical data are relevant to his present prediction problem and that, if he can get a satisfactory relationship, it will be useful in determining whether to change assemblers more often, introduce work breaks, or take other possible corrective actions open to him. As a first step in estimating the relationship, he may plot the data from Table 3–2 using assembler time as the independent variable (see Figure 3–8). The number by each point is the observation number and is taken from the first column of Table 3–2.

TABLE 3–2

Number of Defects by Time Assembler Has Been Working
(Arranged by Time Order of the Observation)

Observation Number	Number of Defects	Assembler Time (hours)
1	2	4
2	5	3
3	6	8
4	8	5
5	1	2
6	1	9
7	3	2
8	10	10
9	4	5
10	1	6
11	4	9
12	6	6
13	7	10
14	8	8
15	3	7
16	3	10
17	4	8

Contrary to previous examples we have examined, but quite realistically, the plotted points do not fall on a single line, curved or straight. In such cases the manager may still use the available data to estimate the underlying relationship. The manager familiar with the operation being studied has a distinct advantage over the mathematician. This is because his experience helps him to judge the appropriate form of the relationship between the two variables.

Suppose the manager in the present example believes that the number of defectives should increase as assembler time increases. This might be due, say, to operator fatigue. Suppose further that he is willing to assume that the relationship is linear. Based on this assumption a given increase in time causes a constant increase in the average number of defectives. (The data slightly suggest that the number of defectives increases more rapidly than linearly with increased assembler time, and this may also be a reasonable operating

FIGURE 3–8

Number of Defects as a Function of Assembler Time

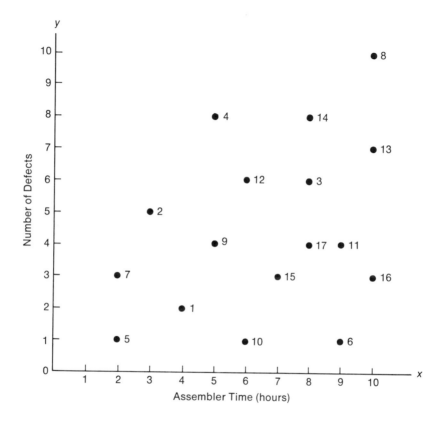

assumption. Nevertheless, a linear relationship over the observed range may still be an adequate and useful approximation. It is not uncommon for mathematical approximations such as this to be used in managerial problems.) The manager then fits a freehand straight line to the data using Figure 3–8. You might try this yourself using a straightedge before looking at the manager's solution in Figure 3–9. There is a tendency for most people to draw the line with a greater slope than is justified by the data. Did you make this mistake?

The manager can now use the estimated line on the graph to predict the average number of defectives. He may, however, prefer to use the equation of the line. We note that the line passes through the points (2, 2) and (10, 6). The slope of the line, the change in the dependent variable, divided by the change in the independent variable, is $(6 - 2) \div (10 - 2) = \frac{1}{2}$. Extending the line two units to the left will therefore cause it to fall by one-half this

FIGURE 3–9

**Number of Defects as a Function of Assembler Time
with Estimated Linear Relationship**

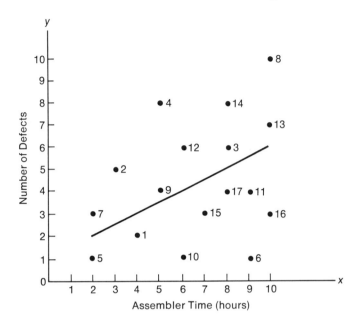

amount, or 1 unit. Thus the y intercept, the value of y when $x = 0$, of the line is 1. The equation of the line can now be written as

$$y \equiv f(x) = 1 + 0.5x, \qquad 2 \leq x \leq 10.$$

It is important to specify that the equation is valid only for the values observed. To extrapolate beyond this set of values requires an assumption of continued linearity for the relationship, an assumption we have already argued may not be valid if assembler time is increased beyond 10 hours. This does not mean that the manager should not extrapolate, only that he should be careful to realize the additional assumption he is making by extrapolating.

But we have not exhausted all the information available in Table 3–2. It may be that the relationship is changing over time. Since we are given the order of observations, it may be possible to obtain some insight into this issue. The numbers in Figures 3–8 or 3–9 indicate the time order of the observations. From these we see that there appears to be a tendency for more recent observations to involve larger values for both variables and for there to be more defects regardless of assembler time. This could be important. If true, it may signal further study using new data as they become available. The cause may be in new and cheaper materials, equipment condition, different operators, or a combination of these.

The graphs also suggest that there is more variability of the points about the line for large values of *x*. In other words, points are farther from the line for larger values of the independent variable *x*. More variability may be due to fatigue when the assembler has been on the job a long time. Suppose this is true and the equation of the line is used to predict *y* for given values of *x*. Then the predictions of *y* for larger values of *x* will have more variability associated with them. More variability suggests more uncertainty in such predictions.

The reader may wonder why the points do not fall on a single curve. There could be several reasons. They include, but are not limited to (1) other factors affecting the number of defects besides assembler time (such as the status of the equipment) and (2) the ability to determine (measure) time spent or the number of defects without error.

As you might expect, there are more sophisticated ways to study relationships similar to the one in this section. You will probably do so some day in a statistics course, where the methods will be discussed under the heading "correlation and regression analysis." Nevertheless, it is important to realize that you are already in a position to obtain one of the more important benefits of these more sophisticated techniques—prediction.

~~ : Circle the best description of what you think the form of the following relationship would be: the relationship between the average total cost of production per unit and the productive capacity for which a plant is built. Let *C* be defined as average total cost per unit and *P* be defined as productive capacity:

1. *C* decreases continuously with increases in *P*,
2. *C* increases continuously with increases in *P*,
3. *C* first increases and then decreases with increases in *P*, or
4. *C* first decreases and then increases with increases in *P*.

Answer. For small levels of productive capacity, average total unit costs are high. For somewhat larger capacity levels, average cost declines as efficiencies of scale take place. But these efficiencies do not continue indefinitely as productive capacity is further increased. Eventually increases in productive capacity cost more than they save in variable costs and average total unit costs rise. Thus answer 4 is correct for most situations.

3-6 INVERSE FUNCTIONS

The first function in Section 3–3 related expected cost to productive activity by the equation

$$y = 400 + 2x, \qquad 100 \leq x \leq 125.$$

Given a value of x, productive activity, we can estimate expected cost. But it is possible to work in the opposite direction as well. Given a level of expected cost, it is possible to find the related productive activity. For example, if an expected cost level of 618 is taken, this value can be substituted into the equation and the associated productive-activity level determined:

$$y = 618 = 400 + 2x.$$

Solving,

$$(618 - 400) \div 2 = x$$

or

$$0.5(618) - 200 = x$$

and

$$109 \ = x.$$

As you might expect, the mathematician can solve generally for x in terms of y. For the present example, he obtains

$$x \equiv f(y) = 0.5y - 200 \qquad 600 \le y \le 650.$$

The function given by this equation is the inverse of the original function

$$y = 400 + 2x.$$

Inverse Function

If it is possible to determine x as a function of y, call it $f(y)$, then $f(y)$ is the inverse function of $f(x)$.

Not all functions have inverses. For example,

$$y = x^2, \qquad \text{where } x \text{ and } y \text{ are real numbers}$$

is an equation for a function from the set over which x is a variable to the set over which y is a variable. But its inverse,

$$x = \sqrt{y}$$

or, squaring both sides,

$$x^2 = y$$

is not a function from the set over which y is a variable to the set over which x is a variable since two elements in set 2, the set of x's here, are associated with each y in set 1. This violates the definition of a function given in Section 3–1. For example, both $x = +2$ and $x = -2$ are associated with $y = 4$. (The equation $x = \sqrt{y}$ is the rule for a function if $\sqrt{y}$ is defined as the positive square root and y is defined to be nonnegative.)

In graphing it is usual, when considering inverse functions, to interchange the axes so that the horizontal axis continues to reflect the independent variable, y in the case of an inverse function.

∿ :   Suppose that sales as a function of advertising are reflected by the equation

$$y = \begin{cases} x, & 0 \le x < 4, \\ 2 + 0.5x, & 4 \le x \le 6. \end{cases}$$

Write the equation for the inverse function which describes advertising as a function of sales.

Answer

$$x = \begin{cases} y, & 0 \le y < 4, \\ 2y - 4, & 4 \le y \le 5. \end{cases}$$

Note that two different equations are required to describe the function over the set of x values allowed. The same was true of the function $y \equiv f(x)$.

3-7 SUMMARY

The concept of a function is one of the most important in all of mathematics. You will have need of it continually from here on. It is important to distinguish between the function and the rule for the function. The function is the set of pairs of values. The rule can be given in several forms, including tabular, graphical, or equation. Once the sets to be associated are determined, the rule tells us what pairs of values are associated, that is, the pairs that make up the function. Where these sets are clear to the parties in a discussion, such as when they are the real numbers, the rule for the function tells us all we need to know.

Whenever the manager specifies relationships or attempts to estimate them, he is using functions. These functions can take on many forms and can have many uses. Some of these forms and uses have been illustrated in this chapter. Others will be illustrated as we continue.

We have not exhausted the subject of functions. For example, only functions involving one independent variable have been discussed. Functions involving more than one independent variable are required for many applications and we shall have reason to resort to them later.

Finally, we have used some terms (such as set) that have very precise mathematical meanings. And we have not been particularly careful in their use in pursuit of the objective of communicating ideas versus mathematical rigor. Chapter 16, which discusses sets, is more precise about this important terminology.

NEW SYMBOLS

Symbol	English Translation
$f(x)$	The value of the function at x (also used to represent the function when the sets involved are clear).

PROBLEMS

Problems for Self-Study: 1, 3, 4, 11, 14

3–1. Which of the following are functions or the rules for functions? (In parts *c* through *f*, *y* is the dependent variable.) Assume that the sets of numbers involved are the real numbers unless otherwise specified.

  a. $\{(1, 2), (2, 4), (3, 6), (4, 8), (5, 1)\}$, where the first set is the set of positive integers less than 6.

  b. $\{(1, 2), (2, 4), (5, 1), (3, 6), (2, 7), (4, 8)\}$, where the first set is the set of positive integers less than 6.

  c. $y^2 = 6x$

  d. $y = (x^2 - 4) \div (x^2 - 4x + 4)$

  e. $y = x^3$

  f. $y = x^{-2}$

3–2.* Represent graphically on an *xy* coordinate system.

  a. $x = 2$

  b. $y = 4$ for $2 \le x \le 4$

  c. $x \ge 0$ and $y \ge 1$

  d. $x < 3$ and $1 \le y$

  e. $y > x - 1$

  f. $1 \le x < 3$

3–3.   Evaluate.

   a. $f(2)$ when $f(x) = 3bx^2 + 6x + 6$
   b. $f(1)$ when $f(x) = (3ax - 6x^2) \div (2x - 2)$
   c. $f(4a)$ when $f(z) = -z^2 + (z - 2a)^2$
   d. $f(z)$ when $f(y) = y^{-1} + a^4$
   e. $f(az^2)$ when $f(x) = (x^2 - a^2z^4) \div x$
   f. $f(x = a^2z)$ when $f(x) = x^2y + y^3 - 2a^4z^2y$

3–4.   The Dundee Corporation has estimated that total production cost in thousands is 100 at a level of activity of 5000 units, and 240 thousand at 40,000 units. Write a linear rule for this function and use it to estimate the level of fixed costs (cost when output equals zero) of the Dundee Company.

3–5.*   Sketch a graph for the following functions:

   a. $3x - 2$, $-3 \leq x \leq 4$
   b. $x^2 - 1$, $-3 \leq x \leq 3$
   c. $4 - x^2$, $-4 \leq x \leq 4$
   d. $(x + 2)(x - 3)^2$, $-2 \leq x \leq 4$
   e. $(x + 1)/(x - 1)(x + 1)$, $-3 \leq x \leq 3$
   f. $-2x^2 + 4x + 1$, $-1 \leq x \leq 3$

3–6.*   The Orsey Company uses accounting data to estimate profits based on sales. The functional relationship is given by

$$y \equiv f(x) = 5x - 200, \qquad x \geq 0,$$

where x and y are in thousands.

   a. What profit is made if there are no sales?
   b. What profit is made at a sales level of 100,000 units?
   c. What is the breakeven sales level? (Breakeven is defined as the sales level where profit is zero.)

3–7.   The Jackson County Hospital estimated its needs for polio treatment facilities in terms of patient hours in hundreds by the function

$$f(x) = -2x + 40, \qquad x \geq 0,$$

where x is time in years and $x = 0$ in 1965.

   a. How much care is required in 1980?
   b. When will there be no further demand for treatment?

3–8.* A store owner quickly jotted down the number of coins removed from his cash register by noting the number of quarters he had removed. Suppose that this number (of quarters) is x. He planned to figure out how much he had in coins as he went to the bank. He noted that the number of dimes is twice the number of quarters, the number of nickels is 3 less than the number of dimes, and there were half again as many 50-cent pieces as quarters. Determine an equation that will allow the store owner to determine how much he is taking to the bank.

3–9. The jaws on a go–no go gauge gradually drift apart. The left jaw moves left at 4 hundredths of a millimeter per hour and the right jaw moves right at 5 hundredths of a millimeter per hour.

    a. If they start at a distance of 20 hundredths of a millimeter apart, how far apart will they be in x hours?

    b. If the right jaw does not begin moving for y hours, how far apart are they after x hours?

    c. In part *a*, if maximum tolerance is 38 hundredths of a millimeter for the gauge, how long will it be before adjustment is necessary?

3–10.* A company makes rectangular-shaped fishing-tackle boxes without tops from rectangular pieces of metal 20 by 32 inches by cutting equal squares of size x on a side from each corner.

    a. Express the volume of the box as a function of x.

    b. If squares of size x are cut from one of the 20-inch ends only, while a lid is formed by cutting rectangles of width x from the other 20-inch end, express the volume of the box as a function of x. (See the figure below.)

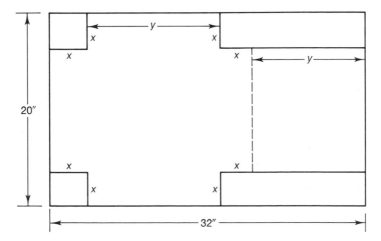

3–11. A manufacturer wishes to mix various grades of coffee in 100-lb lots to produce different grades. He has at his disposal coffee worth 90 cents and \$1.05 per pound. Assume that he uses x lb of the \$1.05 coffee.

    a. How many pounds of the 90-cent coffee does he use in each lot?

    b. What is the value in cents of the mixture?

    c. At what price per pound should he offer the mixture to recover exactly its value?

*3–12.** The change in sales revenues (in units of \$10,000) is related to advertising expenditures (in units of \$1000) by the function

$$f(x) = (x + 1)(x - 1)(x - 2), \qquad -2 \leq x \leq +3.$$

    a. By graphing, find the ranges over which sales revenues increase from their present levels.

    b. Find the level of advertising that most increases sales revenues.

3–13. The estimated monthly cost for a given level of productive activity is given by the function

$$f(x) = x^2 - x + 12, \qquad -5 \leq x \leq 4.$$

    a. By graphing, find the levels of productive activity over which monthly costs are increasing.

    b. Find the level of productive activity that minimizes the monthly cost. What is this monthly cost?

3–14. A certain chemical is produced as it passes through two production processes. In the first process, there is a shrinkage of 10 percent, and in the second there is a shrinkage of 20 percent of the material entering the second process. Develop a functional relationship between the gallons of input as the independent variable, x, and the gallons of output as the dependent variable, y.

    a. Give the rule for the function in equation form and indicate its domain (that is, the values of x for which the function is valid).

    b. Also give the equation for the relationship that allows one to find the number of gallons needed to produce a given output. This is called the *inverse* function of the first.

*3–15.** The government is considering changes in airline safety requirements. The results, unknown at this time, will either increase or decrease the amount of labor required of the maintenance staff by a maximum of

300 hours per week on the average. The benefits, in terms of the change in profits, for the firm in question are expected to follow a pattern described by the equation

$$y \equiv f(x) = x^2 + x - 2,$$

where $y \equiv$ expected profit change in thousands of dollars, and $x \equiv$ average change in average weekly hours worked by the maintenance staff in hundreds of hours. Required:

a. For what values of x is a function defined?

b. Show the function by graphing it.

c. What change in profits is suggested if no change in hours is required?

d. What change in hours leads to no change in profits?

e. Can you find the point where profits are reduced the most?

3–16. Write the equation and the values of x for the following relationships.

a. An investment of $100,000 yields a return of $6000 and an investment of $100 yields a return of $6. The function is linear. Assume the equation holds for all nonnegative investment levels.

b.

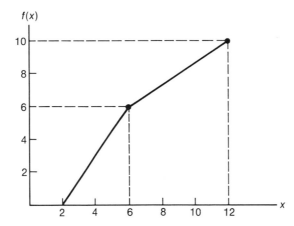

c. The Loma Company finds that when salesmen number between 30 and 50 inclusive, sales volume in dollars increases at a constant rate of $1000 per salesman. It also knows that 40 salesmen, its present number, generate $100,000 in sales at $10 per unit. But sales also respond to price. When price is changed in a range of 25 percent, sales move in the opposite direction at the constant rate of $100 per dollar change in price. Write the functional relationship between sales volume in dollars as a function of price change and the number of salesmen.

3–17.* Represent graphically or by equation.

    a. The total depreciation taken on an asset versus time in years, if depreciation per year is calculated by dividing the initial cost less the final estimated salvage value by the asset's life in years.

    b. For part *a*, graph the remaining book value, original cost less depreciation to date, versus time.

    c. A construction firm estimates that the likelihood *p* of finishing a project is 0.8 by the completion date. The value rises to 1.0 if the completion time is increased 2 months and falls to zero if the completion time is reduced 1 month. If a smooth function is appropriate, graph an approximate curve that depicts this relationship.

3–18. Total manufacturing cost for the Pardee Company is given by the function $f(x) = 200 + 1.5x$, $100 \leq x \leq 1000$, where cost is measured in units of $1000 and *x* in hundreds.

    a. What is the variable cost (the cost of one more unit) per unit?

    b. What do fixed costs (cost at zero output) equal?

    c. What is the total variable cost in dollars as a function of output?

    d. What is total cost at 5000 units?

    e. If a unit sells for $20, what is the breakeven value (where cost equals revenue) of *x*?

3–19.* The Williams Production Company is considering building a new exit from its main production room to facilitate workers getting small parts from their supply shed. One of the advantages is the amount of time saved in worker travel. The layout of the old and new situation is given below. If a worker walks at a rate of *x* feet per minute on the average, develop a relationship that shows the amount of money saved per trip to the supply shed if the hourly wage rate is *m*.

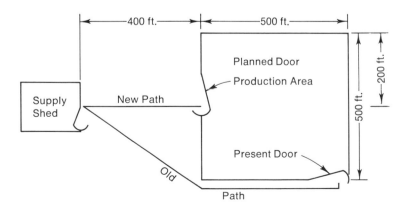

3–20. * The Jones Candy Company manufactures bars of milk chocolate in two sizes: a $2\frac{1}{4}$-oz bar that costs 3.75 cents to produce, and $3\frac{3}{4}$-oz bar at a production cost of 4.75 cents. Jones is considering the introduction of a larger candy bar and needs some quick cost estimates for a preliminary financial analysis. Since the simplest forms of estimation are usable at the early stages, the firm is considering only two possibilities.

(1) Manufacturing costs in line with existing products.

(2) Decreasing costs by 0.5 cents for weights in excess of 5 oz (that is, costs are less by one half cent per ounce).

Supply equations and graphs for management's use depicting these relationships.

3–21. A bank requires that a borrowing corporation keep a proportion, call it p, of its outstanding loan deposited at the bank. These deposits are called *compensating balances*.

a. Express the necessary compensating balance, y, as a function of the total amount borrowed, x, where p is the percentage of the outstanding loan that must be kept deposited.

b. If b is the amount of funds actually needed, how much must be borrowed?

3–22. A repair shop charges its customers on a "cost-plus" basis; that is, it charges a percentage p above its labor costs. Suppose that the hourly wage rate is w.

a. Express the customer's cost, c, as a function of the labor hours, L, needed for any repair.

b. Suppose that the customer wanted to know the percentage "mark up" that the repair shop requires. Assume that he knows c and L from his bill and can find out the wage rate, w. Express the percentage mark up as a function of c, taking L and w as constants.

3–23. * A construction firm has contracted to enclose each of eight square pillars in cylindrical steel tubes. If the pillars are 50 feet high and 2 feet

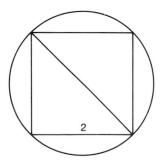

square, how much steel will be required? A cross-sectional view of a pillar is shown on p. 71. (*Hint:* The Pythagorean theorem states that the square of the hypotenuse of a right triangle equals the sum of the squares of the sides. The circumference of a circle is equal to $\pi \cdot d$, where d is the diameter of the circle.)

3–24.* Suppose that the federal corporate income tax structure were the following: Losses are not taxed; the first $25,000 of income is taxed at 25 percent and all income thereafter is taxed at 48 percent.

    a. Write the rule for this function.

    b. Graph the function.

    c. Write the rule for after-tax income as a function of pretax income.

3–25.* The president of a small consulting firm has a staff of people, all of whom are paid a salary of a dollars. In general, each staff member is assigned b clients. The president wishes to know his labor costs, c, as a function of the number of clients, x, the firm handles.

    a. Graph the cost function for $0 \le x \le 5b$.

    b. Give the function rule for $0 \le x \le 5b$.

3–26. Define the inverse of each of the function rules below. If the inverse cannot be defined, give the reason.

    a. $y = 5 + 2x$ for $0 \le x \le 5$ and $5 \le y \le 15$.

    b. $[(1, 6), (2, 7), (3, 9), (4, 9), (5, 10)]$ for x the set of positive integers less than 6 and y the set of positive integers greater than 6 and less than 11.

    c. $y = x^I$: all real x and y, where I is an integer.

    d. $y = x^2$: all real and positive x and y.

3–27. A bank charges interest of a percent per year on the original balance of a 36-month consumer credit loan. Equal payments are made each month.

    a. Express the monthly-payment amount, y, as a function of the amount borrowed, x.

    b. If a borrower can afford to pay back a maximum of y per month, what is the maximum credit that he should be granted?

3–28. A firm has a demand for its product which is a function of the product's price. The function is $x = 10,000 - p$ for x and p real and greater than zero. The cost of production, c, is equal to $4000 + 5x$ for *x* greater than zero. Express the firm's profit, *y*, as a function of only the price it charges and give the range for which the function holds.

3–29.* A plant manager wishes to find the level of output at which the average cost of production is lowest. He has observations on output level and the corresponding cost over several output levels.

No. Units	Total Cost ($)
100	4,100
200	7,800
300	8,700
400	10,400
500	12,500
600	15,600
700	20,300
800	27,200

Find the average costs and graph the average cost as a function of output. Estimate the minimum.

3–30.* Let the function $f(x) = x^2 - x - 6$ be defined for all real x. Evaluate the following.

a. $f(3)$
b. $f(-1)$
c. $f(10)$
d. $f(14 - (-1)1)$
e. $f(3)/f(-3)$
f. $f(7) \cdot f(-2)$
g. Graph $f(x)$ from $-5 \leq x \leq 5$.

4

Exponential and Logarithmic Functions

The manager of the Plunket Company has noted that sales growth of their major product line has continued, but that the amount of the increase in sales of this line has been declining by approximately the same percentage for several periods. He is interested in estimating future sales levels. The Department of Health, Education, and Welfare is interested in how population growth in certain areas will affect particular programs and needs to know the impact of, say, a constant percentage growth rate on future population size. A firm or government agency is concerned with the depletion of resources (say, oil) available to it for use or sale. Another firm is concerned with the decay of the purchase rate of a product as one factor in the decision of whether to continue producing the product.

All of these situations and a host of other managerial decisions involve the notions of growth and decay. Where this growth or decay is in equal amounts per unit of, say, time for example, a linear function can be used to represent the phenomenon. For example, if sales start at 100 units today and increase by 5 units per month, then for any future month starting from the present,

$$\text{sales} = 100 + 5x, \qquad x \geq 0,$$

where x is in months and x equals 0 for the present month.

But quite often growth or decay is not adequately described by linear relationships. More complex curves are necessary, and these typically involve exponential or logarithmic functions.

We have already spent some time in Chapter 2 reviewing exponents. This chapter begins with a review of logarithmic operations before a more practical exploration of the growth and decay functions which they describe.

74

4-1 LOGARITHMS

In Chapter 2 we discussed the concept of an exponent and investigated several equations involving exponents. A simple example is

$$3^2 = 9.$$

This mathematical expression can be translated as: (1) 3 multiplied by itself gives (equals) 9; *or* (2) 3 squared is 9; *or* (3) 2 is the power to which 3 must be raised to yield 9.

Translation (3) is the one we shall focus on here. Mathematicians write this expression using the notation

$$2 = \log_3 9$$

and say "the logarithm of 9 to the base 3 is 2." Slightly expanded, and using statement (3), this expression becomes "the logarithm of 9 to the base 3 is the power (exponent) needed to raise 3 to 9." This power is, of course, 2. Hence a logarithm is an exponent.

Let's try another example.

$$4^3 = 64.$$

In logarithmic form the exponential expression becomes

$$3 = \log_4 64$$

and is phrased as "the logarithm of 64 to the base 4 is 3." This means that 3 is the power that raises 4 to 64. This is a direct translation of $3 = \log_4 64$. The correspondence is "3" in the phrase for the 3 in the mathematical expression, "is" for $=$, "the power which raises" for log, 4 for 4, and "to 64" in the phrase for 64 in the equation.

In more general terms:

$$x = \log_b a,$$

which means that x is the power needed to raise b to a. We write

$$b^x = a.$$

A logarithm is an exponent.

Symbol	*English Translation*
$x = \log_b a$	x is the exponent needed to raise b to the value a.

Logarithm as an Inverse Function

The two equations above the symbol translation suggest the dual or inverse relationship between equations written in logarithmic and exponential form. For example, suppose that we are given the logarithmic equation

$$x = \log_3 81$$

and asked to find x. You may already know the answer, but most of us find it simpler to understand what is going on by first converting this expression to its exponential equivalent (or inverse form). In inverse form we obtain

$$3^x = 81.$$

We suspect that the answer, $x = 4$, is more easily obtained using this form.

Exponential and logarithmic functions are connected by this inverse relationship. Given the exponential equation in general form

$$y \equiv f(x) = b^x,$$

we can write the inverse logarithmic equation

$$x \equiv f(y) = \log_b y.$$

Note that, as has now been illustrated, we can go either way.

⁓ :   Write the following logarithmic equations in exponential form and solve for x.

	Exponential form	Solution
1. $x = \log_3 27$		$x =$
2. $x = \log_3 3$		$x =$
3. $x = \log_3 1$		$x =$
4. $x = \log_{0.1} 0.0001$		$x =$
5. $x = \log_b b^{2a}$		$x =$
6. $x = \log_4 128$		$x =$
7. $x = \log_{10} 0.1$		$x =$

Answers

1. $3^x = 27$	$x = 3$	
2. $3^x = 3$	$x = 1$	
3. $3^x = 1$	$x = 0$	
4. $(0.1)^x = 0.0001$	$x = 4$	
5. $b^x = b^{2a}$	$x = 2a$	
6. $4^x = 128$	$x = 3.5$ since $128 = 4 \cdot 4 \cdot 4 \cdot 2 = 4^3 \cdot 4^{\frac{1}{2}} = 4^{3\frac{1}{2}}$	
7. $10^x = 0.1$	$x = -1$ since $10^{-1} = \frac{1}{10} = 0.1$	

Logarithmic Bases

The previous section indicates that any one of a number of bases can be used for logarithmic functions. Nevertheless, certain bases have found particular favor. The first of these is the base 10. This base is particularly useful in hand numerical calculation. The rules for calculations using logarithms are briefly reviewed in Section 4–4. The advent of electronic computers has made it much less necessary to make use of logarithmic hand calculations, however. (It is interesting to recall from Section 2–3 that the electronic computer uses a base other than 10, namely 2, for making calculations.)

The other major logarithmic base commonly found in practical applications is the mathematical constant $e = 2.71828 \ldots$. This number arises often enough that logarithmic tables have been computed using the constant e as a base. Logarithms using the base e are called *natural logarithms*. Again, for simplification, the mathematician uses shorthand and writes ln for natural logarithm, rather than $\log_e$. In other words, $\ln \equiv \log_e$.

One example of where natural logarithms arise in a managerial setting is illustrated by the topic of compound interest which we studied in Section 2–2. At that time we noted that \$1.00 invested at an annual interest rate of r for t years accumulates to $(1 + r)^t$. We saw further that if interest is compounded semiannually, we obtain $(1 + (r/2))^{2t}$. But suppose the compounding process is carried to days, to hours, to seconds, and so on. Suppose the compounding were carried to the ultimate end by compounding continuously. What would \$1.00 amount to after t years? The answer, which we are not sophisticated enough to derive or even intuit, turns out to be e^{tr}.

For an example, if \$10 is invested at a rate of 0.05 for 2 years, continuously compounded, the amount at the end of 2 years is

$$10e^{2(0.05)}$$

Using Table I at the back of the book $e^{2(0.05)} = e^{0.1} = 1.105$. Therefore, \$10 invested at a rate of 0.05 yields $10(1.105) = \$11.05$ under continuous compounding.

⌇ : What is the yearly advantage to a depositor of having his money invested at a rate of 0.06 compounded continuously versus compounded semiannually?

Answer. Compounding semiannually gives $(1 + 0.03)^2 = (1.03)(1.03) = 1.0609$. Compounding continuously gives $e^{1(0.06)} = e^{0.06} = 1.0618$. The difference is 0.0009 per dollar or 9 cents per \$100. This calculation suggests that it is advantageous to use continuous compounding to approximate the results of daily or even weekly compounding. The approximation is sufficiently close for all practical purposes. After all, $e^{0.06}$ is much easier to evaluate than the precise answer to daily compounding at a 0.06 annual rate, which is given by $(1 + (0.06/365))^{365}$.

4-2 RULES FOR LOGARITHMS

In Section 2–1 we studied several rules for operating with exponents. Related rules exist for logarithms. These rules can be derived using what we already know about exponents and the inverse functional relationship between logarithms and exponents.

Suppose that we desire the logarithm of (4)(16) to the base 2. That is, we wish to find

$$y = \log_2 [(4)(16)].$$

Using the exponential inverse and the first rule of exponents we write

$$2^y = (4)(16) = (2^2)(2^4)$$
$$= 2^6.$$

Hence $y = 6$, since the base is the same. But this is the same answer we get by writing

$$y = \log_2 (4) + \log_2 (16) = 2 + 4 = 6,$$

using the definition of a logarithm as the power needed to raise the base, 2 in this case, to the given number, first 4 and then 16 here. As a check, $(4)(16) = 64 = 2^6$. We have illustrated (but not proved) that, corresponding to the first rule for exponents, we can write the following first rule for logarithms.

Rule 1 for Logarithms: PRODUCTS

The logarithm of a product is equal to the sum of the logarithms. In symbolic form:

$$y = \log_b(a_1 \cdot a_2 \cdot \ldots \cdot a_i \cdot \ldots \cdot a_n)$$
$$= \log_b a_1 + \ldots + \log_b a_i + \ldots + \log_b a_n$$
$$= \sum_{i=1}^{n} \log_b a_i.$$

Suppose that the logarithmic expression desired is

$$y = \log_2 (2^3).$$

Again, using the inverse relationship, we write

$$2^y = 2^3.$$

Hence $y = 3$. But since $\log_2 (2) = 1$, that is, 1 is the power necessary to raise 2 to 2, we can write

$$y = 3(1) = 3 \log_2 2.$$

This illustrates, but again it does not prove, the second rule for logarithms.

Rule 2 for Logarithm: POWERS

The logarithm of any term raised to a power is equal to the power multiplied by the logarithm of the term. In symbolic form:

$$\log_b a^n = n \log_b a.$$

Perhaps another development of this expression is useful. Again, using a numerical example, see if you can follow the algebra. Given

$$8 = 2^3.$$

Now taking logarithms of each side to the base 2,

$$\log_2 8 = \log_2 (2^3)$$

or

$$\log_2 8 = 3$$

since, on the right, 3 is, by definition, the power one must raise the base 2 to get 2^3. Substituting $\log_2 8$ for 3 in the initial equation yields

$$8 = 2^{\log_2 8}.$$

Squaring both sides and then using the second rule for exponents,

$$8^2 = (2^{\log_2 8})^2 = 2^{2 \log_2 8}.$$

Using the definition of a logarithm, $2 \log_2 8$ is the power to which 2 must be raised to give 8^2. Hence $2 \log_2 8$ is the logarithm of 8^2 to the base 2. We write

$$\log_2 8^2 = 2 \log_2 8,$$

which agrees with the second rule for logarithms. The example is complete.

Consider now the logarithm of the quotient of two expressions. For example,

$$y = \log_3(\tfrac{27}{9}) = \log_3 (3) = 1.$$

Using rule 3 for exponents from Section 2–1, we may write

$$y = \log_3 [(27)(9^{-1})],$$

and using rule 1 for logarithms,

$$y = \log_3 (27) + \log_3 (9^{-1}).$$

Now using rule 2 for logarithms,

$$y = \log_3 (27) - \log_3 (9).$$

This is equal to $3 - 2$, or 1, as we previously saw, and hence the manipulations have not altered the correct answer. This example suggests rule 3 for logarithms.

Rule 3 for Logarithms: QUOTIENTS

The logarithm of a quotient is equal to the logarithm of the numerator minus the logarithm of the denominator. In symbolic form:

$$\log_b \left(\frac{a}{c} \right) = \log_b a - \log_b c.$$

～ : See if you can answer the following.

1. $\log_4 (2) =$
2. $\log_r (3^0) =$
3. $\log_2 (8^{-1}) =$
4. $\log_3 (81^{1/4}) =$

Answers

1. The first question asks for the power needed to raise 4 to yield 2; the answer is the $\frac{1}{2}$ power.
2. Using the second rule for exponents, we get $0 \log_r 3$, and zero times anything is zero.
3. Again using rule 2 we get $(-1) \log_2 8 = -3$.
4. Working inside the parentheses, $81^{1/4}$ is the fourth root of 81. This is 3. Hence $\log_3 (81^{1/4}) = \log_3 (3) = 1$.

4-3 GRAPHS OF LOGARITHMIC AND EXPONENTIAL FUNCTIONS

The exponential function given by

$$y = b^x, \qquad b > 1,$$

has the logarithmic equivalent, using the concept of inverse functions, given by

$$x = \log_b y.$$

This function is graphed in Figure 4–1 using the normal Cartesian axes. The reader will note that the function can be viewed as a growth curve for non-negative values of x. The growth is a constant percentage. For example, if $b = 2$, a partial sequence (for $x = 0, 1, 2, \ldots$) is $y = 2^x = 1, 2, 4, 8 \ldots$. This series increases by 100 percent; it doubles for each unit increase in x. A frequently encountered member of this family of functions is where $b = e = 2.71828 \ldots$. This gives the function $y = e^x$.

FIGURE 4–1

Graph of $y = b^x$ or $x = \log_b y$

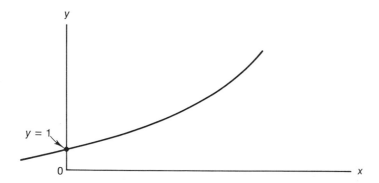

A related but different growth curve is obtained by interchanging the x and y values. This yields

$$x = b^y, \qquad b > 1,$$

or in inverse form,

$$y = \log_b x.$$

The graph of this function is given in Figure 4–2. This function is usually relevant to managerial problems only for $x \geq 1$. Growth in this case continues but, in contrast to that in Figure 4–1, by decreasing amounts.

FIGURE 4–2

Graph of $x = b^y$ or $y = \log_b x$ for $b > 1$

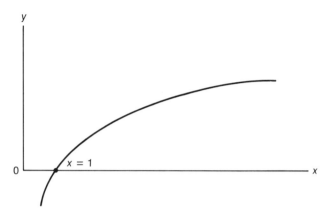

Reading graphs and obtaining values for situations involving curves of the type just described is often easier if the equations are transformed mathematically to straight lines. In the first example, if we consider

$$y = b^x$$

and take logarithms of each side to an arbitrary base, say r, we obtain

$$\log_r y = x \log_r b.$$

Since $\log_r b$ is a constant, this equation will plot as a straight line through the origin, if we plot the logarithm of y to the base r on the y axis. This is illustrated in Figure 4–3. The illustration assumes for simplicity that $r = b = 2$. Thus the function can be written $y = 2^x$. Now if instead of plotting y, we plot $\log_2 y$, the following points appear on the graph:

x	y	$\log_2 y$
0	1	0
1	2	1
2	4	2
3	8	3
4	16	4
.	.	.
.	.	.
.	.	.

FIGURE 4–3

Graph of $\log_2 y$ where $b = 2$ and $y = b^x$

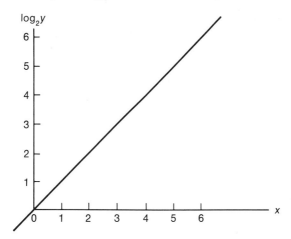

Mathematicians call the graph used in Figure 4–3 a semilogarithmic graph since the logarithms of one of the variables, y, is plotted rather than the values of the variable itself. In this case the vertical scale was transformed. A similar approach could be used on the horizontal scale to transform the exponential equation $x = b^y$ to a linear graph. Sometimes it is necessary to convert both scales to logarithms to obtain a linear relationship. An example is the equation $y = x^b$.

Logarithmic transformations to achieve linearity are often useful in curve-fitting problems, particularly when the data reflect exponential growth. Fitting a curve to population-growth or sales-growth curves is a common example where taking logarithms of the data may be helpful.

The actual data points may not lie on a straight line even after taking logarithms or using some other appropriate procedure to transform the original data. If we still wish to select a single linear equation to represent the data, then we need a technique that selects the "best" linear representation. One means of making this selection is the method of least-squares. This technique is discussed in statistics courses and we will not attempt a rigorous discussion here. However, the technique is consistent with the following six steps:

1. Select a line $y = a + bx$.
2. For each data point with coordinates x', y', solve the equation $\hat{y} = a + bx'$.
3. Compute the difference $y' - \hat{y}$ for each data point.
4. Square each of these differences to obtain $(y' - \hat{y})^2$.
5. Sum these squared differences to obtain $\Sigma(y' - \hat{y})^2$.
6. Select that line which produces the smallest (i. e., minimizes the) sum.

The technique is computerized, including the initial taking of logarithms if necessary to facilitate finding the line that minimizes the sum of the squared differences. In a later chapter we will see that calculus is also involved in shortening the search (the minimizing) process.

Whether or not a logarithmic conversion to obtain linearity is appropriate is best decided by the manager (possibly in consultation with a statistical specialist) with operating experience concerning the phenomenon at hand. He is in the best position to decide whether sales are growing in a way described by, say, a constant percentage growth such as is given by the equation $y = b^x$, or in some other way.

Some Growth Curves of Interest

Using exponential and logarithmic functions, several types of growth functions can be described in equation form. These may be useful to you in practical application situations. We will restrict the discussion to non-negative x.

Function 1

$$y = ab^x, \quad b > 1, \quad a > 0.$$

This function is identical to the one graphed in Figure 4–1, except for the y intercept, the value of y when $x = 0$. The intercept of the present function is the constant a.

Function 2

$$y = k - ab^x, \quad k > 0, \quad 0 < b < 1, \quad a > 0.$$

Function 2 represents a declining-growth-rate situation. The curve begins at the point $k - a$ and increases toward, but never reaches, k. The value k is called an *asymptote* of the function. The distance between the function and k decreases by a constant percent as x increases. The graph is given in Figure 4–4. There is continued growth in y, but the absolute increase in y declines as x increases. The curve might be used to describe the average usage, y, of a storage facility with a fixed capacity k as productive capacity, x, is more fully utilized.

Function 3

$$y = k - b/x, \quad k > 0, b > 0.$$

This is another function, although not an exponential one, that grows toward but never quite reaches a particular value, again denoted by k. One of

FIGURE 4–4

Graph of $y = k - ab^x$

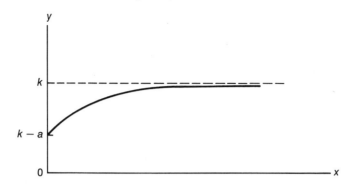

the differences between this function and function 2 is that this one is unde-fined for $x = 0$. Also, it must equal zero for $x = b/k$. The function is graphed in Figure 4–5. This is one form of a commonly encountered function called a *hyperbola*.

FIGURE 4–5

Graph of $y = k - \dfrac{b}{x}$

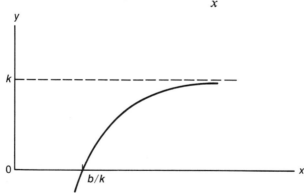

Use of functions 2 and 3 could include estimates of benefits from program expenditures or increases in trade from increased foreign aid.

Function 4

$$y = ax^b, \qquad a > 0, \quad b > 1.$$

Function 4 resembles the graph of $y = ab^x$ graphed in Figure 4–1 for $a = 1$, the difference being that $y = ax^b$ passes through the origin and increases more slowly than the function $y = ab^x$. For $a = 1$ and $b = 2$, the function $y = ab^x$ gives the series $y = 1, 2, 4, 8, 16, 32, 64, \ldots$ using only integer values of x. For the function $y = ax^b$, $a = 1$, $b = 2$, we obtain $y = 0, 1, 4, 9, 16, 25, 36, \ldots$. Total variable production costs may be reflected by one of these two types of functions. (For the case where $0 < b < 1$, the function resembles the graph in Figure 4–4, with $k = a$, except that no asymptote is approached.)

Two other, somewhat more complicated functions have been used to describe sales during the early stages of the life cycle of new products. These functions are:

Function 5: The Gompertz Function

$$y = ka^{b^x}, \quad k > 0, \quad 0 < b < 1, \quad 0 < a < 1.$$

Function 6: The Logistic Function

$$y = \frac{1}{k + ab^x}, \quad k > 0, \quad 0 < b < 1, \quad a < 0 < k$$

These two functions are graphed in Figure 4–6.

FIGURE 4–6

Gompertz and Logistic Functions

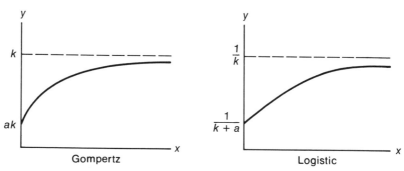

Gompertz

Logistic

The Gompertz function reflects the sales during the early part of the life cycle of a new product with a quick acceptance and then slow growth toward what could be called a saturation level of period sales, represented by k. The logistic function, on the other hand, represents the pattern for a product experiencing slower initial acceptance followed once again by growth toward the saturation level. Neither curve is complicated enough to treat the eventual decline in acceptance experienced by many products. The reader may think of other managerial phenomena that could be approximated with these or similar functional forms.

Decay Curves of Interest

Exponential and logarithmic curves also permit us to describe situations in which sales or costs are decreasing. Several common situations are described in this subsection. We will again deal only with nonnegative x.

Function 7

$$y = ab^{-x}, \qquad a > 0, \quad b > 1.$$

This function has a y-intercept value equal to the constant a and decreases toward, but never reaches, the x axis. The quickness of approach to the x axis is in direct relationship to the value of b. This function is graphed in Figure 4–7. (It is worth noting that by letting $0 < b < 1$, this function will graph as function 1.)

FIGURE 4–7

Graph of $y = ab^{-x}$

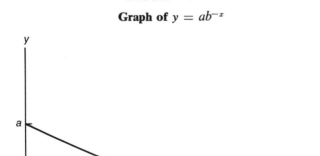

If we desire that the function approach some value of y other than $y = 0$, the x axis, this can be done by writing

$$y = ab^{-x} + k.$$

The function now approaches k and the y intercept is $a + k$. The function is similar to function 2 except that it defines a declining pattern for y.

This function, including its modification, can be used to approximate, among other managerial phenomena, declining sales, the depleted value of resources, the depreciated value of equipment, and the reduced capacity of obsolete plant. In other words, it is a useful function.

Function 8

$$y = k + \frac{b}{x}, \qquad k > 0, \quad b > 0.$$

This function is similar to function 3 but represents a situation in which y decreases as x increases. The function approaches, but does not reach, k. It also does not have a y intercept. An example is average unit cost of production, including a fixed cost component, b, and a constant variable cost component, k. Over some range, the unit variable cost may remain constant, but the portion of total fixed costs not affected by output that is allocated to each unit declines. This example is graphed in Figure 4–8.

FIGURE 4–8

Graph of $y = k + b / x$ (where k is the unit variable cost, b the total fixed cost, y the unit cost, and x the number of units)

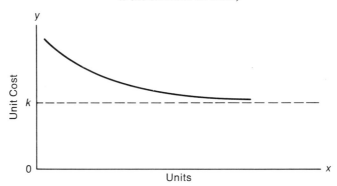

Function 9

$$y = ax^b, \qquad a > 0, \quad b < 0.$$

This gives function 4 except with a negative value for b. Hence function 9 can be written $y = a/x^b$. The function describes a situation similar to that of function 8 for $k = 0$ except that a/x^b decreases faster than b/x. An example might be the average number of defectives in output as the number of inspections or effort spent on inspection increases (at least over some relevant range). This function is graphed in Figure 4–9.

FIGURE 4–9

Graph of $y = ax^b$ $(b < 0)$

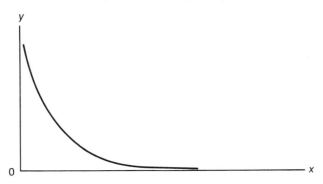

A practical example of this case is supplied by the application of learning theory to cost estimation. Empirical research suggests that, in repetitive operations, a constant percentage reduction takes place in the average labor input time required per unit as the cumulative output doubles. Mathematically this is expressed as $y = ax^b$, where the constant a is the number of hours required for the first unit, x is the cumulative number of units produced, and b is the learning index, which turns out to have a negative value. Estimation of such relationships can be important in estimating manpower needs, predicting order-completion time, deciding on inventory needs, evaluating performance, and so on.

A concrete example is suggested by the case where a reduction of 20 percent in the average labor input time occurs each time output doubles. If the first unit takes 125 hours, the average time for 2 units should be 100 hours, $125 - 0.2(125) = 0.8(125)$. The second unit only takes 75 hours to produce. To find b, we observe that

$$\text{for } x = 1: \quad 125 = a(1)^b,$$
$$\text{for } x = 2: \quad 100 = a(2)^b.$$

Solving the first equation, $a = 125$ since 1 raised to any power is 1. Substituting this value for a into the equation for $x = 2$ gives

$$100 = 125(2)^b.$$

Solving $$\frac{100}{125} = 0.8 = 2^b$$

and taking logarithms to the base 10 (any base would do),

$$\log_{10}(0.8) = \log_{10}2^b = b \log_{10}2$$

using the second rule for logarithms. Hence

$$b = \frac{\log_{10} 0.8}{\log_{10} 2}.$$

Using tables of logarithms, $b = -0.322$. (See Table II at the back of the book.) Hence the relation of average labor input time per unit, y, to the cumulative output in units, x, is

$$y = 125x^{-0.322}.$$

This function is graphed in Figure 4–10.

FIGURE 4–10

Average Labor Hours Required for x Units

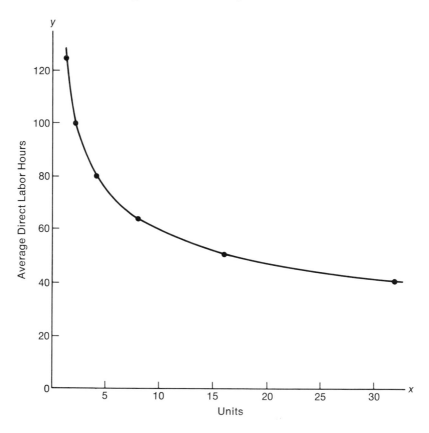

We shall close this section with three remarks. First, only a few of the more common growth and decay functions have been illustrated. And these curves can often be used to describe situations that might not initially be thought of in these terms. Second, the functions have been given in exponential form, even though each could be stated in logarithmic form. For example,

$$y = ax^b$$

becomes, in logarithmic form,

$$b = \log_x \left(\frac{y}{a}\right).$$

We have used the exponential form since it is more easily understood. Finally, there are other exponential and logarithmic curves which have nothing to do with growth or decay but which are very useful to managerial problem solving. Several of these functions were discussed in Chapter 3.

As another example consider

$$y = e^{-x^2},$$

which is graphed in Figure 4–11. This function turns out to have extensive practical use, which you will discover when you study statistics. In a slightly

FIGURE 4–11

Graph of $y = e^{-x^2}$

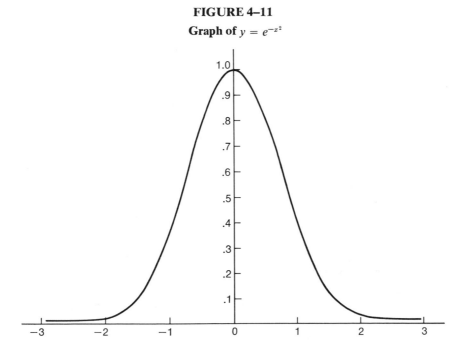

modified form, the function is known to statisticians as the *normal curve*. The distribution of certain phenomena in nature, such as height and intelligence, are reasonably well described by this function. However, its primary importance is based on the fact that it is useful in describing the distribution of arithmetic averages computed from large samples. (If this paragraph is mysterious to you, just remember that e^{-x^2} is another very useful exponential function. Its use will be described to you when you study probability and statistics.)

⌒⌒ :   Many firms prefer to lease rather than purchase high-cost equipment that requires substantial technical maintenance. In making this decision, management may wish to compare the discounted value of the periodic lease payments with the purchase price. Let the y axis be the present value of the periodic payments and the x axis be defined as the life of the lease agreement. Circle the number of the function that most nearly reflects the present value of the lease payments for a time horizon of x years. (You may wish to refer to the figures and to the discussion in this section.)

1. $y = ax^b$ $\qquad\qquad\qquad\qquad$ $a > 0, 0 < b < 1$

2. $y = b^x$ $\qquad\qquad\qquad\qquad$ $b > 1$

3. $y = k - \dfrac{b}{x}$ $\qquad\qquad\qquad$ $k > 0, b > 0$

4. $y = b^{-x}$ $\qquad\qquad\qquad\qquad$ $b > 1$

Answer.   The first point to recognize is that the present value of the leasing obligation increases as the life of the obligation, x, increases. This eliminates any downward-sloping curves, namely alternative 4. Second, the obligation, being a present value, grows more slowly as x increases. Equal payments at equal intervals pose a smaller obligation for future than for present periods. This eliminates alternative 2. Finally, alternative 3 can also be eliminated. The function given by 3 has a large negative value for a zero life; but the obligation would really be zero for a zero life. The correct function passes through the origin and continues to grow but by decreasing absolute amounts as x increases. Only function 1 does this. Alternative 1 is the best of the choices available, but it only approximates the exact solution.

4-4 USING LOGARITHMS FOR CALCULATIONAL PURPOSES*

In Section 4–1 we mentioned that the logarithmic base 10 is used when

---

* This section may be omitted without loss of continuity or sleep.

logarithms are employed for calculational purposes. Let's see how this works for a simple example. Consider

$$y = 10(1,000).$$

We know that the answer is 10,000, and no one needs to use logarithms for this. But to illustrate the way logarithms are used in calculations, we shall do so anyway.

Taking logarithms to the base 10 of each side of the equation,

$$\begin{aligned}
\log_{10} y &= \log_{10}[(10)(1,000)] \\
&= \log_{10}(10) + \log_{10}(1,000) \\
&= 1 + 3 \\
&= 4.
\end{aligned}$$

Using the definition of a logarithm, 4 is the power to which 10 must be raised to yield y: If 10 is raised to the fourth power, this gives y. Hence

$$y = 10^4 = 10,000.$$

Tables of logarithms to the base 10 are common, and a brief one appears as Table II at the back of the book. To find the logarithm of any number in the table, we first convert the number so that its first nonzero digit immediately precedes the decimal. For example, 3,210 becomes $3.21(10^3)$, and 0.0452 becomes $4.52(10^{-2})$. Using the first and second rules for logarithms, we can write

$$\begin{aligned}
\log_{10} 3,210 &= \log_{10} 3.21 + \log_{10} (10^3) = \log_{10} 3.21 + 3 \log_{10} 10 \\
&= \log_{10} 3.21 + 3, \text{ and} \\
\log_{10} 0.0452 &= \log_{10} 4.52 + \log_{10} (10^{-2}) = \log_{10} 4.52 - 2.
\end{aligned}$$

Now if we wish to multiply these two numbers together, that is, find $(3,210)(0.0452)$, we need to add their logarithms since if

$$y = (3,210)(0.0452)$$

then

$$\log_{10} y = \log_{10} 3,210 + \log_{10} (0.0452).$$

Hence

$$\log_{10} y = \log_{10} 3.21 + \log_{10} 4.52 + 3 - 2.$$

The next step is to find $\log_{10} 3.21$ and $\log_{10} 4.52$. But these values are the ones found in a table of logarithms to the base 10. Using Table II, $\log_{10} 3.21 = 0.5065$ and $\log_{10} 4.52 = 0.6551$. Hence

$$\log_{10} y = 0.5065 + 0.6551 + 3 - 2$$
$$= 1.1616 + 1,$$
$$= 0.1616 \mid 2.$$

To find y we now work backward through the table. The integer and decimal portions of the logarithm are separated. Next the decimal portion is looked up in the body of Table II. For 0.1616 we find 1.456. We do not need to look up the integer part. We now write

$$\log_{10} y = \log_{10} 1.456 + \log_{10} 10^2$$
$$= \log_{10} [(1.456)(10^2)]$$
$$= \log_{10} (145.6),$$

and thus

$$y = 145.6$$

to four figures.

Let's try one more example. Consider the equation

$$y = (732)^{0.42}.$$

Using the first and second rules for logarithms,

$$\log_{10} y = \log_{10} (732^{0.42}) = 0.42 \, (\log_{10} 732)$$
$$= 0.42 \, [\log_{10} (7.32)10^2]$$
$$= 0.42 \, [\log_{10} (7.32) + \log_{10} 10^2]$$
$$= 0.42 \, [\log_{10} (7.32) + 2 \log_{10} 10]$$
$$= 0.42 \, [\log_{10} (7.32) + 2].$$

Resorting to Table II we find that $\log_{10} (7.32)$ is 0.8645. Therefore,

$$\log_{10} y = 0.42(0.8645 + 2)$$
$$= 0.42 \, (2.8645).$$

At this stage we can perform the indicated multiplication or use logarithms to do so as was illustrated by the first example. We shall simply carry through the multiplication by hand. This gives

$$\log_{10} y = 1.2031 = 0.2031 + 1$$

separating the decimal from the integer portion.

Now working backward, the number in the table whose logarithm is 0.2031 is 1.596. Thus

$$\begin{aligned} \log_{10} y &= \log_{10} 1.596 + \log_{10} 10^1 \\ &= \log_{10} [(1.596)(10)] \\ &= \log_{10} (15.96) \end{aligned}$$

and

$$y = 15.96.$$

Although we have not needed to resort to special terminology here, mathematicians have given special names to the two components of any logarithm. Since you may have seen these names before, we repeat them here for completeness. After converting the original number (for example, $732 = 7.32 \cdot 10^2$), the power of 10 is known as the *characteristic* of the logarithm, and the tabular value for the decimal is called the *mantissa*. Hence for 3,210, conversion gives $3.21 \cdot 10^3$. The characteristic is 3 and the mantissa from the table is 0.5065. We repeat that it is not necessary to know this to solve computational problems. All we need is the definition and rules for logarithms, a logarithm table in base 10, and a little algebra.

Another notational convention used by mathematicians is to omit the base 10 when writing logarithms. Remember the following two notational simplifications we have encountered: $\log b \equiv \log_{10} b$, $\ln b \equiv \log_e b$. In all other cases the base must be explicitly indicated.

Using Table II we can also find the natural logarithm of any number x, since (see Problem 4-11):

$$\log_e x \equiv \ln x = [\log_e 10][\log_{10} x] = [1/\log_{10} e][\log_{10} x] \approx 2.3026 \log_{10} x.$$

Finally, calculations by logarithms are usually only approximate and may often require extensive numerical work (see the second example). The existence of slide rules for approximating calculations, calculators, and computers now make logarithmic calculations much less necessary. Anyway, who carries a table of logarithms in his pocket?

〰️ : Use logarithms to the base 10 to evaluate the following expressions. Do your work in steps as we have done in the text.

1. (3.75)(302)   *Answer*_____

2. 3.5 ÷ 108   _____

3. $\sqrt[3]{137}$ _____

Answers. (The intermediate steps are omitted)

1. 1,132

2. 0.03243

3. 5.154

4-5 SUMMARY

A logarithm is an exponent. This fundamental fact is critical because it permits us to understand logarithms by thinking in terms of the inverse functional relationship. This chapter examines the rules for logarithms and how functions involving logarithms can be manipulated algebraically. Often transformation of a functional form into logarithms eases the algebraic task. Multiplication becomes addition, division becomes subtraction, and raising to powers is reduced to multiplication.

In Section 4–3 several exponential (and logarithmic) functions are discussed in detail. These functions have numerous managerial applications including, but not limited to, situations involving growth and decay.

The final and optional section of the chapter reviews the means by which logarithms can be used to ease numerical calculations. This section was purposely written in a way that reviews and illustrates what we learned about logarithms in the earlier portion of the chapter since the need for logarithms in numerical calculations is not very great anymore.

NEW SYMBOLS

Symbol	*English Translation*
$x = \log_b a$	x is the exponent needed to raise b to the value a.
$x = \ln a = \log_e a$	x is the exponent needed to raise e to the value a.
$x = \log a = \log_{10} a$	x is the exponent needed to raise 10 to the value a.

RULES FOR LOGARITHMS

Rule 1: Product

$$\log_b(a_1 \cdot a_2 \cdot \ldots \cdot a_i \cdot \ldots \cdot a_n) = \log_b a_1 + \log_b a_2 + \ldots + \log_b a_i + \ldots + \log_b a_n$$

$$= \sum_{i=1}^{n} \log_b a_i$$

Rule 2: Power

$$\log_b a^n = n \log_b a$$

Rule 3: Quotient

$$\log_b \left(\frac{a}{c} \right) = \log_b a - \log_b c$$

PROBLEMS

Problems for Self-Study: 2, 3, 5, 14

4-1.* Write the following expressions in inverse form (that is, if in log form, put in exponential form, and vice versa).

a. $3^x = y$
b. $\log_x 3 = y$
c. $\log_y x = 3$
d. $a^b = x$
e. $\log_x a = b$
f. $e^z = y$

4-2. Compute the following.

a. $\log_2 8$
b. $\log_{10} 1$
c. $\log_4 8$
d. $\log_{4a} (4a)^4$
e. $2^{\log_2 6}$
f. $4^{\log_2 8}$

4-3. Where possible, simplify using the laws of logarithms.

a. $\log_a (2xy)$
b. $\log_a (x^2 y^3 / z^4)$
c. $\log_a (2x + y)$
d. $\log_a (x^a)$
e. $\log_a (a^2 \cdot x^3 / 3)$

4-4.* Using the table of base 10 logarithms compute the following.

a. $\log 13.42$
b. $\log 2.19$
c. $\log 10170000$
d. $\log 0.000497$
e. $\log 4.368$

4-5. Using either the table of base 10 logarithms or the table of powers of e, find the missing value.

a. $\ln 5.7546 = x$
b. $\ln 0.02 = x$

    c. $\log x = 1.8007$

    d. $\ln 12088 = x$

    e. $\log x = 2.6803$

4-6.*   Find the following.

    a. $\log_9 2187 =$

    b. $3^{\ln e^3} =$

    c. $2^{\log_2 17} =$

4-7.   The profits of firm XYZ are now p_0 and are expected to grow at a constant percentage of r per year. Express the logarithm of profits in year n as a function of the logarithms of p_0 and $(1 + r)$. (*Hint:* Write it first in the form p_n equal to some function.)

4-8.   In the situation described in Problem 4-7, compute p_n using logarithms for the following cases.

    a. $p_0 = \$1234,\ r = 0.08,\ n = 7$

    b. $p_0 = \$9786,\ r = -0.05,\ n = 12$

4-9.*   A sales manager knows that the demand for his product, D, is a function of its price, p:

$$D = 1857 \cdot p^{-0.75},$$

where D is the units demanded and p is the unit price in dollars. Calculate the demand for the following prices.

    a. $0.75

    b. $1.00

    c. $1.25

    d. $1.50

4-10.   Demand for a particular product may be expressed as

$$D = (483.6) \cdot p^{-.4} \cdot I^{.3},$$

where D is units demanded, p is the unit price, and I is the average disposable income (in 100s) in the distribution area. Find D for the following cases.

    a. $p = \$4.00, I = \$6$

    b. $p = \$3.00, I = \$5$

4–11.* Show that $\log_a x = C \log_b x$, where $C = 1/\log_b a$. (*Hint:* Start with the fact that $a^{\log_a x} = x$ and take logs to the base b.) This provides a means of going from one base, a, to another, b.

4–12.* Using the answer to Problem 4–10, find the constant C necessary for changing from one base to another in the following cases.

a. base 10 to base e (that is, $C = 1/\log_{10} e$)

b. base e to base 10

c. base 2 to base 8

d. base 9 to base 3

4–13. a. An investor has the choice between investing his dollars at 5 percent compounded continuously or at an annual rate of 5.1 percent. Which should he choose?

b. What should he choose if the annual rate were changed to 5.1 percent compounded quarterly?

4–14. The manager of a cost control center may spend his budget in any of three basic areas. In each area, the amount of cost saving is related to the amount allocated in that area. Describe the function (for example, by the numbers or names in the text) from the following description of the cost savings pattern. Draw the curve.

a. The cost saving increases as budgeted expenditures increases but always by a decreasing amount.

b. Cost savings increase in proportion to the amount budgeted for cost control up to a point at which no further savings will result from further expenditures.

c. Cost savings increase slowly at first, then more sharply.

4–15.* Suppose that a stockholder believes that the dividend of one share of XYZ, Inc., will grow at a percentage of 10 percent for the next 5 years, 15 percent for the following 3 years, followed by 5 percent forever thereafter. The present dividend is $1 per share.

a. Compute the dividends for the next 12 years.

b.*Graph the dividends.

c.*Graph the dividends on semilog paper or plot the logs of dividends on regular graph paper.

4–16.* Sales of the ABC Company have been growing for the last 7 years. The sales figures have been (in millions of dollars) $1.6, $1.92, $2.30, $2.76, $3.31, $3.97, and $4.76. Plot these points on regular graph paper and semilog paper. Does the growth appear to be linear or exponential?

4–17. Suppose the sales in Problem 4–16 had been $1.6, $1.92, $2.3, $2.76, $3.04, $3.34, and $3.67. Graphing on regular and semilog paper, what appears to happen in the growth pattern?

4–18. Suppose that by using semilogarithmic paper, a manager had determined that the level of output, X, was related to the levels of labor, L, and capital, K, in the following way:

$$\log X = 3 + 0.6 \log L + 0.4 \log K.$$

What is the function for X?

4–19.* A man invests $1000 in a savings account that yields 5 percent per year, compounded continuously. How long will it be before his money doubles?

4–20.* A new worker must learn to do a repetitive task. The amount of time it takes for him to accomplish the task decreases until he reaches the point where further time savings are not possible.

  a. Write a function to describe the worker's task time, x, as a function of his time on the job, t.

  b. If the worker works H hours per day, what is his daily output, Y, as a function of t?

4–21. As a plant expands its operations, it must hire additional labor. As the newly hired workers are trained, there will be attrition for various reasons. Suppose that t days after the workers are hired, the numbers of workers left is W, and

$$W = L + m \cdot 2^{-t}.$$

If $L = 50$ and $m = 32$, how many workers will be left at

  a. $t = 0$?

  b. $t = 2$?

  c. $t = 5$?

4–22. Suppose that the effects of the phenomena described in Problems 4–20 and 4–21 were combined, so that

$$Y = \frac{8}{0.5 + 0.5(2^{-t})}, \qquad W = 50 + 32(2^{-t}).$$

Total output per day will be found by multiplying Y and W. Find the daily output rates at

a. $t = 0$

b. $t = 2$

c. $t = 5$

4–23.* The spread of some communicable disease is described as spreading slowly at first, then at an increasing rate until almost all the susceptible population is exposed, at which point the spread of the disease slows. What type of curve would describe the number of people exposed to the disease as a function of time?

4–24. The work on learning curves suggests that in repetitive operations the average time to perform a given task declines by a constant percentage, u, as the number of times the operation is performed doubles. The relevant equation is given by $y = ax^b$. If it takes 200 hours to produce 20 units and 360 hours to produce 40 units, what is the percentage reduction and what are the appropriate values of a and b in the equation? [*Hint*: $b = \log(1 - (u/100) \div \log 2$.]

4–25.* Compute the following using logarithms.

a. $(72.1)(0.376)$

b. $(64.2) \div (127)$

c. $(4.72)^{2.7}$

5

Equations in One Unknown

An investor has $20,000 to invest, and he is interested in making at least $1,600 a year from his investment. He is considering allocating his $20,000 between two interest-bearing corporate bonds. (In buying such a bond, he is in effect loaning the corporation money; the corporation pays interest to him for, say, 20 years, and then repays the principal.) One of the two bonds, bond I, is rated AAA (very safe), and it yields 5 percent per year. The other bond, bond II, is rated A (not as safe), and it yields 9 percent.

Our investor observes that the riskier bond will yield more interest, but he wants to own as little of that bond as possible. He would prefer to invest all his money in bond I, the safer bond, but he cannot do so and still earn his minimum required return of $1,600 per year. He wants to know how much of each of the bonds to buy.

In order to solve the investor's problem, the above information can be put in the form of an equation and solved. You have, no doubt, already run across problems similar to this one; they are called "word problems." Throughout this chapter we shall deal with word problems. Word problems are usually solved using equations, and such problems occur constantly in managerial situations. However, they seldom occur in equation form. (Very few corporation presidents say: "$2x = 3 + x$; give me the answer by 4 P.M.")

The investor's problem above is an example of a linear equation, as we will see when we solve the problem. Before solving the investor's problem, we digress to study techniques for translating (some) word problems into equations and to give some useful results on equations in general. The investor will have to wait 30 minutes for his answer.

5-1 EQUATIONS

The equal sign was introduced in Sections 1–1 and 1–3. An equation simply sets one quantity equal to another. One of these quantities will typically be unknown and the other known. In this chapter the use of equations will center on solving for the unknown quantity. For example:

> $1,600 = amount of money earned from bond I plus amount of money earned from bond II.

This is a partial statement of the equation relating the investor's problem given in the chapter introduction. We want to solve for "dollars invested in bond I." Once we know that, the dollars to be invested in bond II will be $20,000 minus the dollars invested in bond I.

An equation sets two quantities equal to one another:

$$\text{quantity } 1 = \text{quantity } 2.$$

For another example, consider:

> Profit is the same as Revenue minus Cost.

In symbols, where $P \equiv$ profit, $R \equiv$ revenue, and $C \equiv$ cost, the equation is

$$P = R - C.$$

If, for example, revenue = $10,000 and cost = $8,000, we know that

$$P = R - C = \$2,000.$$

If $R = \$10,000$ and $C = \$11,000$, then

$$P = R - C = -\$1,000 \text{ (a \$1,000 loss.)}$$

Still other examples include

$A = \pi r^2$ ($A \equiv$ area of a circle; $r \equiv$ radius, and $\pi = 3.14$),

$2x = 3 - x,$

$x^2 - 2x - 1 = 0,$

$F = MA$ (force = mass times acceleration, one of Newton's laws of motion).

Changing Words into Equations

The profit equation was written first as "profit is the same as revenue minus cost." If word problems are to be the norm, it will be necessary to be able to decipher them. In the profit example the word "minus" can be represented by a minus sign. "Is the same as" can be represented by an equal sign. Some other examples are given below. In this case we have the "English translation," often in a particular dialect, and we want to write the mathematical version. We want to do this so that the equation can be solved.

Words	*Mathematical Representation*
is the same as; equals; is; is equal to	$=$
minus; less; subtracted from	$-$
plus; in addition to	$+$
is the product of	$\cdot$

The examples are, unfortunately, indicative but not exhaustive of the many ways in which these symbols may appear in written form. In addition to words for single symbols, there are words that indicate the type of equation involved. Some of these are given below.

Words	*Equation Type*	*Example*
varies as (varies linearly as)	$y = ax$	Consumption varies as income.

These words say that the first-mentioned variable (the dependent variable) equals a constant, a, times the second-mentioned (independent) variable. We will use "varies as" synonomously with "varies linearly as."

| varies as the square | $y = ax^2$ (or $s = at^2$) | Distance covered during a free fall varies as the square of the time spent in the air (in this case $a = 16.1$). |
| varies inversely | $y = \dfrac{a}{x}$ | Demand varies inversely with the price charged. |

Knowing the mathematical equivalent of phrases such as these helps us to decode word problems into mathematical notation. As an example, suppose we know that a shoe salesman's income varies as the number of pairs of shoes he sells. If he receives $10,000 in a year when he sold 2,000 pairs of shoes, what is the commission on one pair of shoes? The answer to this question is easy, but let's write it as an equation to illustrate the ideas of this section. First, we can write the general form:

$$\text{income} = a(\text{sales})$$

In particular,

$$10{,}000 = a \cdot 2{,}000$$

Solving for a,

$$\frac{10{,}000}{2{,}000} = a = \$5.$$

The salesman's commission is $5 per pair of shoes.

This example has two important characteristics: (1) it is a linear equation, and (2) it is an equation in one unknown. These two concepts are defined below.

A linear equation is one composed of terms consisting of constants and single variables to the 1 power; that is, the highest exponent of any unknown is 1, and no term has two or more unknowns.

An equation in one unknown consists only of constants and terms in one unknown.

For example:

1. $2x = 3 - x$ is a *linear equation*, in one unknown.
2. $2x = 3 - y$ is a *linear equation* in two unknowns.
3. $2x = 3 - x^2$ is an *equation in one unknown*, but it is not linear.
4. $xy = 4$ is a *nonlinear equation* in two unknowns.

Sometimes the difficult part of writing an equation lies in choosing the unknown. As an example, consider the investor's bond-choice problem. What we want to know is how many dollars worth of bond I he should choose, so we could use the number of dollars he holds of bond I (or bond II) as the unknown, or we could use the fraction of his total bond holdings allocated to bond I (or bond II) as the unknown. Using the number of dollars allocated to bond I as the unknown, we proceed as follows.

annual income = interest from bond I + interest from bond II

Let:

$$x = \text{dollars invested in bond I.}$$

Then,

$$20,000 - x = \text{dollars invested in bond II,}$$

since he invests a total of 20,000.

Now, bond I earns 5 percent (0.05) and bond II earns 9 percent (0.09). Thus

$$\text{annual income} = 1,600 = x(0.05) + (20,000 - x)(0.09).$$

This equation satisfies the definition of a linear equation in one unknown. Having written the equation, the hard part is over. The next section discusses how to solve for the unknown quantity, x.

1. Which of the following statements are (or imply) linear equations? Which are equations in one unknown? Which are equations?
   (a) $y^2 + 8y = 16x + 40z$.
   (b) An author's income varies as his ability to communicate.
   (c) An author's income varies inversely as his ability to confuse.
   (d) $3x - 2 = 6x - 5$.
   (e) $y = ax + b$.

2. Write a linear equation in one unknown to describe the following situation. A manufacturing firm makes three products, which cost \$1, \$2, and \$3, respectively. They make 100 of the \$1 items per day, and they want to make as many of the \$3 items as possible to improve the quality image of their firm. However, they must make a total of 300 units (daily total production of items 2 and 6 must be 200), and they have a \$650 total budget to be spent on each day's production.

   Equation _____.

Answers

1. All parts are or imply equations. Parts (b), (d), and (e) are linear equations. Part (d) is the only equation in one unknown, unless you happen to know two of the three terms implied in either of parts (b) or (c).

2. Let x = the number of \$3 units produced:

   $$3x + (200 - x)2 + 100(1) = 650.$$

   This is a linear equation in one unknown. (Although we do not yet know how to solve this, the solution for x is 150. Hence the firm should produce 150 \$3 units and 50 \$2 units. Solving linear equations is our next topic.)

5-2 SOLVING LINEAR EQUATIONS IN ONE UNKNOWN

Starting from the verbal definition of the investor's problem, we have arrived at

$$1,600 = 0.05x + (20,000 - x)0.09$$
$$= 0.05x + 1,800 - 0.09x.$$

Collecting terms, $-200 = -0.04x.$

Dividing by -0.04, $5,000 = x.$

The investor should purchase \$5,000 of bond I and \$15,000 (the remainder of his \$20,000) of bond II. He must spend a majority of his funds on the riskier bond (bond II) if he is to meet his interest objective.

To solve the above problem, we first multiplied out all terms. Then we collected the constants on one side (the left side here, but either side could be used) by subtracting 1,800 from both sides; the unknowns were collected on the other side by adding the two terms in x. Finally, we divided by the coefficient of (the constant that multiplies) the x term. Since we did all of this, it must be legitimate, right? Below we summarize what can be done to equations. These things can be done to all equations, not just linear equations. (Many of them have already been used in earlier chapters.)

Equality-Preserving Operations

If the title seems a little fancy, you can substitute: "Things we can do to an equation without upsetting the equality." As mentioned above, the list below holds for all equations, not just linear equations. We can

1. Add (subtract) the same quantity to (from) both sides.
2. Multiply (divide) both sides by the same quantity. (One exception is that division by zero is not allowed.)
3. Raise both sides to the same power (or take the same root of both sides).
4. Take the logarithm of both sides, if both sides are positive quantities.

In the investor example, we used operations 1 and 2 to obtain a solution. The statement "collect terms" involves operation 1. You can, if you prefer to think of it this way, say that transposing terms from one side of the equation to the other is legitimate if the sign is changed when a term is moved to the other side.

As examples, consider the following:

(i) $3x + 7 = 4x$
   $3x - 4x + 7 = 4x - 4x$ subtracting $4x$ from both sides (or
     $-x + 7 = 0$ transposing terms)

$$-x + 7 - 7 = 0 - 7 \qquad \text{subtracting 7 from both sides}$$
$$x = +7 \qquad \text{dividing by } -1 \text{ (or multiplying by } -1)$$

(ii) $x^{1/2} - 2 = 3$

$$x^{1/2} - 2 + 2 = 3 + 2 \qquad \text{adding 2 to both sides (or transposing}$$
$$x^{1/2} = 5 \qquad \text{terms)}$$
$$(x^{1/2})^2 = 5^2 \qquad \text{raising both sides to the second power}$$
$$x = 25$$

The last example is not a linear equation, but it does demonstrate an application of equality-preserving operations.

Method for Solving Linear Equations in One Unknown

The method for solving linear equations in one unknown is relatively simple. You will usually find that once you manage to state the problem in equation form, the actual solution is much less difficult.

Method for Solving Linear Equations in One Unknown

1. Complete any multiplications. Collect all terms in the unknown on one side and the constant terms on the other (that is, transpose terms to achieve this).
2. Add like terms; the equation is now in the form $ax = b$.
3. Divide both sides by the coefficient of (the constant that multiplies) the unknown (say x) term. The equation now reads $x =$ a constant; the constant is the answer.

For example,

$$3x - 2 = 6x - 5.$$

Step 1: $3x - 6x = -5 + 2.$
Step 2: $-3x = -3.$
Step 3: $x = +1.$

Many of you will be able to solve this type of problem more quickly by your own techniques. Please do so; do not be trapped into using our method unless you find it is the best way for you.

We just would not feel right unless we gave one algebra problem of the following form.   The president of a corporation has a son, whose name is

John. If 3 times John's age is the same as 2 times John's age in 7 years, how old is John?

Let:

$$x = \text{John's current age.}$$

Now we can decode the sentence.

If three times John's age $\qquad$ $3x$
is the same as $\qquad$ $=$
(two) times (John's age in 7 years) $\qquad$ $(2)(x + 7)$

That is,

$$3x = 2(x + 7)$$
$$= 2x + 14.$$

Solving, we find that $x = 14$. John is currently 14 years old. (This is about the age when students of mathematics are introduced to such practical exercises.)

1. If the investor in our earlier problem would be satisfied with a return of $1,200 annual interest, how much of each bond should he buy? What if he wants $2,000 in annual interest? Amount_____. Amount _____.

2. Firm A is currently selling 15,000 units per year, and its major competition (firm B) is selling 20,000 units per year. Firm A's sales are growing at a rate of 1,000 units per year; firm B's sales are growing at a rate of 500 units per year. Firm A will catch firm B in $5,000/500 = 10$ years. Explain how the answer is arrived at in terms of the equality-preserving operations discussed in this section.

Answers

1. $1,200 = 0.05x + (20,000 - x)(0.09)$
   $-600 = -0.04x$
   $x = \$15,000.$

   He should buy $15,000 of bond I (the safer bond) and $5,000 of bond II, if he is satisfied with $1,200 of interest. If he wants $2,000 of interest he is out of luck; it is impossible.

2. We could solve this problem by writing the equation

$$\text{firm A's sales} = \text{firm B's sales}$$

and solve for the time at which this is true. Let $t = $ time, in years. Then

$$15,000 + 1,000t = 20,000 + 500t.$$

Subtracting 15,000 from both sides,

$$1,000t = 20,000 - 15,000 + 500t.$$

Subtracting 500*t* from both sides,

$$1,000t - 500t = 20,000 - 15,000$$
$$500t = 5,000.$$

Dividing by 500,

$$t = \frac{5,000}{500} = 10.$$

We used equality-preserving operations 1 and 2. However, this is a perfect example of an easy problem that can be made difficult by following the rules precisely. It is easier to think: "Firm A has 5,000 units to catch up, and it is catching up at a rate of 500 per year. They will catch up in 10 years." Never let a method keep you from solving a problem the easy way.

5-3 POLYNOMIALS

In the previous section we dealt almost entirely with linear equations. Unfortunately, many real situations cannot be described using linear equations, and we have to know how to work with nonlinear equations. This section deals with a special kind of equation called a *polynomial*.

A polynomial function in *x*, of degree *n*, is given by

$$f(x) = a_n x^n + a_{n-1} x^{n-1} + \cdots + a_1 x^1 + a_0,$$

where $a_o, \ldots, a_n$ are constants. (We assume that $a_n \neq 0$; otherwise the first term drops out and we have a polynominal of degree $n - 1$ at most.)

For example,

$$f(x) = 2x^3 + x - 4$$

defines a polynomial function in *x* of degree 3,

$$f(x, y) = 2x^3y + 4x^2 - 1$$

does not define a polynomial function in *x*, since one term includes the unknown *y*,

$$f(x) = x + 2$$

defines a polynomial function in *x* of degree 1 (usually called a linear function).

For a concrete example, suppose a theater owner believes that demand for theater tickets is very sensitive to the price charged, in that there are several other theaters in town which will not follow a price increase. He believes that the average demand per show (over a price range of \$1.50 to \$5) is given as a function of the price, p, by

$$\text{average demand per show} = D = 180 + 12p - 8p^2; \qquad 1.5 \le p \le 5.$$

He is currently charging \$3 per ticket. His profit on any night is pD minus \$400 of fixed costs, which is the only cost in this example. Thus his profits are given by

$$
\begin{aligned}
\text{profit} &= (\text{price})(\text{demand}) - (\text{fixed cost}) = pD - 400 \\
&= 180p + 12p^2 - 8p^3 - 400.
\end{aligned}
$$

The theater owner wants to raise the price, and he would like to know how much profit he will make at each price higher than \$3. He is especially interested in knowing how high a price he can charge and still break even (make zero profit). This would allow him to establish the higher price, and eventually he thinks that customers would return. However, he also wants to know how low a price he can charge and break even, since a low price would bring in lots of customers and (hopefully) form some "product identification" on the customer's part for his theater. He knows that he is making money at \$3, and the above words simply translate to "find the range over which he will make money." It is bounded, in this case, by two breakeven points.

Mathematically, he wants to find x values for which $f(x) = 0$. This has the special name "polynomial equation." The polynomial equation is formed by setting $f(x) = 0$, where $f(x)$ defines a polynomial function.

A polynomial equation in x of degree n, in standard form, is written

$$a_n x^n + a_{n-1} x^{n-1} + \cdots + a_1 x^1 + a_0 = 0, \qquad a_n \ne 0.$$

Solving a polynomial equation is sometimes called "finding the zeros" of the polynomial function, since the values where $f(x) = 0$ [where $f(x)$ crosses the x axis] are being found. This is an important problem in management applications, although, as you might expect, no one tells another person to "go find the zeros of that polynomial function."

Let's test the owner's statement that he is making money at a ticket price of \$3 ($p = 3$). First we put the problem in standard form:

$$f(p) = -8p^3 + 12p^2 + 180p - 400.$$

That is, $a_3 = -8$, $a_2 = +12$, $a_1 = 180$, and $a_0 = -400$.

$$f(3) = -8(3)^3 + 12(3)^2 + 180(3) - 400 = +32.$$

[If he has 16 shows per week, he is making $16(32) = \$512$ per week.]

He wants to find p values where $f(p) = 0$. Let's try increasing p first. Just for fun, let's try $p = 4$.

$$f(4) = -8(4)^3 + 12(4)^2 + 180(4) - 400 = 0.$$

We've done it! A ticket price of $4 is one breakeven point. Let's try the other direction, $p = 2$.

$$f(2) = -8(2)^3 + 12(2)^2 + 180(2) - 400 = -56.$$

That price is too small. A negative profit results. Let's try going halfway:

$$f(2\tfrac{1}{2}) = -8(2\tfrac{1}{2})^3 + 12(2\tfrac{1}{2})^2 + 180(2\tfrac{1}{2}) - 400 = 0.$$

Now a "zero" in both directions has been found. If he wants to make money, while achieving some marketing objective, he should charge between $2.50 and $4. The pricing policy depends on the objective.

There are still unanswered questions in the theater manager's problem.

1. What do we do if the breakeven price were to be 2.6472 instead of 2.5, and searching for it is tedious?
2. What is the price he should charge to maximize his profit?
3. How can we be sure there are no other "zeros" between $2.50 and $4?

The answers are:

1. Learn an easier way to find them, which we are about to do.
2. This price is $3.33, and we will learn how to find it in Chapter 12.
3. Once we learn the easier way to find zeros, we will know that the only other zero for this function occurs for a negative price. (Chapter 12 will give us yet another method of being sure that no other zeros exist between $2.50 and $4.

The next order of business is learning the easier way. Before doing so we need to (briefly) extend our ability to do arithmetic with polynomials.

Multiplication of Polynomials

As we saw earlier, addition and subtraction of polynomials is relatively easy. [Thus $x + x = 2x$; $(1 + x + x^2) + (2 + x - 2x^2) = 3 + 2x - x^2$.] We just add the constants multiplying the x terms to obtain the coefficient of the x term in the answer; likewise for other terms. Multiplication and division is a little harder. Let's try an example.

$$(a + bx)(c + dx)$$

$$
\begin{array}{r}
a + bx \\
c + dx \\
\hline
adx + bdx^2 \\
\end{array}
$$

$$
\begin{array}{l}
ac \qquad\quad + bcx \\
\hline
ac + (ad + bc)x + bdx^2 \\
\end{array}
$$

This answer is a general form that can be used to multiply specific examples. For example,

$$(3 + x)(1 + 2x) = 3(1) + [3(2) + 1(1)]x + 1(2)x^2 = 3 + 7x + 2x^2.$$

For another example,

$$(a + bx + cx^2)(d + ex). \text{ Then}$$

$$
\begin{array}{l}
a + bx + cx^2 \\
d + ex \\
\hline
\quad\qquad + bex^2 + cex^3 \\
\end{array}
$$

$$
\begin{array}{l}
aex \qquad\qquad\quad + dcx^2 \\
ad \qquad + bdx \\
\hline
ad + (ae + bd)x + (bc + dc)x^2 + cex^3 \\
\end{array}
$$

The general steps in the method for multiplying two polynomials are spelled out next.

Method for Multiplying Polynomials

1. Arrange the two expressions one above the other.
2. Multiply the rightmost term of the lower expression by each term of the upper expression.
3. Continue, using the next term to the left in the lower expression, writing the x term under the x term from the first multiplication, the x^2 term under the x^2 term, and so on.
4. Add the separate multiplication terms, collecting by x terms, then by x^2 terms, and so on.
5. If you see an easier way to do a particular problem, by all means use it!

〰 : Multiply the following polynomials to obtain $f(x)g(x)$.

1. $f(x) = (2 + 3x)$
   $g(x) = (1 + x)$

3. $f(x) = 2x$
   $g(x) = x^2 + 1$

2. $f(x) = 3 + x^2$ 4. $f(x) = 1 + x + x^2$
   $g(x) = 4 + x$ $g(x) = 1 + x$

Answers

1. $(2 + 3x)(1 + x) = 2 + 5x + 3x^2$
2. $(3 + x^2)(4 + x) = 12 + 3x + 4x^2 + x^3$
3. $(2x)(x^2 + 1) = 2x^3 + 2x$
4. $(1 + x + x^2)(1 + x) = 1 + 2x + 2x^2 + x^3$

Division of Polynomials

Example 1

$$(2x^2 - 3x - 2) \div (x - 2)$$

Step 1	Step 2

$$
\begin{array}{r}
2x \\
x - 2 \overline{)\, 2x^2 - 3x - 2} \\
\underline{2x^2 - 4x} \\
\text{Subtracting} \quad x - 2
\end{array}
\qquad
\begin{array}{r}
1 \\
x - 2 \overline{)\, x - 2} \\
\underline{x - 2} \\
0
\end{array}
$$

The answer is $2x + 1$.

Example 2

$$(x^2 + 4x + 9) \div (x + 2)$$

Step 1	Step 2

$$
\begin{array}{r}
x \\
\text{Divisor} \quad x + 2 \overline{)\, x^2 + 4x + 9} \quad \text{dividend} \\
\underline{x^2 + 2x} \\
\text{Subtracting} \quad 2x + 9 \quad \text{intermediate} \\
\text{remainder}
\end{array}
\qquad
\begin{array}{r}
2 \\
x + 2 \overline{)\, 2x + 9} \\
\underline{2x + 4} \\
5 \quad \text{final remainder}
\end{array}
$$

The answer is $x + 2 + \dfrac{5}{x + 2}$.

Method

1. Arrange the expression being divided (the dividend) and the expression doing the dividing (the divisor) as shown in the examples. Be sure both expressions are in descending powers of $x: x^3$, x^2, x, for example.
2. Find a term that multiplies the first term of the divisor to give the first term of the dividend. Write it above the line.
3. Multiply it by the divisor, subtract the result from the dividend, and perform the same operations [steps 1, 2, and 3 on the remainder (called above the intermediate remainder)].

4. Continue steps 1 to 3 until a remainder (called above the final remainder) has a highest power of x lower than the highest power of x in the divisor. The answer is written as the results of steps 1–3, with the final remainder expressed as a fraction over the divisor.

5. The divisor is called a *perfect divisor* of the dividend if and only if the final remainder is zero. (This is analogous to: 2 is a perfect divisor of 4 but not of 5.) The divisor in the first example is a perfect divisor.

6. If you see an easy way to do a problem, use it!

$\sim\!\!\checkmark$: Given the following functions, find $f(x) \div g(x)$.

1. $f(x) = 2x^2 - 3x - 2$
   $g(x) = 2x + 1$
2. $f(x) = x^2 - 4x + 4$
   $g(x) = x - 2$
3. $f(x) = x^2 - 1$
   $g(x) = x + 1$
4. $f(x) = x^2 - 5$
   $g(x) = x - 2$

Answers

Step 1	Step 2

$$1.\quad 2x + 1\,\overline{)\,2x^2 - 3x - 2}$$
$$\underline{2x^2 + x}$$
$$\text{Subtracting } -4x - 2$$

Step 2:
$$-2$$
$$2x + 1\,\overline{)\,-4x - 2}$$
$$\underline{-4x - 2}$$
$$\text{Subtracting } \quad 0$$

We know that $(x - 2)(2x + 1) = 2x^2 - 3x - 2$. We add some terminology here. The terms $x - 2$ and $2x + 1$ are called *factors* of $2x^2 - 3x - 2$. They are both "perfect divisors." Factors are explored in the next subsection. The answers to (*b*) and (*c*) are given without showing the steps.

2. $x - 2$.

3. $x - 1$.

4. $x + 2 - \dfrac{1}{x - 2}$.

Factoring Polynomials

Given a function, defined by $f(x)$, a function $g(x)$ is a *factor* of $f(x)$ if $f(x)$ $\div$ $g(x)$ has zero as a *final* remainder. That is, $g(x)$ is a factor if it is a perfect divisor of $f(x)$. Alternatively, $g(x)$ is a factor of $f(x)$ if there is a polynomial $h(x)$ such that $f(x) = g(x)\,h(x)$.

For example:

1. $x + 1$ is a factor of $x^2 - 1$ since $(x^2 - 1) \div (x + 1) = (x - 1)$, and $x - 1$ is also a factor of $x^2 - 1$ since $(x^2 - 1) \div (x - 1) = (x + 1)$. In fact, $(x + 1)(x - 1) = x^2 - 1$, and these two terms are the only factors of $x^2 - 1$.

2. $(2x + 1)(x - 2) = 2x^2 - 3x - 2$, and $2x + 1$ and $x - 2$ are the only factors of $2x^2 - 3x - 2$.

When looking for factors of a polynomial, $f(x)$, we must be clever. One fact to remember is that the constant terms in the factors must multiply to give the constant term in $f(x)$. A second fact is that the coefficients on the highest power of x in each factor must multiply to give the coefficient of the highest power of x in $f(x)$. For example, given $f(x) = (2x + 1)(x - 2)$, then

1. $(1)(-2) =$ the constant in $2x^2 - 3x - 2$, namely -2.
2. $(2)(1) =$ the coefficient of x^2, namely 2.

These two facts will help us find factors, when they exist, as we shall see shortly.

These are several useful things to know about factors. One of these is called the *factor theorem*.

The Factor Theorem

If $f(x) = a_n x^n + \ldots + a_0$ is a polynomial function, and if $(x-a)$ is a factor of $f(x)$, then $f(a) = 0$, and $x = a$ is called a "root" or "zero" of the polynomial function.

If $(x - a)$ is a factor, the polynomial can be written $(x - a)(b_{n-1}x^{n-1} + \ldots + b_0)$. Now if $x = a$, then $x - a = 0$ and zero times anything is zero, so the factor theorem makes sense. A polynomial equation in x is in *standard form* when written $a_n x^n + \ldots + a_0 = 0$. If you find a factor of $a_n x^n + \ldots + a_0$, you have found one solution to the equation. To illustrate the method, we return to the theater owner's problem. He had

$$f(p) = -8p^3 + 12p^2 + 180p - 400.$$

To find factors, we first notice that (-4) can be factored out of every term.

$$f(p) = -4(+2p^3 - 3p^2 - 45p + 100).$$

The manager wants $f(p) = 0$, so we have to find other factors, if they exist. They do, and we now write the polynomial in factored form without telling you for the moment how we found the factors.

$$f(p) = -4(p - 4)(2p - 5)(p + 5).$$

Thus $f(p) = 0$ when any one of the factors is zero; when $p = 4$, or when $p = -5$, or when $2p = 5$ (that is, when $p = 2.5$). We see that if $(ax - b)$ is a factor, then $x = b/a$ is a root of the polynomial. These three values of p are the roots of the equation.

The two breakeven prices are \$2.50 and \$4. The $p = -5$ solution is not valid since the demand function was only accurate for $1.5 < p < 5$. Next we discuss how to obtain the factors of the theater owner's (or some other) polynomial.

About the only way to find factors, when they exist, is to try the biblical method of "seek and ye shall (may?) find." Using the facts developed earlier about the products of the constant terms and the coefficients of the highest powers of x, we can generate the following possible pairs of values for the factors of $2p^3 - 3p^2 - 45p + 100$. If a polynomial can be factored into n factors it can also be factored into two factors, where one factor is the product of $n - 1$ factors. Thus we initially work to factor the above polynomial into two factors: $(ap + b)(cp^2 + dp + g)$. For b and g, using fact 1, we get the following possible pairs: $(100, 1)$, $(50, 2)$, $(25, 4)$, $(20, 5)$, $(10, 10)$, $(-100, -1)$, $(-50, -2)$, $(-25, -4)$, $(-20, -5)$, and $(-10, -10)$. For a and c, using fact 2, we get the possible pairs $(2, 1)$ and $(-2, -1)$. (Only integer multiples are considered here; factoring with noninteger values is difficult, and we resort to it only in desperation.)

We now have possible values to test for a, b, c, and g. We select a (b, g) pair from the first list and an (a, c) pair from the second list. Suppose that we selected $a = 1$ ($c = 2$) and $b = -4$ ($g = -25$); then the factor $(1p - 4)$ could be checked by dividing $(p - 4)$ into the polynomial as follows:

$$(2p^3 - 3p^2 - 45p + 100) \div (p - 4) = 2p^2 + 5p - 25.$$

The polynomial $-4(+2p^3 - 3p^2 - 45p + 100)$ can now be written as $-4(p - 4)(2p^2 + 5p - 25)$. This checks with the pairs chosen. By first delineating the possibilities and then using trial-and-error methods, the factor $2p^2 + 5p - 25$ can be further broken down into the terms $(2p - 5)$ and $(p + 5)$. You may wish to try to get this result yourself.

Another useful fact about polynomials concerns the number of roots it may have.

A polynomial function in x of degree n has at most n roots. It may have as few as zero. That is, a polynomial equation in x of degree n, in standard form, has at most n solutions.

For example:

1. $f(x) = x^2 + 1$ has no real-valued roots, since it never becomes negative; when $x = 0, f(0) = 1$ is the smallest value of $f(x)$.
2. $f(x) = x^2 - 2x - 1$ has only one root. $f(x) = (x - 1)(x - 1)$. The factor $(x - 1)$ appears twice; $+1$ is the only root.

To summarize the information to date:

1. Polynomial equations can sometimes be solved by factoring; that is, we can find the values of x for which $f(x) = 0$.
2. There are at most as many solutions as the degree of the equation.
3. If we want to find the x values where $f(x) = b$, if $f(x)$ is a polynomial function and b is a constant, we write $g(x) = f(x) - b$ and find values where $g(x) = 0$.
4. We need to know how to divide and multiply polynomials by one another in order to work with factors.

In spite of the last statement, the easiest way to find factors is by trial and error, remembering that the first terms of the factors must multiply to give the first term of the polynomial, and the last terms of the factors must multiply to give the last term of the polynomial.

Graphing Polynomials

Polynomials, like other functions, are graphed by finding $f(x)$ for several values of x. The roots of a polynomial are particularly useful in graphing the function. The roots often have managerial implications as well, as we saw in the theater manager's problem. To plot a polynomial, the following steps can be used.

1. Find all roots of the function $f(x)$. At these values $f(x) = 0$. These points are easily located on a graph.
2. Evaluate the function at some points between (and around) the roots. You will now see where the curve is rising, falling, and where it crosses zero. [Always include $f(0)$ since it is the easiest value to evaluate.] Remember that if $f(x) = 0$ at two adjacent roots, and if $f(x)$ is positive (negative) for one value in between, it is positive (negative) for every value in between.
3. Sketch the curve. It is a good idea to compute a few more points to check your sketch.

Let's try an example. Suppose that

$$f(x) = x^3 + 3x^2 - x - 3.$$

Using the trial-and-error method to factor this equation gives

$$f(x) = (x + 3)(x + 1)(x - 1).$$

The roots are $x = -3$, $x = -1$, and $x = +1$. We next evaluate $f(x)$ at some intermediate point such as $x = -4$, $x = -2$, $x = 0$, and $x = +2$. Using the values obtained for $f(x)$, we can now graph the function. The graph is shown in Figure 5-1. It shows the general shape of a cubic (third-degree) function. We do not claim to be able to obtain the precise graph in this way, but we can come as close as we like by trying more and more values of x. The $f(x)$ values evaluated are as follows:

$$
\begin{aligned}
f(-4) &= -15 & f(-3) &= 0 \\
f(-2) &= +3 & f(-1) &= 0 \\
f(0) &= -3 & f(+1) &= 0 \\
f(+2) &= +15
\end{aligned}
$$

FIGURE 5–1

Graph of $f(x) = x^3 + 3x^2 - x - 3$
$$= (x + 3)(x + 1)(x - 1)$$

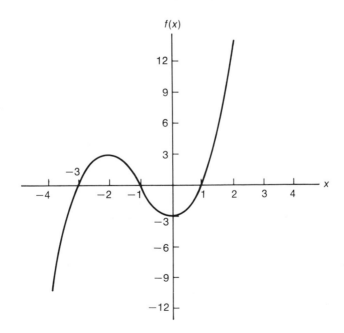

One special polynomial is worth mentioning here: $f(x) = a_1x_1 + a_0$, the linear polynomial. As you may recall, this function is graphed as a straight line, with a slope equal to a_1. It has an intercept [$f(x)$ value when $x = 0$] of a_0. It crosses the $f(x)$ axis at a_0. This value, a_0, is called the *intercept*. The function is graphed as a straight line in which the change in $f(x)$ (the "rise" in the function) for a given change in x (the "run") always equals a_1. The rise divided by the run is called the *slope* of the function. If $f(x) = 2x + 4$, then $f(0) = 4$, and the function crosses the $f(x)$ axis at 4. It has an intercept of 4. Further, if x is changed from 3 to 8, then $f(x)$ changes 10 units from $f(3) = 10$ to $f(8) = 20$. It has a slope of $10 \div 5 = 2$.

⁓ : Find the roots by factoring and sketch the graphs of the following functions.

  1. $f(x) = x^2 - 3x + 2$
  2. $f(x) = 2x^3 - x^2 - 8x + 4$

Answers

  1. $f(x) = x^2 - 3x + 2 = (x - 2)(x - 1)$.
     Thus: $f(0) = +2$ $f(\frac{1}{2}) = +\frac{3}{4}$
           $f(1) = 0$ $f(1\frac{1}{2}) = -\frac{1}{4}$
           $f(2) = 0$ $f(3) = +2$ (Figure 5–2).

FIGURE 5–2

Graph of $f(x) = x^2 - 3x + 2$

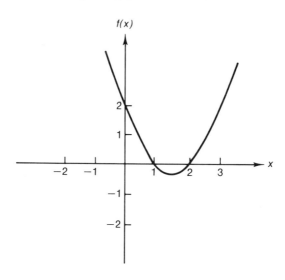

2. $f(x) = 2x^3 - x^2 - 8x + 4 = (2x - 1)(x + 2)(x - 2)$.
Thus: $f(-2) = 0 \qquad f(-1) = +9$
$\qquad f(0) = +4 \qquad f(+1) = -3$
$\qquad f(+\tfrac{1}{2}) = 0 \qquad f(+3) = +25$ (Figure 5-3).
$\qquad f(+2) = 0$

FIGURE 5-3

Graph of $f(x) = 2x^3 - x^2 - 8x + 4$

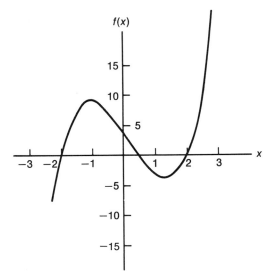

A Special Polynomial—The Quadratic Function

The polynomial function in x of degree 2 is written as $f(x)=a_2x^2+a_1x^1+a_0$ or as $f(x)=ax^2+bx+c$. (The latter form is more common.) It is called a quadratic function. The corresponding polynomial equation, $ax^2+bx^1+c=0$, is called a *quadratic equation*. The curve of the quadratic function is called a *parabola*.

All quadratic functions have the same shape. This shape is illustrated in Figure 5-4.

Figure 5-4a illustrates a quadratic function with no roots; Figure 5-4b illustrates a quadratic function with two roots; and Figure 5-4c shows a

FIGURE 5–4

Graphs of Three Parabolas

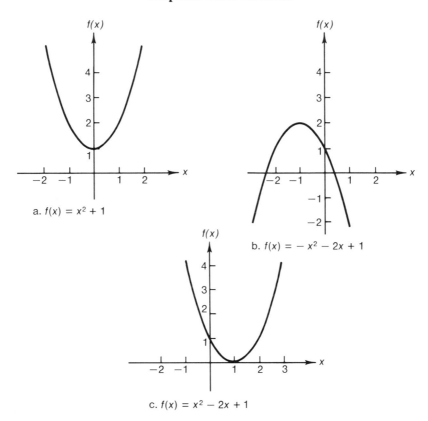

a. $f(x) = x^2 + 1$

b. $f(x) = -x^2 - 2x + 1$

c. $f(x) = x^2 - 2x + 1$

parabola with only one root. The lowest $f(x)$ value in Figures 5-4a and 5-4c and the highest $f(x)$ value in Figure 5-4b is called the *vertex of the parabola.* Using the general form $f(x) = ax^2 + bx + c$ to represent the parabola, the vertex occurs at $x = -b/2a$. This is proved in Chapter 12. For now it is simply given as a fact.

The roots of a quadratic function can be found (sometimes) by factoring, just as they can for other polynomials. In fact, at the end of the previous section we found the roots of $f(x) = x^2 - 3x + 2$ by factoring. But if factors do not exist, or if the factors are nonintegers, obtaining the solution can be difficult. Fortunately, a general solution exists for all quadratic equations, so the roots of a quadratic function can always be found. Let's do some algebra to obtain this general solution.

The general form for a quadratic is

$$f(x) = ax^2 + bx + c.$$

To find the roots of the function we find the x values where $f(x) = 0$; we set

$$ax^2 + bx + c = 0.$$

Subtracting c from each side gives

$$ax^2 + bx = -c.$$

Dividing by a,

$$x^2 + \frac{b}{a}x = -\frac{c}{a}.$$

Adding $(b/2a)^2$ to each side:

$$x^2 + \frac{b}{a}x + \left(\frac{b}{2a}\right)^2 = -\frac{c}{a} + \left(\frac{b}{2a}\right)^2.$$

(This last step is not one you would normally think to do. But someone found that it works.)

Factor the left side:

$$\left(x + \frac{b}{2a}\right)\left(x + \frac{b}{2a}\right) = -\frac{c}{a} + \left(\frac{b}{2a}\right)^2$$

or

$$\left(x + \frac{b}{2a}\right)^2 = -\frac{c}{a} + \left(\frac{b}{2a}\right)^2.$$

Taking the square root of both sides,

$$\left(x + \frac{b}{2a}\right) = \pm\sqrt{-\frac{c}{a} + \left(\frac{b}{2a}\right)^2}.$$

(The $\pm$ sign is used to remind us that a positive number has both a positive and a negative square root.) Subtracting $b/2a$ gives

$$x = -\frac{b}{2a} \pm \sqrt{-\frac{c}{a} + \left(\frac{b}{2a}\right)^2}.$$

There are two solutions to any quadratic equation, and we have found them both. They are

$$x = -\frac{b}{2a} + \sqrt{-\frac{c}{a} + \left(\frac{b}{2a}\right)^2} \quad \text{and} \quad x = -\frac{b}{2a} - \sqrt{-\frac{c}{a} + \left(\frac{b}{2a}\right)^2}.$$

In more compact form,

$$x = -\frac{b}{2a} \pm \sqrt{-\frac{c}{a} + \frac{b^2}{4a^2}}$$

$$= -\frac{b}{2a} \pm \sqrt{\frac{-4ac + b^2}{4a^2}} = \frac{-b \pm \sqrt{b^2 - 4ac}}{2a}$$

The above is partly an exercise in equality-preserving operations and partly one in algebra. You should be able to understand each step, but you should not try to memorize or be able to reproduce the steps. We have derived the quadratic formula, and once you accept the steps, you may use it without having to derive it every time you need it. The most useful (and common) form is

$$x = \frac{-b \pm \sqrt{b^2 - 4ac}}{2a}.$$

For an example we can use the quadratic formula to find the roots of $f(x) = x^2 - 3x + 2$. The roots occur at

$$\frac{-(-3) \pm \sqrt{(-3)^2 - 4(1)2}}{2(1)} = \frac{3 \pm \sqrt{9 - 8}}{2} = 1\tfrac{1}{2} \pm \tfrac{1}{2},$$

or at $x = 1$ and $x = 2$. These are the same roots we found when we factored this quadratic function into $f(x) = (x - 2)(x - 1)$.

As you may have guessed, sometimes a negative number will appear under the square-root sign. In that event the quadratic function has no real roots; it has only what are called *complex* roots, which we will not be dealing with here.

A few more things about the function can be discovered by examining the expression $b^2 - 4ac$ in the quadratic formula.

The expression $b^2 - 4ac$ is called the *discriminant* **of a quadratic equation. If**

1. It is zero, both roots are identical, real numbers.
2. It is greater than zero, both roots are real, and they are unequal.
3. It is less than zero, both roots are complex numbers.

Let us try a managerial example. Suppose that a production control manager knows that his total inventory-related cost equals the sum of two terms. The first is the inventory cost per unit multiplied by the average number of units in inventory. The second term is the number of setups (the number of production runs) per year multiplied by the setup cost (cost incurred preparing for a production run). If $x =$ the number of units produced each time, and if

(i) inventory holding cost = $1 per unit per year
(ii) setup cost = $10 per setup
(iii) annual rate of demand = 1,000,

then we can write total inventory cost as the sum of inventory holding cost and setup cost:

$$\text{cost} = \frac{x}{2}(1) + \left(\frac{1,000}{x}\right)10.$$

Suppose further that the manager has a budget of $150 for inventory cost on this item. How many units can he order to exactly meet the budget? The answer is supplied by the equation

$$\$150 = \frac{x}{2} + \frac{10,000}{x}.$$

Multiply by x (otherwise, how do you proceed?):

$$150x = \frac{x^2}{2} + 10,000,$$

or transposing,

$$\tfrac{1}{2}x^2 - 150x + 10,000 = 0.$$

Using the quadratic formula

$$x = \frac{150 \pm \sqrt{(150)^2 - 20,000}}{1} = 150 \pm 50.$$

He can meet his budget by ordering either 100 or 200 units each time he orders. (You might be surprised to learn that he meets demand and simultaneously minimizes his cost by ordering 141.4 units each time. Exactly how we arrive at that magical number is something you will learn in Chapter 12.)

1. If, in the above inventory example, the manager had to stay within a budget of $100 \sqrt{2}$ ($\approx$ $141.42), how many units should he order? _____units.
2. What if he wanted to meet a budget of $140? _____units.

Answers

1. $\dfrac{100\sqrt{2} \pm \sqrt{(100\sqrt{2})^2 - 20,000}}{1} = 100\sqrt{2}.$

There is only one root in this case. The cost of $100\sqrt{2}$ units is the minimum cost of meeting demand.

2. $\dfrac{140 \pm \sqrt{19,600 - 20,000}}{1} = 140 \pm \sqrt{-400}.$

This is a complex number, and it means that he cannot meet both the demand for 1,000 units per year and a budget of $140.

5-4 SOLVING A FEW OTHER TYPES OF EQUATIONS

Without elaboration, this section discusses the solution to a few other common functions. Most of the previous sections dealt only with the equality-preserving operations of addition and multiplication. The solution to some equations requires raising to a power (perhaps a fractional power) or taking a logarithm. We have already illustrated the process of taking roots in deriving the quadratic formula. Finally, solving some equations is accomplished only through trickery. Let's do a few examples of each of these.

Example. Taking a root to solve an equation

(i) If $x^2 - 4x + 4 = 4$ (ii) If $(x - 3)^3 = 54$

Then $(x - 2)^2 = 4$ Then, taking the cube root of

Taking the square root: both sides:

$\quad x - 2 = \pm 2$ $\quad (x - 3) = \sqrt[3]{27(2)}$

and $\quad x = 3 + 3\sqrt[3]{2}.$

$\quad x = 4$ and $x = 0.$

Example. Taking a logarithm to solve an equation

As we learned in Chapter 4, exponential curves can represent growth patterns of new products. As a simplified example, suppose that sales for a new product are given by

$$s(t) = e^{2t - 0.2t^2}, \qquad 0 < t < 5,$$

where time is measured in years and sales are measured in thousands of units. The company wants to know when sales will reach 20,000 units. They want to solve:

$$20 = e^{2t - 0.2t^2}.$$

To solve this equation, take the logarithm of both sides to the base e.

$$\ln(20) = 2t - 0.2t^2.$$

Using Table I at the back of the book, ln 20 is about 3. Hence we may write

$$3 = 2t - 0.2t^2 \quad \text{or} \quad -0.2t^2 + 2t - 3 = 0.$$

Using the quadratic formula,

$$t = \frac{-2 \pm \sqrt{4 - 2.4}}{0.4} = 5 \pm \frac{\sqrt{1.6}}{0.4}$$

$$= 1.82 \quad \text{or} \quad 8.18.$$

The $t = 8.18$ value is not allowed since $0 < t < 5$ is specified, so $t = 1.82$ is the answer; they will reach 20,000 sales in 1.82 years if their growth curve is correctly specified.

Example.   Using trickery to solve an equation

Being clever is useful in mathematics. Seeing the correct trick to use can often make what seemed to be an insolvable problem solvable. For example, find x values such that

$$5x^{-1} + 2x^{-2} + 3 = 0.$$

One trick is to let $y = 1/x$; then we have

$$5y + 2y^2 + 3 = 0.$$

Solving by the quadratic formula,

$$y = \frac{-5 \pm \sqrt{25 - 24}}{4} = -\frac{5}{4} \pm \frac{1}{4} = -\frac{6}{4} \text{ and } -1.$$

Since $x = 1/y$, $x = -\frac{2}{3}$ and $x = -1$ are solutions to the original equation. Another trick we could have used here is to multiply by x^2; then we have

$$3x^2 + 5x + 2 = 0.$$

Solving by the quadratic formula,

$$x = \frac{-5 \pm \sqrt{25 - 24}}{6} = -\frac{5}{6} \pm \frac{1}{6}, \quad \text{so} \quad x = -1 \text{ and } x = -\frac{2}{3}.$$

(It is comforting to get the same answer both ways.) Unfortunately, trickery is an art learned only after considerable practice.

Finally, we should mention the fact that there are computer programs written (by someone else) to solve complicated equations. The computer, being more patient than we are, can use a trial-and-error approach and not get tired. If an equation is very complex, it is best to let a computer do the job.

⌇ : Solve the following equations. Leave the answers in square-root form.

1. $\sqrt{x} = x + 1$ $x = $ _____.

2. $\dfrac{1}{e} = e^{x^2 - 4}$ $x = $ _____.

3. $-\dfrac{1}{x} + \dfrac{1}{x^2} = 1$ $x = $ _____.

Answers

1. Squaring both sides and then using the quadratic formula:

$$x = x^2 + 2x + 1 \quad \text{or} \quad x^2 + x + 1 = 0$$
$$x = \frac{1 \pm \sqrt{1 - 4}}{2} = \frac{1}{2} \pm \frac{\sqrt{-3}}{2}.$$

The answers are complex numbers, so we quit trying to solve it.

2. Rewriting, taking logarithms to the base e, and then taking square roots, we obtain

$$e^{-1} = e^{x^2 - 4},$$
$$-1 = x^2 - 4,$$
$$x^2 = 3,$$
$$x = \pm \sqrt{3}.$$

3. Multiplying by x^2 and then using the quadratic formula,

$$-x^2 - x + 1 = 0,$$
$$x = \frac{1 \pm \sqrt{1 + 4}}{-2} = -\frac{1}{2} \pm \frac{\sqrt{5}}{2}.$$

5-5 SUMMARY

This chapter gives a formal introduction to the equation, the most important mathematical relation. We learn that we can add, multiply, divide, raise to a power, and take logarithms of both sides (all in an appropriate manner) and still have an equation, if we started with one. The chapter also discusses how one can decode "word problems" into equations. Unfortunately, this is an art, and only practice will make you good at it.

A method of solving linear equations in one unknown is given in Section 5–2, and we see that equations in one unknown can be useful in finding breakeven points. A much more general class of functions, polynomial functions, is investigated at some length. One useful method of solving polynomial equations is factoring. A special and very common polynomial is the quadratic function, given by $f(x) = ax^2 + bx^1 + c$. A method for solving all such functions for their roots [that is, finding x values such that $f(x) = 0$] is to use the quadratic formula. This method always works, although it may give answers that are complex numbers (in which case there is no real solution). The chapter ends with some examples of using logarithms and raising to a power to solve special types of equations. Some important ideas are repeated here for convenience in reference.

$f(x) = a_n x^n + \cdots + a_1 x + a_0$	a polynomial function in x of degree n
$a_n x^n + \cdots + a_1 x + a_0 = 0$	a polynomial equation in x, of degree n, in standard form
$f(x) = ax^2 + bx + c$, or $f(x) = a_2 x^2 + a_1 x + a_0$	a quadratic function; the graph is called a parabola
$x = \dfrac{-b \pm \sqrt{b^2 - 4ac}}{2a}$	the quadratic formula, for solving quadratic equations
$f(x) = a_1 x + a_0$	a linear function; the graph is a straight line

Equality-preserving operations are:

1. Add (subtract) the same value to both sides.
2. Multiply (divide) both sides by the same value (other than zero).
3. Raise both sides to the same power (take the same root).
4. Take logarithms of both sides.

PROBLEMS

Problems for Self-Study: 1, 3, 7, 9, 11, 12, 14

5–1.　Express the following word problems in equation form. Define the terms you need.

a. Income tax varies as the square of pretax income.

b. After-tax income is pretax income minus taxes.

c. Income tax varies as pretax income but at a different rate depending on whether pretax income is more or less than \$25,000.

d. The number of students in a professor's class varies with the number of jokes he knows.

e. The number of students who frequent the local pizzeria varies with the amount of cheese on the pizzas.

5–2.*　Solve each linear equation below for the value of x.

a. $x = 2x - 3$

b. $7(x + 1) = 4(x + 3)$

c. $x - 3 = 6(x + 1)$

d. $17x = x + 48$

e. $3(x - 1) = 6 - 3(x - 2) + x$

5–3. A small construction firm is considering purchasing a large bulldozer, costing $50,000. The bulldozer costs $14 per hour to operate (including the operator's pay and all transportation and maintenance costs). How many hours must they operate the bulldozer in order to break even if they can charge for its use at a rate of $28 per hour?

5–4.* An office manager must replace some of the desks and chairs in his office. He needs one new chair for every new desk but must stay within his budget of $2000. Chairs cost $30 and desks $85. How many chairs can he order if he wants to exactly meet his budget? (Then round the answer to the nearest integer.)

5–5. Multiply the following polynomials.

a. $(x + 2)(x - 1)$
b. $(x - 6)(x - 7)$
c. $(x^2 - 2x + 1)(x - 1)$
d. $(x + 1)(x - 2)(x - 4)$
e. $(x^2 - 3)(x + 1)(x - 5)$

5–6.* Divide the following polynomials.

a. $(x^2 - 2x - 8) \div (x + 2)$
b. $(x^2 - 2x - 10) \div (x - 4)$
c. $(x^4 + 3x^2 - 7x + 4) \div (x + 3)$
d. $(x^3 - 12x^2 + 6x + 5) \div (x - 1)$

5–7. Given $f(x) = x + 2$, $g(x) = x^2 - 1$, and $h(x) = x + 1$, find

a. $f(x) \cdot g(x) \cdot h(x)$
b. $f(x) \cdot g(x) \div h(x)$
c. $g(x) \div f(x)$

5–8.* A health insurance plan has found that the number of patient visits covered by their insurance is increasing linearly with time while the average cost per visit is increasing according to a quadratic function with time. In particular:

Patient visits $= 10,000 + 40t$,   where t is time in years.
Average cost per visit $= \$8 + t + t^2/10$.

a. Find the function that describes total dollar cost of patient visits covered by the insurance company.
b. At what rate will they be paying for visits when $t = 2$ (that is, 2 years from now)?

5-9. Find the values of x such that $f(x) = 0$.

    a. $f(x) = x - 3$

    b. $f(x) = x + a$

    c. $f(x) = 17x - 3$

    d. $f(x) = 43x$

5-10.* Find the roots of the following functions when they exist.

    a. $f(x) = 2x^2 - 3x + 1$

    b. $f(x) = 3x^2 + 10x + 3$

    c. $f(x) = x^2 - 2x - 35$

    d. $f(x) = 2x^2 - 12x + 18$

    e. $f(x) = 10x^2 - 3x + 3$

5-11. Suppose that the supply, S, and demand, D, for a product are functions of the product's price, p.

$$S = 10 + 10p - p^2,$$
$$D = 110 - 10p.$$

At what price will the supply equal the demand?

5-12. A manager knows that his demand function (number of units he will sell as a function of price) is given by $(20 - p)$, so the revenue is

$$R = p(20 - p) = 20p - p^2.$$

He wants revenues to be 75. Solve for possible prices he may choose by (a) factoring and (b) using the quadratic formula.

5-13.* Suppose that the manager in Problem 5-12 wants revenues of $\$A$. Solve for the possible prices as a function of A. For what value of A is there only one possible price, and what is that price?

5-14. Find the roots of the following functions.

    a. $f(x) = x^3 - 6x^2 + 11x - 6$

    b. $f(x) = x^4 - 2x^3 + 2x - 1$

    c. $f(x) = x^3 - x^2 + x$

5-15.* Find the solutions to the following equations.

    a. $x^{1/2} = x - 4, \ x \geq 4$

    b. $\dfrac{1}{x^2} + \dfrac{3}{x} - 2 = 0$

    c. $1 = e^{1 - x^2}$

    d. $x^2 - 10x + 17 = 0$

5-16.* At what points does the function $f(x) = e^{-x^2}$ take on the following values?

    a. $f(x) = 1$

    b. $f(x) = \frac{1}{2}$

    c. $f(x) = -\frac{1}{3}$

    Leave the answers in logarithmic form.

5-17.* Graph the functions given by the following.

    a. $f(x) = x - 4 - x^{1/2}, x \geq 0$

    b. $f(x) = \dfrac{1}{x^2} + \dfrac{3}{x} - 2$

    c. $f(x) = e^{1-x^2} - 1$

    d. $f(x) = x^2 - 10x + 17$

5-18. A manager knows that for each product unit he sells he receives its price p, but the cost of producing another unit increases as the square of the number produced. Let $C(x)$ be the cost of producing the xth unit. Then the incremental profit from selling one more unit is $P = p - C(x)$. Find the general solution for the point where $P = 0$. Let $C(x) = a + bx^2$. (When incremental profit is zero, the price that maximizes profit has been found.)

5-19.* Suppose that the theater owner in the chapter had an average demand function given by $D = 200 + 30p - 10p^2$ and his fixed costs were $500. Where are the breakeven points? (The price is denoted by p; try $p = 5$.)

5-20. A machine may be used to produce either of two products. When producing product 1, it costs $10 per hour to run the machine and it produces 10 units per hour. For product 2 it is $20 per hour and 8 units per hour. The daily (24-hour) operating budget is $380, and at least 100 units of product 1 must be produced. The firm would like to produce as much of product 2 as possible. How much machine time during each day should be devoted to product 2?

5-21.* Suppose that in Problem 5-20 there was no minimum product 1 level but rather a particular product mix desired. How many hours should be spent producing each product for a product mix of 3:2 (3 units of product 1 to 2 units of product 2)? Ignore the budget constraint. What is the daily cost?

5-22. a. A marketing manager wants to spend his entire budget, B, on advertising in two media, magazines and television. A unit of magazine advertising costs $a and a unit of television costs $c. The manager wishes to buy twice as many television units as magazine units. In terms of a, c, and B, how many magazine units should he buy?

b. Substitute $B = \$5{,}000{,}000$, $a = \$10{,}000$, and $c = \$20{,}000$ into your solution for part a.

5–23.* a. Sales for a new product are expected to be

$$S(t) = S_0 \ln(t) \qquad \text{for } t > 1.$$

When will sales reach S_G? That is, solve for that time, t, in terms of S_G and S_0.

b. Substitute $S_G = 6$, $S_0 = 2$ into the solution to part a.

5–24. A manufacturing company has found that as a new group of workers are trained, their output level in units per day, X, increases as their number of days on the job, t, increases.

$$X = f(t) = 100 - 50(\tfrac{1}{2})^t.$$

The production scheduler wants to know how many days must go by before production reaches the level of 95. Can you tell him?

5–25.* The population, P, of an area can be described as a function of time t so that

$$P = f(t) = \frac{1000}{1 + (e^{\ln 99})(e^{-2t})} = \frac{1000}{1 + 99e^{-2t}}.$$

What is the population level at

a. $t = 0$?

b. $t = \ln 10$?

c. What type of function is P?

d. When will $P = 900$? (Leave in log form.)

6

Simultaneous Equations

The Stumptown National Bank believes its consumer loan applications are a function of the interest rate they charge and the expenditure made on advertising. In particular, they think the relationship can be expressed as a linear function:

$$\text{consumer loan applications} = f(r, A) = ar + bA$$

where r is the interest rate, A is the advertising expenditure during the period, and a and b are constants.

This relationship has two independent variables (r and A) and two constants (a and b). The bank has information from the two previous quarter-year periods.

	Quarter 1	Quarter 2
Consumer loan applications	1,000	1,100
Interest rate	0.10	0.12
Advertising expenditure (in thousands)	5	7

They want to estimate the constants a and b. The constants specify the equation, and the bank can then intelligently set interest rates and advertising budgets. The techniques we learned in Chapter 5 are of no help since there is more than one unknown. The methods of this chapter will enable us to help the bank manager. Notice that, once again, a and b, the coefficients of the equation, are the unknowns.

134

6-1 EQUATIONS IN MORE THAN ONE UNKNOWN

As we see in the bank's problem, some functions are functions of more than one variable. Leaving the bank's problem for a moment, a general function in two variables can be defined by $f(x, y)$. For example,

$$f(x, y) = x^2y^2 + y + y^3$$

defines a polynomial function in x and y. Polynomials are not restricted to one variable, but little of our attention will be given to polynomials of two or more variables. This is because polynomials in two variables are more difficult to handle, and because many managerial situations can be adequately described by a function of one variable. We will, on occasion, deal with non-linear functions with at most two unknowns, and linear equations with more than one variable are very important in management applications. The linear function using interest rate and advertising above is one example of a linear function in more than one unknown. An example of a more complicated polynomial in two variables is given next.

The output of a firm is often treated by economists as a function of two basic inputs, labor and capital. That is,

output quantity $= Q(L, C) =$ a function of labor and capital.

For example,

$$Q(L, C) = aL + bC + cLC + dL^2 + gC^2,$$

over some allowable range of L and C. Thus $Q(L, C)$ is a polynomial in L and C. If all the constants are known, a manager might use this relationship in choosing the amount of both inputs to use in planning a new plant or an addition to an old plant. In other words, he may wish to decide how "capital intensive" or "labor intensive" the operation should be.

The major thrust of this chapter, however, is toward linear functions, not the more complex polynomials illustrated by the labor–capital problem. Another example of a linear function (and a linear equation) is as follows:

$$f(x, y) = .5x - .5y + 4 \qquad \text{defines a linear function;}$$
$$0 \le x \le 8, \qquad 0 \le y \le 4$$
$$0 = .5x - .5y + 4$$

A linear function in two variables can be graphed if you are clever or an accomplished draftsman (see, as an example, Figure 6–1).

The function $f(x, y) = .5x - .5y + 4$ graphs as a plane in three dimensions. Try thinking first of the corner of a room. The xy plane is the floor, the other two planes are the walls. Now the function plane is like a table top with

FIGURE 6–1

Linear Function in Two Unknowns

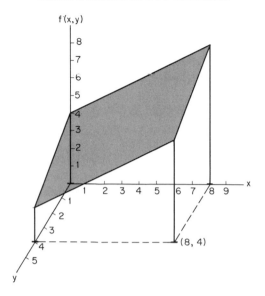

unequal sized legs. (If that doesn't help, don't worry, we can still muddle along.) Although we have difficulty graphing in three dimensions (two independent variables), we cannot even begin to graph a function with more than two independent variables. For these reasons we will make little use of graphing in this chapter, and instead use more general methods of making sense from the relationships given: The linear equation given above can be solved using the techniques given in Chapter 5.

$$0 = 2x + 4y + 7,$$
$$-2x = 4y + 7,$$
$$x = -2y - \tfrac{7}{2}.$$

This is a solution for x in terms of y. Now, if we know what y is, we know the x value. In the case of the linear function, given x and y we know $f(x, y)$. These two facts are supported by the following calculations.

Linear Function: $f(x, y) = .5x - .5y + 4$ *Linear Equation:* $0 = .5x - .5y + 4$
$\quad x = 0, y = 0; f(x, y) = 4$ $y = 0; x = -8$
$\quad x = 2, y = 0; f(x, y) = 5$ $y = 1; x = -7$
$\quad x = 0, y = 2; f(x, y) = 3$ $y = 2; x = -6$
$\quad x = 2, y = 2; f(x, y) = 4$ $y = 3; x = -5$

Given some values, we can find others. But this is all we can do if we only have one equation but two unknowns. The next section examines systems of linear equations. In most of these cases, we will be able to solve for values of all the unknowns.

$\sim\!\!\checkmark$: Which of the following are linear equations in two unknowns?

1. $xy = 0$.
2. $x + 3y - 4 = 0$.
3. $x^2 + y + 2 = 0$.
4. $x + y + 3z = 0$.

Answers. Number 3 is nonlinear and number 4 is a linear equation in three variables. Number 2 is a linear equation in two variables. Number 1 plots as the axes of the graph, and is thus composed of straight lines (plot it and see). Even so, it is not thought of as a linear equation, since it plots as two lines, not one.

6-2 SYSTEMS OF LINEAR EQUATIONS

Let's get back to the managers of the Stumptown National Bank. They maintained that

$$\text{consumer loan applications} = ar + bA,$$

where $r \equiv$ the interest rate and $A \equiv$ advertising expenditure. They also had some data. For example, when $r = 0.10$ and $A = 5$, consumer loan applications equaled 1,000. That is,

$$1,000 = a(0.10) + b(5).$$

We can solve for a in terms of b (and the bank's in-residence mathematician did so), obtaining

$$a(0.10) = 1,000 - 5b,$$
$$a = 10,000 - 50b.$$

The bank also knows that when $r = 0.12$ and $A = 7$, consumer loan applications equaled 1,100. That is,

$$1,100 = a(0.12) + b(7).$$

Now watch carefully, as we substitute (with nothing up either sleeve) the previous solution for a into the last equation:

$$1,100 = (10,000 - 50b)0.12 + 7b.$$

That looks like one linear equation in one unknown, namely b. Solving,

$$b = -100$$

and substituting this value of b into the equation already solved for a, we obtain

$$a = 10,000 - 50b$$
$$= 10,000 - 50(-100) = 15,000.$$

The solution says that a is positive, so raising interest rates will increase loan applications; it also says that b is negative, so lowering advertising will increase loan applications. There is something odd about that solution. However, the bank president believed it and promptly set $r = 0.14$ and $A = 4$. The result, unfortunately, was that consumer loan applications dropped to 700 during the quarter. That value does not fit in with the previous estimates of a and b. Using those estimates we would predict

consumer loan applications $= (0.14)(15,000) - 100(4) = 1,700.$

So it appears that the bank cannot trust its mathematician. Well, mathematics can be trusted if you use common sense, and we will return to the bank's problem in a little while to see how we can use common sense. For the moment, we will say only that they misspecified the relationship. Before giving a more correct relationship, let's examine what we have done above in solving the system of (two) equations in two unknowns.

First, a few general definitions.

A system of (linear) simultaneous equations is more than one (linear) equation involving more than one common unknown. All equations must hold simultaneously. (This is why they are called simultaneous equations.)

A system of n simultaneous equations in n unknowns may have

   (*i*) one unique solution, in which case the equations are *consistent* and *independent*.
   (*ii*) an infinite number of solutions, in which case the equations are *consistent* and *dependent*.
   (*iii*) no solution, in which case the equations are *inconsistent*.

Case (i) is the most common in managerial situations and hence of most interest to us. We just solved such a case for a and b. An example of case (ii) is $x + y = 1, 2x + 2y = 2$. These two equations are really just one equation since the second equation is two times the first equation. There is an infinite number of pairs of x, y values that satisfy them. The equations are dependent. An example of case (iii) is $x + y = 1, x + y = 2$. These two equations cannot simultaneously hold. There are no pairs of x, y values that work simultaneously for both equations.

⌒✓ : Which of the following systems of equations are systems of linear equations in more than one unknown? Are any of them dependent or inconsistent?

1. $x + y = 1$
   $x - y = 1$
2. $x^2 + 2 = 1$
   $x + y^2 = 4$

3. $x + y - z = 1$
   $2x + 2y - z = 1$
   $3x - 4y - 2z = 2$
4. $x + y = 4$
   $3x + 3y = 7$

Answers. Systems (1), (3), and (4) are systems of linear equations; (2) is nonlinear. System (4) is an inconsistent set of equations. (The second equation can be rewritten as $x + y = \frac{7}{3}$, and $x + y$ cannot equal both 4 and $\frac{7}{3}$ at the same time.)

6-3 SOLVING TWO LINEAR EQUATIONS IN TWO UNKNOWNS

In the above bank example, we solved for the unknowns using a substitution ($a = 10,000 - 50b$). This section will examine a formal method for solving equations by substitution as well as other methods. We begin with a graphical method for solving two equations in two unknowns. (In this section, two equations always means two linear equations.)

Graphical Method

Method of Graphical Solution for Two Equations in Two Unknowns

Plot both equations on "Cartesian coordinates" (ordinary graph paper), plotting one variable on the horizontal axis and the other variable on the vertical axis.

1. If the equations cross, the crossing point is the solution [this is case (i); there is a unique solution].
2. If they are both the same line, there is an infinite number of solutions [case (ii)].
3. If they are parallel, then the lines never touch, and there is no solution [case (iii)].

An example of each of these situations, including pathological cases (ii) and (iii), is given next.

$$\text{(i)} \quad x + y = 7,$$
$$x - y = 1.$$

FIGURE 6–2

Case (i) Illustrated

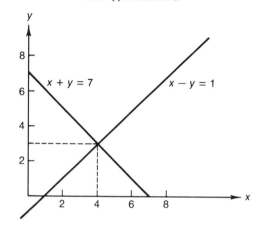

The solution is

$$x = 4, \qquad y = 3.$$

This is the point where the lines cross in Figure 6-2.

$$\text{(ii)} \quad 2x + 2y = 6,$$
$$3x + 3y = 9.$$

FIGURE 6–3

Case (ii) Illustrated

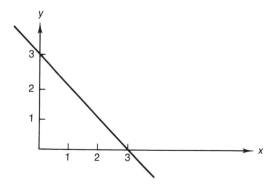

Both equations plot as the same line (see Figure 6-3). There is an infinite number of solutions.

$$\text{(iii)} \quad 2x + y = 1,$$
$$4x + 2y = 4.$$

The lines are parallel (see Figure 6-4), and there is no solution.

FIGURE 6–4

Case (iii) Illustrated

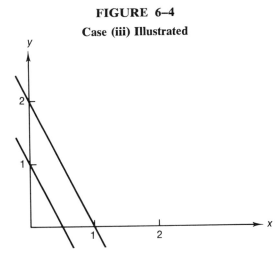

Graphical solution helps our understanding; where the lines cross we are simultaneously on both lines, and both equations are satisfied. However, the method depends on how well we draw the graph, and it can become quite tedious. Fortunately, we have two other methods.

Substitution Method

Method of Solution by substitution for Two Equations in Two Unknowns

1. Using either equation, express one variable in terms of the other. (For example, express x in terms of y, in the form $x = ay + b$.)
2. Substitute this solution into the other equation. (For example, substitute $x = ay + b$ into the other equation.)
3. The two equations are now reduced to one equation in one unknown. Solve for that unknown value.
4. Substitute the numerical value of the variable just found into the expression obtained in step 1; obtain a numerical value for the second unknown.
5. If at some stage you have $a = a$, you are in case (ii), the case of many solutions. If you get $a = b$ (where actually $a \neq b$), you are in case (iii), where there is no solution.

Let's try some examples.

$$\text{(i)} \quad x + y = 7,$$
$$x - y = 1.$$

Expressing x as a function of y using the first equation:

$$x = 7 - y.$$

This completes step 1. Then

$$7 - y - y = 1,$$

and this completes step 2. Solving for y,

$$6 = 2y, \quad \text{or} \quad y = 3$$

and we have completed step 3. Substituting $y = 3$ into $x = 7 - y$, as required by step 4,

$$x = 4.$$
$$\text{(ii)} \quad 2x + 2y = 6,$$
$$3x + 3y = 9.$$

Using the first equation to express x as a function of y,

$$x = 3 - y.$$

This completes step 1. Now substituting for x in the second equation,

$$3(3 - y) + 3y = 9.$$

This completes step 2. Solving as required in step 3, we find

$$9 = 9,$$

and we are in case (ii), where there is an infinite number of solutions.

$$\text{(iii)} \quad 2x + y = 1,$$
$$4x + 2y = 4.$$

Using the first equation, we express y as a function of x this time to show you how versatile we are:

$$y = 1 - 2x.$$

This completes step 1. Now substituting as required in step 2:

$$4x + 2(1 - 2x) = 4.$$

Solving, we obtain for step 3,

$$2 = 4,$$

and we are in case (iii), where there is no solution.

The method of substitution is valuable because it uses the methods for solving one equation in one unknown that we learned in Chapter 5.

To bring the point home about reducing a problem to one we already know how to solve, we relate a story about the difference between a mathematician and an engineer. When confronted with the problem of how to move a box from a chair to a table, both picked up the box and placed it on the table. Then when confronted with the problem of how to move the box from the floor to the table, the engineer picked up the box and placed it on the table. The mathematician picked up the box, moved it to the chair, and announced that he was through since the chair-to-table problem had been previously solved. By using what we previously knew we are acting like the mathematician.

The next method, the method of elimination, carries over more easily to more than two equations in more than two unknowns. Actually, you will, after some practice, develop your own mixture of the techniques presented here. Use whatever works for you; even a guess is helpful at times.

Elimination Method

Method of Solution by Elimination for Two Equations in Two Unknowns

The two equations are

$$a_1x + b_1y + c_1 = 0,$$
$$a_2x + b_2y + c_2 = 0.$$

1. Multiply one of the equations by a constant such that the coefficient of one of the unknowns is the same as the coefficient of that unknown in the other equation. (For example, multiply the first equation by a_2/a_1, making both coefficients in x be a_2.)
2. Subtract one equation from the other. The result is one equation in one unknown.
3. Solve that one equation in one unknown for a numerical value.
4. Substitute that numerical value into either equation and solve for the other unknown.
5. Cases (ii) and (iii) are identified as in the substitution method.

Let's work some examples.

$$\text{(i)} \quad x + y = 7,$$
$$x - y = 1.$$

Since the x coefficients are the same, step 1 can be omitted. Subtract the second equation from the first equation as required by step 2, to obtain

$$2y = 6,$$

and solving according to step 3 yields

$$y = 3.$$

Substituting the numerical value of y into the first equation as required by step 4:

$$x + 3 = 7 \quad \text{and} \quad x = 4.$$

$$\text{(ii)} \quad 2x + 2y = 6,$$
$$3x + 3y = 9.$$

Multiplying the first equation by $\frac{3}{2}$ as required by step 1, and then subtracting the second equation from the first equation according to step 2:

$$0 = 0,$$

and this is a case (ii) situation.

$$\text{(iii)} \quad 2x + y \; = 1,$$
$$4x + 2y = 4.$$

Multiplying the first equation by 2, according to step 1, and subtracting the second equation from the first equation as required by step 2 yields

$$0 = 2,$$

and this is a case (iii) situation.

$$\text{(iv)} \quad a_1x + b_1y + c_1 = 0,$$
$$a_2x + b_2y + c_2 = 0.$$

Multiplying the first equation by (a_2/a_1) and subtracting the second equation from the first equation as required by steps 1 and 2 gives

$$\left(\frac{a_2 b_1}{a_1} - b_2 \right) y = \left(c_2 - \frac{a_2 c_1}{a_1} \right).$$

Solving for y as required by step 3:

$$y = \frac{c_2 - (a_2c_1/a_1)}{(a_2b_1/a_1) - b_2} = \frac{a_1c_2 - a_2c_1}{a_2b_1 - a_1b_2}.$$

Substituting that value into the second equation and solving for x according to step 4:

$$a_2x + b_2\left(\frac{a_1c_2 - a_2c_1}{a_2b_1 - a_1b_2}\right) + c_2 = 0,$$

so that

$$x = \frac{b_2}{a_2}\left(\frac{a_2c_1 - a_1c_2}{a_2b_1 - a_1b_2}\right) - \frac{c_2}{a_2} \qquad \text{or} \qquad x = \frac{-b_2y - c_2}{a_2}.$$

The equations $(y =)$ and $(x =)$ constitute a general solution, for any a, b, and c values. We require that $a_2b_1 - a_1b_2 \neq 0$ for a solution. If $a_2b_1 - a_1b_2 = 0$, the two equations plot as either parallel or coincident lines.

If you think the last example does not look like any fun to solve, you are right. It is presented only to show that the 2 by 2 case can be solved in general, assuming none of the required divisions are by zero. General solutions are often useful; in this case, it will usually be just as easy to solve the problem by one of the other methods as to plug into the general solution just found.

1. Use the general solution to solve the example: $x + y - 7 = 0$, $x - y - 1 = 0$. That is: $a_1 = b_1 = 1$, $c_1 = -7$, $a_2 = 1$, $b_2 = c_2 = -1$.
2. Solve the following system of equations by all three methods:

   $3x - 2y = 16,$
   $x + y = 2,$ $\qquad x = \underline{\hspace{1cm}},$ $\qquad y = \underline{\hspace{1cm}}.$

Answers

1. $y = \dfrac{-1 + 7}{1 + 1} = \dfrac{6}{2} = 3,$

   $x = \dfrac{+1(+3) + 1}{1} = 4$, using $x = \dfrac{-b_2y - c_2}{a_2}$. It works!

2. Substitution:

   $$3x - 2y = 16,$$
   $$x + y = 2.$$

   Using the second equation: $x = 2 - y$. Then

   $$3(2 - y) - 2y = 16.$$

Hence

$$y = -2 \quad \text{and} \quad x = +4.$$

Elimination:

$$3x - 2y = 16,$$
$$x + y = 2.$$

Multiply the second equation by 2 and add the equations (you are allowed to do it this way since it is equivalent to multiplying by -2 and subtracting) to obtain

$$5x = 20.$$

Solving

$$x = 4 \quad \text{and} \quad y = -2.$$

Graphical: See Figure 6–5. The intersection is at $x = 4$ and $y = -2$.

FIGURE 6–5

Graphical Solution of
$$3x - 2y = 16$$
$$x + y = 2$$

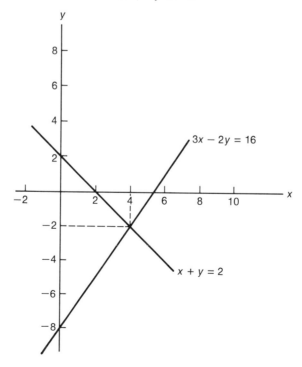

6-4 MORE COMPLEX SYSTEMS OF EQUATIONS

Solving Three Equations in Three Unknowns

We left our Stumptown National Bank president in trouble. His third-quarter prediction of consumer loan applications was off by 1,000 applications (1,700 predicted versus 700 actual). Their initial solution suggested that raising interest rates will increase loan applications. One of the bank's junior vice-presidents says that this is nonsense. He believes that if $r = 0$ (free loans), loan applications would increase. In fact, he thinks there would be some applications at $r = 0$ even if $A = 0$ also. (He thinks the word would spread about free loans.) His suggestion implies that

$$\text{consumer loan applications} = ar + bA + c,$$

where c is the number of applications they expect when $r = 0$ and $A = 0$. Given the previous data, we estimate

$$1,000 = a(0.1) + b(5) + c,$$
$$1,100 = a(0.12) + b(7) + c,$$

and using third-quarter data,

$$700 = a(0.14) + b(4) + c.$$

It makes sense to add the constant since loan applications would not be zero when $r = A = 0$. But how do we solve for a, b, and c? There are now three unknowns, but fortunately there are also three equations. The elimination method can be used for solving three equations in three unknowns.

Method of Elimination for Solving Three Equations in Three Unknowns

1. Using any two equations, eliminate one variable, forming one equation in two unknowns.
2. Using the third equation and either of the two equations used in step 1, eliminate the same variable, forming one equation in two unknowns.
3. We now have (from steps 1 and 2) two equations in two unknowns. Solve them, using a method for solving two equations in two unknowns, and substitute the two values into any one of the three original equations to obtain a value for the third variable.

For an example, let's solve the banker's problem.

$$(0.1)a + 5b + c - 1,000 = 0,$$
$$(0.12)a + 7b + c - 1,100 = 0,$$
$$(0.14)a + 4b + c - 700 = 0.$$

Choose the first and second equations to eliminate c:

$$-(0.02)a - 2b + 100 = 0.$$

Using the second and third equations, eliminate c:

$$-(0.02)a + 3b - 400 = 0.$$

Using the two new equations, eliminate a by subtracting the second equation from the first equation to obtain:

$$5b = 500 \quad \text{and} \quad b = 100$$

Substituting $b = 100$ into the equation $-(0.02)a - 2b + 100 = 0$ gives

$$-(0.02)a - 2(100) + 100 = 0$$

and

$$a = -5,000.$$

Finally, using the first equation in the original problem statement,

$$(0.1)(-5,000) + 5(100) + c - 1,000 = 0$$

and

$$c = 1,000, \quad b = 100, \quad a = -5,000$$

is the answer. The equation for predicting consumer loan applications is: applications $= -5,000r + 100A + 1000$. This answer makes more sense than the answer based only on data for the first two quarters. It suggests that loan applications rise as the interest rate falls (a is negative) and as advertising increases (b is positive). In the fourth quarter the president tries $r = 0.12$ and $A = 8$ (thousand) based on (and to check) the new relationship. The resulting loan applications number 1,200. To check their new answer:

$$(0.12)(-5,000) + 100(8) + 1,000 = 1,200.$$

It worked.

In the real world, of course, it would never work exactly. The manager works with averages, not individual readings, and he must accept a good answer, not a perfect one. He may use a statistical technique (which you may learn in a statistics course). But, at least, he must specify the problem well enough to avoid the nonsense answer we saw first. This problem illustrates the importance of the manager and what he knows in solving real problems. Recall that it was a manager who saw the fact that the initial solution was nonsense.

The elimination method can be extended to more than two equations if necessary. The method is stated below.

Method for Solving n Linear Equations in n Unknowns

Method of Elimination for Solving n Equations in n Unknowns

1. Using the first and second equations, and eliminate one variable.
2. Using the second and third equations, eliminate the same variable as in 1; also, using the third and fourth, fourth and fifth, and so on to $n - 1$ and n, eliminate the same variable.
3. We now have $n - 1$ equations in $n - 1$ unknowns. Proceed as in steps 1 and 2 to obtain $n - 2$ equations in $n - 2$ unknowns, then $n - 3$, and so on, until you have two equations in two unknowns.
4. Solve the two equations in two unknowns using the methods introduced above.
5. Using the two values from the solution in step 4 and one of the equations you had when you had three equations in three unknowns, solve for a third variable.
6. Using one of the four variable equations and the results of step 5, solve for the fourth value and so on until all values are known.
7. Avoid dealing (by hand) with large systems of equations, if at all possible. Let a computer do it.

We will not do an example larger than the 3 by 3 just done, since simpler techniques are introduced in Chapter 7, and another general technique is introduced in the next section. Unfortunately, not all systems of equations involve linear equations. The final topic of this section discusses how to make (some) nonlinear systems of equations look linear, and hence make them yield to the methods we already know.

Solving Nonlinear Equations by Trickery

Once again, we will only do (two) examples to illustrate the fact that some problems can be made linear by looking at them in the right way.

$$(i) \quad a_1 x^{b_1} y^{c_1} z^{d_1} = g_1,$$
$$a_2 x^{b_2} y^{c_2} z^{d_2} = g_2,$$
$$a_3 x^{b_3} y^{c_3} z^{d_3} = g_3,$$

where the a_i, b_i, c_i, d_i, and g_i ($i = 1, 2, 3$) are known constants. Each equation in this set is nonlinear. But we learned in Chapter 4 that such equations are linear when transformed to logarithms. Taking the logarithm of both sides of each equation and using rule 2 for logs gives in general:

$$\log a_i + b_i \log x + c_i \log y + d_i \log z = \log g_i; \qquad i = 1, 2, 3.$$

Each of these equations is linear in $\log x$, $\log y$, and $\log z$. We can now solve for $\log x$, $\log y$, and $\log z$. Once these values are known, the x, y, and z values can be found using a logarithm table.

$$\text{(ii)} \quad \frac{1}{x} + \frac{1}{y} = 4,$$

$$\frac{2}{x} + \frac{3}{y} = 5.$$

To solve this problem, treat $(1/x)$ and $(1/y)$ as the variables. Then

$$1\left(\frac{1}{x}\right) + 1\left(\frac{1}{y}\right) = 4,$$

$$2\left(\frac{1}{x}\right) + 3\left(\frac{1}{y}\right) = 5.$$

Solving by elimination, we obtain

$$\left(\frac{1}{y}\right) = -3, \text{ so } y = -\frac{1}{3}; \quad \text{then } \frac{1}{x} = 7 \text{ and } x = \frac{1}{7}$$

$\sim\!\!\sqrt{}$: Solve the following systems of equations.

1. $3x + y - 2z = -8$,

$\qquad -3x + 2y - z = -7$,

$\qquad\quad x + y + z = 8$.

$x = \underline{} y = \underline{} z = \underline{}$.

2. $\dfrac{1}{x} + y + \dfrac{1}{z} = 10$,

$\qquad \dfrac{1}{x} + 2y + \dfrac{4}{z} = 12$,

$\qquad x \qquad\qquad = \frac{1}{2}$.

$x = \underline{} y = \underline{} z = \underline{}$.

Answers

1. The values for x, y, and z are 1, 1, and 6, respectively.
2. Even though x and $1/x$ both appear, the third equation tells us their value, so we can proceed with a 2 by 2 problem. The answers are $x = \frac{1}{2}$, $y = 11$, and $z = -\frac{1}{4}$.

6-5 DETERMINANTS AND THEIR USE IN SOLVING SYSTEMS OF LINEAR EQUATIONS

Given a system of two linear equations in two unknowns written as

$$a_1x + b_1y = c_1,$$
$$a_2x + b_2y = c_2,$$

the "determinant" of that system is written

$$D = \begin{vmatrix} a_1 & b_1 \\ a_2 & b_2 \end{vmatrix}.$$

It is an ordered array of the coefficients in the equations. The straight vertical lines do not mean absolute value in this case. The determinant is evaluated as a number (or "is" that number). The formula for computing the value is as follows.

Determinant of the System of Equations

$$a_1x + b_1y = c_1,$$
$$a_2x + b_2y = c_2$$

is a number,

$$D \equiv \begin{vmatrix} a_1 & b_1 \\ a_2 & b_2 \end{vmatrix} = a_1b_2 - a_2b_1,$$

Symbol	*English Translation*
$D \equiv \begin{vmatrix} a_1 & b_1 \\ a_2 & b_2 \end{vmatrix}$	The determinant of the coefficients of a 2 by 2 system of linear equations. D is a number, computed as $a_1b_2 - a_2b_1$. It can be used to solve the system of equations.

For example, consider the system of equations

$$8x - y = 11,$$
$$2x + y = 9.$$

$$D = \begin{vmatrix} 8 & -1 \\ 2 & +1 \end{vmatrix} = 8(1) - (2)(-1) = 10.$$

N_x (or N_y, N_z, or N-sub any variable name) is the determinant formed
when you replace the coefficients of the xs (or ys or other variables) with
the constant terms on the right-hand side of the equation. For example,
using the general form above:

$$N_x \equiv \begin{vmatrix} c_1 & b_1 \\ c_2 & b_2 \end{vmatrix} = c_1 b_2 - c_2 b_1 \quad \text{and} \quad N_y \equiv \begin{vmatrix} a_1 & c_1 \\ a_2 & c_2 \end{vmatrix} = a_1 c_2 - a_2 c_1.$$

For example, using

$$8x - y = 11,$$
$$2x + y = 9,$$
$$N_x = \begin{vmatrix} 11 & -1 \\ 9 & +1 \end{vmatrix} = 20,$$
$$N_y = \begin{vmatrix} 8 & 11 \\ 2 & 9 \end{vmatrix} = 50.$$

Symbol	*English Translation*
N_x	The determinant formed by replacing the coefficients of the x variable with the constants from the right-hand side (N_y is defined in an analogous fashion).

Determinant Method for Solving Two Equations in Two Unknowns

Method for Solving an n by n System of Linear Equations Using
Determinants.

$$x = \frac{N_x}{D}, \quad y = \frac{N_y}{D} \quad \text{(and so on if there are more than two unknowns)}$$

This method holds in general. Of all the material so far, only the method
of computing D is tied to a 2 by 2 set of equations. We will use all the other
material again when discussing n equations in n unknowns.

Notice that to find x and y we divide by D. Thus $D \neq 0$ is necessary for a
solution to be found by this method. The implications of $D = 0$ will be
discussed later.

Example

$$8x - y = 11,$$
$$2x + y = 9,$$
$$D = 10, \qquad N_x = 20, \qquad N_y = 50$$
$$x = \frac{20}{10} = 2, \qquad y = \frac{N_y}{D} = \frac{50}{10} = 5$$

To check the answer, we substitute $x = 2$ and $y = 5$:

$$8(2) - 5 = 11,$$
$$2(2) + 5 = 9.$$

Higher-Order Determinants

This subsection is necessary for completeness. It is relatively difficult, and you should try it only after mastering the preceding material.

A system of n linear equations in n unknowns can be written as follows:

equation 1 $a_{11}x_1 + a_{12}x_2 + \ldots + a_{1j}x_j + \ldots + a_{1n}x_n = c_1$
equation 2 $a_{21}x_1 + a_{22}x_2 + \ldots + a_{2j}x_j + \ldots + a_{2n}x_n = c_2$

equation i $a_{i1}x_1 + a_{i2}x_2 + \ldots + a_{ij}x_j + \ldots + a_{in}x_n = c_i$

equation n $a_{n1}x_1 + a_{n2}x_2 + \ldots + a_{nj}x_j + \ldots + a_{nn}x_n = c_n$

The dots stand for items not explicitly listed. The constants are a_{ij}, and a_{ij} is the jth constant in the ith equation (appears in the ith row, jth column). The determinant of this system of equation is, again, written using these coefficients.

$$D \equiv \begin{vmatrix} a_{11} & a_{12} & \ldots & a_{1j} & \ldots & a_{1n} \\ a_{21} & a_{22} & \ldots & a_{2j} & \ldots & a_{2n} \\ \cdot & \cdot & & \cdot & & \cdot \\ \cdot & \cdot & & \cdot & & \cdot \\ \cdot & \cdot & & \cdot & & \cdot \\ a_{i1} & a_{i2} & \ldots & a_{ij} & \ldots & a_{in} \\ \cdot & \cdot & & \cdot & & \cdot \\ \cdot & \cdot & & \cdot & & \cdot \\ \cdot & \cdot & & \cdot & & \cdot \\ a_{n1} & a_{n2} & \ldots & a_{nj} & \ldots & a_{nn} \end{vmatrix}$$

N_{x_j}, as before, is the determinant formed by replacing the jth constant of each equation (the jth column of D) with the c_i value for that equation. For example,

$$N_{x_1} \equiv \begin{vmatrix} c_1 & a_{12} & \cdots & a_{1j} & \cdots & a_{1n} \\ c_2 & a_{22} & \cdots & a_{2j} & \cdots & a_{2n} \\ & \cdot & & \cdot & & \cdot \\ & \cdot & & \cdot & & \cdot \\ & \cdot & & \cdot & & \cdot \\ c_i & a_{i2} & \cdots & a_{ij} & \cdots & a_{in} \\ & \cdot & & \cdot & & \cdot \\ & \cdot & & \cdot & & \cdot \\ & \cdot & & \cdot & & \cdot \\ c_n & a_{n2} & \cdots & a_{nj} & \cdots & a_{nn} \end{vmatrix}$$

The equations are solved in exactly the same manner as in the two-equation case.

$$x_1 = \frac{N_{x_1}}{D}, \ldots, x_i = \frac{N_{x_i}}{D}, \ldots, x_n = \frac{N_{x_n}}{D}.$$

That looks fine, you might say, but how do we evaluate determinants that are n by n, when n is larger than 2?

Method for Evaluating Determinants That Are n by n

1. Choose any row (column) of the determinant. (A row with zeros in it will save you some work.) Suppose that it is row i.
2. Let $M_{\text{row column}} = M_{ij}$ be the $(n-1)$-order determinant formed by crossing out the ith row and the jth column of D. Then

$$D = (-1)^{i+1}a_{i1}M_{i1} + (-1)^{i+2}a_{i2}M_{i2} + \cdots + (-1)^{i+j}a_{ij}M_{ij} + \cdots$$
$$+ (-1)^{i+n}a_{ij}M_{ij} = \sum_{j=1}^{n} (-1)^{i+j}a_{ij}M_{ij}.$$

(If you use a column instead of a row, we move down the column $a_{1j}M_{1j}$ to $a_{2j}M_{2j}$, and so on. The subscripts always read $M_{\text{row column}}$. The first subscript is the row and the second subscript is the column.)
3. If the M_{ij} are of order 2, evaluate them and evaluate D. If they are of order greater than 2, use steps 1 and 2 to reduce them further. Once the M_{ij} are of order 2, you can evaluate them. Then the 3 by 3 M_{ij}'s can be evaluated using those values, and so on until D is evaluated.

Symbol	English Translation
M_{ij}	The determinant (of size $n-1$ by $n-1$) formed by crossing out the ith row and the jth column of an n by n determinant.

For an example of the computational method, a 3 by 3 determinant can be evaluated as

$$\begin{vmatrix} a_{11} & a_{12} & a_{13} \\ a_{21} & a_{22} & a_{23} \\ a_{31} & a_{32} & a_{33} \end{vmatrix} = a_{11} \begin{vmatrix} a_{22} & a_{23} \\ a_{32} & a_{33} \end{vmatrix} - a_{12} \begin{vmatrix} a_{21} & a_{23} \\ a_{31} & a_{33} \end{vmatrix} + a_{13} \begin{vmatrix} a_{21} & a_{22} \\ a_{31} & a_{32} \end{vmatrix}.$$

We chose the first row, and multiplied a_{11} (the first entry in the first row) by the determinant formed by crossing out the first row and column. The second coefficient in the first row, with a minus sign since $(-1)^{1+2} = -1$, is multiplied by the determinant formed by crossing out the first row and second column.

Since we know how to evaluate a 2 by 2 determinant, the above example shows us how to evaluate a 3 by 3 determinant. A 4 by 4 then becomes the sum of four 3 by 3 determinants. With enough arithmetic and patience, we can evaluate any size of determinant. This method is often called *expansion by minors*. We will not discuss the validity of this method nor will we give alternative definitions of and methods for evaluating determinants. Furthermore, we encourage you to do large and messy problems using a computer.

For example, let's solve the following set of equations using expansion by minors.

$$x - 3y + 4z = 9,$$
$$2x - 6y + 3z = -2,$$
$$x + y = 5,$$
$$D = \begin{vmatrix} 1 & -3 & +4 \\ 2 & -6 & +3 \\ 1 & 1 & 0 \end{vmatrix}.$$

Choose the third row. Then

$$D = 1 \begin{vmatrix} -3 & +4 \\ -6 & +3 \end{vmatrix} - 1 \begin{vmatrix} 1 & 4 \\ 2 & 3 \end{vmatrix} = 15 - (-5) = 20,$$

$$N_x = \begin{vmatrix} 9 & -3 & +4 \\ -2 & -6 & +3 \\ 5 & 1 & 0 \end{vmatrix}.$$

Choose the third row. Then

$$N_x = 5 \begin{vmatrix} -3 & +4 \\ -6 & +3 \end{vmatrix} - 1 \begin{vmatrix} 9 & 4 \\ -2 & 3 \end{vmatrix} = 75 - 35 = 40.$$

Thus

$$x = \frac{N_x}{D} = \frac{40}{20} = 2.$$

Now let's be clever and not compute N_y and N_z. We know

$$x + y = 5, \text{ so } y = 3 \quad \text{(since } x = 2\text{).}$$

Also,

$$x - 3y + 4z = 9, \text{ so } z = 4 \quad \text{(since } x = 2 \text{ and } y = 3\text{).}$$

The answer is $x = 2$, $y = 3$, and $z = 4$. Also note how we reduced the computational task by picking a row with a zero in it.

Determinants can also be used to indicate whether there is one unique solution or not. This is especially useful if we cannot graph the equations.

Given an $n \times n$ system of linear equations with determinant, D, if

   (i) $D \neq 0$, there is one unique solution.

   (ii) $D = 0$ and $N_x, N_y, \ldots$ all are zero, the equations are dependent, and there may or may not be a solution. (In the 2 by 2 case, dependent equations meant the two lines were the same; it is not so simple for n equations.)

   (iii) $D = 0$ and at least one of the $N_x, N_y, \ldots$ are nonzero, the equations are inconsistent, and there is no solution.

For example, consider the three examples we had in the two-equation subsection.

   (i) $x + y = 7,$
       $x - y = 1,$
       $D = \begin{vmatrix} 1 & 1 \\ 1 & -1 \end{vmatrix} = -2$; we are in case (i).

   (ii) $2x + 2y = 6,$
        $3x + 3y = 9,$
        $D = \begin{vmatrix} 2 & 2 \\ 3 & 3 \end{vmatrix} = 0,$

   $N_x = \begin{vmatrix} 6 & 2 \\ 9 & 3 \end{vmatrix} = 0, \qquad N_y = \begin{vmatrix} 2 & 6 \\ 3 & 9 \end{vmatrix} = 0$; we are in case (ii).

   (iii) $2x + y = 1,$
         $4x + 2y = 4,$
         $D = \begin{vmatrix} 2 & 1 \\ 4 & 2 \end{vmatrix} = 0,$

   $N_x = \begin{vmatrix} 1 & 1 \\ 4 & 2 \end{vmatrix} = -2$; we are in case (iii).

1. Solve, using determinants:
$$2x - y = 1,$$
$$3x + y = 4.$$
$$x = \underline{\hspace{2cm}}, \quad y = \underline{\hspace{2cm}}.$$

2. A government has decided there are three types of people: landowners, who have a lot of capital but very little income; wage earners, who have large incomes but very little capital; and people who have small amounts of both. Sales taxes fall most heavily on the last group, income taxes on the second, and property taxes on the first. The taxes can be represented by

People Type	Sales	Tax Property	Income
Landowners	$0.2x$ +	$0.7y$ +	$0.2z = c_1$
Wage earners	$0.4x$ +	$0.2y$ +	$0.6z = c_2$
Lower income	$0.4x$ +	$0.1y$ +	$0.2z = c_3$

where $x \equiv$ sales tax dollars raised, $y \equiv$ property tax dollars raised, and $z \equiv$ income tax dollars raised.

The government must raise 10 (billion) dollars; that is, it has decided that $c_1 + c_2 + c_3 = 10$. They want to choose tax rates such that landowners pay 4, wage earners pay 4, and lower income people pay 2 of the total. What taxes should be imposed? (Use determinants to obtain the solution.)

Answers

1. $D = 5$, $N_x = 5$, $N_y = 5$, so $x = y = 1$.
2. They want

$$0.2x + 0.7y + 0.2z = 4.0$$
$$0.4x + 0.2y + 0.6z = 4.0$$
$$0.4x + 0.1y + 0.2z = 2.0$$

$$D = \begin{vmatrix} 0.2 & 0.7 & 0.2 \\ 0.4 & 0.2 & 0.6 \\ 0.4 & 0.1 & 0.2 \end{vmatrix} = 0.10$$

$N_x = 0.20$, $N_y = 0.40$, and $N_z = 0.40$. Thus $x = 2$, $y = 4$, and $z = 4$.

They should go light on the sales tax and heavy on income and property taxes. Naturally, a change in the desired payments by different kinds of people would change the amounts of each tax chosen. The above numbers are for example only. Techniques such as these could be used, but the size of the problem would have to be much larger to be realistic.

6-6 SUMMARY

This chapter discusses equations in more than one unknown, and systems of equations in more than one unknown. Systems of n linear equations in n unknowns can, sometimes, be solved for the appropriate unknown values. The system will either have one solution (the most important case), no solutions (the equations are inconsistent), or an infinite number of solutions. One test that can be applied is that if $D \neq 0$ (the determinant is nonzero), then the system has one unique solution.

Several methods of finding a solution are discussed for two equations in two unknowns; a graphical technique and the methods of substitution and elimination are described and examples are given. For more than two equations, solution by elimination is suggested and illustrated. The final method of solution given works for any n by n system, and it uses the determinant. The formulas are

$$x = \frac{N_x}{D}, \quad y = \frac{N_y}{D}, \quad \text{and so on for any other variables if } D \neq 0.$$

N_x and D are defined, and methods for evaluating them are given in Section 6–5.

NEW SYMBOLS

Symbols	*English Translation*
$D = \begin{vmatrix} a_{11} & \cdots & a_{1n} \\ \cdot & & \cdot \\ \cdot & & \cdot \\ \cdot & & \cdot \\ a_{n1} & \cdots & a_{nn} \end{vmatrix}$	The determinant of a system of equations whose coefficients are a_{11}, a_{12}, $\ldots$, a_{1n} in the first equation, and so on. Methods for evaluating D are discussed in the text.
$N_x = \begin{vmatrix} a_{11} & \cdots & c_1 & \cdots & a_{1n} \\ \cdot & & \cdot & & \cdot \\ \cdot & & \cdot & & \cdot \\ \cdot & & \cdot & & \cdot \\ a_{1n} & \cdots & c_n & \cdots & a_{nn} \end{vmatrix}$	The determinant formed by replacing the coefficients of the x variable by the constants from the right-hand side of the equation. It is used to solve for x, $N_x/D = x$.
$M_{\text{row column}} = M_{ij}$	The $n - 1$ by $n - 1$ determinant formed by crossing out the ith row and jth column of an n by n determinant. This is used to evaluate higher-order determinants.

PROBLEMS

Problems for Self-Study: 2, 4bc, 8ab, 11, 13

6–1.* Which of the following are systems of linear equations? Are any of them dependent or inconsistent?

    a. $x + 2y = 6$
        $3x - y = 8$
    b. $x + 3 = 9$
    c. $x + 2xy + y = 7$
        $x - y = 4$
    d. $2x + 3y = 4$
        $-4x - 6y = -8$
    e. $7x + 6y = 3$
        $-7x - 6y = 0$

6–2. Solve the following systems of linear equations using the substitution method.

a. $x + 2y = 6$
$3x - y = 8$

b. $x + 3 = 9$
$x - y = 2$

c. $4x - 6y = 3$
$-2x + 3y = \frac{3}{2}$

d. $7x + 12y = 19$
$12x - 7y = 5$

6–3. Solve the systems of linear equations in Problem 6–2 by the method of elimination.

6–4. Solve the following systems of linear equations by substitution or elimination.

a.*$3x - y + z = 5$
$x - y - 3z = 5$
$-2x + 2y + z = -5$

b. $x + y + z = 2$
$-x + y + z = 6$
$4x + 7y + 3z = 8$

c. $3x + y - z = 7$
$6x - 2y + 2z = 3$
$3x - 3y + 3z = -4$

d. $w + x + y + z = 1$
$3w + 2y - z = -1$
$w - x - y + 6z = -13$
$w + 4x + 2y - z = 17$

6–5. Solve the following systems of equations.

a. $3x^2y = 12$
$4xy^2 = 8$

b. $\dfrac{6}{x} - \dfrac{8}{y} = -1$

$\dfrac{9}{x} + \dfrac{6}{y} = 3$

c. $\dfrac{6y}{x^2} = 2$

$\dfrac{9}{xy^2} = \dfrac{1}{3}$

6-6.* Solve the following systems of equations.

a. $xyz = 1$
$x^2yz = e$
$x^2y/z = e^{-1}$

b. $\dfrac{1}{x} + \dfrac{1}{y} = 1\frac{1}{2}$

$\dfrac{2}{x} + \dfrac{1}{y} = 2$

6-7. Calculate the determinants.

a. $\begin{vmatrix} 1 & 2 \\ 3 & 4 \end{vmatrix}$

b. $\begin{vmatrix} 7 & -3 \\ -4 & 6 \end{vmatrix}$

c. $\begin{vmatrix} 1 & 2 & 3 \\ 2 & 4 & 6 \\ 7 & 1 & 1 \end{vmatrix}$

d. $\begin{vmatrix} 1 & 2 & 3 \\ 4 & 5 & 6 \\ 7 & 8 & 9 \end{vmatrix}$

6-8. Use the determinant method for solving the following systems of equations. (Part *d* is relatively more difficult.)

a. $x + y = 6$
$x - y = 2$

b. $x + y + z = 3$
$2x - y - z = 0$
$x - 2y + 3z = 2$

c. $3x + y + z = 6$
$x - y + z = 2$
$2x + 3y - 2z = 4$

d. $4w + 2x - y - z = 1$
$w - x + y - z = -2$
$w - x - y + z = 0$
$w + x + 3y - 2z = 4$

6-9. Output, x, is a linear function of labor, L, and capital, K. That is,

$$x = aL + bK.$$

For two production periods, the following were observed.

$$\text{Period 1: } x = 1000, L = 40, K = 100;$$
$$\text{Period 2: } x = 1200, L = 60, K = 110.$$

Find a and b.

6–10.* A new housing development will use modular housing with two types of units. One model costs $10,000 per unit, and the other costs $15,000 per unit. The housing authority has a budget of $1,500,000 and wants to buy 130 units, while spending its entire budget. How many of each model should be bought?

6–11. The cost of a patient's stay in a hospital may be a function of the length of the stay (in days) and the amount of medical attention (in hours). Two patients had the following bills.

Patient	Days in Hospital (H)	Hours of Attention (A)	Total Bill (C)
1	4	10	$ 500
2	7	30	$1125

If the cost is a linear function of length of stay, H, and hours of attention, A, such that $C = aH + bA$, find the values of the constants a and b.

6–12.* A hospital personnel administrator must hire 20 new orderlies. Some orderlies have had special training; others have not. The trained man is preferred but must be paid $4.00 per hour; the untrained man must be paid only $2.75 per hour. The budgeted total wages for the 20 new men is $70 per hour. How many trained men can be hired?

6–13. A sales manager knows that sales, S, are a linear function of magazine advertising, M, and television advertising, T. Thus

$$S = a + bM + cT.$$

The manager has three quarter-years of data:

$$\text{Quarter 1: } S = 1000, M = 20, T = 40;$$
$$\text{Quarter 2: } S = 900, M = 25, T = 35;$$
$$\text{Quarter 3: } S = 1200, M = 25, T = 45.$$

Find the values of a, b, and c.

6–14.* The cost of operating a particular plant is a linear function of the labor used, L, and the amount of capital invested, K. Thus

$$C = aL + bK.$$

The general manager knows that for the first quarter the cost of operation was 100,000 while the values of L and K were 10,000 and 100,000, respectively. For the second quarter, the same figures were $C = 80,000$, $L = 9000$, and $K = 70,000$. Find the values of a and b.

6–15.* The owner of a hot-dog stand wishes to have sales at the rate of 200 per hour. He knows that the number of hot dogs he sells, H, depends on his price, P, and the number of advertisements, A, he has on the local radio station. In particular,

$$H = a + \frac{b}{P} + cA.$$

For 3 weeks he varied price and advertising, and he has the following data.

Week	Price	Advertisements	Sales per Hour
1	0.20	3	180
2	0.25	5	190
3	0.40	6	185

Find the values of a, b, and c and then find one set of values for P and A that cause sales to be 200 per hour.

6–16. Let $f(x)$ be a polynomial of degree 2. Then $f(x) = a + bx + cx^2$. Given the following values of x and $f(x)$, find the values of a, b, and c.

x	$f(x)$
1	9
-2	0
3	25

6–17. The prices of wheat and bread are P_W and P_B, respectively. The demand (denoted by D) and supply (denoted by S) for each commodity are dependent on the two prices.

$$S_W = 50 + 20P_W - 5P_B, \quad D_W = 50 - 10P_W + 5P_B,$$
$$S_B = -10P_W + 10P_B, \quad D_B = 400 + 10P_W - 10P_B.$$

Find the values of P_W and P_B such that both markets are in equilibrium. That is, solve for P_W and P_B such that $D_W = S_W$ and $D_B = S_B$.

6–18.* A commercial farming operation believes that the yield (in bushels) per acre planted in corn is described by

$$\text{yield} \equiv Y = a + bx_1 + cx_2,$$

where $x_1 =$ amount (in pounds) of fertilizer 1 put on 1 acre of land, and $x_2 =$ amount (in pounds) of fertilizer 2 put on 1 acre of land. They know that the following yields occurred when x_1 and x_2 were applied in the indicated amounts.

Yield	x_1	x_2
400	40	30
500	60	40
550	60	50

Corn sells for $3 per bushel, and x_1 and x_2 both cost $10 per pound. The accountant told the farmer to use $x_1 = 20$ and $x_2 = 20$ to cut costs. The farmer prefers $x_1 = 40$ and $x_2 = 40$. Which one has a better solution if the goal is to make as much profit as possible?

6–19.* A marketing manager believes that his demand as a function of price is given by

$$\text{demand} = a + bp - cp^2, \quad \text{over a range of } p.$$

The manager has the following data:

Price	Demand
2	100
3	97
4	92

The manager wants you to estimate a, b, and c, then use those values to see if a price of 5 will produce more revenue (price times demand) than a price of 4.

6–20. The director of a public playground is ordering a supply of baseball equipment. He wishes to have two gloves for every ball and one bat for every three gloves. The unit prices for gloves, bats, and balls are $4.00, $3.00, and $0.50, respectively. The director has a budget of $157.50. What equipment should be ordered?

6–21.* Suppose that the amount that a company must borrow each month on a short-term basis, B, is a function of its cash sales, S, and credit sales, C, that month, so that

$$B = a + \frac{b}{S} + dC.$$

For the last 3 months, the values of B, S, and C have been as follows,

Month	B	S	C
1	32	10	20
2	16	20	5
3	29	5	15

Find a, b, and d.

6–22.* A plant has a machine that must run 24 hours a day. This machine produces 2 products, product 1 at the rate of 40 units per hour and product 2 at the rate of 70 units per hour. A product mix of 3 units of product 1 for every 7 units of product 2 is desired. How much of a 24-hour day should be spent producing product 1? Use a simultaneous system of equations.

6–23. The amount of tax an individual must pay, T, is a function of his income, I, such that

$$T = a + bI.$$

Two men have incomes of $10,000 and $15,000, respectively, and have to pay $2000 and $4000 in taxes, respectively. What are the values of a and b?

6 24.* A manufacturer who makes two products knows that product A requires 6 hours on machine 1 and 3 hours on machine 2. Product B requires 3 hours on machine 1 and 7 hours on machine 2. He has available 36 hours per week of machine 1 time (4 hours are lost in start-up procedures) and 40 hours per week on machine 2. He wants to use all machine time. Set up the problem as two simultaneous equations and compute the number of production units of both products.

6–25.* A state government is instituting an income tax as in Problem 6-23; $T = a + bI$, where T is tax and I is income. They know that they want a total of $5000 from two persons, one with a $10,000 income and one with a $15,000 income. They want the person with a $15,000 income to pay twice as much as the person with a $10,000 income. Set the problem up as two equations in two unknowns and solve for a and b.

7

Matrices

A marketing manager believes there are essentially three types of people who make up the major market for his product. They are (1) housewives, (2) persons from families having more than $15,000 income, and (3) persons in the 30- to 50-year-old age bracket. Unfortunately, some people belong to all three of these groups. Nevertheless, the manager has data that he thinks are sufficient for making his periodic advertising decision.

In particular, he is considering spending money in three different media: newspapers (medium 1, denoted x_1), television (medium 2, denoted x_2), and radio (medium 3, denoted x_3). His information says that:

$2x_1 + 3x_2 + 5x_3 =$ number of housewives reached by the company's message,

$7x_1 + 1x_2 + 0x_3 =$ number of persons from families with over $15,000 income reached by the message,

$4x_1 + 5x_2 + 1x_3 =$ number of persons of age 30 to 50 reached by the message.

The manager wants to reach 30,000 housewives, 20,000 persons from over $15,000 income families, and 20,000 persons of age 30 to 50, without regard to the fact that some persons may be counted more than once. How many dollars must he spend to reach his goal? First, let's write his problem in equation form. There are three equations in three unknowns:

$$2x_1 + 3x_2 + 5x_3 = 30,000,$$
$$7x_1 + 1x_2 \qquad\;\; = 20,000,$$
$$4x_1 + 5x_2 + 1x_3 = 20,000.$$

The manager solves his problem if he finds values for x_1, x_2, and x_3 that satisfy all three equations simultaneously.

We can solve the above problem using the techniques of Chapter 6, but this chapter will introduce another (more general) method. The inclusion of this chapter is based largely on the fact that writing systems of equations in the above form and solving them (or performing other operations) can be very tedious. (Certainly you will agree that writing out systems of equations can be a bother.)

7-1 MATRIX AND VECTOR NOTATION

The determinant of the above system of equations can be evaluated using the last column:

$$D = \begin{vmatrix} 2 & 3 & 5 \\ 7 & 1 & 0 \\ 4 & 5 & 1 \end{vmatrix} = 5 \begin{vmatrix} 7 & 1 \\ 4 & 5 \end{vmatrix} + 1 \begin{vmatrix} 2 & 3 \\ 7 & 1 \end{vmatrix} = 155 - 19 = 136.$$

We can use this value to solve the system of equations as we learned how to do in Chapter 6, but, if we can contain our enthusiasm a moment, we will find still another way to solve this system. Suppose that we write an array of the coefficients. It would look like the array in D, but we put brackets, [ ], around it rather than vertical straight lines. Let's call it $\mathbf{A}$, using boldface type:

$$\mathbf{A} = \begin{bmatrix} 2 & 3 & 5 \\ 7 & 1 & 0 \\ 4 & 5 & 1 \end{bmatrix}.$$

$\mathbf{A}$ is called a *matrix of coefficients.*

A matrix is a rectangular array of numbers. It is identified by writing it in boldface type and using brackets to enclose the array.

We can also array the unknowns and the constants on the right-hand side of the equation set. Call them $\mathbf{x}$ and $\mathbf{b}$ respectively:

$$\mathbf{x} = \begin{bmatrix} x_1 \\ x_2 \\ x_3 \end{bmatrix}, \qquad \mathbf{b} = \begin{bmatrix} 30{,}000 \\ 20{,}000 \\ 20{,}000 \end{bmatrix}.$$

These two matrices are called the *vector of unknowns* and the *vector of constants*, respectively. We will use small letters to indicate that the matrix is a vector.

A matrix composed of a single column is called a *column vector.*
A matrix composed of a single row is called a *row vector.*

Given these definitions, we can (although as yet you do not know why) write
the equation system in much more compact form as

$$\mathbf{Ax} = \mathbf{b}.$$

The $\mathbf{A}$ matrix has 3 rows and 3 columns. We say it is a 3 by 3 matrix
(written 3×3). The two vectors are both 3 rows by 1 column. We say they
are 3 by 1 (3×1). Since the entries in each vector are arranged in a column,
both $\mathbf{x}$ and $\mathbf{b}$ are column vectors. If we wish to indicate the size (or order as it
is often called) of the matrices used, we can write the equations as

$$\mathbf{A}_{3\times3}\mathbf{x}_{3\times1} = \mathbf{b}_{3\times1}.$$

We have added only a means of indicating the size of the matrix. A summary
of the notation up to this point follows.

Symbols	*English Translation*
$\mathbf{A}_{m\times n}, \mathbf{B}_{m\times n}$	An m by n matrix. An array with m rows and n columns. We usually will use $\mathbf{A}, \mathbf{B}, \mathbf{C}$ to denote matrices. They are nearly always, in this book, composed of constants. The order (size) is not always indicated. Thus $\mathbf{A}$ is a matrix.
$\mathbf{a}_{n\times1}, \mathbf{b}_{n\times1}, \mathbf{t}_{n\times1}$	An n by 1 column vector (n rows, one column). Vectors may be composed of constants or unknowns. These vectors are called column vectors.
$\mathbf{a}'_{1\times n}, \mathbf{b}'_{1\times n}$	A 1 by n row vector (1 row, n columns). This is called a row vector since the entries are arranged in a single row. We will use a prime ($'$) to indicate a row vector.

We observe again that all matrix symbols are in boldface type, to distinguish
them from constants and variables. Also we note that a matrix need not have
the same number of rows as columns; m need not equal n. As mentioned
above, we will deal mainly with matrices composed completely of constants
and vectors composed completely of either unknowns or constants. Matrices
are not so restricted, but our use of them here will be. For example:

$$\begin{bmatrix} 3 & 0 & 2 & 1 \\ 4 & 0 & 0 & 5 \\ 1 & 1 & 2 & 4 \end{bmatrix} = \mathbf{A}_{3\times4}$$ 3 by 4 matrix of constants

$$[x_1 \ x_2 \ x_3] = \mathbf{x}'_{1\times3}$$ 1 by 3 row vector of unknowns

$$\begin{bmatrix} 2 & 1 \\ 3 & 4 \\ 1 & 0 \end{bmatrix} = \mathbf{B}_{3\times2}$$ 3 by 2 matrix

$$\begin{bmatrix} 1 \\ 2 \end{bmatrix} = \mathbf{t}_{2\times1}$$ 2 by 1 column vector

$$\begin{bmatrix} a_{11} & a_{12} & \cdots & a_{1j} & \cdots & a_{1n} \\ a_{21} & a_{22} & \cdots & a_{2j} & \cdots & a_{2n} \\ \cdot & & & \cdot & & \cdot \\ \cdot & & & \cdot & & \cdot \\ \cdot & & & \cdot & & \cdot \\ a_{i1} & a_{i2} & \cdots & a_{ij} & \cdots & a_{in} \\ \cdot & & & \cdot & & \cdot \\ \cdot & & & \cdot & & \cdot \\ \cdot & & & \cdot & & \cdot \\ a_{m1} & a_{m2} & \cdots & a_{mj} & \cdots & a_{mn} \end{bmatrix} = \{a_{ij}\} = \mathbf{A}_{m\times n}$$ m by n matrix

In this last and most general case, each a_{ij} value is an element of the matrix. The first subscript refers to the row of the element, and the second subscript refers to the column. Thus a_{ij} is the element in the ith row and the jth column. In fact, matrices can be written as the set of a_{ij} values.

Symbol	*English Translation*
$\mathbf{A}_{m\times n} = \{a_{ij}\}, i = 1, \ldots, m$ and $j = 1, \ldots, n$	$\mathbf{A}_{m\times n}$ is the set of a_{ij} values, arranged in an array of m rows and n columns; a_{ij} represents the element in the ith row and jth column.

The definition of a_{ij} may seem tedious, but it will be useful from time to time. The size of a matrix or vector ($m \times n$) is critical when discussing matrix arithmetic and other topics. For example, a determinant only exists for a square matrix $\mathbf{A}_{n\times n}$. In general, we only want to solve a system of equations involving a square matrix.

Symbol	*English Translation*
$\mathbf{A}_{n\times n}$	A square matrix, consisting of n rows and n columns.

Rewriting the marketing manager's set of equations in matrix form, we have

$$\mathbf{Ax} = \mathbf{b}, \text{ or } \begin{bmatrix} 2 & 3 & 5 \\ 7 & 1 & 0 \\ 4 & 5 & 1 \end{bmatrix} \begin{bmatrix} x_1 \\ x_2 \\ x_3 \end{bmatrix} = \begin{bmatrix} 30{,}000 \\ 20{,}000 \\ 20{,}000 \end{bmatrix}.$$

The product of the coefficient matrix by the vector of unknowns yields a vector of constants. Here a 3 × 3 matrix times a 3 by 1 column vector equals a 3 by 1 column vector. But how is this multiplication of matrices accomplished? The next section describes how matrices are added, subtracted, and multiplied.

1. Given the following matrix, answer the indicated questions.

$$\begin{bmatrix} 3 & 2 & 0 & 1 & 2 \\ 1 & 1 & 7 & 4 & 2 \\ 4 & 2 & 6 & 0 & 2 \end{bmatrix} = \mathbf{A}_{m \times n}$$

(a) Is it a square matrix?   Yes_____   No_____
(b) What values do m and n have? $m =$ _____ $n =$ _____
(c) What is a_{13}? a_{42}? a_{33}? $a_{13} =$ ____ ; $a_{42} =$ ____ ; $a_{33} =$ ____
(d) Does a determinant exist for $\mathbf{A}_{m \times n}$?   Yes_____   No_____

2. Give an example in the space at the right of
   (a) a 2 by 1 column vector.
   (b) a square matrix.
   (c) a row vector.

3. Given the system of equations below, write the matrix of coefficients, $\mathbf{A}$; the vector of unknowns, $\mathbf{t}$; and the vector of right-hand-side constants, $\mathbf{c}$. Finally, write the system of equations in matrix form, following the example used in this section.

$$2x + y = 4,$$
$$3x - y = 1.$$

Answers

1. $\mathbf{A}_{m \times n}$ is $3 = m$ by $5 = n$, so it is not square and a determinant does not exist; $a_{13} = 0$, a_{42} does not exist, and $a_{33} = 6$.

2. (a) $\begin{bmatrix} 1 \\ 2 \end{bmatrix}$ (b) $\begin{bmatrix} 1 & 2 \\ 2 & 1 \end{bmatrix}$ (c) $[1 \quad 2]$

   These are only examples.

3. $\mathbf{A}_{2 \times 2} = \begin{bmatrix} 2 & 1 \\ 3 & -1 \end{bmatrix}$, $\mathbf{t}_{2 \times 1} = \begin{bmatrix} x \\ y \end{bmatrix}$, $\mathbf{c}_{2 \times 1} = \begin{bmatrix} 4 \\ 1 \end{bmatrix}$.

   Then

$$\mathbf{A}_{2 \times 2}\mathbf{t}_{2 \times 1} = \mathbf{c}_{2 \times 1}.$$

7-2 MATRIX ARITHMETIC: ADDITION, SUBTRACTION, AND MULTIPLICATION

Division is missing from this section title because division of matrices does not exist as such; its analogue, the inverse, is more complicated than the other topics of this section. We will discuss the relatively easy topics of addition, subtraction, and multiplication, and gather strength for the task ahead.

Addition and Subtraction

Addition and Subtraction of Matrices

1. Two matrices can be added (subtracted) only if they are of the same size (order). That is, $A_{m \times n} + B_{m \times n}$ can be accomplished. $A_{m \times n} + B_{r \times s}$ cannot be done, unless $r = m$ and $s = n$. (The fancy term for "$A + B$ can be accomplished" is "A and B are conformable for addition and subtraction.")
2. Addition of $A_{m \times n} + B_{m \times n}$ is accomplished by adding $a_{11} + b_{11}$, $a_{12} + b_{12}$, $\ldots, a_{ij} + b_{ij}, \ldots, a_{mn} + b_{mn}$: that is, by adding elements term by term. For

   subtraction, $A_{m \times n} - B_{m \times n}$ is accomplished in general by obtaining $a_{ij} - b_{ij}$: that is, by obtaining $a_{11} - b_{11}$ and so on.

Consider some examples:

(i)
$$A = \begin{bmatrix} 2 & 1 \\ 3 & 1 \end{bmatrix}, \quad B = \begin{bmatrix} 1 & 4 \\ 2 & 1 \end{bmatrix},$$
$$A + B = \begin{bmatrix} (2+1) & (1+4) \\ (3+2) & (1+1) \end{bmatrix} = \begin{bmatrix} 3 & 5 \\ 5 & 2 \end{bmatrix}.$$

(Notice that the size, 2×2, does not have to be included.)

$$A - B = \begin{bmatrix} (2-1) & (1-4) \\ (3-2) & (1-1) \end{bmatrix} = \begin{bmatrix} 1 & -3 \\ 1 & 0 \end{bmatrix},$$
$$B - A = \begin{bmatrix} (1-2) & (4-1) \\ (2-3) & (1-1) \end{bmatrix} = \begin{bmatrix} -1 & +3 \\ -1 & 0 \end{bmatrix}.$$

(ii)
$$C = \begin{bmatrix} 1 & 0 & 0 \\ 0 & 1 & 0 \\ 0 & 0 & 1 \end{bmatrix}, \quad A \text{ and } B \text{ as above.}$$

$A + C$ cannot be accomplished!

(iii)
$$A - A = \begin{bmatrix} 0 & 0 \\ 0 & 0 \end{bmatrix}.$$

Since matrices are arrays of numbers and unknowns, two matrices may be equal. One requirement for equality is that the matrices be of the same size, but this is not sufficient.

For the examples used in addition and subtraction:

$$\mathbf{A} \neq \mathbf{B}, \mathbf{A} \neq \mathbf{C} \text{ and } \mathbf{B} \neq \mathbf{C}.$$

Equality only holds if the matrices have identical elements in every position. That is, $\mathbf{A}$ and $\mathbf{B}$ are equal if and only if $a_{ij} = b_{ij}$ for all i and j.

Multiplication by a Constant (Scalar)

A constant is sometimes referred to as a scalar in matrix terminology. Any matrix may be multiplied by a constant. The result is written as

$$c\mathbf{A}, \qquad \text{where } c \text{ is a constant.}$$

Multiplication of a Matrix by a Constant (Scalar)

$$\text{If } \mathbf{A} = \{a_{ij}\}, \text{ then } c\mathbf{A} = \{ca_{ij}\}.$$

That is, every element of A is multiplied by the constant.

An example of multiplication by scalars is

$$3\begin{bmatrix} 4 & 0 \\ 1 & 2 \end{bmatrix} - 2\begin{bmatrix} 8 & 1 \\ 1 & 1 \end{bmatrix} = \begin{bmatrix} 12 & 0 \\ 3 & 6 \end{bmatrix} - \begin{bmatrix} 16 & 2 \\ 2 & 2 \end{bmatrix} = \begin{bmatrix} -4 & -2 \\ +1 & +4 \end{bmatrix}.$$

For a more realistic example, suppose that a producer of toy wagons has the following sales, by region of the country and color of the wagon (entries are sales, in thousands of units, per month):

Color \ Regions	I	II	III
Red	10	4	8
Blue	10	6	4

A matrix of the firm's sales can be written using that data:

$$\mathbf{A} = \begin{bmatrix} 10 & 4 & 8 \\ 10 & 6 & 4 \end{bmatrix}.$$

Suppose that the total fixed costs of the firm are $60 (thousand). These costs are independent of the number of region–colors as long as this number exceeds zero. Now, suppose that the contribution (selling price minus the variable cost) per wagon is $2. The company wants to know how much each region–color contributes to the total profits of the company if each region–color must carry an equal share of the fixed costs. This answer is given by

$2\mathbf{A} - \mathbf{B}$, where $\mathbf{B} = \begin{bmatrix} 10 & 10 & 10 \\ 10 & 10 & 10 \end{bmatrix}$ is the matrix of fixed-cost shares;

$$2\mathbf{A} - \mathbf{B} = 2\begin{bmatrix} 10 & 4 & 8 \\ 10 & 6 & 4 \end{bmatrix} - \begin{bmatrix} 10 & 10 & 10 \\ 10 & 10 & 10 \end{bmatrix} = \begin{bmatrix} 20 & 8 & 16 \\ 20 & 12 & 8 \end{bmatrix} - \begin{bmatrix} 10 & 10 & 10 \\ 10 & 10 & 10 \end{bmatrix}$$

$$= \begin{bmatrix} 10 & -2 & 6 \\ 10 & 2 & -2 \end{bmatrix}.$$

In words, each region–color contributes $2 per item sold, 2**A**, and is charged (in thousands) $10 (one-sixth the fixed costs), denoted by subtracting $10 from each item in 2**A**. Suppose, further, that the manager wishes to know whether they should quit selling blue wagons in region 3 and red wagons in region 2 since those values in 2**A** − **B** are negative. This question is not solved using matrix arithmetic, but the matrix may help you see the answer. Think about what would happen. If they eliminate those two pairs, the fixed cost of 60 would not change, but the contribution of $4 + 4 = 8$ would be lost. Hence the answer is no!

Suppose that the manager insists that each region–color pair continue to cover an equal share of the allocated fixed costs. If the two pairs with negative entries in the matrix 2**A** − **B** are eliminated, the $60 fixed cost would be split four ways among the remaining region–color pairs. Each remaining region–color pair would be charged $15. The firm would then be forced to eliminate blue in region 2. Then the $60 is split three ways, or $20 per region, and region 3–red would have to go. Finally, both colors in region 1 would go, since neither can pay half of $60 without showing a loss. By this means the firm would systematically drive itself out of business, even though it is currently making $24,000. The moral of the story is: do not make marginal decisions based on fixed cost. Decisions about single product lines here do not change the fixed costs.

Multiplication of Matrices

Two matrices $\mathbf{A}_{m \times n}$ and $\mathbf{B}_{r \times s}$ can be multiplied (are conformable for multiplication) if (and only if) the number of columns in **A** equals the number of rows in **B**, $n = r$. The result is an m by s matrix. That is,

$$\mathbf{A}_{m \times n}\mathbf{B}_{n \times s} = (\mathbf{AB})_{m \times s}.$$

The steps are messy and you should not stop with the definition, but try some of the examples.

Matrix Multiplication

The product of two matrices $A_{m \times n}$ and $B_{n \times s}$ is given by

$$\mathbf{A}_{m\times n}\mathbf{B}_{n\times s} = \begin{bmatrix} \sum\limits_{k=1}^{n} a_{1k}b_{k1} & \cdots & \sum\limits_{k=1}^{n} a_{1k}b_{kj} & \cdots & \sum\limits_{k=1}^{n} a_{1k}b_{ks} \\ \cdot & & \cdot & & \cdot \\ \cdot & & \cdot & & \cdot \\ \sum\limits_{k=1}^{n} a_{ik}b_{k1} & \cdots & \sum\limits_{k=1}^{n} a_{ik}b_{kj} & \cdots & \sum\limits_{k=1}^{n} a_{ik}b_{ks} \\ \cdot & & \cdot & & \cdot \\ \cdot & & \cdot & & \cdot \\ \sum\limits_{k=1}^{n} a_{mk}b_{k1} & \cdots & \sum\limits_{k=1}^{n} a_{mk}b_{kj} & \cdots & \sum\limits_{k=1}^{n} a_{mk}b_{ks} \end{bmatrix} = \left\{ \sum\limits_{k=1}^{n} a_{ik}b_{kj} \right\}$$

for $i = 1, 2, \ldots,$ m and $j = 1, 2, \ldots, s$.

That is, the element in the ith row and the jth column of the product matrix is the sum of products (element by element) of the n elements in the ith row of the first matrix with the corresponding n elements of the jth column of the second matrix. For each element of the product matrix, move across a row of the first matrix and down a column of the second matrix, multiplying term by term.

Multiplying matrices requires practice. Let's try a few examples.

$$\mathbf{A} = \begin{bmatrix} 1 & 3 \\ 2 & 4 \end{bmatrix}, \qquad \mathbf{B} = \begin{bmatrix} 2 & 1 \\ 2 & 1 \end{bmatrix}, \qquad \mathbf{C} = \begin{bmatrix} 0 & 1 \\ 1 & 0 \end{bmatrix},$$

$$\mathbf{AB} = \begin{bmatrix} 1 & 3 \\ 2 & 4 \end{bmatrix} \begin{bmatrix} 2 & 1 \\ 2 & 1 \end{bmatrix} = \begin{bmatrix} [(1)2 + 3(2)] & [1(1) + 3(1)] \\ [2(2) + 4(2)] & [2(1) + 4(1)] \end{bmatrix} = \begin{bmatrix} 8 & 4 \\ 12 & 6 \end{bmatrix},$$

$$\mathbf{AC} = \begin{bmatrix} 1 & 3 \\ 2 & 4 \end{bmatrix} \begin{bmatrix} 0 & 1 \\ 1 & 0 \end{bmatrix} = \begin{bmatrix} [1(0) + 3(1)] & [1(1) + 3(0)] \\ [2(0) + 4(1)] & [2(1) + 4(0)] \end{bmatrix} = \begin{bmatrix} 3 & 1 \\ 4 & 2 \end{bmatrix},$$

$$(\mathbf{AB})\mathbf{C} = \begin{bmatrix} 8 & 4 \\ 12 & 6 \end{bmatrix} \begin{bmatrix} 0 & 1 \\ 1 & 0 \end{bmatrix} = \begin{bmatrix} [8(0) + 4(1)] & [8(1) + 4(0)] \\ [12(0) + 6(1)] & [12(1) + 6(0)] \end{bmatrix} = \begin{bmatrix} 4 & 8 \\ 6 & 12 \end{bmatrix}.$$

Omitting some parentheses as we get more familiar with the method,

$$\mathbf{BA} = \begin{bmatrix} 2 & 1 \\ 2 & 1 \end{bmatrix} \begin{bmatrix} 1 & 3 \\ 2 & 4 \end{bmatrix} = \begin{bmatrix} 2+2 & 6+4 \\ 2+2 & 6+4 \end{bmatrix} = \begin{bmatrix} 4 & 10 \\ 4 & 10 \end{bmatrix}.$$

The above examples point out several facts worth noting.

(*i*) **ABC** (assuming the matrices can be multiplied) can be accomplished by first finding **AB**, and then multiplying by **C**. This is written in conventional form (**AB**)**C**.

(*ii*) The matrix product **AB** does not usually equal the matrix product **BA**. Also **AB** can exist even though **BA** does not.

Let's try some more complex examples now.

$$A = \begin{bmatrix} 1 & -1 & 0 \\ 0 & 1 & 1 \end{bmatrix}, \qquad B = \begin{bmatrix} 1 & 0 & 0 \\ 0 & 1 & 0 \\ 0 & 2 & 1 \end{bmatrix}, \qquad c = \begin{bmatrix} 1 \\ 1 \\ 1 \end{bmatrix}, \qquad d' = [0 \ 1]$$

Then

$$AB = \begin{bmatrix} 1 & -1 & 0 \\ 0 & 1 & 1 \end{bmatrix} \begin{bmatrix} 1 & 0 & 0 \\ 0 & 1 & 0 \\ 0 & 2 & 1 \end{bmatrix} = \begin{bmatrix} 1 & -1 & 0 \\ 0 & 3 & 1 \end{bmatrix}.$$

A 2 × 3 matrix times a 3 × 3 matrix gives a 2 × 3 matrix.

BA does not exist!

$$(AB)c = \begin{bmatrix} 1 & -1 & 0 \\ 0 & 3 & 1 \end{bmatrix} \begin{bmatrix} 1 \\ 1 \\ 1 \end{bmatrix} = \begin{bmatrix} 0 \\ 4 \end{bmatrix}.$$

A 2 × 3 matrix times a 3 × 1 matrix gives a 2 × 1 matrix (a column vector).

$$((AB)c)d' = \begin{bmatrix} 0 \\ 4 \end{bmatrix} [0 \ 1] = \begin{bmatrix} 0 & 0 \\ 0 & 4 \end{bmatrix}.$$

A 2 × 1 matrix times a 1 × 2 matrix gives a 2 × 2 matrix.

$$d'(ABc) = [0 \ 1] \begin{bmatrix} 0 \\ 4 \end{bmatrix} = [4].$$

A 1 × 2 matrix times a 2 × 1 gives a 1 × 1 matrix.

As a final illustration, let's return to the marketing manager's advertising problem. We had

$$A = \begin{bmatrix} 2 & 3 & 5 \\ 7 & 1 & 0 \\ 4 & 5 & 1 \end{bmatrix}, \qquad x = \begin{bmatrix} x_1 \\ x_2 \\ x_3 \end{bmatrix}, \qquad b = \begin{bmatrix} 30{,}000 \\ 20{,}000 \\ 20{,}000 \end{bmatrix}.$$

Then the manager's problem was stated as: find **x** such that **Ax** = **b**. To show that **Ax** = **b** is equivalent to the longer version, let's multiply.

$$Ax = \begin{bmatrix} 2 & 3 & 5 \\ 7 & 1 & 0 \\ 4 & 5 & 1 \end{bmatrix} \begin{bmatrix} x_1 \\ x_2 \\ x_3 \end{bmatrix} = \begin{bmatrix} 2x_1 + 3x_2 + 5x_3 \\ 7x_1 + x_2 \\ 4x_1 + 5x_2 + x_3 \end{bmatrix}.$$

Now we can see that **Ax** = **b** is exactly the same as the longer version of the system of equations. In fact, any set of *n* equations in *n* unknowns can be written as: $\mathbf{Ax} = \mathbf{b}$, where $\mathbf{A}$ is the matrix of coefficients, $\mathbf{x}$ is the vector of unknowns, and $\mathbf{b}$ is the vector of constants. How to solve a set of equations written in matrix form is the topic of Sections 7–3 and 7–4.

$\sim\!\!\sim$: Let

$$A = \begin{bmatrix} 1 & 0 & 0 \\ 0 & 1 & 0 \\ 0 & 0 & 1 \end{bmatrix}, \quad B = \begin{bmatrix} 1 & -1 \\ 4 & -1 \end{bmatrix}, \quad C = \begin{bmatrix} 1 & 0 \\ 2 & 0 \\ 0 & 1 \\ 1 & 1 \end{bmatrix}, \quad d = \begin{bmatrix} 1 \\ 0 \end{bmatrix}, \quad e' = [0\ 0\ 1].$$

1. Circle each of the following multiplications that are not allowed. Multiply the first two that are allowed. What is the size of the final product matrix for any others that are allowed?

    (*a*) $\mathbf{e'A}$ (*e*) $\mathbf{CB}$

    (*b*) $\mathbf{Ae'}$ (*f*) $\mathbf{CBd}$

    (*c*) $\mathbf{AB}$ (*g*) $\mathbf{CBdd}$

    (*d*) $\mathbf{BC}$ (*h*) $\mathbf{Bd}$

2. Circle each of the following operations that is allowed. Perform the first two that are allowed.

    (*a*) $\mathbf{Bd} - \mathbf{d}$ (*d*) $\mathbf{C} - \mathbf{CB}$

    (*b*) $\mathbf{A} - \mathbf{B}$ (*e*) $\mathbf{C} + 2\mathbf{A}$

    (*c*) $2\mathbf{A}$ (*f*) $\mathbf{B} + \mathbf{B}$

Answers

1. $e'A = [0 \quad 0 \quad 1], \quad CB = \begin{bmatrix} 1 & -1 \\ 2 & -2 \\ 4 & -1 \\ 5 & -2 \end{bmatrix}.$

CBd and **Bd** are also allowed and give rise to a 4×1 and a 2×1 matrix (column vector), respectively. Parts (b), (c), (d), and (g) cannot be accomplished.

2. $Bd - d = \begin{bmatrix} 0 \\ 4 \end{bmatrix}, \quad 2A = \begin{bmatrix} 2 & 0 & 0 \\ 0 & 2 & 0 \\ 0 & 0 & 2 \end{bmatrix}.$

Parts (*d*) and (*f*) are also allowed, but (*b*) and (*e*) are not.

7-3 INVERSE OF A MATRIX

Before solving the marketing manager's problem, we must learn how to take the inverse of a matrix. This section and the next discuss how to solve systems of equations using the inverse of a matrix. We will examine only systems of n equations in n unknowns. A few preliminary ideas are necessary.

An identity matrix, $I_{n \times n}$, has 1s along the diagonal and 0s everywhere else.

For example:

$$I_{3\times 3} = \begin{bmatrix} 1 & 0 & 0 \\ 0 & 1 & 0 \\ 0 & 0 & 1 \end{bmatrix}.$$

I is the analog of 1 in arithmetic because (as you should verify)

    (*i*) **IA = AI = A**   if **I** and **A** are both *n* by *n*.
    (*ii*) **IA = A**   if **I** is *n* by *n* and **A** is *n* by *m*.
    (*iii*) **AI = A**   if **I** is *n* by *n* and **A** is *m* by *n*.

We illustrate situation (i) by the example

$$\begin{bmatrix} 2 & 1 \\ 3 & 1 \end{bmatrix}\begin{bmatrix} 1 & 0 \\ 0 & 1 \end{bmatrix} = \begin{bmatrix} 2 & 1 \\ 3 & 1 \end{bmatrix}.$$

Symbol	*English Translation*
I	An identity matrix, for example $I_{2\times 2} = \begin{bmatrix} 1 & 0 \\ 0 & 1 \end{bmatrix}$. **I** is the matrix analogue of 1 in arithmetic.

The transpose of a matrix, *A*, is denoted *A′*. It is formed by putting the *ij*th element in the *ji*th location.

Roughly speaking, rotate the matrix around the diagonal. Since a row vector is a transposed column vector, we have used a prime to indicate it. (A vector without a prime will always be a column vector in this text.)

Symbol	*English Translation*
A′	The transpose of the matrix **A**, formed by putting the *ij*th element in the *ji*th location. The rows of the matrix **A** are the columns of the transpose, **A′**.

For example:

$$\text{if } A = \begin{bmatrix} 4 & 6 \\ 8 & 5 \end{bmatrix}, \quad \text{then } A' = \begin{bmatrix} 4 & 8 \\ 6 & 5 \end{bmatrix};$$

$$\text{if } B = \begin{bmatrix} 1 & 2 & 3 \\ 4 & 5 & 6 \end{bmatrix}, \quad \text{then } B' = \begin{bmatrix} 1 & 4 \\ 2 & 5 \\ 3 & 6 \end{bmatrix}.$$

Notice that the rows of **A** are the columns of **A′**. The first row is the first column and so on.

The only other material we need to recall in order to define and compute the inverse of a matrix is on determinants. We need to remember the definitions of D and M_{ij}:

D is the determinant of a matrix;

M_{ij} is the determinant formed by crossing out the ith row and jth column of the original determinant.

The inverse of a square matrix, A, is written A^{-1}. It is the (only) matrix that, when multiplied by A, gives the identity matrix, I. (A^{-1} only exists if $D \neq 0$.)

$$A^{-1}A = AA^{-1} = I.$$

The inverse is defined only for square matrices.

Symbol	English Translation
A^{-1}	The inverse of the matrix A:
	$AA^{-1} = A^{-1}A = I.$

For example, the coefficient matrix in the marketing manager's problem was

$$A = \begin{bmatrix} 2 & 3 & 5 \\ 7 & 1 & 0 \\ 4 & 5 & 1 \end{bmatrix}. \quad \text{Let us try} \quad A^{-1} = \begin{bmatrix} \frac{1}{136} & \frac{22}{136} & -\frac{5}{136} \\ -\frac{7}{136} & -\frac{18}{136} & \frac{35}{136} \\ \frac{31}{136} & \frac{2}{136} & -\frac{19}{136} \end{bmatrix}.$$

Then

$$AA^{-1} = \begin{bmatrix} 1 & 0 & 0 \\ 0 & 1 & 0 \\ 0 & 0 & 1 \end{bmatrix}.$$

It works.

But how on earth did we ever find an A^{-1} to check? Let's look at another (easier) example before we tell you the method we used to find A^{-1}. Suppose that

$$A = \begin{bmatrix} 1 & 2 \\ 3 & 4 \end{bmatrix}.$$

Suppose that we try

$$A^{-1} = -\frac{1}{2} \begin{bmatrix} 4 & -2 \\ -3 & 1 \end{bmatrix} = \begin{bmatrix} -2 & 1 \\ \frac{3}{2} & -\frac{1}{2} \end{bmatrix},$$

$$AA^{-1} = \begin{bmatrix} 1 & 2 \\ 3 & 4 \end{bmatrix} \begin{bmatrix} -2 & 1 \\ \frac{3}{2} & -\frac{1}{2} \end{bmatrix} = \begin{bmatrix} 1 & 0 \\ 0 & 1 \end{bmatrix}.$$

In this case the multiplication is easier, and you can see that it works. Perhaps in this simpler example you can also see some similarities between A and A^{-1}. We shall try to pinpoint these similarities as we describe a method for finding the inverse of a matrix.

To Find the Inverse of a Matrix, A (Method 1)

1. Evaluate D and every M_{ij}.

2. $A^{-1} = (1/D)\{M_{ij}(-1)^{i+j}\}'$.

That is, form a matrix with the M_{ij} values instead of a_{ij}, and give each M_{ij} the sign indicated by $(-1)^{i+j}$. Then take the transpose of that matrix and divide each element by D. (The matrix $\{M_{ij}(-1)^{i+j}\}$ is often called the *adjoint matrix*. The *ij*th element of the adjoint matrix is called the *cofactor* of a_{ij}. We will not use these terms in this book.)

Using the example whose inverse we established above:

$$A = \begin{bmatrix} 1 & 2 \\ 3 & 4 \end{bmatrix}, \qquad D = 4 - 6 = -2.$$

$$M_{11} = 4, \qquad M_{12} = 3, \qquad M_{21} = 2, \qquad M_{22} = 1.$$

Remembering to include the $(-1)^{i+j}$ term, we now form A^{-1} using the definition.

$$A^{-1} = \frac{1}{-2}\begin{bmatrix} 4 & -3 \\ -2 & 1 \end{bmatrix}' = \frac{1}{-2}\begin{bmatrix} 4 & -2 \\ -3 & 1 \end{bmatrix} = \begin{bmatrix} -2 & 1 \\ \frac{3}{2} & -\frac{1}{2} \end{bmatrix}.$$

If the method of computation looks complicated, take heart. It is important for you to know what an inverse is and what an identity matrix and a transpose matrix are, as well as how to use them (which we will discuss later). You should find some inverses by hand and use them in small problems to become comfortable with the notions. However, when (not if) you forget how to find inverses, there is always method 2!

To Find the Inverse of a Matrix, A (Method 2)

Give the matrix to a computer. There are efficient computer routines written which can find a matrix inverse.

Other useful methods of finding inverses exist, but these two are adequate for our purposes. Some of the important facts about inverses are summarized below:

(*i*) A^{-1} exists only for square matrices and only if the determinant of A is not zero.

(*ii*) A^{-1} is unique; there is only one A^{-1} for a given matrix A.

(*iii*) $AA^{-1} = A^{-1}A = I$.

In the next section the inverse is used in solving systems of equations.

1. (*a*) Write a 3 by 3 identity matrix.

(*b*) Find I'.

(*c*) Find I^{-1}.

(*d*) Compute $\begin{bmatrix} 1 & 0 & 0 \\ 0 & 1 & 0 \\ 0 & 0 & 1 \end{bmatrix}\begin{bmatrix} 1 \\ 1 \\ 1 \end{bmatrix}$.

2. Find the inverse and transpose of the following matrices. Verify the inverse by multiplying by the original matrix to obtain I.

$$A = \begin{bmatrix} 3 & -4 \\ 7 & 14 \end{bmatrix} \qquad B = \begin{bmatrix} -1 & 3 & 0 \\ 0 & 2 & 1 \\ 1 & 0 & 4 \end{bmatrix}.$$

Answers

1.
$$I_{3\times3} = \begin{bmatrix} 1 & 0 & 0 \\ 0 & 1 & 0 \\ 0 & 0 & 1 \end{bmatrix} = I' = I^{-1}, \qquad \begin{bmatrix} 1 & 0 & 0 \\ 0 & 1 & 0 \\ 0 & 0 & 1 \end{bmatrix}\begin{bmatrix} 1 \\ 1 \\ 1 \end{bmatrix} = \begin{bmatrix} 1 \\ 1 \\ 1 \end{bmatrix}.$$

2.
$$A' = \begin{bmatrix} 3 & 7 \\ -4 & 14 \end{bmatrix}; \qquad B' = \begin{bmatrix} -1 & 0 & 1 \\ 3 & 2 & 0 \\ 0 & 1 & 4 \end{bmatrix};$$

$$A^{-1} = \frac{1}{70}\begin{bmatrix} 14 & 4 \\ -7 & 3 \end{bmatrix}; \qquad B^{-1} = -\frac{1}{5}\begin{bmatrix} 8 & -12 & 3 \\ 1 & -4 & 1 \\ -2 & 3 & -2 \end{bmatrix}.$$

7-4 SOLVING SYSTEMS OF EQUATIONS USING THE INVERSE

Let's look at the marketing manager's problem once more. In matrix notation,

$$Ax = b.$$

As long as we multiply or add in accordance with the rules of matrix algebra, we can add to and multiply by the same quantity on both sides of a matrix equation just as we did for single equations. But for *matrix* equations we can only use *matrix* addition and multiplication. (*Caution:* If we multiply in the front of the left-hand side, that is, before **A**, we must do the same on the right-hand side. Thus if **A** = **B**, then **bA** = **bB**. It is not proper to multiply **bA** on the left and **Bb** on the right as one could do for single equations.)

Let's premultiply the manager's matrix equation by $\mathbf{A}^{-1}$ to get the matrix of unknowns to stand alone.

$$\mathbf{A}^{-1}\mathbf{A}\mathbf{x} = \mathbf{A}^{-1}\mathbf{b}.$$

(Premultiplication by $\mathbf{A}^{-1}$ means making $\mathbf{A}^{-1}$ be the first term on both sides.) But $\mathbf{A}^{-1}\mathbf{A} = \mathbf{I}$ and $\mathbf{I}\mathbf{x} = \mathbf{x}$. Thus

$$\mathbf{A}^{-1}\mathbf{A}\mathbf{x} = \mathbf{x} = \mathbf{A}^{-1}\mathbf{b}.$$

We have just solved for the vector of unknowns, **x**.

$$\mathbf{x} = \mathbf{A}^{-1}\mathbf{b}.$$

To solve a system of equations (a matrix equation) written as

$$\mathbf{A}\mathbf{x} = \mathbf{b},$$

premultiply by $\mathbf{A}^{-1}$. Then:

$$\mathbf{x} = \mathbf{A}^{-1}\mathbf{b} \text{ is the solution.}$$

Continuing the marketing manager's example:

$$\mathbf{A} = \begin{bmatrix} 2 & 3 & 5 \\ 7 & 1 & 0 \\ 4 & 5 & 1 \end{bmatrix}, \quad \mathbf{A}^{-1} = \frac{1}{136} \begin{bmatrix} 1 & 22 & -5 \\ -7 & -18 & 35 \\ 31 & 2 & -19 \end{bmatrix}, \quad \mathbf{b} = \begin{bmatrix} 30,000 \\ 20,000 \\ 20,000 \end{bmatrix}.$$

The solution of the marketing manager's problem regarding how much he must spend on advertisements in each of the three media is

$$\mathbf{x} = \mathbf{A}^{-1}\mathbf{b} = \frac{1}{136} \begin{bmatrix} 1 & 22 & -5 \\ -7 & -18 & 35 \\ 31 & 2 & -19 \end{bmatrix} \begin{bmatrix} 30,000 \\ 20,000 \\ 20,000 \end{bmatrix} = \frac{1}{136} \begin{bmatrix} 370,000 \\ 130,000 \\ 590,000 \end{bmatrix}$$

$$= \begin{bmatrix} \dfrac{370,000}{136} \\ \dfrac{130,000}{136} \\ \dfrac{590,000}{136} \end{bmatrix} = \begin{bmatrix} 2721 \\ 957 \\ 3603 \end{bmatrix}.$$

The manager should allocate \$2,721 to newspaper advertising, \$957 to television advertising, and \$3,603 to radio advertising. He needs to spend a total of $2,721 + 957 + 3,603 = \$7,281$, or approximately \$7,300, to reach the goals he has set for total individual exposures to the company's message.

The determinant technique given in Chapter 6 for solving systems of equations and the inverse method used here both employ the same numbers in similar ways. There is a relationship between the two methods, but we need not go into it here. The inverse technique has the advantage of generating the entire solution vector at once, and it also is a better way (once mastered) to understand what is happening. Let's do another example to test our skill with this new technique.

$$\begin{aligned} x_1 + 2x_2 - 2x_3 &= 2, \\ 3x_1 - x_2 - x_3 &= 2, \\ x_1 + x_2 + x_3 &= 6. \end{aligned}$$

$$\mathbf{A} = \begin{bmatrix} 1 & 2 & -2 \\ 3 & -1 & -1 \\ 1 & 1 & 1 \end{bmatrix}, \qquad \mathbf{x} = \begin{bmatrix} x_1 \\ x_2 \\ x_3 \end{bmatrix}, \qquad \mathbf{b} = \begin{bmatrix} 2 \\ 2 \\ 6 \end{bmatrix}.$$

Then the equation system can be written in matrix notation as

$$\mathbf{Ax} = \mathbf{b} \qquad \text{and} \qquad \mathbf{x} = \mathbf{A}^{-1}\mathbf{b};$$

$$\mathbf{A}^{-1} = \frac{1}{-16} \begin{bmatrix} 0 & -4 & -4 \\ -4 & 3 & -5 \\ 4 & 1 & -7 \end{bmatrix} = \begin{bmatrix} 0 & \frac{1}{4} & \frac{1}{4} \\ \frac{1}{4} & -\frac{3}{16} & \frac{5}{16} \\ -\frac{1}{4} & -\frac{1}{16} & \frac{7}{16} \end{bmatrix}.$$

Then

$$\mathbf{x} = \begin{bmatrix} 0 & \frac{1}{4} & \frac{1}{4} \\ \frac{1}{4} & -\frac{3}{16} & \frac{5}{16} \\ -\frac{1}{4} & -\frac{1}{16} & \frac{7}{16} \end{bmatrix} \begin{bmatrix} 2 \\ 2 \\ 6 \end{bmatrix} = \begin{bmatrix} 2 \\ 2 \\ 2 \end{bmatrix}.$$

The solution is $x_1 = 2$, $x_2 = 2$, and $x_3 = 2$.

One final point is in order. Suppose, as an example, that the marketing manager insists on reaching more people in each category. Must we solve the problem again? The answer is no; let's see why.

We had

$$\mathbf{x} = \mathbf{A}^{-1}\mathbf{b}.$$

Now $\mathbf{A}^{-1}$ will not change, so we can find the new $\mathbf{x}$ vector simply by matrix multiplication ($\mathbf{A}^{-1}$ by the new vector $\mathbf{b}$). Suppose the manager would like to consider obtaining 5,000 more message exposures in the over-\$15,000 category, and he wants to know the cost before he decides whether or not to go ahead. Then the new **b** vector is

$$\mathbf{b} = \begin{bmatrix} 30,000 \\ 25,000 \\ 20,000 \end{bmatrix} \quad \text{and} \quad \mathbf{x} = \mathbf{A}^{-1}\mathbf{b}$$

so

$$\mathbf{x} = \frac{1}{136} \begin{bmatrix} 1 & 22 & -5 \\ -7 & -18 & 35 \\ 31 & 2 & -19 \end{bmatrix} \begin{bmatrix} 30,000 \\ 25,000 \\ 20,000 \end{bmatrix} = \frac{1}{136} \begin{bmatrix} 480,000 \\ 40,000 \\ 600,000 \end{bmatrix},$$

which is approximately

$$\begin{bmatrix} 3,529 \\ 294 \\ 4,412 \end{bmatrix}.$$

He has to spend a total of \$3,529 + \$294 + \$4,412, or about \$7,735, to achieve the new exposure requirements. This is about \$650 more than before. Notice that, even though only one element on the right-hand side changed, every media has a different dollar allocation than it had with the old goal.

1. What is the mathematical solution if the marketing manager in the above example wants to increase the over-\$15,000 category to 30,000? Does the solution make sense?

2. Solve the following systems of equations using the inverse technique.

$$(a) \quad \begin{aligned} 3x_1 - 2x_2 - x_3 &= 3, \\ x_1 + x_2 - 4x_3 &= -17, \\ -x_1 - x_2 + x_3 &= 5. \end{aligned} \qquad (b) \quad \begin{aligned} y_1 + y_2 &= 2, \\ 2y_1 - y_2 &= 1. \end{aligned}$$

Answers

1.

$$\mathbf{b} = \begin{bmatrix} 30,000 \\ 30,000 \\ 20,000 \end{bmatrix} \quad \text{so } \mathbf{x} = \begin{bmatrix} \dfrac{590,000}{136} \\ \dfrac{-50,000}{136} \\ \dfrac{610,000}{136} \end{bmatrix}.$$

The solution does not make sense because you can buy very little television time with $-\$50,000/136$.

2. (a) The answers are $x_1 = 1$, $x_2 = -2$, and $x_3 = 4$. The inverse is

$$\mathbf{A}^{-1} = \frac{1}{-15} \begin{bmatrix} -3 & +3 & +9 \\ 3 & 2 & 11 \\ 0 & 5 & 5 \end{bmatrix}.$$

(*b*) The answers are $y_1 = y_2 = +1$. The inverse is

$$\mathbf{A}^{-1} = \frac{1}{-3} \begin{bmatrix} -1 & -1 \\ -2 & +1 \end{bmatrix}.$$

7-5 SUMMARY

This chapter gives a very brief introduction to the algebra of matrices. We have been particularly interested in matrix equations (systems of linear equations) and how to solve them.

A matrix of size m by n, $\mathbf{A}_{m \times n}$, is an array of elements in m rows and n columns. The element in the ith row and jth column is designated by a_{ij}. Vectors are matrices of only one row or one column. Vectors and matrices can be added and subtracted if they are of the same size (m by n) by adding (subtracting) the elements. Multiplication is more complicated. Matrices can be multiplied if the number of columns in the first equals the number of rows in the second. The rules for matrix arithmetic are easy to learn, but they are easier to look up. These rules are found in Section 7–2 and we encourage you to look them up when you need them. Don't try to memorize them.

Division, as such, does not exist, but the inverse of a matrix, $\mathbf{A}$, denoted by $\mathbf{A}^{-1}$, is a matrix such that $\mathbf{A}^{-1}\mathbf{A} = \mathbf{I}$. (This is analogous to $a^{-1}a = 1$ for numbers.) The matrix $\mathbf{I}$ is the identity matrix, the matrix that when multiplied by $\mathbf{A}$ gives $\mathbf{A}$ again as the result. That is, $\mathbf{IA} = \mathbf{AI} = \mathbf{A}$. The reason that all of this is of interest is that the inverse can be used to solve systems of equations. If

$$\mathbf{Ax} = \mathbf{b},$$

then

$$\mathbf{x} = \mathbf{A}^{-1}\mathbf{b}$$

is the solution to the system of equations.

The method for finding the inverse involves the determinant D, the smaller determinant (or minor) M_{ij}, and the concept of a transpose. In particular,

$$\mathbf{A}^{-1} = \frac{1}{D} \{M_{ij}(-1)^{i+j}\}'.$$

The inverse technique is a very powerful method for solving systems of linear equations. Matrices are also useful in representing both data and systems of equations in compact form. Chapter 8 shows how matrices can be used to describe systems of inequalities, which have important applications to managerial problems.

As you might have expected, there are many topics in matrix algebra that we have not discussed. For example, there are other useful methods for finding inverses. The subject is just too big to do more than introduce it. Whole courses in mathematics curriculums are devoted to it if you find you like this sort of thing. We have only touched on some of the major ideas that you will find useful in management applications.

NEW SYMBOLS

Symbols	English Translation
$A_{m \times n}$	An m by n matrix. An array of m rows and n columns. If $m = n$, this is called a *square matrix*. Each element is denoted as a_{ij}. A matrix is sometimes written using just the a_{ij}. That is, $A = \{a_{ij}\}$, $i = 1, \ldots, m$ and $j = 1, \ldots, n$.
$a_{n \times 1}$	An n by 1 vector. An array of n elements in one column, called a *column vector*.
$a'_{1 \times n}$	A *row vector*, n elements in one row.
$I_{n \times n}$	The *identity matrix* of n rows and columns. It consists of 1s in the $a_{11}, a_{22}, \ldots,$ and a_{nn} positions and 0s elsewhere. For example, $$I_{2 \times 2} = \begin{bmatrix} 1 & 0 \\ 0 & 1 \end{bmatrix}.$$
A'	The *transpose* of the matrix A. The rows of A become the columns of A'. The first row of A becomes the first column of A', and so on.
$A^{-1}{}_{n \times n}$	The *inverse* of the square matrix A. If it exists, A^{-1} is unique, and $AA^{-1} = A^{-1}A = I$.

PROBLEMS

Problems for Self-Study: 1, 4, 5, 12, 19

7-1. Which of the following matrices are square? Give the values for m and n if they are denoted as $A_{m \times n}$. Indicate the a_{23} value if there is one.

a. $\begin{bmatrix} 3 & 5 \\ 1 & 0 \\ 2 & 7 \end{bmatrix}$ b. $\begin{bmatrix} 2 & 1 \\ 1 & 4 \end{bmatrix}$ c. $\begin{bmatrix} 1 & 4 & 8 \\ 2 & 1 & 7 \\ -4 & -5 & -6 \end{bmatrix}$ d. $\begin{bmatrix} 1 & 6 & 4 & 2 \\ 1 & 6 & 4 & 2 \\ -1 & -6 & 4 & 2 \end{bmatrix}$

7-2. Evaluate the determinant of the following matrices. Does an inverse exist for each one?

a. $\begin{bmatrix} 2 & 4 \\ 1 & 3 \end{bmatrix}$ b. $\begin{bmatrix} 6 & 1 \\ 3 & 2 \end{bmatrix}$ c. $\begin{bmatrix} 1 & 2 & -1 \\ 2 & 4 & -2 \\ 0 & 1 & 1 \end{bmatrix}$

7–3. Write the following systems of equations in matrix form.

a. $4x - y + z = 14$ b. $2x + 2y = 1$
$\quad x + y - 2z = 12$ $\quad 2x + y = 5$
$\quad\quad y \quad\quad = 7$

7–4. Perform the following matrix operations (if the operations are allowed). Let

$$A = \begin{bmatrix} 7 & -4 \\ 1 & -2 \\ 2 & -1 \end{bmatrix}, \quad B = \begin{bmatrix} 6 & 1 \\ 2 & -3 \end{bmatrix}, \quad C = \begin{bmatrix} 1 & -2 & -1 \\ 0 & 0 & 1 \end{bmatrix}$$

$$a = \begin{bmatrix} 1 \\ 0 \end{bmatrix}, \quad b' = [0 \ 1 \ 1], \quad c = \begin{bmatrix} 1 \\ 4 \\ 3 \end{bmatrix}$$

a. AB   d. cb′
b. Ab′   e. Cc
c. b′c   f. BA

7–5. Suppose that our toy manufacturer in Section 7–2 also makes tricycles, in the same three regions, in red, blue, and yellow. The sales data, in thousands of units, are as follows.

	Region		
Color	I	II	III
Red	6	4	5
Blue	4	3	2
Yellow	4	4	3

Each tricycle makes a contribution (selling price minus variable cost) of $3. If a total of $72 (thousand) fixed cost must be shared equally by the regions, show the matrix arithmetic to obtain the net contribution of each region–color combination. Should they get rid of region–color combinations with negative values in this final matrix?

7–6. a. In Problem 7–5 suppose that the three colors of tricycles sold for $3 (red), $4 (blue), and $5 (yellow). Show that multiplying the matrix of sales by a *row vector*, [3 4 5], gives total revenue from each color to the firm. What is the total revenue over all colors?

b. If the selling price differential was not made by colors but by regions — $3 (region I), $4 (region II), $5 (region III) — what multiplication should be done to obtain total revenue in each region? What is the total revenue in this case?

7–7.   Write the following systems of equations in matrix form.

a. $3x_1 + x_2 - 7x_3 = -14$
   $x_1 - 3x_2 - x_3 = -12$
   $-x_1 + x_2 - 2x_3 = -2$

b. $4a + b + c = 6$
   $2a + 3b + c = 6$
   $a - b + 4c = 3$

7–8.*   A distributor has lost his inventory records, and he does not want to count his inventory (take "physical inventory") until next month. He has three items, and sales of each are denoted x_1, x_2, and x_3; they sell for \$1, \$8, and \$10, respectively. He had 500 units of each as of the last physical inventory. He knows (1) that he has sold a total of 400 units, (2) that he has received total revenue of \$2550, and (3) $4x_2 = x_3$ since he has sold 4 times as many of x_3 as of x_2.

a. Write a system of equations in matrix form that can be solved for x_1, x_2, and x_3.

b. Write a vector equation to determine how many units of inventory he has on hand, using $\begin{bmatrix} x_1 \\ x_2 \\ x_3 \end{bmatrix}$ as one vector.

7–9.*   Perform the following matrix operations (if the operations are allowed). Let

$$A = \begin{bmatrix} 4 & 0 \\ -2 & -2 \end{bmatrix}, \qquad B = \begin{bmatrix} 1 & -1 & 0 \\ 4 & 0 & 3 \end{bmatrix},$$

$$a = \begin{bmatrix} 1 \\ 3 \\ 1 \end{bmatrix}, \qquad b' = [1 \quad -4].$$

a. AB d. aB g. $b'a$
b. BA e. Ba
c. aA f. ab'

7–10.*   Using the inverse, solve the distributor's problem from Problem 7–8. That is, how much inventory does he have of each product?

7–11.*   Find the determinant, transpose, and inverse of the following matrices where possible.

a.
$$A = \begin{bmatrix} 2 & 3 \\ 4 & 6 \end{bmatrix}$$

b.
$$B = \begin{bmatrix} 1 & -2 \\ 1 & 1 \end{bmatrix}$$

c.
$$C = \begin{bmatrix} 1 & 1 & 0 \\ 0 & 0 & 2 \\ 1 & 3 & 0 \end{bmatrix}$$

7–12. In Problem 6–7, four determinants are computed. Which of the associated matrices have inverses? Find those inverses.

*7–13.** In Problem 6–11, you were asked to find the function describing the cost of a patient's stay in the hospital. Set the same problem up in matrix form and solve using the matrix inverse.

7–14. A consumer wishes to buy 7 times as much of product X as product Y and 42 units more of product X than product Y. Using matrix algebra, solve for the units of products X and Y purchased.

*7–15.** A purchasing manager must buy a product, X, which is a mixture of two other products, Y and Z. The cost of X depends on the mixture ordered. The manager wants to know the cost of one unit of X as a (linear) function of the fractions of Y and Z. He has the following data:

Order No.	Cost/Unit of X	Y	Z
1	12.00	0.40	0.60
2	12.75	0.55	0.45

Solve the purchasing manager's problem using matrix algebra.

7–16. The daily cost of operating a hospital, C, is a linear function of the number of in-patients, I, and out-patients, P, plus a fixed cost, a. That is, $C = a + b \cdot P + d \cdot I$. Given the following data from 3 days, find the values of a, b, and d by setting up a linear system of equations and solve using the matrix inverse.

Day	Cost	No. In-Patients: I	No. Out-Patients: P
1	$6950	40	10
2	$6725	35	9
3	$7100	40	12

7–17. In a 2 by 2 system of equations, if one equation is simply a multiple of the other equation, there is an infinite number of solutions. As you may recall, the determinant is then zero, and the inverse does not exist.

a. Verify that $D = 0$ if

$$\mathbf{A} = \begin{bmatrix} a_{11} & a_{12} \\ ca_{11} & ca_{12} \end{bmatrix}$$

where all entries are constants.

b. If, in an n by n system of equations, one equation is a "linear combination" of some others, $D = 0$. A fancy term that applies here is: "The matrix is not of full rank." If $D \neq 0$, the matrix has rank $= n$; it is of full rank. The following 3 by 3 matrix has a third row that equals the first plus the second. Verify that $D = 0$.

$$B = \begin{bmatrix} 1 & -2 & 1 \\ 0 & 2 & 2 \\ 1 & 0 & 3 \end{bmatrix}$$

7–18.* Find the inverse of the following 4 by 4 matrix. (It is designed to help you if you are clever.) Check the answer by multiplying AA^{-1}.

$$A = \begin{bmatrix} 1 & -1 & 0 & 1 \\ 0 & 2 & 0 & 4 \\ 1 & 0 & 0 & 0 \\ 0 & 2 & 1 & 1 \end{bmatrix}$$

7–19. A marketing manager is in charge of a relatively new product. He believes that the demand is, as with the Stumptown Bank, a linear function of advertising and price. He has 3 months of data.

Month	Advertising (in thousands)	Price	Sales (in thousands)
1	10	4	22
2	12	3	26
3	14	3	28

a. What is the manager's best estimate of the demand function? (It will be of the form $a + bA + cp$.)

b. If the manager sets advertising $= 14$ and price $= 5$, what is his forecast of sales?

7-20.* Suppose that the manager in Problem 7–19 believes that sales are growing linearly with time (in addition to the price and advertising effects). The demand function then is of the form:

demand $= a + bA + cp + dt$,   where t is time, in months;

   $t = 1, 2, 3$ are the first 3 months.

a. Their forecast was 24; the actual demand now turns out to be 25. Their 4 months of data now include sales of 22, 26, 28, and 25.

Write the matrix equations, including the time variable and all four data points. Indicate how you would solve for a, b, c, and d.

b. The answers are $a = 24$, $b = \frac{1}{2}$, $c = -2$, and $d = 1$. Check to see that they fit with all four data points.

7–21. A distributor has given three customers a deal on three products. He sold 10 units of product A, 5 units of product B, and 12 units of product C to the first customer for $66. He sold 5, 7, and 10 units of A, B, and C, respectively to the second customer for $54. Finally, the third customer received 6 units of each product for $42. Government regulations require that the distributor make individual product prices known and that the prices be the same for all customers. Solve for the implicit prices he charged to his customers.

7–22.* The Brand Wheat Company has found that the yield of wheat (in bushels) per acre is 100 plus 2 times the pounds of fertilizer 1 added to the ground plus 3 times the pounds of fertilizer 2 added.

a. What is the equation representing yield?

b. The firm has put the following amounts of additives on four plots of ground.

Plot	Additive 1	Additive 2
1	20	20
2	30	20
3	30	30
4	40	30

Find the vector of yields per acre using matrix multiplication.

7–23.* A manufacturing company that produces heavy equipment has found that weekly sales of two similar items are a linear function of personal selling effort (in hours per week) and advertising in a specific trade journal (in column inches). In particular:

$$\text{sales of product } 1 = 2x + 8y,$$
$$\text{sales of product } 2 = 5x + 4y,$$

where $x \equiv$ hours of personal selling and $y \equiv$ inches of advertising.

a. If the company has a sales goal of 100 for product 1 and 120 for product 2, what values of x and y should they choose? Use the inverse technique.

b. They want to increase product 2 sales to 150 while product 1 sales remain the same; what values of x and y should they choose?

c. The firm makes a contribution (selling price less variable cost) of $100 on product 1 and $50 on product 2; personal selling hours cost $20 per hour, and inches of advertising cost $40 each. Which of the two sales goals above lead to a higher value for total contribution less selling and advertising cost (which we call "net contribution")?

7–24. The company in Problem 7-23 is really unsure about their sales goal.

a. If the company's goals are 100 and $120 + a$, where a is any constant, what x and y values should they choose? For what value of a is one of the x, y values driven to zero?

b. If the firm's goals are b for product 1 and c for product 2, where b and c are any constants, what x, y values should they choose?

c. Substitute $b = 100$ and $c = 120$ and check to see that you get $17\frac{1}{2}$ and $8\frac{1}{8}$.

7–25.* A gasoline producer has a basic regular gasoline to which the firm adds two high performance additives. They try three blends, with the following results.

Amount of Additive 1	Amount of Additive 2	Amount of Octane Rating
2	3	100
3	3	102
1	1	94

(The additive numbers are in cubic centimeters per gallon.) The firm believes that the additives relate to octane rating linearly; what is the linear relationship? (*Hint:* Do not forget to include the constant term for the octane rating of the basic gasoline.)

8

Inequalities and
Linear Programming

The All-Sports Trophy Manufacturing Company makes two types of trophies in their large trophy department. Both types are large and relatively expensive, but they are not identical. Trophy type 1 has a contribution to profit (sales price less variable cost) of $20, and trophy type 2 has a contribution to profit of $30. The company has two machines, and both trophies require time on both machines. Trophy type 1 requires 3 hours on machine 1 and 4 hours on machine 2. Trophy type 2 requires 4 hours on machine 1 but only 2 hours on machine 2. The company operates each of these machines 40 hours per week, but if it had more time available every additional unit made could be sold. The company has recently had greater demand than it can satisfy.

The president would like to know how many of each type of trophy the company should make. He also has been considering adding overtime on either or both machines, up to 8 hours additional time on each. If each additional overtime hour on either machine costs $6, how much time should be added? Also, how much contribution to profit does the firm make in 1 week from this department's operation?

This problem is not a problem of solving equations, but one of dealing with inequalities. The firm has 40 hours of usable regular time on each machine. The firm can use no more than this amount, but they could use less. No more than 8 hours of overtime can be used on each machine, but the president could decide to use less. These ideas are summarized in the following inequalities.

$$\text{regular time on machine } 1 \leq 40$$
$$\text{regular time on machine } 2 \leq 40$$
$$\text{overtime on machine } 1 \leq 8$$
$$\text{overtime on machine } 2 \leq 8$$

Regular time on machine 1, for example, must involve the facts that trophy type 1 requires 3 hours of machine 1 time per unit and trophy type 2 requires 4 hours of machine 1 time per unit. The overtime constraints have similar interpretations. Finally the company must satisfy all the inequalities, and it wishes to maximize the contribution of these products to profits. In fancy language, the firm wishes to maximize contribution subject to several constraints on available machine time.

The problem looks, and is, complicated. However, by the end of this chapter we will be able to solve this problem and other similar ones. Before we can solve the trophy company's problem, we must learn how to work with inequalities.

8-1 INEQUALITIES

A set of mathematical relations that are very important, although not so important as the equality relationship, is the set of inequality relations. These are shown below, to refresh your memory of Chapter 1.

Symbol	English Translation
$<$	less than
$\leq$	less than or equal to (no more than)
$>$	greater than
$\geq$	greater than or equal to (no less than)

The inequality relations can be used to place a set of numbers in a precise order. For example, the following set of numbers is ordered using $<$:

$$-3, 1, 4, 7, 8.$$

Any two real numbers can have one or more of the inequalities applied to them. We can, as examples, answer the following questions. Is

(1) $5 < 6$?	Yes.
(2) $6 < 5$?	No.
(3) $5 < 5$?	No.
(4) $5 \leq 5$?	Yes.
(5) $5 \geq 5$?	Yes.
(6) $4 \leq 5$?	Yes.

The last three relations are worth further discussion. The question asked in (4) is: Is 5 less than or equal to 5? In other words, is 5 either less than or equal to 5; is 5 no more than 5? The answer is yes; since $5 = 5$, it is also true that $5 \leq 5$. Question (5) is similar, but what about question (6)? Is 4 either less than or equal to 5? Is 4 no more than 5? Yes, since 4 is less than 5, it is no more than 5.

These relations often cause difficulty. Some persons try to read $\geq$ (for example) as greater than *and* equal to. But both conditions cannot hold simultaneously. The "or" type of relations ($\leq$, $\geq$) require that one and only one of the two situations, $<$ or $=$ in the case of $\leq$, hold. It is exactly analogous to pointing at a hedgetoad and saying: "Is that either a hedgetoad or a hippopotamus?" The answer is yes, it is. Since it is a hedgetoad it is "either a hedgetoad or a hippopotamus."

Inequalities do not have to be applied to ordinary numbers since we usually know their order. Some more complicated inequalities are as follows. Is

(1)	$15^{1/2} < 4$?	Yes.
(2)	$2.5^2 < 6$?	No.
(3)	$x^2 \geq 0$?	Yes (always).
(4)	$x > 10$?	Sometimes.
(5)	$x \geq 7$?	Sometimes.

The last three inequalities involve variables rather than constants. Whereas inequalities involving only numbers either hold or do not hold, inequalities involving variables can hold "sometimes." In the latter cases, we must specify (or be told) for what values of the variables the relations hold.

Inequalities involving a variable(s), and which hold for some values of the variable(s) but not others, are called *conditional inequalities.*

Inequalities involving a variable(s), and which hold for all values of the variable(s), are called *absolute inequalities.*

For example, using numbers (3), (4), and (1) from the above list of inequalities:

(3) $x^2 \geq 0$ is an absolute inequality; it holds for all real numbers.

(4) $x > 10$ is a conditional inequality; it holds (only) for all values of x greater than 10.

(1) $15^{1/2} < 4$ does not involve a variable. It is an inequality that always holds.

As the final topic of this section, before discussing the solution of inequalities, we discuss inequality-preserving operations. As with equalities, the phrase "inequality-preserving operation" means something we can do to an inequality without upsetting or changing it. Since inequalities are fussier fellows than equalities, the list of things we can do to them is shorter.

Inequality-Preserving Operations

1. We may add (subtract) the same quantity to (from) both sides.

2. We may multiply (divide) both sides by the same *positive* number.

If both sides of the inequality are always positive:

3. We may raise both sides to the same positive power.

4. We may take the logarithm of both sides.

If two inequalities are of the same type ($\leq$, $<$, $\geq$, or $>$):

5. We may add (but not subtract) the inequalities and obtain an inequality of the same type.

Operations 3 through 5 illustrate some of the difficulties in dealing with inequalities. We had to put so many qualifiers in the statements that these operations are not so useful as their counterparts in equality-preserving operations.

Actually, operation 2 also displays this difficulty, since the qualifier "positive" must be included. Let us try these operations on two examples.

	(*i*) $3 < 4$	(*ii*) $3x < 4x$	(*for* $x > 0$)
(*a*) add 5	$8 < 9$? Yes.	$3x + 5 < 4x + 5$?	Yes, for $x > 0$.
(*b*) multiply by 5	$15 < 20$? Yes.	$15x < 20x$?	Yes, for $x > 0$.
(*c*) multiply by -1	$-3 < -4$? No.	$-3x < -4x$?	No; holds only for $x < 0$.
(*d*) raise to the 2 power	$9 < 16$? Yes.	$9x^2 < 16x^2$?	Yes.
(*e*) raise to the -2 power	$\dfrac{1}{9} < \dfrac{1}{16}$? No.	$\dfrac{1}{9x^2} < \dfrac{1}{16x^2}$?	No.

Part (c) leads us to the following conclusion.

Multiplying both sides of an inequality by the same *negative* number reverses the "sense" of the inequality. (Changing the "sense" means changing the direction in which the sign points; the relation $>$ replaces $<$, $\geq$ replaces $\leq$ or vice versa.)

For example:

$3 < 4$ holds, so, multiplying by -1, $-3 > -4$ holds.

$-1 \leq 0$ holds, so, multiplying by -1, $1 \geq 0$ holds.

A complete outline of what raising to powers does to an inequality is compli-cated enough that we will not go into it. The five inequality-preserving opera-tions, coupled with the (important) rule for multiplying by a negative number, are sufficient for nearly all managerial applications of inequalities.

1. Order the following set of numbers using $\leq$.
   $\{1, -4, 5, -1, 3, 104\}$ $\{\underline{\hspace{0.4cm}}, \underline{\hspace{0.4cm}}, \underline{\hspace{0.4cm}}, \underline{\hspace{0.4cm}}, \underline{\hspace{0.4cm}}, \underline{\hspace{0.4cm}}\}$

2. Which of the following inequalities hold?
   (a) $4 \leq 4$ Yes_____   No_____   (d) $42 > 4$ Yes_____   No_____
   (b) $7 \leq 10$ Yes_____   No_____   (e) $-7 < -1$ Yes_____   No_____
   (c) $1 > 0$ Yes_____   No_____   (f) $7 < 1$ Yes_____   No_____

3. Circle those of the following inequalities that hold. Correct any that are incorrect. Assume that $2x < 3y - 1$. Start with (a) and work on one at a time.
   (a) $2x \leq 3y - 1$ (e) $-2x > -3y$
   (b) $2x - 5 \leq 3y - 6$ (f) $-2x < -3y + 1$
   (c) $2x - 6 \leq 3y - 6$ (g) $-2x > 3y - 1$
   (d) $2x < 3y$ (h) $x < \frac{3}{2}y - \frac{1}{2}$

Answers

1. $\{-4, -1, 1, 3, 5, 104\}$.
2. All except part (f) hold; $+7$ is not less than $+1$.
3. If $2x < 3y - 1$ holds, $2x \leq 3y - 1$ holds. In part (b), 5 is subtracted from both sides, and it holds. In part (c), the left side is reduced still further, and the equality continues to be valid. In (d), we increase the right (larger) side of $2x < 3y - 1$, so the inequality still holds. If (d) holds, (e) holds using the rule for multiplying by a negative number (-1). Part (f) does not hold. It should read $-2x > -3y + 1$. We cannot be sure that (g) holds since only one side was multiplied by -1. Dividing the original inequality by 2, part (h) holds. Parts (f) and (g) are the only incorrect parts.

8-2 SOLVING INEQUALITIES IN ONE UNKNOWN

Solving an inequality means finding the region in which it holds, in other words, finding the set of real numbers for which it is true. For $x \geq 10$, the region where it holds is, not surprisingly, for x values greater than or equal to 10. Unfortunately, most inequalities are not this easy to solve. In this section we consider only conditional inequalities in one unknown: that is,

$$f(x) \geq 0, \quad f(x) > 0, \quad f(x) < 0, \quad f(x) \leq 0.$$

All inequalities can be written in standard form with zero to the right of the symbol. Thus $x \geq 10$ becomes $x - 10 \geq 0$ in standard form.

A conditional inequality in one variable can be graphed on a straight line, and this will often be useful in solving an inequality. For example, Figure 8–1 shows several graphs of conditional inequalities in one variable.

FIGURE 8–1

Graphs of Four Inequalities

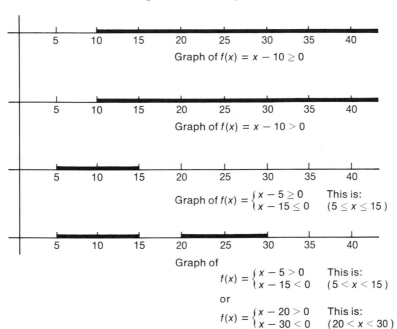

The line segments $x - 10 > 0$ and $x - 10 \geq 0$ cannot be distinguished from each other. In all four graphs, regions where the inequalities hold are the darkened portions of the lines. Equalities of the type $x - y \geq 0$ can also be graphed, but we will defer that to the next section.

The method for solving conditional inequalities begins with the solution of an equation. In particular, we always first solve as if the inequality were an equality; that is, we find x such that $f(x) = 0$. The x values found will separate the horizontal line on the graph into regions where the inequality holds and regions where it does not hold. The method is spelled out below.

Method for Solving Conditional Inequalities

1. Given an inequality, write it in standard form using inequality-preserving operations.

2. Solve for all x values such that $f(x) = 0$ (if there are any). Mark those values on a line as was done in Figure 8–1. Thus the line is broken into segments by these x values.

3. For one point in each segment, evaluate $f(x)$. If the inequality holds for the point chosen, it holds for the entire segment. [The line segments where the inequality holds are thus identified. If $f(x) = 0$ never occurs, the inequality holds everywhere or nowhere and testing one point will tell you which.]

For most cases, you need evaluate $f(x)$ only for one segment. The inequality alternately holds and does not hold for the segments found in step 2. [There are occasional exceptions to this. If when $f(x) = 0$, $f(x)$ touches, but does not cross (is tangent to) the x axis, the regions will not alternate at that point.]

For an example, suppose that a company has a selling price for a particular product of $5 per unit. The variable cost of production is $3 per unit, and they have fixed costs of $1,000. They would like to know the values of sales that will give them some positive profit. They want to find

$$f(x) = 5x - 3x - 1{,}000 > 0,$$

where $x \equiv$ units sold.

Step 1.   Solve as an equality:

$$5x - 3x - 1{,}000 = 0$$
$$x = 500.$$

Step 2.   Evaluate in the regions implied:

For $x < 500$, try $x = 0$. $\qquad$ $f(x) = -1{,}000.$
For $x > 500$, try $x = 1{,}000$. $\qquad$ $f(x) = +1{,}000.$

The inequality holds for $x > 500$.

But, you say, "that's just the breakeven point, and any dummy knows that the more sales the better. There is an easier way to solve this problem." You are right, and you should use that easier way whenever possible. There is not always an easier way available. Suppose that, for example, the firm has low variable costs initially, and that as space becomes limited, costs begin to rise. In particular, for the same firm, suppose that variable cost per unit is given by

$$c(x) = 1 + 0.001x.$$

Then they want to find x values such that

$$f(x) = 5x - (1 + 0.001x)x - 1,000 \geq 0.$$

Step 1. $f(x) = 0 = 4x - 0.001x^2 - 1,000.$

Solving using the quadratic formula (and using the fact that $\sqrt{12} = 3.464$), we obtain $x = 268$ and $x = 3,732$.

Step 2.
$$\text{at } x = 0, f(x) = -1,000;$$
$$\text{at } x = 500, f(x) = +750;$$
$$\text{at } x = 10,000, f(x) = -61,000.$$

The inequality holds for $268 < x < 3,732$.

The company will make money if sales are between 268 and 3,732. If sales are above 3,732, they lose money. In Chapter 12 we will discuss how to find the value of sales that will maximize profits.

✓ : Find and graph on the lines provided the regions where the following inequalities hold.

1. $x + 7 > 4x - 17$
2. $2x^2 + 4x + 6 > x^2 + 10 + 4x$
3. $x^2 - 1 \leq 0$
4. $x^2 - 2x + 1 \leq 0$

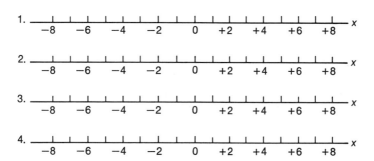

Answers

1. $x < 8$
2. $x^2 - 4 = 0$ at $x = +2$ and $x = -2$. This inequality holds for $x < -2$ and $x > +2$.
3. $-1 \leq x \leq +1$ [Note that $\leq$ is used here, and $<$ is used in parts (1) and (2).]
4. This is greater than zero in both regions. It equals zero at $x = +1$. Thus the inequality holds for (only) $x = +1$.

FIGURE 8–2

Graphs of Inequalities

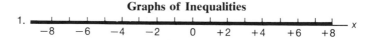

8-3 SYSTEMS OF LINEAR INEQUALITIES

Just as with equalities, some very important managerial problems involve not one inequality in one unknown, but several inequalities in several unknowns. For example, there are two unknowns in the All-Sports Trophy Manufacturing Company problem: how many units of trophy type 1 to make, and how many units of trophy type 2 to make. There are also several inequalities.

The easiest way to work simple problems involving no more than two unknowns is to graph them. This is the method we will use to resolve the All-Sports Company's problem. However, before tackling their problem, let's try graphing an easier example. Consider

$$x \geq y.$$

Does this relation hold if:

$x = 1$ and $y = 1$? Yes;

$x = 1$ and $y = 0$? Yes;

$x = 1$ and $y = 2$? No.

We can represent the points where it holds graphically. The area where the relation holds is the lined area in Figure 8–3. The method for drawing such graphs is given next.

FIGURE 8–3

Graph of $x \geq y$

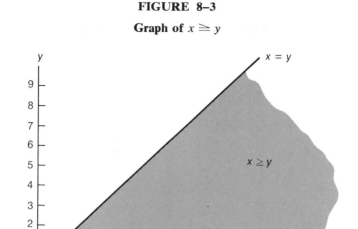

To plot a linear inequality in two unknowns, draw the line representing the relationship as though it were an equality. The inequality holds for all points on one side of the line and for no points on the other side. Evaluate the inequality for one point (not on the line) to determine which side is which. (After a while you will know which side is which without evaluating anything.)

The same graph can be used to plot more than one inequality. The region where all these inequalities are satisfied simultaneously can then be identified, if it exists. For example, let us plot $y \geq 0$ and $x \leq 5$ on a picture that has $x \geq y$ already graphed. This is shown in Figure 8–4.

The darkly shaded region shows the only area where $x \geq y$, $y \geq 0$, and $x \leq 5$ are all simultaneously satisfied. Any point in that region satisfies all three inequalities. The unmarked regions show areas where two inequalities are simultaneously satisfied, and the dotted areas show regions where only one inequality holds. (There is no area where none of the inequalities is satisfied.) If we have a problem where several inequalities hold, simultaneously, the region where all are simultaneously satisfied (the darkly shaded area in Figure 8–4) is called the *solution space*.

FIGURE 8–4

Simultaneous Inequalities: $x \geq y;\ y \geq 0;$ **and** $x \leq 5$

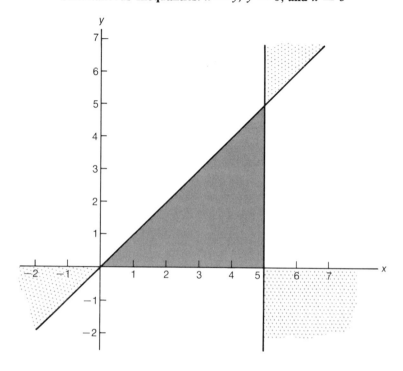

Given a set of m linear inequalities in n unknowns, the region where all inequalities are simultaneously satisfied (if it exists) is called the *solution space*.

There are several useful and even interesting facts about a solution space formed by linear inequalities. They are:

   i. If you pick any two points in the solution space, the entire line segment between the two points is within the solution space. (A region of this type is called *convex*.)

  ii. The boundary of the space is composed entirely of straight lines, which change direction at places called *corner points*. The corner points are the intersection of some number (two in Figure 8–4) of equations; that is, a corner point in Figure 8–4 is where two of the inequalities simultaneously hold as equalities. In a problem involving two unknowns we may have a point defined by the intersection of two inequalities, but the point of intersection is not in the solution space. These points are called "potential corner points" and they do not belong to the solution space. Examples are shown in Figure 8–5.

iii. There might be an inequality that does not affect the solution space. For example, if $x \leq 1$, then it is of no value to *also* say that $x \leq 2$. The latter constraint is a *redundant constraint.*

iv. It is possible for the solution space to be empty. The simultaneous satisfaction of the inequalities $x > 7$ and $x \leq 6$ is not possible.

Allow us now to add three constraints to the problem graphed in Figure 8–4. The three new constraints are

$$x + y \leq 8,$$
$$x + y \geq 2,$$

and

$$x \qquad \geq 0.$$

The new picture is shown in Figure 8–5.

FIGURE 8–5

Simultaneous Inequalities:

$$x \geq y;\ y \geq 0;\ x \leq 5;\ x + y \leq 8;\ x + y \geq 2;\ x \geq 0$$

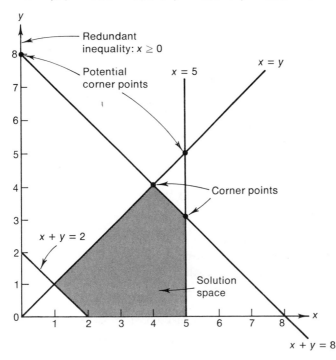

In Figure 8–5 we have represented the following inequalities. (The redundant constraint, $x \geq 0$, has been deleted.)

$$
\begin{array}{lll}
x \geq y & \text{or} & -x + y \leq 0 \\
x \leq 5 & & x \quad\;\; \leq 5 \\
y \geq 0 & & -y \leq 0 \\
x + y \leq 8 & & x + y \leq 8 \\
x + y \geq 2 & & -x - y \leq -2.
\end{array}
$$

All the corner points, in this example, can be obtained by solving the five inequalities two at a time as equations. Some points so found are not in the solution space. For example, the point $x = y = 5$ is not in the solution space, and it is a "potential corner point." The point where $x = y$ and $x + y = 8$, on the other hand, is in the solution space. See if you can identify these two points on the graph. Also, check the four facts given above regarding solutions spaces using the graph in Figure 8–5.

We now have five inequalities in two unknowns. The system of linear inequalities can be written using matrix notation:

$$
\begin{bmatrix}
-1 & +1 \\
1 & 0 \\
0 & -1 \\
1 & 1 \\
-1 & -1
\end{bmatrix}
\begin{bmatrix} x \\ y \end{bmatrix}
\leq
\begin{bmatrix}
0 \\ 5 \\ 0 \\ 8 \\ -2
\end{bmatrix}
\qquad \text{or} \qquad \mathbf{Ax} \leq \mathbf{b},
$$

where $\mathbf{A}$, $\mathbf{x}$, and $\mathbf{b}$ are defined as the three matrices in the brackets. Any system of m linear inequalities in n unknowns can be written in matrix form.

Now let's see if we can write the All-Sports Trophy Manufacturing Company's problem using inequalities. For the moment we will not consider the overtime question; we will solve the problem using only regular time. Let

$x \equiv$ number of trophies of type 1 they produce per week,

$y \equiv$ number of trophies of type 2 they produce per week.

These two variables are the decision variables. We want to write the inequalities using them. Each unit of x uses 3 hours of machine 1 time and 4 hours of machine 2 time. Each unit of y uses 4 hours on machine 1 and 2 hours on machine 2. Thus recalling that we have only 40 hours of time available on each machine, we have

total time required of machine 1 $= 3x + 4y \leq 40$,

total time required of machine 2 $= 4x + 2y \leq 40$.

This is an important step. Be sure you understand it. We now have

$$3x + 4y \leq 40,$$
$$4x + 2y \leq 40,$$
$$x \qquad \geq 0,$$
$$y \geq 0.$$

These last two inequalities tell us that we cannot produce a negative number of trophies (that seems logical). They are additional constraints. The four inequality constraints faced by the All-Sports Trophy Company are shown in Figure 8–6. The solution space is the shaded area. Only points in this area meet all the constraints placed on the firm.

FIGURE 8–6

**Graph of the All-Sports Trophy Problem:
Solution Space**

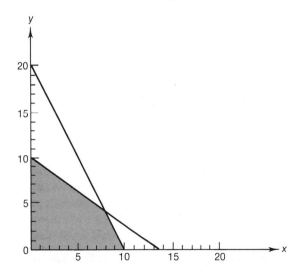

There is one other facet to this problem. We need to express the firm's objective in functional form. We recall that they wish to maximize the contribution made by these products. Since the firm makes a $20 contribution on each trophy type 1 and $30 on each trophy type 2, they wish to:

$$\text{maximize:} \quad 20x + 30y$$

$$\text{subject to:} \quad 3x + 4y \leq 40,$$
$$4x + 2y \leq 40,$$
$$x \qquad \geq 0,$$
$$y \geq 0.$$

In this form the problem is called a linear programming (L.P.) formulation. It starts with a function stating the objective and continues with a set of inequality constraints. Further, all the relations are linear in form. In the next section we deal (very briefly) with how optimal solutions to linear programming problems are found.

A linear programming formulation can also be written in matrix form. (This discussion, and other references to matrix form, can be skipped without losing continuity.) For example, the All-Sports problem can be written:

$$\text{maximize:} \quad \mathbf{c}'\mathbf{x}$$

$$\text{subject to:} \quad \mathbf{Ax} \leq \mathbf{b},$$
$$\mathbf{x} \geq \mathbf{0},$$

where

$$\mathbf{c}' = [20 \ 30],$$

$$\mathbf{x} = \begin{bmatrix} x \\ y \end{bmatrix},$$

$$\mathbf{A} = \begin{bmatrix} 3 & 4 \\ 4 & 2 \end{bmatrix},$$

$$\mathbf{b} = \begin{bmatrix} 40 \\ 40 \end{bmatrix},$$

and $\mathbf{0}$ is a vector containing all zeros, $\begin{bmatrix} 0 \\ 0 \end{bmatrix}$ in this case.

The $\mathbf{x} \geq \mathbf{0}$ constraints are always necessary; they are written separately. The problem now is to choose $\mathbf{x}$ to make $\mathbf{c}'\mathbf{x}$ as large as possible while satisfying $\mathbf{Ax} \leq \mathbf{b}$ and $\mathbf{x} \geq \mathbf{0}$. In terms of the graph in Figure 8–6, we wish to find the point in the shaded area that makes $20x + 30y$ as large as possible.

1. Identify the corner points in the All-Sports problem (there are four). All four are the intersection of two constraints solved as equalities. For example, $x = 0$, $y = 0$ is one corner point. Solve for the other three corner points, each as the solution to two equations in two unknowns.

(*a*) _____ (*b*) _____ (*c*) _____

2. Draw a solution space for the following systems of inequalities:

$$2x + y \le 5,$$
$$x + 2y \le 6,$$
$$x + y \le 4,$$
$$x \ge 0,$$
$$y \ge 0.$$

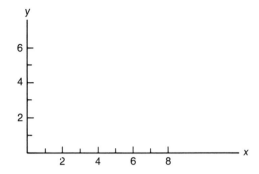

Identify and solve for the corner points. Identify any redundant constraints.

Answers

1. The corner points are the corners of the solution space in Figure 8–6. The points are $x = 0, y = 0$ (solution of $x = 0, y = 0$); $x = 0, y = 10$ (solution of $x = 0$, $3x + 4y = 40$); $x = 10$, $y = 0$ (solution of $4x + 2y = 40$, $y = 0$); and $x = 8, y = 4$ (solution of $3x + 4y = 40, 4x + 2y = 40$).

2.

FIGURE 8–7

Solution Space for Problem 2

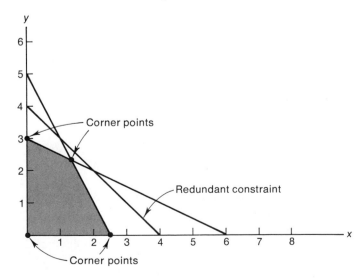

The corner points and corresponding equations are:

$$x = 0, \quad y = 0 \qquad (x = 0, y = 0)$$
$$x = 0, \quad y = 3 \qquad (x = 0, x + 2y = 6)$$
$$x = 2\tfrac{1}{2}, y = 0 \qquad (2x + y = 5, y = 0)$$
$$x = 1\tfrac{1}{3}, y = 2\tfrac{1}{3} \qquad (2x + y = 5, x + 2y = 6)$$

8-4 LINEAR PROGRAMMING

In the previous section we wrote the All-Sports Trophy Manufacturing Company's problem as:

$$\text{maximize:} \quad 20x + 30y$$

$$\text{subject to:} \quad 3x + 4y \le 40,$$
$$4x + 2y \le 40,$$
$$x \quad\quad\ge 0,$$
$$y \ge 0.$$

The solution space was graphed in Figure 8–6. There is an infinite number of points in the solution space. How do we choose one? The following statement, which we cannot prove here, makes the choice of an optimal point less difficult.

An optimal solution to any linear programming problem is found at a corner point.

That sounds easy enough. There are only four corner points in the All-Sports problem. We can evaluate the objective function at each of them.

Corner Point	*Value of Objective Function*
$x = 0, \quad y = 0$	0
$x = 10, y = 0$	$20(10) + 0 = \$200$
$x = 0, \quad y = 10$	$0 + 30(10) = \$300$ (maximum)
$x = 8, \quad y = 4$	$8(20) + 4(30) = \$280$

There are also two potential corner points ($x = 13\tfrac{1}{3}$, $y = 0$ and $x = 0$, $y = 20$), but they can be rejected because they are not in the solution space. For example, $x = 0$, $y = 20$ breaks the constraint $3x + 4y \le 40$. The All-Sports Trophy Company should produce 10 units of trophy type 2 per week and no trophy type 1 units. Let's see if they have any unused machine time. Substituting the optimal answer into the machine constraint inequalities gives

$3(0) + 4(10) = 40$ All time on machine 1 is used.
$4(0) + 2(10) = 20$ Only 20 hours on machine 2 is used.
   Twenty hours are unused.

Now let's answer the question of whether the firm should add any overtime. How many units of overtime should the firm add on machine 2? None! One does not need to know linear programming to know that if there is unused machine time already, overtime should not be used.

Should the firm use any of the 8 hours of overtime on machine 1? If they use all 8 hours, they must pay $8 \times \$6 = \$48$ additional cost ($6 is the per hour cost of overtime). The firm can produce two more trophies in 8 hours, so they would obtain $60 ($30 per trophy) at a cost of $48. The two additional trophies require a total of 4 additional hours on machine 2, but this creates no problem since there are 20 hours of unused time available. Hence the firm should use 8 hours of overtime on machine 1, and they should produce a total of 12 trophies of type 1 per week. The company will make $300 + (60 - 48)$ or $312 per week.

Well, you thought we would never make it but here we are at last. We have solved a product-choice problem, a classic application of linear programming. We solved it by examining corner points. For a two-unknown problem, that method will work for either $\leq$ or $\geq$ constraints and for either maximization or minimization problems.

The corner-point idea also forms the basis for a more general mathematical technique, called the *simplex method*, that will give an optimal solution, if one exists, to any linear programming problem. The computer does all the calculating. The important task for a manager is to formulate the problem. A linear programming problem contains a linear objective function and a set of linear constraints; the constraints can include some $\leq$, some $\geq$, and even some $=$ constraints. The objective can be to maximize or to minimize the linear objective function. Once the problem is formulated the computer program, which someone else has written for you, does nearly all the remaining work. A general version of a linear programming formulation can be written in matrix form as:

maximize or minimize: $\mathbf{c'x}$

subject to: $\mathbf{A_1 x} \leq \mathbf{b_1},$
           $\mathbf{A_2 x} \geq \mathbf{b_2},$
           $\mathbf{A_3 x} = \mathbf{b_3},$
           $\mathbf{x} \geq \mathbf{0}.$

(A_1, A_2, and A_3 are different matrices; b_1, b_2, and b_3 are different vectors. In any problem, some of these may not be necessary.)

You will probably learn more about the computer solution of linear programming problems in other courses or books. We will deal with small problems here that can be solved graphically. Graphical solution is more intuitive and will hopefully increase our basic grasp of linear programming problems. Thus we can recognize opportunities for applying this powerful technique. Three examples are used to illustrate graphical solution of linear programming problems.

(i) Maximize y subject to   *(ii) Maximize x subject to*   *(iii) Maximize 2x + y subject to*

$$x + y \leq 4,$$
$$2x - y \leq 4,$$
$$x \quad\;\; \geq 0,$$
$$y \geq 0.$$

$$x + y \leq 4,$$
$$2x - y \leq 4,$$
$$x \quad\;\; \geq 0,$$
$$y \geq 0.$$

$$x + y \leq 4,$$
$$2x - y \leq 4,$$
$$x \quad\;\; \geq 0,$$
$$y \geq 0.$$

All three problems have the same constraints and thus the same solution space. The solution space is graphed as the shaded area in Figure 8–8.

FIGURE 8–8

Solution Space for $x + y \leq 4$; $2x - y \leq 4$; $x \geq 0$; $y \geq 0$

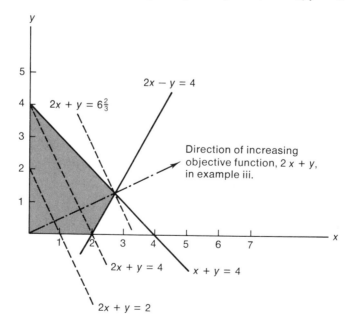

Consider example (i) first. What is the maximum value of y? $y = 4$. That's easy. You simply find the highest point in the solution space. Now try example (ii). What is the maximum value of x? $x = 2\frac{2}{3}$. This is also easy (although you may not be able to read the graph that closely).

Now comes the hard part. What is the maximum value of $2x + y$? Is it 2? That is, is $2x + y = 2$ the maximum? The line $2x + y = 2$ is plotted in Figure 8–8. But so is $2x + y = 4$, and it has some points that are in the solution space. Hence we can at least get $2x + y = 4$. We have improved on a value of 2 by moving up and to the right. Why not continue to do so? In fact, plot lines $2x + y = c$, for different c values, until you cannot increase c any further without leaving the solution space. Rather than plot the lines, we will simply use a pencil as the line, and move it in a direction such that it remains parallel to $2x + y = 2$ and $2x + y = 4$, until any further movement would cause the pencil to be entirely out of the solution space. This usually happens when the pencil touches the solution space at a corner point. That is the optimum. It occurs at $x = 2\frac{2}{3}$, $y = 1\frac{1}{3}$, as shown. The optimal solution then is $2(2\frac{2}{3}) + (1\frac{1}{3})$, or $6\frac{2}{3}$. Do you see intuitively why the solution occurred at a corner point? (It is possible for the line representing the objective function to be parallel to one of the constraints and lie along it when optimization occurs. In this case, two corner points and all points on the line segment connecting them are optimal.)

Graphical Technique for Solving Linear Programming Problems in Two Unknowns

1. Plot the solution space. (If there is no solution space, that is, points where all constraints are simultaneously satisfied, there is no solution.)
2. Plot the objective function, $f(x, y) = c$, for some value c such that part of the line falls in the solution space.
3. (*a*) Maximization Problems. Plot the objective function for $c + \Delta$ ($\Delta = $ a small amount). Keeping your pencil parallel to these lines, move it in the direction of increasing objective function: that is from c to $c + \Delta$ and beyond, until any further movement causes the pencil (and hence the line representing the objective function) to leave the solution space entirely. The last point touched (or any one of the last points touched) is the optimal solution.

   (*b*) Minimization Problems. Plot the objective function for $c - \Delta$. Move your pencil in that direction until, as above, the line would leave the solution space. The last point (or points) in the solution space that also falls on the objective function line is the optimal solution.

Let's illustrate the technique for a new problem already in linear programming form. Suppose we wish to:

minimize: $3x + y$

subject to: $x + y \geq 2,$
$2x - y \geq 1,$
$x \qquad \geq 0,$
$y \geq 0.$

The solution space is shaded in Figure 8–9. It extends to infinity in the first quadrant. (Note that $y \geq 0$ is a redundant constraint in this problem.)

FIGURE 8–9

Minimization Problem

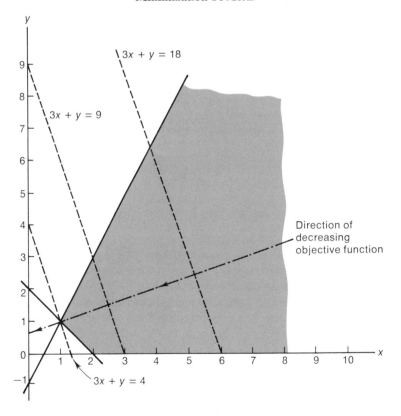

Instead of moving up and to the right, the lines leading to a decrease of the objective function (say, cost) move down and to the left. The optimal solution occurs at the corner point $x = 1, y = 1$, where the objective function equals $3(1) + 1$ or 4. The minimization problem does not present any additional difficulties.

The reader should not expect to feel completely at ease with linear programming after this cursory introduction. However, after doing some problems he should have a better idea about how and when to use linear programming. The details can be studied again, and the computer is on our side when it comes to working out a problem, believe it or not. We conclude this chapter and the algebra portion of the text by asking you to work another applied linear programming problem.

$\sim\!\!\curvearrowright$: A local marketing manager is considering purchasing time on radio and television. Each "spot" on radio costs $100, and he wants the number of spots to be between 5 and 15. Each TV spot costs $500 and he wants the number of spots to be between 2 and 8. Each radio spot reaches 5,000 people; each TV spot reaches 20,000 people. He wants to send the message to as many people as possible (he is not concerned that some of the messages are duplicate messages), subject to spending no more than $3,000.

1. Formulate the linear programming problem. Write it in matrix form.
2. Draw the solution space. Indicate the corner points, including any potential corner points that are not in the solution space.
3. Solve the manager's problem; indicate both his decisions and the value of the objective function.

Answers

1. Let $x \equiv$ radio spots and $y \equiv$ TV spots. The manager's problem is:

$$\text{maximize:} \quad 5{,}000x + 20{,}000y$$

$$\text{subject to:} \quad 100x + 500y \leq 3{,}000,$$
$$x \qquad\quad \leq 15,$$
$$x \qquad\quad \geq 5,$$
$$y \leq 8,$$
$$y \geq 2.$$

($x \geq 0$, $y \geq 0$ are not needed since we have $x \geq 5$, $y \geq 2$.)

Figure 8–10 portrays the solution space; you can see that $y \leq 8$ is a redundant constraint.

If we write

$$\mathbf{A}_1 = \begin{bmatrix} 100 & 500 \\ 1 & 0 \\ 0 & 1 \end{bmatrix}, \quad \mathbf{b}_1 = \begin{bmatrix} 3{,}000 \\ 15 \\ 8 \end{bmatrix}, \quad \mathbf{A}_2 = \begin{bmatrix} 1 & 0 \\ 0 & 1 \end{bmatrix}, \quad \mathbf{b}_2 = \begin{bmatrix} 5 \\ 2 \end{bmatrix}$$

$$\mathbf{x} = \begin{bmatrix} x \\ y \end{bmatrix}, \quad \mathbf{c}' = [5{,}000 \quad 20{,}000],$$

then the problem can be written as:

$$\text{maximize:} \quad \mathbf{c}'\mathbf{x}$$

$$\text{subject to:} \quad \mathbf{A}_1\mathbf{x} \leq \mathbf{b}_1,$$
$$\mathbf{A}_2\mathbf{x} \geq \mathbf{b}_2.$$

FIGURE 8–10

Media Problem Solution Space

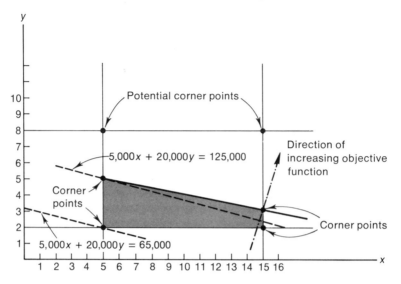

3. The lines $5,000x + 20,000y = 65,000$ and $= 125,000$ are shown. Continuing to move up to the right we will reach $5,000x + 20,000y = 135,000$ at $x = 15, y = 3$. We could also obtain this solution by evaluating the objective function at the four corner points.

8-5 SUMMARY

Inequalities are a very important mathematical relation for managerial applications of mathematics. This chapter studies the four basic inequality relations, $\leq$, $\geq$, $<$, and $>$. An absolute equality is one that always holds. A conditional inequality is one that holds for some, but not all, values of the unknown(s). Solving for the values where the inequality holds is often important.

One inequality in one unknown, $f(x) \leq 0$ for example, is solved by finding x values where $f(x) = 0$; this identifies potential regions where the inequality can be tested. Systems of inequalities in more than one unknown lead to regions where they hold simultaneously. In a system of linear inequalities involving two unknowns, the region, if it exists, where the inequalities hold simultaneously can be graphed. The region where two or more inequalities hold simultaneously is called a *solution space*. Corner points are points on the boundary of the solution space where the boundary changes direction.

Linear programming makes a linear objective function as large (or small) as possible, subject to staying within a solution space defined by a set of simultaneous linear inequality constraints. An optimal solution always occurs at one of the corner points. If there are only two unknowns, we can find the solution by graphing the solution space and either checking the objective function value at all corner points or using the "pencil (graphical) technique." For larger problems, we can concentrate on formulating the problem, then let a computer do the calculations for us.

Many optimization problems in managerial situations involve nonlinear functions and constraints. More complex techniques are required to solve such problems. However, often these problems can be adequately approximated in the region of interest by linear equations and inequalities, and linear programming may give a sufficiently accurate solution. Owing to the relatively greater cost of the more sophisticated techniques, this fact is very important. It remains the responsibility of the manager to decide if the linear programming approximation is adequate.

PROBLEMS

Problems for Self-Study: 2, 6, 8, 11, 14, 15

8–1. Order the following sets of numbers using $>$.
  a. $14, 0.5, \frac{3}{4}, \sqrt{2}, -8, 1$
  b. $2, 3, 4, 7, 14, -1$
  c. $\sqrt{2}, \sqrt{3}, \pi, 3$

8–2. Which of the following statements are correct?
  a. $1000 < 4$ e. $x \geq 1$
  b. $1000 \leq 4$ f. $x^2 \geq 0$
  c. $2 \leq 4$ g. $x^2 \geq 1$
  d. $2 \geq 2$ h. $x^2 + 1 \geq 1$

8–3. Assume that $x \geq 2$. Which of the following inequalities follow from that assumption? State which inequality-preserving operation has been used for those that do follow.
  a. $x + 1 \geq 3$ e. $-x - 1 \leq -3$
  b. $x^2 \geq 4$ f. $x > 2$
  c. $4x \geq 8$ g. $-x \geq -2$
  d. $x - 1 \geq 2$ h. $\log x \geq \log 2$

8–4.* Assuming that $x + 1 \leq y$, indicate which step below is the first incorrect step and state why it is incorrect.

a. $x + 1 \leq y$

b. $x + 1 \leq y + 1$

c. $-x - 1 \geq -y - 1$

d. $-x - 7 \geq -y - 7$

e. $-x \geq -y$

f. $(-x)^2 \geq (-y)^2$

g. $x^2 \geq y^2$

h. $x \geq y$

i. $x + 1 \geq y$

8–5.* Graph the following conditional inequalities.

a. $x > -2$

b. $-4 \leq x \leq -1$

c. $4 \leq x \leq 6$

d. $4 \leq x \leq 4$

e. $4 < x < 4$

8–6. Put the following linear inequalities in one unknown in standard form [$f(x) < 0$, for example]. Then write as $x \geq a$, $x > a$, $x \leq a$, or $x < a$, where a is a constant.

a. $x + 2 \leq 3x - 4$

b. $2x - 1 > x - 8$

c. $7x < 2x - 6$

8–7.* Hack Dike is a cabby, and he knows that having any cars costs him $1000 (fixed cost). He also knows that each car costs an additional $400 per year, and each car brings in revenue of $550 per year. He wants revenue to be greater than cost. How many cars must he maintain, at a minimum? Use inequality notation to solve.

8–8. In Chapter 5 we discussed an investor's problem. The investor was considering two commercial bonds, one with a 5 percent yield and one with a 9 percent yield. Suppose that instead of saying he wanted to make exactly $1600 on a $20,000 investment, he said his goal was to make at least $1500. What possible investments can he consider?

8–9. Solve for the x values where the following conditional inequalities hold.

a. $x^2 + 4x + 4 \geq 0$

b. $x^3 - 2x^2 - x + 2 > 0$

c. $x^2 - 1 < 0$

d. $x^2 < 0$

8-10.* In Chapter 5 we examined the problem of a production control manager who is in charge of inventories. He had an inventory-related cost of

$$\text{cost} = \frac{x}{2}(1) + \frac{1000}{x}(10)$$

He said he wanted to meet a budget of \$150. Solve for x values that allow cost to be less than or equal to the \$150 budget. You must assume that $x > 0$; when you need this assumption, say so.

8-11. A product manager believes his demand function is

$$\text{sales units} = 400 - 10p.$$

The product costs \$5 per unit to make and the price is p. Find the set of prices that guarantee that he will make a profit of at least his \$3000 fixed cost.

8-12.* Graph the following set of linear inequalities in two unknowns. Indicate the solution space, corner points, and any redundant constraints.

$$x \leq y$$
$$x + y \geq 2$$
$$y \leq 3$$
$$x < 4$$

8-13.* Suppose, in Problem 8-12, that we add the standard linear programming constraints $x \geq 0$, $y \geq 0$.

a. Indicate which of the new constraints, if any, is redundant.

b. Describe the new solution space.

c. How many corner points are removed? Added?

8-14. Suppose in Problem 8-8 that the investor wanted to invest no more than \$20,000, make at least \$1500, and have no more than \$15,000 invested in the 9 percent bond. Let $x \equiv$ the amount of the 9 percent bond he purchases and $y \equiv$ the amount of the 5 percent bond he purchases. Draw a graph of the possible bond purchases he can make (that is, a solution space) while satisfying all the constraints.

8–15. The investor in Problem 8–14 is unsure about his objective. He wants to satisfy all the constraints given in Problem 8–14 and

(*1*) maximize the interest he receives,

(*2*) minimize the amount of the riskier 9 percent bond, or

(*3*) minimize the amount of money he must invest.

a. Write all three versions of the problem as linear programming problems.

b. On the solution space you drew for Problem 8–14, indicate which corner point is optimal for each objective.

c. Solve for each corner point and evaluate the first objective at each of the three points, to verify your solution in part *b.*

8–16.* Write the following linear programming formulations in matrix form.

a. minimize: $\qquad x + y + z$

subject to: $\qquad x - 2y \geq 4$

$\qquad\qquad\qquad x - 3z \geq 7$

$\qquad\qquad 4x - 2y - z \geq 10$

$\qquad\qquad\qquad\qquad x \geq 0$

$\qquad\qquad\qquad\qquad y \geq 0$

$\qquad\qquad\qquad\qquad z \geq 0$

b. maximize: $\qquad 2x - y$

subject to: $\qquad x + y \leq 4$

$\qquad\qquad x + 3y \leq 6$

$\qquad\qquad x + y \geq 2$

$\qquad\qquad\qquad x \geq 0$

$\qquad\qquad\qquad y \geq 0$

8–17.* Solve part *b* of Problem 8–16 graphically. (*Note:* You need not have done Problem 8–16 to complete Problem 8–17.)

8-18.* Using the same set of constraints as in Problems 8-16b, minimize

a. $x + 3y$

b. $2x + y$

8–19. Write the following linear programming problems in matrix form.

  a. minimize: $\qquad\qquad x + 2y - z$

  subject to: $\qquad\qquad x + 4y \leq 10$
  $$4x + 3y \leq 10$$
  $$z \leq 4$$
  $$x \geq 0$$
  $$y \geq 0$$
  $$z \geq 0$$

  b. maximize: $\qquad\qquad 2x + 3y$

  subject to: $\qquad\qquad 8x + 6y \leq 40$
  $$4x + 10y \leq 40$$
  $$2x + 7y \leq 40$$
  $$x \geq 0$$
  $$y \geq 0$$

8–20. A commercial dairy farmer is interested in feeding his cattle at minimum cost, subject to meeting some constraints. The cattle are fed two feeds: oats and NK-34, a commercial preparation. The constraints are that each cow must get at least 400 grams per day of protein, at least 800 grams per day of carbohydrates, and no more than 100 grams per day of fat. Oats contains 10 percent protein, 80 percent carbohydrates, and 10 percent fat. NK-34 contains 40 percent protein, 60 percent carbohydrates, and no fat. Oats cost $0.20 per 1000 grams, and NK-34 costs $0.50 per 1000 grams.

  a. Write a linear programming formulation to solve for the optimal amounts of each type of feed.

  b. Solve the problem graphically.

  c. Check your solution by finding the three corner points of interest and evaluating the objective function.

8–21.* A chemical company is producing a cough medicine using grain alcohol, water, and a previously marketed patent medicine. They make it in batches of 10 gallons; the grain alcohol costs $8 per gallon and the patent medicine costs $4 per gallon. The company says that the alcohol content must be at least 2.1 gallons per batch if the medicine is to have sufficient shelf life. However, the amount of pure grain alcohol must be no more than 2 gallons per batch and the amount of the previous patent medicine must be no more than 3 gallons per batch. We also know that grain alcohol contains 95 percent pure alcohol and the patent medicine contains 20 percent pure alcohol.

What should the mixture contain if the company wants to minimize cost? [*Note:* Since amount of water $= 10 -$ amount of patent medicine $-$ amount of alcohol, there are really only two unknowns (water can be eliminated) and a graphical solution is possible.]

8–22.* A small machine shop has two machines and makes two products. Product I requires 3 hours on machine A and 2 hours on machine B per unit. Product II requires 2 hours on machine A and 3 hours on machine B per unit. Machine A is available 8 hours per day, but machine B, which takes an hour to prepare for operation, is only available 7 hours per day. If both products sell for $50 per unit, how many units of each should they produce per day and how much profit do they make? (Fractional answers are acceptable since a unit can be completed the next day.) Is there any slack machine time?

8–23. A tomato cannery has 5000 pounds of grade A tomatoes and 10,000 pounds of grade B tomatoes, from which they will make whole canned tomatoes and tomato paste. Whole tomatoes must be composed of at least 80 percent grade A tomatoes, whereas tomato paste must be made with at least 10 percent grade A tomatoes. Whole tomatoes sell for $0.08 per pound and paste sells for $0.05 per pound. Formulate a linear program to solve for how much of each product to make, if the company wants to maximize revenue. (*Hint:* Let $x_{WA} =$ pounds of A grade tomatoes used in whole tomatoes, $x_{WB} =$ pounds of B grade tomatoes used in whole tomatoes; the amount of whole tomatoes produced can be found as $x_{WA} + x_{WB}$ after x_{WA} and x_{WB} are chosen.)

8–24.* The planner for a new housing development may buy any combination of two types of modular housing. The one-bedroom models cost $8000 per unit, and the two-bedroom models cost $12,000 per unit. He must have at least 50 of each unit, and he has a budget of $1,500,000. The average number of people that live in a one-bedroom unit is 1.5 and the average number of people that live in a two-bedroom unit is 2.5. If the planner wishes to maximize the average number of people housed, subject to the specified constraints, how many units of each model should be bought?

8–25. A marketing manager wishes to maximize the number of people exposed to the company's advertising. He may choose television commercials, which reach 20 million people per commercial, or magazine advertising, which reaches 10 million people per advertisement. Magazine advertisements cost $40,000 each while a television advertisement costs $75,000. The manager has a budget of $2,000,000 and must buy at least 20 magazine advertisements. How many units of each type of advertising should be purchased?

8–26.* If for any constants b and d and variable x, it is true that $b \leq x \leq d$, then b and d may be thought of as the lower and upper limits, respectively, of the values that x may have. These concepts are used in this problem. Suppose that a manager believes that sales, S, are expected to be between \$100 and \$125 and that his costs, C, will be between \$80 and \$105. Express these expectations in the form $b \leq x \leq d$. Using these results, derive a similar expression for profits, $P = S - C$.

9

Limits and Continuity

The Atwood Company's variable cost of producing a particular product is composed of material costs and labor costs in the total amount of $100 per unit. The fixed costs of production, such as plant, selling, and administration, which can be identified with the production of the product in question, amount to $10,000 per period. These fixed costs do not change regardless of the number of units produced.

The sales manager maintains that if production is increased sufficiently, unit costs can be reduced to the point where a profit can be made at the current market price of $110 per unit. Indeed, he argues that the firm can at least break even, assuming all output can be sold at no additional cost, as long as the price does not fall below $100. The production manager, on the other hand, believes it is impossible to reduce costs to the point where the firm can break even at a price of $100 even if (and this both he and the sales manager agree is impossible) costs and price both remain unchanged as production per period increases to larger and larger values. Who is right here?

9-1 LIMITS

The functional relationship giving Atwood's average unit cost as a function of productive activity for a period is

$$y = k + \frac{b}{x} = 100 + \frac{10,000}{x}, \qquad x > 0,$$

where

    $y \equiv$ average unit cost for the period,
    $b \equiv$ total fixed cost for the period,
    $k \equiv$ unit variable cost for the period (assumed constant),
    $x \equiv$ number of units produced.

(You should have been able to write this function yourself by now.)

We first met this type of function in Section 4–3, and at that time we studied its graph, which is reproduced in Figure 9–1. As *x* increases the value of the function gets closer and closer to the value 100. We can see from the functional relationship that for *x* greater than 1,000, *y* is less than 110, and, as the sales manager claimed, average unit costs are less than the present unit sales price of 110, assuring a profit on the item.

But no matter how large productive activity is, average unit cost never quite reaches $100. Thus no matter how large the production volume, the firm, as the production manager maintained, cannot achieve break even at a price

FIGURE 9–1

Atwood Company Cost Function

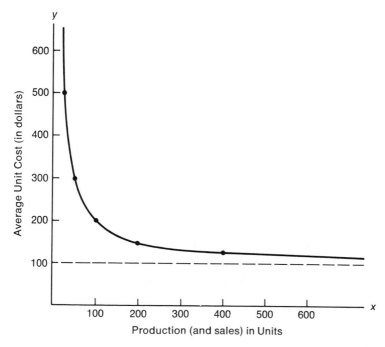

Production (and sales) in Units

of $100. At such a price it will exactly recover its variable production costs on each unit. It will never recover the fixed investment.

However, in one sense this is hair splitting. Given the assumed facts, it is true that average unit cost cannot be reduced to $100. But the company can get average unit cost as close to $100 per unit as it desires by increasing production sufficiently. More technically, the value of the average-unit-cost function can be made as close to this specific value of 100 as is desired if x is taken sufficiently large. When, by judicious selection of x, a function can be made to assume a value as close as we like to some number, say L, then L is said to be the limit. Hence 100 is the limit for Atwood's average unit cost as x increases without bound.

Let's look at a very simple mathematical function and be more precise about just what a limit is. For our purposes

$$y \equiv f(x) = 2x$$

will do nicely. Further, let us consider a specific value of x, say $x = 3$, and ask whether the function approaches a limit as x approaches 3. Intuitively, can we get as close as we like to a single number, L, if we take x values closer and closer to 3? Our intuition tells us that we can do so and, further, that the value of L equals 6: $6 = f(3) = 2(3)$.

Let's try some values and see if we get closer and closer to $y = 6$ as we take x values closer and closer to 3.

Value of x < 3	Values of y = 2x	Values of x > 3	Values of y = 2x
1	2	5	10
2	4	4	8
2.5	5	3.5	7
2.9	5.8	3.1	6.2
2.99	5.98	3.01	6.02
2.999	5.998	3.001	6.002
.	.	.	.
.	.	.	.
.	.	.	.

The table suggests that we can get as close as we like to 6 by taking x values close enough to 3 on either side of 3. Indeed, if someone demanded that we be within 0.0000002 of 6 using $y = 2x$, we could do so by taking values of x within 0.0000001 of 3. Perhaps you can see this more easily from the graph in Figure 9–2. This condition is summarized by saying that the function given by $f(x) = 2x$ has a limit of 6 as x approaches 3. (This function has a different limit for some other value of x.) We write formally:

$$\lim_{x \to 3} 2x = 6.$$

FIGURE 9–2

Limit of the Function
Given by
$$y \equiv f(x) = 2x \text{ at } x = 3$$

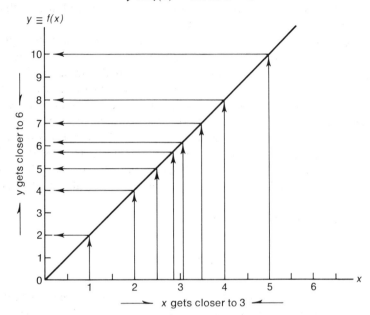

x gets closer to 3

A function given by $f(x)$ has a limit, L, as x approaches some constant, call it a, if we can make $f(x)$ as close to L as we wish for all values of x sufficiently close but not equal, to a (on both sides of a). In symbolic form:

$$\lim_{x \to a} f(x) = L.$$

Symbol	English Translation
$\lim_{x \to a} f(x) = L$	The function given by $f(x)$ gets as close as we like to the value L as x gets close to the value a. (The arrow means as x approaches a.)

For another example, what is the limit of the function given by $y = x^2$ as x gets close to 3? The answer is 9, and we write

$$\lim_{x \to 3} x^2 = 9$$

since the value of this function can be made as close to 9 as we wish by taking values of x sufficiently close to 3. In fact, in this case, and in the case of $y = 2x$, we can even attain the limit precisely by letting $x = 3$. But this is not necessary. In fact, the definition does not permit us to let $x = 3$. The definition, then, does not require that we be able to attain the limit but only that we be able to get as close as anyone might require.

Consider two examples, the first practical, the second mathematical. The other day one of the authors' children was sufficiently naughty to merit his father's wrath and a potential spanking. The boy, realizing his peril, quickly scampered to the other side of the room and, now feeling quite safe, informed his father that it was impossible for the spanking to be carried out. "After all," announced the precocious child, "before you can spank me you must cross to the middle of the room. From there you will need to go halfway again, and then again halfway and so on forever. Since you continually must go halfway each time, you can never get to me." His glee was, however, short-lived when he discovered that his father could approach close enough for all practical purposes.

As a second example, consider

$$f(x) = \frac{2x^2}{x}$$

as x approaches the value zero. If the reader will graph $2x^2/x$ by substituting x values into the function to find the corresponding y value, he will notice that the graph is identical to that in Figure 9–2 except for one point. This is the point where $x = 0$. Since, as we learned in Section 1–2, division by zero is undefined, $2x^2/x$ is undefined at $x = 0$. There is a "hole" in the graph (no y value) for the place where $x = 0$. In other words, when $x = 0$ the y value is "not there." This, naturally, reminds us of the Hughes Mearns verse:

> As I was walking up the stair,
> I saw a man who wasn't there.
> He wasn't there again today.
> I wish, I wish he'd go away.

But, even though $f(x) = 2x^2/x$ is undefined at $x = 0$, it still has a limit as x approaches zero. If we take values of x sufficiently close (but not equal) to zero, we find that the values of $f(x)$ are very close to zero. In fact, we can make $f(x)$ as close to zero as we like by taking values of x sufficiently close to zero. This is all that is needed, according to the definition, for a limit. Hence $f(x) = 2x^2/x$ has the limit zero as x approaches 0 and we write

$$\lim_{x \to 0} \frac{2x^2}{x} = 0.$$

The Atwood case is similar. If we take ever larger production levels, x, average unit cost can be made as close to $100 as we wish. Again the limit value is never taken on by the function for any x, but this is not required. To write the limit in the Atwood case, we let $x \to \infty$. (x approaches infinity) represent the process of taking ever larger values of x. We write

$$\lim_{x \to \infty} 100 + \frac{10,000}{x} = 100.$$

The value 100 was described in Section 4–3 as an asymptote. An *asymptote* is another name for the limiting value of $f(x)$ as x gets very large or very small.

⁓ : What limit would you suggest in the following situations at the value of x indicated?

1. $\lim_{x \to 3} x$ limit suggested_____

2. $\lim_{x \to 1} (1 - x)$ limit suggested_____

3. $\lim_{x \to \infty} e^{-x}$ limit suggested_____

Answers. In case 1, as x approaches 3, the function also approaches 3. In case 2, as x approaches 1, the function approaches zero. In case 3, as x gets very large (that is what $x \to \infty$ means), $1/e^x$ becomes very small but remains positive. By taking x large enough, $1/e^x$ can be made as small as we wish, but it will never quite reach the limit of zero.

Finding Limits

Several different methods exist for locating the limit of a function at a point. The trial-and-error method tends to be time consuming and may lead to mistakes. It should be avoided where possible.

A useful approach, and one we have already used, is to substitute the x value in question into the function and try the result. Thus for the limit of $f(x) = 2x$ as x approaches 3, we substitute and try $f(3) = 2(3) = 6$ as the limit. Substitution worked in this case, and it will generally work for us.

Occasionally, however, the substitution method fails. For example, we could not use it to find the limit of $f(x) = 2x^2/x$ as x approaches zero, because $2x^2/x$ is not defined at $x = 0$. A useful trick in such cases is to simplify and then try substitution to find the limit. Hence canceling,

$$\lim_{x \to 0} \frac{2x^2}{x} = \lim_{x \to 0} 2x.$$

The limit of $f(x) = 2x$ as x approaches zero is zero. This, as we have seen, is also the limit of $f(x) = 2x^2/x$ as x approaches zero.

Another method that is often helpful is to graph the function. Unless you can see what happens to the unit cost function in the Atwood case as x gets large, you may not realize that the limit concept is involved.

〰️ : What are the limits in the following cases?

1. $\lim\limits_{x \to 2} x^2.$ $L = \underline{\hspace{2cm}}.$

2. $\lim\limits_{x \to 3} \dfrac{x - 3}{x^2 - 9} .$ $L = \underline{\hspace{2cm}}.$

3. $\lim\limits_{x \to 0} \left(k - \dfrac{1}{x^2} \right) .$ $L = \underline{\hspace{2cm}}.$

Answers. The first limit is found by substituting directly for x. The limit is 2^2 or 4. For case 2 we can simplify, and this should be done before trying to find the limit. Simplifying,

$$\frac{x - 3}{x^2 - 9} = \frac{x - 3}{(x - 3)(x + 3)} = \frac{1}{x + 3} .$$

This expression approaches $1/6$ as x approaches 3 and so does the original expression. For case 3, as x approaches zero, the second term gets as large negatively as we like. The first term is a constant, so the entire expression gets as large negatively as we like. We say the function goes to minus infinity and express this concept by writing

$$\lim_{x \to 0} \left(k - \frac{1}{x^2} \right) = -\infty .$$

A graph might help you see this result.

Rules for Limits

Just as we have rules for operating with exponents and logarithms, so too there are rules that apply to the operation of taking a limit. We shall illustrate and then state the important rules for limits. We will not prove or derive them. Each rule holds, of course, only if the limits involved exist.

One of the limit rules is illustrated using the function given by $f(x) = 2x$. We saw earlier that as x approaches 3 this function has a limit of 6. Similarly, we could show that the limit of the function given by $f(x) = x$ as x approaches 3 is 3. Hence

$$\lim_{x \to 3} 2x = 6 = 2(3) = 2 \left[\lim_{x \to 3} x \right] .$$

This illustration suggests the first rule for limits.

Rule 1 for Limits: CONSTANT MULTIPLIER

The limit of a function multiplied by a constant is equal to the constant times the limit of the function. In symbolic form:

$$\lim_{x \to a} cf(x) = c \left[\lim_{x \to a} f(x) \right].$$

Using algebra, we can quickly demonstrate another rule for limits. Since taking limits is an operation and given

$$f(x) = 2x$$
$$= x + x,$$

we take the limit of both sides as x approaches 3. This gives,

$$\lim_{x \to 3} f(x) = \lim_{x \to 3} (x + x).$$

Substituting,

$$\lim_{x \to 3} 2x = \lim_{x \to 3} (x + x)$$

and

$$6 = \lim_{x \to 3} (x + x),$$

but

$$3 + 3 = \lim_{x \to 3} (x + x)$$

thus

$$3 + 3 = \lim_{x \to 3} x + \lim_{x \to 3} x.$$

This development suggests the second rule for limits.

Rule 2 for Limits: SUMS

The limit of a sum is equal to the sum of the limits. In symbolic form:

$$\lim_{x \to a} [f_1(x) + \ldots + f_i(x) + \ldots + f_n(x)] = \lim_{x \to a} f_1(x) + \ldots + \lim_{x \to a} f_i(x)$$
$$+ \ldots + \lim_{x \to a} f_n(x)$$

or using more compact notation:

$$\lim_{x \to a} [\sum_{i=1}^{n} f_i(x)] = \sum_{i=1}^{n} \lim_{x \to a} f_i(x).$$

The third rule for limits can be illustrated using

$$f(x) = x^2 = x \cdot x.$$

Taking limits of both sides as x approaches 3 gives

$$\lim_{x \to 3} f(x) = \lim_{x \to 3} x^2 = \lim_{x \to 3} (x \cdot x).$$

But we know from earlier work that

$$\lim_{x \to 3} x^2 = 9 \qquad \text{and} \qquad \lim_{x \to 3} x = 3.$$

Hence we may write

$$\lim_{x \to 3} x^2 = 9 = 3 \cdot 3 = [\lim_{x \to 3} x][\lim_{x \to 3} x].$$

This illustration suggests the third rule for limits.

Rule 3 for Limits: PRODUCTS

The limit of a product is equal to the product of the limits. In symbolic form:

$$\lim_{x \to a} [f(x)][g(x)] = [\lim_{x \to a} f(x)][\lim_{x \to a} g(x)].$$

The fourth and last rule we will consider can be illustrated using $f(x) = 2x^2/x$, which was treated earlier. What is the limit as x approaches 3? Simplifying,

$$\lim_{x \to 3} \frac{2x^2}{x} = \lim_{x \to 3} 2x = 6 = \frac{18}{3} = \frac{2(9)}{3} = 2 (\lim_{x \to 3} x^2) \div (\lim_{x \to 3} x)$$

since we know from previous work that

$$\lim_{x \to 3} x^2 = 9 \qquad \text{and} \qquad \lim_{x \to 3} x = 3.$$

We would not expect you to know that the above steps are the ones that are needed. We used them because someone told us they would work. Fortunately, that someone was right. But the rule itself rather than the derivation is the important thing. This illustration suggests the fourth rule for limits.

Rule 4 for Limits: QUOTIENTS

The limit of a quotient is equal to the quotient of the limits. In symbolic form:

$$\lim_{x \to a} [f(x) \div g(x)] = [\lim_{x \to a} f(x)] \div [\lim_{x \to a} g(x)].$$

One warning: This rule holds only if $g(x) \neq 0$ when $x = a$ and $\lim_{x \to a} g(x) \neq 0$.

: Find the limits of the following functions:

1. $\lim_{x \to 2} 7(x^2 - 3x)$. $L =$ _____.

2. $\lim_{x \to 1} x^2(2x - 3)$. $L =$ _____.

3. $\lim_{x \to 4} 2\left(\dfrac{x + 2}{x - 2}\right)$.

                $L =$ _____.

Answers. The first limit is found using rules 1 and 2. It is -14. For case 2, we use rule 3 and obtain -1. (*Note:* The multiplication could be carried out first and rules 2 and 1 used.) The last problem is solved using rule 4. The limit is 6.

9-2 DEFINED VALUE OF A FUNCTION AT A POINT

When we discussed the limit of the function given by $f(x) = 2x$ as x approaches 3, we concluded that not only was this limit 6, but the function actually assumes the value 6 when x takes on the value 3; that is, $f(3) = 6$. We say that the function is defined at the point $x = 3$ since the function assumes a value, namely 6, which is given by a real number at that point.

A function given by $f(x)$ is defined at the point $x=a$, if $f(a)$ exists as a real number.

As an example of a function that is not defined at a point, we can use the function given by $f(x) = 2x^2/x$ for the point $x = 0$. Although this function has a limit of zero as x approaches zero, it is not defined at $x = 0$ since division by zero is undefined. Hence a function may have a limit at a point, although the function is undefined at the point.

Actually, it is contrary to the definition of a function, given in Section 3–1, to call $f(x) = 2x^2/x$ a function unless we explicitly exclude $x = 0$ from the first set, the set of values x may assume. This is true for two reasons. First, it could at most be the rule for a function, not the function itself. (But we have agreed in Section 3–3 to call rules for functions simply functions.) Second, and more important, the definition of a function requires a value for every choice of x, but no value can be assigned to $x = 0$. Hence there is no function unless $x = 0$ is explicitly excluded. We are, then, guilty of imprecision of terms here in trying to make a point. Perhaps a good way to summarize this section is to point to the fact that a limit can exist even at points excluded from a function for definitional reasons.

$\mathcal{M}$: Circle those functions given by the expressions below which are defined at $x = 3$.

1. $f(x) = x^3/3$.

2. $f(x) = \begin{cases} 3x - 9, & x \neq 3, \\ 9, & x = 3. \end{cases}$

3. $f(x) = \dfrac{1}{3 - x}$.

Answers. The first two cases are both defined at $x = 3$, and both are equal to 9. In case 2, the second part of the function's specification defines $f(x)$ for $x = 3$. In case 3, the denominator takes on a value of zero at $x = 3$ and hence $f(x) = 1/(3 - x)$ is undefined at $x = 3$. [Note that $f(x) = 1/(3 - x)$ approaches minus infinity as we approach 3 through values greater than 3, and it approaches plus infinity as 3 is approached through numbers less than 3.]

9-3 CONTINUITY

The concept of continuity is important to the solution of managerial problems. Its presence is required if certain powerful mathematical tools are to be used. Unfortunately, some functions arising in managerial problems lack this important characteristic.

We shall break the notion of continuity into two subnotions. These are continuity at a point and continuity over an interval.

Continuity at a Point

For a function to be continuous at a point, it must satisfy three conditions. These are listed in the definition.

A function given by $f(x)$ **is continuous at the point** $x = a$ **if**

1. The function is defined at $x = a$.
2. The function has a limit as x approaches a.
3. The defined value, $f(a)$, equals the limit as x approaches a; that is, $f(a) = \lim\limits_{x \to a} f(x)$.

The first condition is redundant since a function is defined at all values of x by definition. However, since the defined value is a part of condition 3, condition 1 is included for completeness. The following examples may help clarify the definition. Consider a productive output of 100 units with

(a) Variable unit cost $\quad f(x) = 2x, \quad x > 0.$

(b) Fixed costs of activity $\quad g(x) = \begin{cases} 20{,}000, & 0 \le x \le 100 \\ 30{,}000, & 100 < x \end{cases}$

Consider the variable-unit-cost function at $x = 100$. We have:

1. The function is defined at $x = 100$ since $f(100) = 200$.
2. The function has a limit as x approaches 100, since by rule 1 for limits,

$$\lim_{x \to 100} 2x = 2 \left[\lim_{x \to 100} x \right] = 2(100) = 200.$$

3. The defined value at $x = 100$ equals the limit as x approaches 100.

$$f(100) = 200 = \lim_{x \to 100} 2x.$$

Thus the function defining variable cost is continuous at the point $x = 100$. For the fixed-cost function at $x = 100$, we have

1. The function is defined at $x = 100$ since $f(100) = 20{,}000$.
2. The function does *not* approach the same value as x approaches 100 through values greater than 100 as it does for x approaching 100 through values less than 100. For values of x greater than 100, the value of $g(x)$ remains at 30,000, while for x values less than 100, the function is always 20,000. There is a jump in the function from a value of 20,000 to a value of 30,000 as x passes through the value 100, moving through increasing values.

Without examining the third condition for continuity at a point, we conclude that this function is discontinuous at $x = 100$. Figure 9–3 illustrates the discontinuity.

FIGURE 9–3

Graph of the Fixed-Cost Function

$$g(x) = \begin{cases} 20,000, & 0 \le x \le 100 \\ 30,000, & 100 < x \end{cases}$$

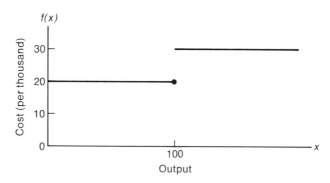

Three other cases in which continuity does not exist at a point are illustrated in Figure 9–4. In each case the discontinuity occurs at $x = 3$. The equation graphed in Figure 9–4a has a limit of 6 as x approaches 3, but it is not defined at $x = 3$. The equation graphed in Figure 9–4b has no limit as x approaches 3, getting increasingly large as x approaches 3 through values larger than 3 and increasingly small (large, negatively) as x approaches 3 through values less than 3. (We have been careful here not to call these two

FIGURE 9–4

Three Examples of Discontinuity

at the Point $x = 3$

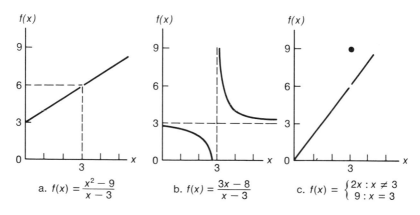

a. $f(x) = \dfrac{x^2 - 9}{x - 3}$ b. $f(x) = \dfrac{3x - 8}{x - 3}$ c. $f(x) = \begin{cases} 2x : x \ne 3 \\ 9 : x = 3 \end{cases}$

cases functions, since there is no value that can be matched to $x = 3$ as is required by the definition.) In Figure 9–4c, the function has a limit of 6 as x approaches 3, and it is defined at $x = 3$. However, the limit of 6 is not equal to the defined value of 9. These pathological cases are somewhat rare in managerial situations, but they help to illustrate the concept of continuity at a point.

Sometimes it is possible to construct or define a continuous function from a case that is discontinuous by "patching" the holes. One must be careful, however, that the new function does not misrepresent the actual situation he is attempting to reflect. The situations illustrated by Figures 9–4a and 9–4c provide examples where this patching process is quite easily accomplished. Two continuous functions that do everything the graph in Figure 9–4a does and that are continuous at $x = 3$ are given by

$$f(x) = x + 3 \quad \text{and} \quad f(x) = \begin{cases} \dfrac{x^2 - 9}{x - 3}, & x \neq 3 \\ 6, & x = 3. \end{cases}$$

Similarly, for Figure 9–4c, we could write

$$f(x) = 2x,$$

or

$$f(x) = \begin{cases} 2x, & x \neq 3, \\ 6, & x = 3. \end{cases}$$

This simple patching process is not always possible, as is suggested perhaps by Figures 9–4b and 9–3.

$\checkmark$: Which of the statements below best completes the following intuitive description of continuity at a point?

A function is continuous at a point if

1. You can't see any holes in it.
2. You can put your pencil on the function to the left of the point and, never lifting it from the function, move the pencil along the function to the right of the point.
3. There are no xs in the denominator.

Answer. Holes made by removing a single point on a function are too small to see. The function in Figure 9–4c has no x in the denominator, but it is discontinuous. Hence, by elimination, statement 2 correctly completes the intuitive description of a limit at a point. Try it out on Figures 9–2 and 9–4a at $x = 3$ to see that it works.

Continuity over an Interval

Continuity over an interval is a straightforward extension of continuity at a point. We simply extend the notion of continuity at a point to all points in the interval.

A function is continuous over an interval if it is continuous at every point in the interval.

Figure 9–2 provides an example of a function, $f(x) = 2x$, that is continuous for any interval of x values we might select. For some other functions this is not the case. Thus for the Atwood Company cost function (see Figure 9–1), we must restrict the interval to values of x greater than zero in order to have continuity. For the fixed-cost function graphed in Figure 9–3, only intervals for x equal to or greater than zero are appropriate. Moreover, in this case any interval including values of x less than 100 must not include x values greater than 100. And any interval including values greater than 100 must not include values of x equal to or less than 100. The function is not continuous at $x = 100$, and it is therefore not continuous over any interval containing $x = 100$.

Intuitively, the best description of continuity over an interval is given by the pencil-tracing notion.

If you can trace out the entire function over some interval without lifting your pencil from the paper, the function is continuous over this interval.

Try this technique on Figure 9–3 for the interval $0 \leq x \leq 50$. This should satisfy you that the function is continuous over this interval and it is, you will agree, easier than checking for continuity at every point in the interval—an impossible task anyway. Try the technique again for the interval $50 \leq x \leq 150$. Try as you may you must lift the pencil from the paper as you move across the point $x = 100$ where the function is discontinuous. Hence the function is discontinuous over this interval. But what about the interval $0 \leq x \leq 100$? Using the same pencil-tracing technique, we conclude that the function is continuous. There is no need to go beyond 100, the end point. End points can be troublesome but if you use the pencil-tracing method you should be able to avoid most of the difficulties. The function in Figure 9–3 is discontinuous over the interval $100 \leq x \leq 150$, since $f(100) = 20,000$, but for any x greater than 100 the function jumps to 30,000. However, if 100 is excluded from this interval (we write $100 < x \leq 150$), the function is continuous over the revised interval.

One final example of a continuous function over all values of x is given by

$$f(x) = \begin{cases} x, & x \leq 4, \\ 8 - x, & x \geq 4. \end{cases}$$

This function is graphed in Figure 9–5. This triangular-shaped function is continuous over any interval and the sharp point at $x = 4$ where the function changes direction does not destroy the continuity for intervals including it.

Although it is helpful to use the pencil-tracing method, the reader may not wish to graph a function to see if it is continuous over some interval. Yet there are infinitely many points in an interval and he, reasonably, wishes to avoid checking each one. What can be done? Familiarity with functions and graphs helps. Thus the reader may already know that

$$f(x) = a + bx$$

and, in fact, all polynomials in x of the form

$$f(x) = a_n x^n + a_{n-1} x^{n-1} + \ldots + a_1 x + a_0$$

are continuous over any intervals. Discontinuities tend to arise at special points, and usually it is sufficient to check the function's behavior at these points.

FIGURE 9–5

Graph of $f(x) = \begin{cases} x, & x \leq 4 \\ 8 - x, & x > 4 \end{cases}$

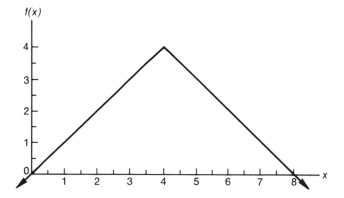

Several examples of such points are

1. Where the denominator of some term in the equation becomes zero.
2. At the end points of the function or of the separate intervals for which different equations are used to define the function. (Examples include $x = 4$ in Figure 9–5 and $x = 3$ in Figure 9–4c.)

$\sim\!\!\sim\!\!\!\!^{\checkmark}$: The questions below refer to Figure 9–4a. Check the appropriate response for the interval given

Interval	Continuous over the Interval	Discontinuous over the Interval
1. $-1 \leq x \leq 2$		
2. $0 \leq x \leq 4$		
3. $1 \leq x \leq 3$		
4. $1 \leq x < 3$		
5. $3 \leq x < 5$		
6. $3 < x < 5$		

Answers. Since the function is only defined for $x \neq 3$, there is no point on the function at $x = 3$. Hence it is impossible to have a continuous function for any interval including $x = 3$. The function is continuous over the intervals represented by cases 1, 4, and 6 only. It is discontinuous over the intervals given by cases 2, 3, and 5.

9-4 SUMMARY

The notion of a limit of a function at a point is one of approaching but not necessarily reaching some value. Intuitively, it means that we can get as close to the limit as we wish by suitable selection of values of x close to the point. In other words, if a function has a limit [the value approached by $f(x)$ as x approaches some specific value], then no matter how close someone may demand that we get to the limit, there are values of x that will permit us to get even closer.

The notion of a function being defined at a point is not new. It means that at some point, call it b, the value of the function is a real number, and this value is equal to $f(b)$. But this is simply one of the requirements in the definition of a function as we learned in Section 3–1.

Given a function that it is defined for all x values considered, continuity at a point requires that (a) the function have a limit at that point and (b) that the limit equal the defined value of the function at that point. Continuity over an interval requires that the function be continuous at every point included in the interval. End points and points where the function is either undefined or is described by a different equation are the usual trouble spots. They are the points of potential discontinuities. If the function is graphed, a useful way to check for continuity over an interval is to see if the function can be traced over the interval with a pencil without removing the pencil from the page.

NEW SYMBOLS

Symbol	*English Translation*
$\lim_{x \to a} f(x) = L$	The function given by $f(x)$ gets as close as we like to the value L as x gets close to the value a.

RULES FOR LIMITS

Rule 1: Constant multiplier

$$\lim_{x \to a} cf(x) = c \lim_{x \to a} f(x)$$

Rule 2: Sums

$$\lim_{x \to a} \sum_{i=1}^{n} f_i(x) = \sum_{i=1}^{n} \lim_{x \to a} f_i(x)$$

Rule 3: Products

$$\lim_{x \to a} [f(x) \cdot g(x)] = [\lim_{x \to a} f(x)] \cdot [\lim_{x \to a} g(x)]$$

Rule 4: Quotients

$$\lim_{x \to a} [f(x) \div g(x)] = [\lim_{x \to a} f(x)] \div [\lim_{x \to a} g(x)]$$

$$\text{if } g(a) \neq 0 \text{ and } \lim_{x \to a} g(x) \neq 0$$

PROBLEMS

Problems for Self-Study: 11, 15, 19, 29

9–1.* Often we hear statements in our everyday life that use the idea of a limit. For example, you may have said as you tried to understand the ideas in this book: "I have reached the limit of my patience." Can you think of other everyday uses of the limit idea?

9–2. Translate into symbolic form the statement

$$\text{``} f(x) = (1 - x^2)/(2 - \sqrt{x^2 + 3})$$

is as close to 4 as we please whenever x is sufficiently close to but different from 1."

9–3.* Sequences of numbers such as 8, 4, 2, 1, $\frac{1}{2}$, . . . may have limits. Using your intuition, indicate the limits of the following sequences by specifying the limit value or using a symbol that suggests the limit (such as ∞).

   a. 8, 4, 2, 1, $\frac{1}{2}$, $\frac{1}{4}$, . . .

   b. 2, 4, 6, 8, 10, . . .

   c. $\dfrac{3}{1}, \dfrac{4}{2}, \dfrac{5}{3}, \ldots, \dfrac{n+2}{n}, \ldots$

   d. $-1, \dfrac{2}{4}, -\dfrac{3}{9}, \ldots, \dfrac{n}{(-1)^n(n^2)}, \ldots$

   e. 1, 3, 1, . . ., $2 + (-1)^n$, . . .

9–4. Sometimes sequences of numbers approach limits. Can you find the limits of the following sequences by using your intuition or any other means at hand?

   a. $1, 2, 3, 4, \ldots, n, \ldots$

   b. $\frac{1}{2}, (\frac{1}{2})^2, (\frac{1}{2})^3, \ldots, (\frac{1}{2})^n, \ldots$

   c. $\lim \sum\limits_{n=0}^{\infty} (\frac{1}{2})^n$ [*Hint:* Let $f(n) = (\frac{1}{2})^n$ and try adding the first 5 to 10 terms and see what value is approached.]

   d. $\lim\limits_{n \to \infty} [(n+2)/n]$

   e. $\lim\limits_{n \to \infty} [n/(n+2)]$

   f. $\lim\limits_{n \to \infty} \left(1 + \dfrac{1}{n}\right)^n$ [*Hint:* Let $f(n) = (1 + (1/n))^n$ and evaluate for larger and larger values of n.]

9–5. Suppose that the contribution to sales in terms of thousands of dollars, $f(n)$, of the nth salesman is given by

$$f(n) = \left(\frac{1}{2}\right)^n.$$

   a. What is the contribution of the second salesman?
   b. What is the total sales generated by 5 salesmen?
   c. What is added by adding a second 5 salesmen?

9–6.* Using the properties of limits, find the following limits.

   a. $\lim\limits_{x \to 2} \left(\dfrac{x^2 - 4}{x - 2}\right)$

   b. $\lim\limits_{x \to 2} \left[\dfrac{x^2 - 4}{x - 2} + 3x^2(2\sqrt{x})\right]$

9-7.* We observe that

$$\lim_{x\to 1} (3x + 1)^1 = 4 = \left[\lim_{x\to 1} (3x + 1)\right]^1$$

$$\lim_{x\to 1} (3x + 1)^2 = 16 = \left[\lim_{x\to 1} (3x + 1)\right]^2$$

$$\lim_{x\to 1} (3x + 1)^3 = 64 = \left[\lim_{x\to 1} (3x + 1)\right]^3$$

What rule about limits do these examples suggest?

9-8. Find the following limits.

a. $\lim\limits_{x\to 2} \left(\dfrac{x^2}{x^3} + \dfrac{3}{x^m} - \dfrac{t}{x + 2}\right)$

b. $\lim\limits_{n\to 2} \left[\left(\dfrac{x^2}{x^3}\right)(\log_2 x)2^x\right]$

9-9.* Find the following limit.

$$\lim_{\Delta x\to 0} \left[\frac{f(x + \Delta x) - f(x)}{\Delta x}\right]$$

if $f(x) = x^2$.

9-10.* The definition of a limit states that in order for the limit L to exist at x_0, we must be able to choose an x^* close to x_0 such that $f(x^*)$ is within a specified distance, ϵ, from that limit. (See the example in Section 9-1.) For each of the following limits and specified distances, find such an x^*. That is, if $\lim\limits_{x\to x_0} f(x) = L$ exists, find an x^* close to x_0 such that $|L - f(x^*)|$ is less than ϵ.

a. $\lim\limits_{x\to 3} x^2 ; \epsilon = 0.1$

b. $\lim\limits_{x\to 1} \dfrac{(x - 1)^2}{x - 1} ; \epsilon = 0.01$

c. $\lim\limits_{x\to 0} \dfrac{1}{x} ; \epsilon = 0.0001$

d. $\lim\limits_{x\to \infty} \dfrac{1}{x} ; \epsilon = 0.0001$

9-11. Find the limits.

a. $\lim\limits_{x\to 2} (3x - 6)$

b. $\lim\limits_{x\to 3} (x^3 + x^2)$

    c. $\lim\limits_{x\to 4}\ [x(x-3)]$

    d. $\lim\limits_{x\to 3}\ \dfrac{1}{x-4}$

    e. $\lim\limits_{x\to 3}\ \dfrac{x^2-5x+6}{x-2}$

9–12.* Find the limits.

    a. $\lim\limits_{x\to 4}\ [(x-2)(2x-12)]$

    b. $\lim\limits_{x\to -3}\ (x^3+4x^2-1x-12)$

    c. $\lim\limits_{x\to 3}\ \dfrac{x^2-6x+8}{x^3-5x^2+7x-3}$

    d. $\lim\limits_{x\to 0}\ \dfrac{x^3}{27x^2}$

9–13. Find the limits.

    a. $\lim\limits_{x\to \infty}\ \dfrac{x+10000}{2x}$

    b. $\lim\limits_{x\to \infty}\ \dfrac{x-4}{x^2+2}$ (*Hint:* Compare to $\lim\limits_{x\to \infty}\ [(x-4)/(x^2-16)]$).

    c. $\lim\limits_{x\to \infty}\ e^{-x}$

    d. $\lim\limits_{x\to \infty}\ \dfrac{x^2-x}{x^2+x}$

9–14.* Find $\lim\limits_{x\to 0}\ \dfrac{1}{x}[(c+x)^3-c^3]$.

9–15. The function given by $f(x)=(x^2-5x+6)/(x^2-x-6)$ is not defined at two points. Find those points and the limit of the function at those points (if the limit exists).

9–16. A geometric series is of the form $a+ar+ar^2+\ldots+ar^n+\ldots$. If $-1<r<+1$, then

$$\sum_{x=0}^{\infty} ar^x = \frac{a}{1-r} \qquad \text{and} \qquad \sum_{x=1}^{\infty} ar^x = \frac{ar}{1-r}\ .$$

Using these facts, answer the following:

a. $\lim\limits_{n \to \infty} \left[\sum\limits_{x=0}^{n} \left(\frac{1}{2}\right)^x \right]$

b. $\lim\limits_{n \to \infty} \left(\sum\limits_{k=2}^{n} \frac{1}{2^{k-1}} \right)$

9–17.* Compute the limit

$$\lim_{x \to 0} g(x) = \frac{f(5ax) - f(x)}{x}$$

for the following definitions of $f(x)$.

a. $f(x) = 3x$
b. $f(x) = b$
c. $f(x) = x^2$
d. $f(x) = x \div b$

9–18.* In some cases a function approaches different values at a point depending on the side from which the point is approached. Find both of the values approached for the functions given below as x approaches the points indicated.

a. $f(x) = x^2$ at $x = 2$

b. $f(x) = a + \dfrac{b}{x}$ at $x = 0$

c. $f(x) = \begin{cases} a \text{ for } x \le c \\ b \text{ for } x > c \end{cases}$ at $x = c$

d. $f(x) = \begin{cases} 3x \text{ for } x \neq 3 \\ 12 \text{ for } x = 3 \end{cases}$ at $x = 3$

9–19. A *perpetuity* is defined as an annuity with an infinite life. In Chapter 2 the present value of an annuity of A for n years was shown to be

$$\text{P.V.} = A \left[\frac{1 - (1 + r)^{-n}}{r} \right].$$

Find the present value of a perpetuity by taking the limit of P.V. as $n \to \infty$. Assume that $r > 0$.

9–20.* A sales manager knows that a dollar spent on advertising will generate S_1 extra sales in the next period. In addition, some consumer loyalty results, so that in the following period S_2 extra sales will result from the same dollar of advertising, and so on for the succeeding periods. However, this loyalty decreases over time by a constant proportion, so that for some λ, $0 < \lambda < 1$:

$$S_2 = (1 - \lambda)S_1,$$
$$S_3 = (1 - \lambda)S_2 = (1 - \lambda)^2 S_1,$$

.

.

.

$$S_n = (1 - \lambda)^{n-1} S_1.$$

Find

a. $\lim_{n \to \infty} S_n$

b. $\lim_{n \to \infty} \sum_{i=1}^{n} S_i$ (This is a difficult problem. See Problem 9–16 for help.)

9–21. Which of the following are continuous at $x = 1$?

a. $f(x) = \dfrac{x - 1}{x}$

b. $f(x) = \begin{cases} x^2, & x \le 1 \\ 2x - 1, & x > 1 \end{cases}$

c. $f(x) = \begin{cases} 0, & x < \frac{1}{2} \\ 1, & \frac{1}{2} \le x < \frac{3}{2} \\ 2, & x \ge \frac{3}{2} \end{cases}$

d. $f(x) = \dfrac{x + 1}{x - 1}$

9–22.* Which of the functions with values given by the expressions in Problem 9–21 are continuous over the following intervals?

a. $0 < x < 1$

b. $\frac{1}{2} \le x \le \frac{3}{2}$

9–23. Consider the limit

$$y = 1 + \frac{1}{2^n}, \qquad n \text{ an integer } (n = 1, 2, \ldots).$$

We write $\lim_{n \to a} y = L$.

a. y is a function of _____ ?

b. The limit is a value determined only after _____ is specified.

c. The limit of y as n increases without bound $(n \to \infty)$ is _____?

d. Is this a continuous function over the set of real numbers between 1 and 10?

9-24.* Can a function be discontinuous at a point if the function is defined at that point and has a limit at the same point?

9-25. Is it possible for a function to have a limit at a point if the function is discontinuous at that point?

9-26.* a. Can a function have a limit at a point if it is discontinuous at that point?

b. Can the function be discontinuous at a point if it is defined at the point?

c. Can the function be undefined at a point if it has a limit at that point and is continuous at that point?

9-27. Find a value y such that the function with values given by

$$f(x) = \begin{cases} \dfrac{x^2 + 2x - 8}{x - 2}, & x \neq 2, \\ y, & x = 2 \end{cases}$$

is continuous for all x.

9-28.* A firm estimates that the interest rate it has to pay is a function of the amount borrowed (in millions of dollars), x. The function is given by

$$f(x) = \begin{cases} 0.06 & \text{for } 0 \leq x \leq 3, \\ 0.03 + 0.01x & \text{for } 3 < x \leq 5, \\ 0.09 & \text{for } 5 < x. \end{cases}$$

Graph the function. At what points is the function not continuous?

9-29. The cost, C, of producing x units at a particular plant can be expressed as

$$C(x) = \begin{cases} 10,000 + 20x + 10x^{1/2} & \text{for } 0 < x \leq 1,000,000, \\ 15,000 + 20x + 10x^{1/2} & \text{for } x > 1,000,000. \end{cases}$$

a. Find $\lim\limits_{x \to 1,000,000} C(x)$

b. Find $\lim\limits_{x \to \infty} \dfrac{C(x)}{x}$. This is the unit cost in the limit as an infinite number of units is produced.

c. Where is the function given by $C(x)$ discontinuous?

d. Where is the function given by $C(x)/x$ discontinuous?

9–30.* A management consultant was attempting to approximate a demand curve in the range 0 to 10 thousand units with a particular mathematical function. The instructions for use of the computer program specify that any function so used must be continuous over the entire appropriate range. Which of the following could not be used to give values of such a function (x in thousands)?

a. $y = \dfrac{(x - 2)^3}{x^2 - 4x + 4}$

b. $y = \dfrac{x^2 - 225}{x - 15}$

c. $y = e^{-x}$

d. $y = \begin{cases} 2x, & x \le 5 \\ 20 - 2x, & x > 5 \end{cases}$

e. $y = \begin{cases} x^2, & x \ne 0 \\ 1, & x = 0 \end{cases}$

9–31. In Problem 9–30a find a value of y for the function with values given by

$$f(x) = \begin{cases} \dfrac{(x - 2)^3}{x^2 - 4x + 4} + 4, & \text{for } x \ne 2, \\ y, & \text{for } x = 2, \end{cases}$$

so that the function can be used in the computer program.

9–32.* Any investigation conducted in a technical organization invariably has as its end result the publication of a report. Soon sizable stacks of such reports and associated memorandums appear in everyone's incoming mail. These increase rapidly with the size of the organization (for example, consider the federal government) until essentially the whole day can easily be taken up perusing these communications.

Suppose that $m \equiv$ the number of reports turned out per year and $k \equiv$ the fraction of reports received and read by the average employee. Assuming that he reads each report received in t days on the average and assuming there are 240 total working days per year, an employee has

$$240 - kmt$$

days left to produce reports of his own (and do other things).

If *d* is the time required on the average to produce a report, he can produce

$$(240 - kmt) \div d$$

reports per year. If there are *n* employees, the number of reports turned out per year could be as high as

$$n(240 - kmt) \div d.$$

But this is *m*, the number of reports turned out per year. Hence

$$m = n(240 - kmt) \div d,$$

and solving for *m* yields

$$m = 240n \div (d + ktn).$$

a. What happens to the number of reports as *n* becomes very large?

b. What happens to the number of reports as the fraction of reports received and read by the average employee is reduced?

9–33. One number we have run into several times is the constant *e*. The value of e^z is given by the sum of an infinitely long series of the form

$$1 + x + \frac{x^2}{2!} + \frac{x^3}{3!} + \frac{x^4}{4!} + \dots,$$

where $n! = n(n-1)(n-2)\dots 1$. Write the general term of this series and calculate the value of $e^{0.5}$ using the first five terms of the series given above. Write the first four terms of *e* and evaluate.

10

The Derivative

One often hears the position expressed that increases in wages should be in line with increases in productivity. Suppose that we hear the statement: "Last year's wages increased twice as fast as productivity." This statement tells us how fast wages changed relative to productivity. It expresses a rate of change. In this case the rate of change of wages with respect to productivity. The speaker tells us this rate of change was 2.

Some time ago the following headline appeared in the local paper. "Prices rose at 0.4 percent a month." This statement also expresses a rate of change: the rate of change of prices with respect to time. This rate is 0.004 per month. It is common to hear advertising men claim that increasing the level of advertising will more than pay for itself in increased sales. This view could be phrased as, "the rate of increase in profits from higher sales exceeds the rate of increase in the cost of advertising."

Similar types of statements can be made concerning numerous pairs of variables: cost and production, quality and inspection activity, program effectiveness and program expenditure, morale and participation in goal setting, and so on. Relations involving a rate of change, that is, relations that tell us how fast one variable is changing with respect to another variable, exist whenever two variables are related through a function. The functional relationship allows us to graph the function and to graph its rate of change.

10-1 THE DERIVATIVE AS A RATE OF CHANGE

Suppose that labor cost and output are related by

$$y \equiv f(x) = x^2, \qquad x \geq 0,$$

where

$$x \equiv \text{output in thousands of units,}$$
$$y \equiv \text{total labor cost in thousands of dollars.}$$

This function is plotted as the curved line from the origin in Figure 10–1. At an output level of 1,000 units, labor cost is also equal to $1,000. But this does not tell us how fast labor costs change with changes in output. The answer to this question is given by the "steepness" of the curve at the point $x = 1$. Steepness can be thought of as "how sharply $f(x)$ rises as we move a little in the x direction."

FIGURE 10–1

Labor Cost and Output

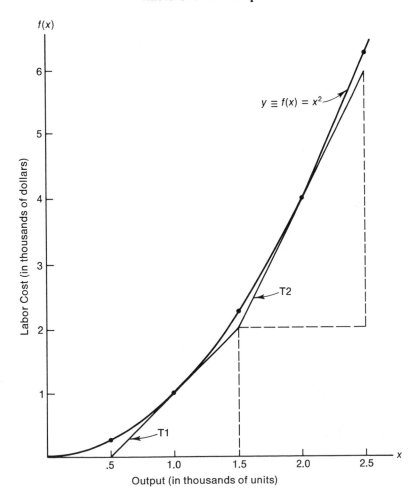

Output (in thousands of units)

If the curve were flat, as is the case when $y \equiv f(x)$ equals a constant, say $y \equiv f(x) = 2$, then wages would not change at all with a change in output. But that is not the case here. The steepness of the present curve at any point is represented by "the slope of the curve" at the point. By definition, "the slope of the curve" equals the slope of the tangent to the curve at the point in question. The tangent at that point has the same slope [the rise ÷ run or the change in $y \equiv f(x)$ divided by the change in x] as the curve. (See the discussion of the slope in Section 3–3.) The slope of the tangent to the curve *at a point* is a constant. The slope of the curve, however, may change from point to point as it does in Figure 10–1.

For the labor–cost output curve in Figure 10–1, we have drawn the tangent to the curve at $x = 1$. This tangent is labeled T1 in the figure. The slope of this tangent line is identical to the slope of the curve $y \equiv f(x) = x^2$ at the particular point $x = 1$. The slope of a straight line is given by the change in $y \equiv f(x)$ divided by the change in x, or the rise divided by the run. Using the unit interval around $x = 1$, that is, x values of $\frac{1}{2}$ and $1\frac{1}{2}$, respectively, the slope of the tangent, read from the graph, is

$$\frac{\text{change in } y}{\text{change in } x} = \frac{\Delta y}{\Delta x} = \frac{2 - 0}{1.5 - 0.5} = \frac{2}{1} = 2.$$

Hence, although the level of labor cost is \$1,000 when output is 1,000 units, labor cost is increasing at a rate of \$2,000 per unit increase in output *at this output level*. In other words, the rate of change of labor cost with a change in output is \$2,000 when the output level is 1,000 units.

Specification of the output level (the x value), where the rate of change is being measured, is very important since the rate of change may be different at different output levels. Indeed, in this case the rate of change in y is different for each value of x. By reference to the curve in Figure 10–1, you can observe that the curve is steeper for values of x exceeding 1. Hence we would expect the rate of change of labor cost with respect to output to be greater at larger output levels. If the curve is steeper, larger changes in y occur for a 1-unit change in x.

The reader can verify these observations by again making reference to Figure 10–1, this time observing the function at $x = 2$. The tangent, T2, to the curve has again been drawn and we find for a unit change in x from 1.5 to 2.5:

$$\frac{\text{change in } y}{\text{change in } x} = \frac{\Delta y}{\Delta x} = \frac{6 - 2}{2.5 - 1.5} = \frac{4}{1} = 4$$

at $x = 2$. The rate of change depends on what value of x is being considered.

A new symbol was introduced in the previous discussion, but we did not stop to translate it then. We do so now.

Symbol	English Translation
Δx	The change in x (called delta x).

The concept of a derivative is closely related to the concept of the rate of change. The *derivative* of a function at a point is defined to be the slope of the tangent to the curve at that point. Thus we have in fact found that the derivative of the function given by $y \equiv f(x) = x^2$ is 4 at $x = 2$, and it is 2 at $x = 1$. To do this we drew the tangent to the function at the point and computed its slope. But it is not easy to draw these tangents accurately. It is better to work with the ratio of the change in x to the change in $y \equiv f(x)$ for the curve itself. As we let the change in x, Δx, approach zero, this ratio will equal the slope of the tangent line in the limit.

The limit of the ratio of the change in x to the change in $y \equiv f(x)$ as the change in x approaches zero is the derivative. In symbols:

$$\lim_{\Delta x \to 0} \frac{\Delta f(x)}{\Delta x} = \lim_{\Delta x \to 0} \frac{\Delta y}{\Delta x}.$$

The Derivative Function

So far we have seen how graphing a function and drawing tangents allows us to find the derivative (and hence the rate of change) of a function at a point. But this method is cumbersome. It would be more efficient if we could find a general function which would give us the derivative in terms of x for any value of x in which we might have an interest. Such a function, if it exists, is called the *derivative function*, and its rule is written $f'(x)$.

Given a function $f(x)$, then another function (if it exists) which gives the slope of the function $f(x)$ for all x values is called the derivative function or simply the derivative. Its rule is written $f'(x)$.

Symbol	English Translation
$f'(x)$	The derivative function.

A very simple example is provided by the straight line $y \equiv f(x) = 2x$. The graph is a straight line through the origin with constant slope 2. In other words, the change in y for a unit change in x is equal to 2 no matter what value of x is considered. For example, consider the ratio of the change in the function to the change in x for an interval 1 unit wide around the following x values. We obtain:

$$\text{at } x = 1: \quad \frac{\text{change in } y}{\text{change in } x} = \frac{\Delta y}{\Delta x} = \frac{3 - 1}{1.5 - 0.5} = 2,$$

$$\text{at } x = 4: \quad \frac{\text{change in } y}{\text{change in } x} = \frac{\Delta y}{\Delta x} = \frac{9 - 7}{4.5 - 3.5} = 2,$$

$$\text{at } x = 20: \quad \frac{\text{change in } y}{\text{change in } x} = \frac{\Delta y}{\Delta x} = \frac{41 - 39}{20.5 - 19.5} = 2.$$

Now consider the ratio of the change in the function to the change in x for an interval $\frac{1}{2}$ unit wide around the same x values as before. We obtain:

$$\text{at } x = 1: \quad \frac{\text{change in } y}{\text{change in } x} = \frac{\Delta y}{\Delta x} = \frac{2.5 - 1.5}{1.25 - 0.75} = 2,$$

$$\text{at } x = 4: \quad \frac{\text{change in } y}{\text{change in } x} = \frac{\Delta y}{\Delta x} = \frac{8.5 - 7.5}{4.25 - 3.75} = 2,$$

$$\text{at } x = 20: \quad \frac{\text{change in } y}{\text{change in } x} = \frac{\Delta y}{\Delta x} = \frac{40.5 - 39.5}{20.25 - 19.75} = 2.$$

Since the function given by $f(x) = 2x$ is a straight line, it has a constant slope of 2 at all values of x. Furthermore, the ratio of the change in y to the change in x remains constant at 2 even though the change in x was only half as large for the second set of ratios. This suggests that the ratio would not change no matter how small the change in x. Hence $\lim_{\Delta x \to 0} \Delta y / \Delta x = 2$ for this function. The derivative of the function given by $y \equiv f(x) = 2x$ is 2 for all x. We write $f'(x) = 2$.

✓ : What is the derivative function for a constant function?
$f'(x) =$ _____ .

Answer. A constant function by definition does not change. It has the same value for any x. Hence the derivative is zero for all x. If $f(x) = c$ where c is any constant, then $f'(x) = 0$.

Delta Method for Finding the Derivative Function

Let's turn to a somewhat more difficult problem. Consider again the labor cost and output function given by

$$y \equiv f(x) = x^2$$

at the point where $x = 1$. At $x = 1$, $y = 1$. Suppose we consider a small change in x, Δx, of say, $+0.1$. Then y moves from $f(x)$ to $f(x + \Delta x)$. The change in y, Δy, is

$$\Delta y = f(x + \Delta x) - f(x) = f(1.1) - f(1) = (1.1)^2 - (1)^2 = 0.21.$$

If we consider a still smaller change in x, say a Δx of 0.01, we obtain

$$\Delta y = f(1.01) - f(1) = 0.0201.$$

Let's summarize these results and add one even smaller change in x:

If x changes from	Δx *is*	*and y changes from*	Δy *is*	*so* $\dfrac{\Delta y}{\Delta x}$ *is*
1 to 1.1	0.1	1 to 1.21	0.21	2.1
1 to 1.01	0.01	1 to 1.0201	0.0201	2.01
1 to 1.001	0.001	1 to 1.002001	0.002001	2.001

As Δx gets smaller and smaller, the ratio of $\Delta y/\Delta x$ approaches 2. The same result occurs if we take small negative changes in x. (Try it and see.) In other words, at the value $x = 1$ the limit of the ratio $\Delta y/\Delta x$ as Δx approaches zero is 2. We write compactly $\lim_{\Delta x \to 0} (\Delta y/\Delta x) = 2$ at $x = 1$. But, as we know, this is the derivative of the function $y = x^2$ at $x = 1$.

Now let's try the same reasoning at $x = 2$.

If x changes from	Δx *is*	*and y changes from*	Δy *is*	*so* $\dfrac{\Delta y}{\Delta x}$ *is*
2 to 2.1	0.1	4 to 4.41	0.41	4.1
2 to 2.01	0.01	4 to 4.0401	0.0401	4.01
2 to 2.001	0.001	4 to 4.004001	0.004001	4.001

As Δx approaches zero, the ratio $\Delta y/\Delta x$ approaches 4. The ratio also approaches 4 as Δx approaches zero through negative values, although we have not shown it here. We may say that the limit of the ratio $\Delta y/\Delta x$ as Δx goes to zero is 4 at the value $x = 2$. We write $\lim_{\Delta x \to 0} (\Delta y/\Delta x) = 4$ at $x = 2$. But, as we showed earlier, this is the derivative of the function $f(x) = x^2$ at $x = 2$. The value of the derivative depends on the value of x, where the limit is taken. It would take a long time to find the derivative at every x value using this approach. You will be glad to know (at least momentarily) that there is an easier way.

What we have shown so far is that the derivative at a value of x can also be thought of as the limit of the ratio $\Delta y/\Delta x$ as $x + \Delta x$ approaches x, that is, as Δx approaches zero. Using this ratio, we can generalize and find a function that will give us the derivative at any value of x we wish. Let's see how this works.

If
$$y \equiv f(x),$$

then
$$y + \Delta y = f(x + \Delta x),$$

so
$$\Delta y = f(x + \Delta x) - y = f(x + \Delta x) - f(x)$$

and
$$\frac{\Delta y}{\Delta x} = \frac{f(x + \Delta x) - f(x)}{\Delta x}.$$

So, we can write the limit of the ratio on the left as $\Delta x \to 0$ as the limit of the ratio on the right as $\Delta x \to 0$:

$$\lim_{\Delta x \to 0} \left[\frac{\Delta y}{\Delta x} \right] = \lim_{\Delta x \to 0} \left[\frac{f(x + \Delta x) - f(x)}{\Delta x} \right].$$

The limit on the right of the above equality can be used to find the derivative at any value of x. Let's try it for $f(x) = x^2$. For our example,

$$f(x + \Delta x) = (x + \Delta x)^2 = x^2 + 2\Delta x + (\Delta x)^2.$$

Thus

$$\lim_{\Delta x \to 0} \left[\frac{f(x + \Delta x) - f(x)}{\Delta x} \right] = \lim_{\Delta x \to 0} \left[\frac{x^2 + 2x\,\Delta x + (\Delta x)^2 - x^2}{\Delta x} \right]$$

$$= \lim_{\Delta x \to 0} \left[\frac{2x\,\Delta x + (\Delta x)^2}{\Delta x} \right]$$

$$= \lim_{\Delta x \to 0} [2x + \Delta x].$$

Now as Δx goes to zero, the term $2x + \Delta x$ goes to $2x + 0$ or just $2x$. Hence

$$\lim_{\Delta x \to 0} [2x + \Delta x] = 2x.$$

The final answer is that $2x$ gives the derivative of $f(x) = x^2$ at any point x. The function given by $2x$ is the *derivative function* and we write it $f'(x) - 2x$. The function given by $f'(x) = 2x$ provides the derivative of the original function given by $f(x) = x^2$ at any point x. Let's try it and see if it works. We have already found that the derivative of $f(x) = x^2$ at $x = 1$ is 2 and at $x = 2$, it is 4. Using $f'(x) = 2x$, we obtain $f'(1) = 2$ and $f'(2) = 4$. (It works!)

It may be hard for you to swallow just yet, but the limit expression above is the operational definition of the *derivative function*. It is a limit. (Ah, you say, so that is why all that limit stuff is in Chapter 9.) The formula is not very intuitive, but it does provide a means of finding derivative functions (when they exist) that is both easier and more efficient than graphing.

The derivative function gives us the answers we seek in general form. The derivative function, evaluated at any output level x, tells us in our labor-cost problem that labor cost is increasing twice as fast as that output level. Thus, for small increases in current output, labor cost will increase at a rate twice the current output level. If current output is 4,000 units, a small increase in current output causes labor costs to increase at a rate of $8,000 per unit increase in output. (A symmetrical argument holds for decreases.)

The derivative function can be found, if it exists, by evaluating the limit

$$\lim_{\Delta x \to 0} \left[\frac{f(x + \Delta x) - f(x)}{\Delta x} \right].$$

It is useful to do another example of this method for finding the derivative function, or simply the derivative as we shall call it from now on. Consider

$$y \equiv f(x) = x^3 + 2x + 6.$$

We have

$$f(x + \Delta x) = (x + \Delta x)^3 + 2(x + \Delta x) + 6$$
$$= [x^3 + 3x^2 \, \Delta x + 3x(\Delta x)^2 + (\Delta x)^3] + 2x + 2\Delta x + 6$$

and

$$f(x + \Delta x) - f(x) = x^3 + 3x^2 \, \Delta x + 3x(\Delta x)^2 + (\Delta x)^3 + 2x + 2\Delta x$$
$$+ 6 - x^3 - 2x - 6$$
$$= 3x^2 \, \Delta x + 3x(\Delta x)^2 + (\Delta x)^3 + 2\Delta x.$$

Dividing by Δx gives

$$\frac{f(x + \Delta x) - f(x)}{\Delta x} = 3x^2 + 3x(\Delta x) + (\Delta x)^2 + 2.$$

Taking the limit as Δx approaches zero yields

$$\lim_{\Delta x \to 0} \left[\frac{f(x + \Delta x) - f(x)}{\Delta x} \right] = 3x^2 + 2,$$

because both $3x(\Delta x)$ and $(\Delta x)^2$ go to zero in the limit as Δx goes to zero. We may write

$$f'(x) = 3x^2 + 2.$$

The derivative takes on a value 5 at $x = 1$ which tells us that this function has a rate of change (slope) of 5 at $x = 1$. A small increase in x near $x = 1$ produces an increase five times as great in $y = f(x)$. If the derivative function had been given by $f'(x) = -3x^2 - 2$, then, at $x = 1$, a small increase in x would yield a *decrease* in $y \equiv f(x)$ five times as great.

In order, it seems, to complicate the initiation rites of the newcomer, there are several symbols used to denote the derivative. The more common include

$$f'(x); \frac{dy}{dx}; \frac{d}{dx}f(x); D_x y; D_x f(x); y'; \lim_{\Delta x \to 0} \left[\frac{\Delta y}{\Delta x}\right]; \lim_{\Delta x \to 0} \left[\frac{f(x + \Delta x) - f(x)}{\Delta x}\right].$$

The last symbol will be used occasionally here to obtain a derivative but not to represent one. Rather, we will use either

$$f'(x), \qquad \frac{dy}{dx}, \qquad \text{or} \qquad \frac{d}{dx}(f(x))$$

interchangeably to indicate the derivative. [We note that different functions of x are given by $g(x)$ and $h(x)$, etc. Hence the derivative of these representations would be written using $g'(x)$ and $h'(x)$, respectively.]

One more point. It is possible to take the derivative of a derivative. For example, we can take the derivative of the function given by

$$f'(x) = 3x^2 + 2.$$

Mentally ignoring the prime and using the operational delta-method formula gives

$$\lim_{\Delta x \to 0} \left[\frac{f(x + \Delta x) - f(x)}{\Delta x}\right] = \lim_{\Delta x \to 0} \left[\frac{3(x + \Delta x)^2 + 2 - 3x^2 - 2}{\Delta x}\right]$$

$$= \lim_{\Delta x \to 0} \left[\frac{3x^2 + 6x\,\Delta x + 3(\Delta x)^2 + 2 - 3x^2 - 2}{\Delta x}\right]$$

$$= \lim_{\Delta x \to 0} (6x + 3\Delta x)$$

$$= 6x.$$

This yields the second derivative with respect to x of the initial function given by $f(x) = x^3 + 2x + 6$. It gives the rate of change of the derivative function at any point x. Symbolically, we write

$$f''(x) = 6x \quad \text{or} \quad \frac{d^2 y}{dx^2} = 6x \quad \text{or} \quad \frac{d}{dx}f'(x) = 6x.$$

The second derivative is the derivative of $f'(x)$. It is the derivative of the derivative. Formally, we can continue the process and find third, fourth, and higher derivatives, if they exist. There is, generally speaking, little use for these higher-order derivatives in managerial applications.

Symbol	*English Translation*
$f''(x)$; $\dfrac{d^2y}{dx^2}$; $\dfrac{d^2}{dx^2}f(x)$; D_x^2y; $D_x^2f(x)$; y''	The value of the second derivative function.

The superscripts in the second, third, fifth, and sixth methods of indicating the derivative are part of the symbol and should be interpreted as meaning the second derivative. They have nothing to do with squaring anything.

〜 : Circle the correct second derivative of $6x^2 + ex$. (Use the delta method.)

1. $12x + e$.

2. $12 + e$.

3. 12.

Answer. Using the delta method,

$$\lim_{\Delta x \to 0}\left[\frac{f(x + \Delta x) - f(x)}{\Delta x}\right] = \lim_{\Delta x \to 0}\left[\frac{6(x + \Delta x)^2 + e(x + \Delta x) - 6x^2 - ex}{\Delta x}\right]$$

$$= \lim_{\Delta x \to 0}\left[\frac{12x\,\Delta x + 6(\Delta x)^2 + e\,\Delta x)}{\Delta x}\right]$$

$$= \lim_{\Delta x \to 0}\left[12x + \Delta x + e\right]$$

$$= 12x + e.$$

The second derivative is obtained by repeating the delta method on $12x + e$.

$$\lim_{\Delta x \to 0}\left[\frac{f(x + \Delta x) - f(x)}{\Delta x}\right] = \lim_{\Delta x \to 0}\left[\frac{12(x + \Delta x) + e - 12x - e}{\Delta x}\right]$$

$$= \lim_{\Delta x \to 0}\left[\frac{12\Delta x}{\Delta x}\right]$$

$$= 12.$$

10-2 CONDITIONS FOR THE EXISTENCE OF THE DERIVATIVE

The definitions of the derivative and the means of finding derivatives all include the phrase "if it exists." It is not unusual for functions found in managerial problems to fail to have a derivative for certain values of x. We will examine the conditions for the derivative to exist at a point and then, using this result, the condition for the derivative to exist over an interval is given.

For the derivative to exist at a point, two conditions must be satisfied. They are: (1) the function must be continuous at the point, and (2) the limit

$$\lim_{\Delta x \to 0} \left[\frac{f(x + \Delta x) - f(x)}{\Delta x} \right]$$

must exist at that point. — (Note: Condition 2 implies Condition 1.)

In Chapter 9 several functions are illustrated that are not continuous at a particular value of x. For example, the fixed-cost function graphed in Figure 9–3 is discontinuous at $x = 100$. You cannot trace out this function without lifting your pencil at the point $x = 100$. The function has no derivative at $x = 100$. Similarly, in Figure 9–4, three functions are graphed, all of which are discontinuous at $x = 3$. They have no derivative at $x = 3$.

But it is possible for a function to be continuous at a point and still not have a derivative at that point. An example is the wedge-shaped function graphed in Figure 9–5 at the point $x = 4$. The function, as you can see, is continuous at that point. But consider the value of the limit required by condition (2) for a derivative to exist. For small negative changes in x, the rate of change in the function, its derivative, is given by the slope of the straight line $f(x) = x$. The slope of this line is $+1$, as can be seen from the graph (or by using the delta method if you are masochistically inclined). Similarly, for small positive values of Δx, the derivative is given by the slope of the straight-line function $f(x) = 8 - x$. The slope of this line is -1. Hence for negative Δx the slope is $+1$, and for positive Δx the slope is -1. This is the case regardless of how small we select Δx. Hence there is no limit as Δx approaches zero and hence no derivative. (For the limit to exist, the same limit value must be approached for both negative and positive Δx).

Visually, a way to satisfy yourself of this fact is to try to draw a tangent to the function at the point $x = 4$. Recall that the slope of such a tangent gives the slope of the function at that point, and that value is the value of the derivative for the function at that point. You will see that there are many lines that could be drawn which would just touch this curve at the point $x = 4$. Cases such as this occur in managerial situations. An example is found in describing the cost of electricity for certain regions. Suppose that the cost is 2.5 cents per kilowatt-hour for the first 2,000 kilowatt-hours in any month, and 1.5 cents per kilowatt-hour thereafter. The total cost can be written symbolically as

$$f(x) = \begin{cases} 0.025x, & 0 < x \le 2,000, \\ 20 + 0.015x, & x > 2,000. \end{cases}$$

Curves of this type are called *piecewise linear* because the segments can be described by straight lines. The function is differentiable at every point except for $x = 2,000$. The function is graphed in Figure 10–2.

FIGURE 10–2

Electricity Cost and Usage

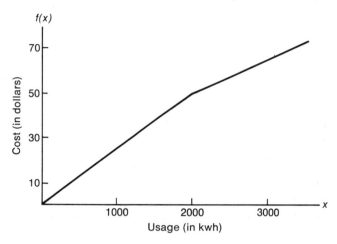

It is also possible for the limit described in condition 2 to exist at a point, but because the function is discontinuous at that point, there is no derivative. The function graphed in Figure 9–4a offers an example at $x = 3$. The limit of

$$\frac{f(x + \Delta x) - f(x)}{\Delta x}$$

as Δx approaches zero exists and is 6, but the function is not continuous and has no derivative at $x = 3$. Figure 9–4c provides another example. Functions without derivatives at a point are characterized by holes or sharp corners at the point in question. An example is the point $x = 2,000$, $f(x) = 50$ in Figure 10–2.

We are now ready to describe the condition required for the derivative of a function to exist over an interval. The definition parallels that for continuity over an interval.

The derivative of a function over an interval exists if the derivative exists at every point in the interval.

We say the function is differentiable over the interval if the derivative exists for every point in the interval.

⌇ : Does the derivative function exist (is the function differentiable) in the following case?

over the interval $-1 < x < +1$?   Yes_____   No_____
over the interval $+1 < x < +3$?   Yes_____   No_____

$$f(x) = \begin{cases} x^2, & -5 \le x \le 2, \\ x + 2, & 2 < x \le 5. \end{cases}$$

Answer. For the first interval under consideration, the function is entirely specified by $f(x) = x^2$, and it is continuous everywhere. Further, the limit of

$$\frac{f(x + \Delta x) - f(x)}{\Delta x}$$

as Δx approaches zero exists. This can be seen from the graph or verified using the delta method. There are no "sharp corners." There is such a corner at $x = 2$ and the derivative does not exist there because the relevant limit does not exist. Thus the derivative does not exist over any interval containing $x = 2$. The function is not differentiable over the interval $+1 < x < +3$ since $x = 2$ belongs to this interval.

10-3 SUMMARY

We have made relatively little use yet of the concept of a derivative. The purpose of this chapter is to explain the concept and the conditions under which it exists.

The derivative at a point is the "slope of the curve at that point." Visually this slope can be defined as the slope of the tangent to the curve at the point. The value of the derivative at the point is the slope of the tangent line. Obtaining this value precisely can be a difficult task if we are forced to resort to drawing tangents. The use of the delta method makes it easier to obtain the derivative of the function. The delta method gives us the derivative at any point x, if it exists. This method employs the limit definition of the derivative to find the derivative function. In Chapter 11 the delta method is used to help derive rules for finding derivatives in common situations. These rules, once established, are easier to use than the delta method.

The limit of the ratio

$$\frac{f(x + \Delta x) - f(x)}{\Delta x}$$

as Δx approaches zero must exist at a point if the function is to have a derivative at the point. But although it is necessary for this limit to exist, by itself it is not sufficient to assure the existence of the derivative at the point in question. The function must also be continuous at this point.

The derivative of a function over an interval exists if the derivative exists at every point in the interval.

NEW SYMBOLS

Symbol	*English Translation*
Δx	The (small) change in x (also called delta x).
$f'(x)$; $\dfrac{dy}{dx}$; $\dfrac{d}{dx}f(x)$; $D_x y$; $D_x f(x)$; y'	The derivative function.
$f''(x)$; $\dfrac{d^2y}{dx^2}$; $\dfrac{d^2}{dx^2}f(x)$; $D_x^2 y$; $D_x^2 f(x)$; y''	The second derivative function.

PROBLEMS

Problems for Self-Study: 2, 12, 17, 20

10–1.* Make up five examples of derivatives (the rate of change of one variable with respect to another) that would be of interest in business applications.

10–2. Which of the following expressions describe a rate of change? Where a rate of change is implied, state it.

 a. The speed (velocity) of my car is 30 miles per hour.

 b. My car will accelerate from 0 to 10 miles per hour in 100 feet.

 c. A thousand new cases of Asian flu are being reported each week.

 d. Only a major inoculation program has kept the number of new cases from increasing beyond 1000 per week.

10–3. For Problem 10–2 describe in equation form the rate of change suggested by each statement. Define all variables. Let $r \equiv$ rate of change in each case. Also write down to what this rate of change applies.

10–4.* In the graph of the quadratic equation given below, does the slope of the line, L, define the derivative at the point p? [A quadratic equation is one of the form $f(x) = ax^2 + bx + c$.]

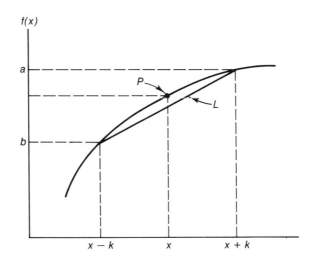

$$a = ax^2 + (2ak + b)x + (ak + bk + c),$$
$$b = ax^2 - (2ak - b)x + (ak - bk + c)$$

10–5.   Given that the rate of change of cost is $2000 or that the Consumer Price Index rose 0.5 points, which of the following facts are important to the interpretation of the significance of these figures?

   a. The independent variable.

   b. The time to which the change relates.

   c. The slope of the function relating to the dependent and independent variable.

10–6.*   If the rate of change of cost in dollars with respect to units produced is 6 over all output levels, then

   a. If total cost is 30 when output is 3, what is the total cost of 10 units?

   b. If total cost is 50 when output is 3, what is the total cost of 10 units?

10–7.   Mr. Grotshawk is considering a new job. The starting salary is $18,000 with a guaranteed annual raise of $1000 per year. He also knows that if he works hard his raise will be increased by $100 per year.

   a. What is the guaranteed rate of change of Mr. Grotshawk's salary with respect to time (in years)?

b. What is the rate of change of his raise with respect to time if he works hard?

c. What is the derivative of his guaranteed salary with respect to time?

d. What is the derivative of his salary with respect to time if he works hard?

e. Write his salary, S, as a function of time ($t = 0, 1, 2, \ldots$) if he works hard. Do the same for the derivative dS/dt of his salary with respect to time.

10-8.* Determine the slope of the functions with the following rules:

a. $f(x) = 3 + 17x$
b. $f(x) = a - bx$
c. $g(y) = 14(y - 2)$
d. $h(z) = a(x + b) - 0.5(x + 4)$

10-9. Plot the functions suggested by the rules given below and estimate their slope at the points indicated:

a. $f(x) = x^3$ at $x = -1$ and $x = 2$
b. $f(x) = \sqrt{x}$ for $x \geq 0$ at $x = 1$ and $x = 4$

10-10.* Using the definition of the derivative without the limit,

$$g(x, \Delta x) = \frac{f(x + \Delta x) - f(x)}{\Delta x},$$

find successively more accurate approximations of the slope of $f(x) = x^2 + 2x - 3$ at $x = 1$.

a. For $\Delta x = 0.1$
b. For $\Delta x = -0.01$
c. For $\Delta x = 0.001$
d. Find $\lim_{\Delta x \to 0} g(1, \Delta x)$.

10-11. Using the definition of the derivative without the limit and the intervals in Problem 10-10, find successively more accurate approximations of the slope of $f(x) = 2x^3 - 3x + 7$ at $x = -1$.

10-12. Is the derivative of a function itself a function? Using the function given by $y \equiv f(x) = 3x$, find the derivative function. Using the answer, can you find a derivative for this expression?

10–13.* Use the delta method to find the derivative functions for
    a. $f(x) = -6x^2$
    b. $f(x) = x^2 + 2x + 1$
    c. $f(x) = x^3 - 4x + 6$
    d. $f(x) = 7x^2 - 19b$

10–14.* Use the delta method to find the derivative functions for
    a. $f(x) = a^2x^2 + c$
    b. $g(y) = aby + cy^3$
    c. $h(z) = az^2 + bz + c$
    d. $f(y) = cy^3 + by^2 + d$

10–15. Use the delta method to find the second derivative functions for the functions with the rules given in Problem 10–13.

10–16.* Use the delta method to find the second derivative functions for the functions with rules given in Problem 10–14.

10–17. The supply of one raw material available to a small electronics producer can be expressed by the equation

$$S = 2p + 4p^2,$$

where p is price in cents and the supply is in units of 100.
    a. What is the instantaneous (or marginal) rate at which supply is changing when the price is 5 cents?
    b. What is the average rate of change when the price is changed from 4 to 6 cents? Do you expect the same result?

10–18.* A manager wishes to know the rate of change of profits with respect to units sold, x, where profits are a function of sales given by

$$f(x) = px - (a + bx^2),$$

where p is the unit price and $(a + bx^2)$ is the cost of producing x units. Use the delta method to find the rate of change as a function of x.

10–19.* Find the derivative function of the function given by

$$y \equiv f(x) = e^x$$

using the delta process and given that $\lim_{\Delta x \to 0} \left[\dfrac{e^{\Delta x} - 1}{\Delta x} \right] = 1.$

10–20. Do the derivatives of the functions whose rules are given below exist at the points indicated?

a. $f(x) = 2x^4$ at $x = -1$

b. $f(x) = \begin{cases} 2x & \text{for } x \leq 6 \\ 12 & \text{for } x > 6 \end{cases}$ at $x = 13$

c. Same as part *b* at $x = 6$

d. $f(x) = \begin{cases} x^2 & \text{for } x \leq 1 \\ 2x - 1 & \text{for } x > 1 \end{cases}$ at $x = 1$

10–21.* Given the function with rule

$$f(x) = \begin{cases} x^2, & x < 1, \\ 2x - 1, & x \geq 1. \end{cases}$$

a. Is it continuous over the interval $0 \leq x \leq 5$?

b. Is it differentiable over the interval $0 \leq x \leq 5$?

10–22. Given the function with rule

$$f(x) = \begin{cases} x^2 - 1, & x \neq 4, \\ 12, & x = 4. \end{cases}$$

a. Is the function continuous for $x \geq 0$?

b. Is the function differentiable for $x \geq 0$? If not, alter the function to make it so.

10–23.* Is the graph of the following expression continuous and is the expression differentiable for $x \geq 0$?

$$f(x) = \frac{x^2 - 4}{x - 2}$$

If not, redefine $f(x)$ so that it has the same values wherever it was defined before and so that it is continuous.

10–24.* Suppose that the demand for a product, D, was expressed as a function of its price, p. Suppose that the function was $D = 1857 \cdot p^{-1}$. Use the delta method to find the rate of change of D with respect to p.

10–25. Find, using the delta method, the derivative function of

$$y \equiv f(x) = a_n x^n.$$

[*Hint:* Separate out only terms involving $(\Delta x)^0$ and $(\Delta x)^1$. The rest will go to zero when the limit is taken.]

11

Rules for Differentiation

In Chapter 10 we developed the conditions necessary for the existence of the derivative and the definitional or delta method of finding derivatives. Although we should always satisfy ourselves concerning the existence of the derivative as a first step, this chapter will assume such conditions are met for the examples discussed.

Most of our task in this chapter is a mechanical one. We concentrate here on finding easier ways to obtain the derivative of a function than using the definitional delta process each time. The results of our endeavors will be a set of rules that allow us to find quickly the derivatives of most of the simple functions found in management applications.

11-1 RULES FOR DIFFERENTIATION

In Section 10–1 we used the delta method to find that the derivative of $f(x) = x^2$ is $f'(x) = 2x$. We can write in this case

$$f'(x) = 2x = 2(x^{2-1}).$$

In words, to find the derivative of a variable raised to a constant exponent, bring down the exponent as a constant multiplier and reduce the exponent of the variable by 1.

Rule 1 for Differentiation: POWERS

The derivative of a variable raised to a constant exponent is the product of the exponent and the variable raised to the exponent reduced by 1. In symbolic form:

$$f'(x) = \frac{d}{dx}[x^n] = nx^{n-1},$$

where n is a constant.

The letter n can be any real number. It does not need to be an integer. (Problem 10–25 requires the reader to derive this rule in the general case.)

A special application of this rule is when $n = 0$. When $n = 0$,

$$f(x) = x^0 = 1$$

and the derivative using rule 1 is zero:

$$f'(x) = 0x^{0-1} = 0.$$

Since the derivative of x^0 is the derivative of the constant, 1, it seems natural to inquire into the derivative of any constant, call it k. Letting $f(x) = k$ and using the delta method,

$$\lim_{\Delta x \to 0} \left[\frac{f(x + \Delta x) - f(x)}{\Delta x} \right] = \lim_{\Delta x \to 0} \left[\frac{k - k}{\Delta x} \right]$$

$$= \lim_{\Delta x \to 0} \left[\frac{0}{\Delta x} \right] = 0.$$

You might think that the limit of the ratio $0/\Delta x$ as Δx approaches zero would be indeterminant, but Δx only approaches zero while the numerator is always zero. Hence the ratio is always zero as Δx approaches zero. The result should not surprise you since the derivative is a slope and the slope of a constant function is zero everywhere. Plot it and see.

Rule 2 for Derivatives: CONSTANTS

The derivative of any constant is zero.

Using rules 1 and 2 for derivatives, we can write

(*i*) If $f(x) = x^{1/2}$, then $f'(x) = \frac{1}{2}x^{-1/2}$.
(*ii*) If $f(z) = z^\pi$, then $f'(z) = \pi z^{\pi-1}$.
(*iii*) If $f(y) = e^{1/2}$, then $f'(y) = 0$.

We turn now to the third rule for derivatives.

Again in Section 10–1, we found the derivative of

$$f(x) = x^3 + 2x + 6$$

by the delta method. The derivative is given by

$$f'(x) = 3x^2 + 2.$$

But using rules 1 and 2 for derivatives, we know that

$$\frac{d}{dx}[x^3] = 3x^2,$$

$$\frac{d}{dx}[2x] = 2,$$

and

$$\frac{d}{dx}[6] = 0.$$

Thus we observe that the derivative of this sum of several expressions is the sum of the derivatives. (This result mirrors the rule that states: the limit of a sum equals the sum of the limits. This is not surprising since the derivative is a limit.) This leads us to the third rule for derivatives.

Rule 3 for Derivatives: SUMS AND DIFFERENCES

The derivative of a sum (difference) is the sum (difference) of the derivatives. In symbolic form:

$$\frac{d}{dx}[f_1(x) \pm f_2(x)] = \frac{d}{dx}[f_1(x)] \pm \frac{d}{dx}[f_2(x)].$$

This rule extends in a straightforward fashion to a sum or difference of several functions. We can write

$$\frac{d}{dx}\left[\sum_{i=1}^{n} f_i(x)\right] = \sum_{i=1}^{n} \frac{d}{dx}[f_i(x)].$$

The rule implies that we can differentiate one term at a time.

Rule 3 can also be derived formally from the delta method. Let $h(x) = f_1(x) + f_2(x)$; then

$$\frac{d}{dx}[h(x)] = \frac{d}{dx}[f_1(x) + f_2(x)] = \lim_{\Delta x \to 0}\left[\frac{h(x + \Delta x) - h(x)}{\Delta x}\right]$$

$$= \lim_{\Delta x \to 0}\left[\frac{f_1(x + \Delta x) + f_2(x + \Delta x) - f_1(x) - f_2(x)}{\Delta x}\right]$$

$$= \lim_{\Delta x \to 0}\left[\frac{f_1(x + \Delta x) - f_1(x)}{\Delta x} + \frac{f_2(x + \Delta x) - f_2(x)}{\Delta x}\right].$$

Now by rule 3 for the limit of sums:

$$\frac{d}{dx}[h(x)] = \lim_{\Delta x \to 0}\left[\frac{f_1(x + \Delta x) - f_1(x)}{\Delta x}\right] + \lim_{\Delta x \to 0}\left[\frac{f_2(x + \Delta x) - f_2(x)}{\Delta x}\right]$$

$$= \frac{d}{dx}[f_1(x)] + \frac{d}{dx}[f_2(x)].$$

Using rules 1, 2, and 3 for derivatives, let's try some examples.

(*i*) If $f(x) = x^{1/3} + 3^e + x^{-1}$, then $f'(x) = \frac{1}{3}x^{-2/3} - x^{-2}$.

(*ii*) If $f(x) = x - 3x^{2m} - \sqrt[4]{x}$, then $f'(x) = 1 - 6mx^{2m-1} - \frac{1}{4}x^{-3/4}$.

The fourth rule for derivatives involves products. We can motivate this rule using a simple example that is solved using rule 1 and what we know about exponents. Consider the function given by

$$f(x) = x^2 \cdot x = x^3.$$

Then by rule 1 for derivatives:

$$f'(x) = 3x^2 = x^2 + 2x^2 = x^2(1) + x(2x).$$

The reason for writing the derivative in this peculiar form will be evident in a minute. Suppose we write $g(x) = x^2$ and $h(x) = x$, just to complicate things further. Then $g'(x) = 2x$ and $h'(x) = 1$. Now rewriting $f(x) = x^3$,

$$f(x) = x^2 \cdot x = [g(x)][h(x)]$$

and

$$f'(x) = x^2(1) + x(2x) = [g(x) \cdot h'(x)] + [h(x) \cdot g'(x)].$$

The rule suggested by this example is generally true and is called the *product rule*. This apparently complex rule is worth referring to when complicated expressions are involved even though the example here is solved more easily by other means. It is often easier to work with rule 4 than to try to simplify an expression to be differentiated.

Rule 4 for Derivatives: PRODUCTS

The derivative of a product of two functions is the first times the derivative of the second plus the second times the derivative of the first. In symbolic form:

$$\frac{d}{dx}[g(x) \cdot h(x)] = [g(x) \cdot h'(x)] + [h(x) \cdot g'(x)].$$

One important example of the product rule is the derivative of $f(x) = kx^n$. Letting $g(x) = k$ and $h(x) = x^n$, then by rule 2, $g'(x) = 0$ and by rule 1, $h'(x) = nx^{n-1}$. Hence $f'(x) = knx^{n-1}$: The constant multiplier k does not affect the differentiation process.

Rule 4 can also be derived using the delta method. Let $y \equiv f(x) = u \cdot v$, where $u \equiv g(x)$ and $v \equiv h(x)$. Then if x is given a small increment, Δx, the function u is changed by a small increment, Δu, and the function v is changed by a small increment Δv. Hence

$$y + \Delta y \equiv f(x + \Delta x) = (u + \Delta u)(v + \Delta v)$$
$$= uv + u(\Delta v) + v(\Delta u) + (\Delta u)(\Delta v)$$

and

$$\frac{f(x + \Delta x) - f(x)}{\Delta x} = u\left(\frac{\Delta v}{\Delta x}\right) + v\left(\frac{\Delta u}{\Delta x}\right) + \Delta u\left(\frac{\Delta v}{\Delta x}\right).$$

Taking limits as Δx approaches zero gives

$$\lim_{\Delta x \to 0}\left[\frac{f(x + \Delta x) - f(x)}{\Delta x}\right] = \lim_{\Delta x \to 0}\left[u\left(\frac{\Delta v}{\Delta x}\right) + v\left(\frac{\Delta u}{\Delta x}\right) + \Delta u\left(\frac{\Delta v}{\Delta x}\right)\right].$$

Using rule 2 for the limit of a sum, we obtain

$$= \lim_{\Delta x \to 0}\left[u\left(\frac{\Delta v}{\Delta x}\right)\right] + \lim_{\Delta x \to 0}\left[v\left(\frac{\Delta u}{\Delta x}\right)\right] + \lim_{\Delta x \to 0}\left[\Delta u\left(\frac{\Delta v}{\Delta x}\right)\right].$$

Using rule 3 for the limit of a product gives

$$= \left[\lim_{\Delta x \to 0} u\right]\left[\lim_{\Delta x \to 0}\frac{\Delta v}{\Delta x}\right] + \left[\lim_{\Delta x \to 0} v\right]\left[\lim_{\Delta x \to 0}\frac{\Delta u}{\Delta x}\right] + \left[\lim_{\Delta x \to 0}\Delta u\right]\left[\lim_{\Delta x \to 0}\frac{\Delta v}{\Delta x}\right].$$

Since the functions u and v are not affected by letting Δx approach zero but Δu goes to zero as Δx approaches zero, we can write

$$= u\frac{dv}{dx} + v\frac{du}{dx} + 0\frac{dv}{dx}$$
$$= [g(x)\cdot h'(x)] + [h(x)\cdot g'(x)].$$

Using the rules developed so far, we can differentiate the following examples:

(i) If $f(x) = x^4\cdot x^{1/2}$, then $f'(x) = \frac{1}{2}x^4x^{-1/2} + 4x^3x^{1/2} = 4\frac{1}{2}x^{7/2}$.
(ii) If $f(x) = x^{2m}\cdot x^6$; then $f'(x) = 6x^{2m+5} + 2mx^{2m+5} = (2m+6)x^{2m+5}$.
(iii) If $f(x) = (x^2 + m)(x^m - a)$, then $f'(x) = m(x^2 + m)x^{m-1} + 2(x^m - a)(x)$.

Try, as a check, solving examples (i) and (ii) using rule 1 and the laws of exponents.

For completeness and for ease of computation, we will also develop the rule for quotients. A separate rule is not required because $1/x = x^{-1}$. Hence, any quotient can be converted into a product. Consider another simple example involving the functions given by $g(x) = x^2$ and $h(x) = x$, with $g'(x) = 2x$ and $h'(x) = 1$, used in the development of rule 4.

Suppose that we wish to find the derivative of

$$f(x) = \frac{x^2}{x} = x.$$

Using rule 1 for derivatives we obtain

$$f'(x) = 1$$

or rewriting to motivate the next rule,

$$f'(x) = 1 = \frac{x^2}{x^2} = \frac{2x^2 - x^2}{x^2} = \frac{x(2x) - x^2(1)}{x^2}$$
$$= \frac{h(x)g'(x) - g(x)h'(x)}{[h(x)]^2}.$$

Once again we have only suggested a rule, but it turns out that this procedure always works as long as $h(x) \neq 0$. (This rule, too, can be derived using the delta method, but, you will be happy to hear, we will not do so.)

Rule 5 for Derivatives: QUOTIENTS

The derivative of a quotient is given by the denominator multiplied by the

derivative of the numerator minus the numerator multiplied by the derivative of the denominator, with the whole of this result divided by the square of the denominator. In symbolic form:

$$\frac{d}{dx}\left[\frac{g(x)}{h(x)}\right] = \frac{h(x)g'(x) - g(x)h'(x)}{[h(x)]^2}.$$

In this case, unlike rule 4, it is important to combine the terms in the numerator of the answer in the proper order, owing to the negative sign between them. Using the rules we now have, we can write

(*i*) If $(fx) = x^5/x^3$, then $f'(x) = \dfrac{5x^4 \cdot x^3 - 3x^5 \cdot x^2}{[x^3]^2} = 2x.$

(*ii*) If $f(x) = x^{3r}/mx$, then $f'(x) = \dfrac{3rmx \cdot x^{3r-1} - mx^{3r}}{(mx)^2} = \dfrac{3r-1}{m}x^{3r-2}.$

Checking these results using the laws of exponents and rule 1 for derivatives yields

(*i*) $f(x) = x^5/x^3 = x^2$ and $f'(x) = 2x.$

(*ii*) $f(x) = \dfrac{x^{3r}}{mx} = \dfrac{1}{m}x^{3r-1}$ and $f'(x) = \dfrac{3r-1}{m}x^{3r-2}.$

We are comforted by the identity of the results obtained using the two independent procedures. As a final example and one that cannot be verified using rule 1 (and rule 2):

(*iii*) If $f(x) = \dfrac{x^2+1}{x^3+1}$, then $f'(x) = \dfrac{(x^3+1)2x - (x^2+1)3x^2}{(x^3+1)^2}$

$\qquad\qquad = \dfrac{-x^4+3x^2+2x}{x^6+2x^3+1}$

⤳ : Find the derivatives of the following functions. Use the product rule for 3 and the quotient rule for 4 and check your answers to 3 and 4 using rule 1.

1. $f(x) = 3x^3$ $f'(x) =$ _____

2. $f(x) = 4x^{1/2} - x^a$ $f'(x) =$ _____

3. $f(x) = (x^t)(x^e)$ $f'(x) =$ _____

4. $f(x) = x^t \div x^e$ $f'(x) =$ _____

Answers

1. $f'(x) = 9x^2$.
2. $f'(x) = 2x^{-1/2} - ax^{a-1}$.
3. $f'(x) = ex^t x^{e-1} + tx^{t-1}x^e = (t + e)x^{t+e-1}$.
4. $f'(x) = \dfrac{tx^e x^{t-1} - ex^t x^{e-1}}{x^{2e}} = \dfrac{(t - e)x^{t+e-1}}{x^{2e}} = (t - e)x^{t-e-1}$.

11-2 THE CHAIN RULE FOR DIFFERENTIATION

Sometimes the expression to be differentiated is quite complex, and we would prefer to work with only a portion of it at a time. A procedure of substitution to make the expression simpler will often help. For example, the derivative of the expression

$$y \equiv f(x) = (2x^2 + x)^{3m}$$

is somewhat difficult unless this procedure is used. [If you don't agree, and even if you do agree, make a guess as to what the derivative of $f(x) = (2x^2 + x)^{3m}$ is and write it down. We will see later how well you did.]

$$\frac{d}{dx}[(2x^2 + x)^{3m}] = \underline{\hspace{3cm}}: \text{(Your guess)}$$

To show how the procedure works, we resort first to a different and more simple example for which we can find the answer using rules that are already familiar.

Consider the function given by

$$y \equiv f(x) = (x^2)^3.$$

Now using rule 2 for exponents, we may write

$$y \equiv f(x) = x^6$$

and, using rule 1 for derivatives,

$$\frac{dy}{dx} = f'(x) = 6x^5.$$

Now let us try to find the answer using substitution.
Let $u = x^2$. Then we can write

$$y \equiv f(x) = u^3.$$

The derivative of $y \equiv f(x) = u^3$ with respect to u is

$$\frac{dy}{du} = 3u^2.$$

Next, we make a very important observation. Since u is a function of x, we can also find du/dx:

$$\frac{du}{dx} = 2x, \qquad \text{since } u = x^2.$$

Multiplying these two results gives

$$\frac{dy}{du} \cdot \frac{du}{dx} = (3u^2)(2x).$$

Recalling that u is a function of x, we substitute x^2 for u to give the answer in terms of the original variable x:

$$\frac{dy}{du} \cdot \frac{du}{dx} = 3(x^2)^2 2x$$
$$= (3x^4)2x$$
$$= 6x^5.$$

But, as we showed directly without substitution, this is the derivative dy/dx. Thus, in this case, $dy/du \cdot du/dx = dy/dx$. This example suggests the very important chain rule.

Rule 6 for Derivatives: THE CHAIN RULE

If $y \equiv f(x)$ is written as a function of u with derivative dy/du, and u is a function of x with derivative du/dx, then the derivative of $y \equiv f(x)$ with respect to x, dy/dx, is given by the derivative of y with respect to u multiplied by the derivative of u with respect to x. In symbolic form:

$$\frac{dy}{dx} = \frac{dy}{du} \cdot \frac{du}{dx}.$$

where $y \equiv f(u)$ and $u \equiv f(x)$.

The best way to get a handle on the chain rule is to do some examples. Using the chain rule, let us differentiate

$$y \equiv f(x) = (2x^2 + x)^{3m}.$$

The substitution that is usually most helpful is to let u be the expression within the parentheses.

Letting $u = 2x^2 + x$, we obtain

$$y \equiv f(u) = u^{3m}$$
$$\frac{dy}{du} = 3mu^{3m-1}$$

and

$$\frac{du}{dx} = \frac{d}{dx}(2x^2 + x) = 4x + 1.$$

Now using the chain rule:

$$\frac{dy}{dx} = \frac{dy}{du}\cdot\frac{du}{dx} = 3mu^{3m-1}(4x + 1).$$

Substituting back for u to obtain an answer expressed in terms of x gives

$$= 3m(2x^2 + x)^{3m-1}(4x + 1).$$

Did you obtain this answer when you tried it? Look back to the answer you wrote down and see. If not, we suspect you may have omitted the $(4x + 1)$ term, the derivative of what is inside the parentheses: the du/dx term. This is an easy step to forget and that is why the rule is valuable.

Let's try another example for practice. Differentiate

$$y \equiv f(x) = (x^3 + 2x^2 + 1)^5.$$

One way to do this is to first expand it by multiplying $(x^3 + 2x^2 + 1)$ by itself four times and then using rules 1, 2, and 3 for differentiation. But this is much longer than using the chain rule. Using this more efficient method, let

$$u = x^3 + 2x^2 + 1 \qquad \text{so that } y = u^5.$$

Then

$$\frac{du}{dx} = 3x^2 + 4x \qquad \text{and} \qquad \frac{dy}{du} = 5u^4.$$

Hence

$$\frac{dy}{dx} = \frac{dy}{du}\cdot\frac{du}{dx} = 5u^4(3x^2 + 4x)$$
$$= 5(x^3 + 2x^2 + 1)^4(3x^2 + 4x).$$

When you have had lots of practice you may be able to do this substitution in your head and immediately write down the answer. The mental process might proceed as follows for this last example: Using rule 1 for derivatives, we obtain five times the expression $(x^3 + 2x^2 + 1)$ to the exponent reduced by 1, and we must multiply this result by the derivative of what is inside the parentheses. It is this last portion of the mental process that tends to be forgotten. If you tend to forget it, resort to the formal rule. The mental process for applying the chain rule to each example differentiated in this section is summarized below:

Expression	Derivative of Expression to a Power	× "What's inside"
$y \equiv f(x) = (x^2)^3$	$3(x^2)^2$	$2x$
$y \equiv f(x) = (2x^2 + x)^{3m}$	$3m(2x^2 + x)^{3m-1}$	$4x + 1$
$y \equiv f(x) = (x^3 + 2x^2 + 1)^5$	$5(x^3 + 2x^2 + 1)^4$	$3x^2 + 4x$

Note that the chain rule works even for x^3 since

$y \equiv f(x) = x^3$	$3x^2$	1

Not all problems are so easy, but the chain rule can often be used to advantage in difficult cases.

Practical application of the chain rule to managerial problems occurs most frequently when one variable, say profit, is given as a function of a second, say sales, and this second variable is given as a function of a third variable, say advertising. Now suppose that management wishes to know the rate of change of the first variable, profit, with respect to a change in the third variable, advertising. The chain rule is directly applicable. For example, let

$$\text{Profit} \equiv P = 3S - 6,$$
$$\text{Sales} \equiv S = 8A - 2A^2, \quad \text{where } A \text{ is the level of advertising.}$$

Then $dP/dS = 3$ and $dS/dA = 8 - 4A$.

The rate of change of profit with respect to advertising is

$$\frac{dP}{dA} = \frac{dP}{dS} \cdot \frac{dS}{dA} = 3(8 - 4A) = 24 - 12A.$$

The rate of change of profit with respect to advertising is 24-12 times the level of advertising. The need for information of this type in managerial problems is common.

A device to help you remember the chain rule is given below. Treating the symbols as fractions and canceling,

$$\frac{dy}{du} \cdot \frac{du}{dx} \quad \text{leaves} \quad \frac{dy}{dx}.$$

(This is only a memory device. One can't really cancel since dy/du and du/dx are symbols not fractions. We use the memory device only because it's helpful.)

⌇ : A local government unit is interested in the crime rate as a function of the income level in the local community. It knows that the local crime rate, r, is strongly influenced by the amount of money spent on community youth activities, m. Further, the amount of money available to spend on community youth activities is a function of the average disposable income level, y, in the community. Suppose the estimated relationships are

$$r = \frac{50}{m^2} + 20 = 50m^{-2} + 20$$

and

$$m = 0.4(y - 2), \qquad y > 2.$$

Then what is the rate of change in the crime rate with respect to changes in local average disposable income level?

Answer

$$\frac{dr}{dm} = -100m^{-3},$$

$$\frac{dm}{dy} = 0.4.$$

Hence

$$\frac{dr}{dy} = \frac{dr}{dm} \cdot \frac{dm}{dy} = 0.4(-100m^{-3}) = -40m^{-3} = \frac{-40}{[0.4(y-2)]^3}, \quad y > 2.$$

The rate of change is negative (for $y > 2$), and hence the effect of larger income levels, here, is to reduce crime.

11-3 DERIVATIVES OF SOME SPECIAL FUNCTIONS

Exponential and logarithmic functions present special problems for differentiation. One of the more unpleasant problems is that we are forced to resort to faith rather than intuition to begin.

Exponential Functions

We begin by asking you to accept by faith and faith alone the fact that if

$$y \equiv f(x) = e^x,$$

then

$$\frac{dy}{dx} = f'(x) = e^x.$$

The fact that the slope of $f(x) = e^x$ is e^x is certainly not intuitive. However, proof of this fact (you will be happy to know) requires mathematical skills beyond those studied in this book. But this ornery constant e is a very special fellow.

Having accomplished this piece of legerdemain, the chain rule will help us develop a more general expression for handling exponentials. Consider the function given by

$$y \equiv f(x) = 6^{x^2},$$

and suppose that we wish to find the derivative with respect to x, $f'(x)$. Since we just resorted to a little hocus-pocus to obtain the last result, we have no reservations about using a few more tricks to get the next one. The trick (one we have often resorted to) is to write the present function in terms of one for which we already know the derivative, namely e^x. To do so, we first write

$$e^b = 6 \qquad \text{where } b = \ln 6 = \log_e 6.$$

Now substituting e^b for 6 in the original expression gives

$$y = e^{bx^2}.$$

Now, as a further substitution in order to use the chain rule, let

$$u = bx^2; \quad \text{then } y = e^u.$$

From what we accepted on faith, we know that

$$\frac{dy}{du} = e^u.$$

Further,

$$\frac{du}{dx} = 2bx.$$

Now using the chain rule

$$\frac{dy}{dx} = \frac{dy}{du} \cdot \frac{du}{dx} = e^u \cdot 2bx = e^{bx^2} \cdot 2bx.$$

But $b = \ln 6$, so

$$\frac{dy}{dx} = (e^{\ln 6})^{x^2}(\ln 6)2x.$$

Now, by the definition of logarithms $e^{\ln 6} = 6$, and we can write

$$\frac{dy}{dx} = 6^{x^2} (\ln 6)2x.$$

Comparing this to the original function given by $f(x) = 6^{x^2}$, we see that the derivative is the original expression multiplied by the natural logarithm of the constant (which is raised to the variable power) times the derivative of the power. This example suggests the sixth rule for differentiation. It was a long example and only the result is important. Once you accept each step, forget the example and be concerned only with the rule it motivates.

Rule 7 for Derivatives: EXPONENTIAL FUNCTIONS

The derivative of a constant to a variable power is the product of the original expression, multiplied by the natural logarithm of the constant, multiplied by the derivative of the power. In symbolic form:

$$\frac{d}{dx}[a^{g(x)}] = a^{g(x)} (\ln a)(g'(x)),$$

where a is any constant.

Several examples are useful at this point.

(i) $f(x) = a^x$, $f'(x) = a^x(\ln a)1.$
(ii) $f(x) = e^x$, $f'(x) = e^x (\ln e)1 = e^x.$
(iii) $f(x) = bc^{2x^3}$, $f'(x) = bc^{2x^3} (\ln c)6x^2.$

Logarithmic Functions

Once again an example is a useful means of introducing the general rule for the derivative of logarithmic functions. For an example, consider:

$$y \equiv f(x) = \log_6 x^2.$$

Using the exponential inverse

$$x^2 = 6^y = 6^{f(x)}.$$

Taking derivatives of both sides with respect to x and using rule 1 (on the left-hand side) and rule 7 (on the right-hand side) gives

$$2x = 6^{f(x)} (\ln 6) f'(x).$$

Solving for $f'(x)$, which is what we want to find,

$$f'(x) = 2x \div [6^{f(x)} (\ln 6)]$$
$$= 2x \div [x^2 (\ln 6)]$$

since $x^2 = 6^{f(x)}$.

A further simplification requires an aside at this point. The following examples suggest a means of altering the last expression if desired.

(*i*) $\log_{10} 1{,}000 = 3 = \dfrac{1}{1/3} = \dfrac{1}{\log_{1{,}000} 10}$.

(*ii*) $\log_3 81 = 4 = \dfrac{1}{1/4} = \dfrac{1}{\log_{81} 3}$.

These two examples suggest that in general

$$\log_b a = \frac{1}{\log_a b}$$

and hence

$$\ln 6 = \log_e 6 = \frac{1}{\log_6 e}.$$

Thus returning to the last expression for $f'(x)$ before the aside, we can write

$$f'(x) = 2x \div x^2 \ln 6 = \frac{2x \log_6 e}{x^2}.$$

This example suggests the eighth rule for derivatives. Again it is the rule (not the example) that is important. Try to understand the steps in the example because they use ideas we are learning. But once you have worked your way to the rule you can forget the example and simply use the rule.

Rule 8 for Derivatives: LOGARITHMIC FUNCTIONS

The derivative of the logarithm of a function to the base "a" is one over (the reciprocal of) the original function multiplied by the derivative of the function, all multiplied by the logarithm of e to the base a. In symbolic form.

$$\frac{d}{dx} [\log_a g(x)] = \frac{g'(x)}{g(x)} \log_a e.$$

Again some examples are useful.

(i) $f(x) = \ln x$, $\qquad f'(x) = \dfrac{1}{x}\log_e e = \dfrac{1}{x}$.

(ii) $f(x) = \log_3 x^2$, $\qquad f'(x) = \dfrac{2x}{x^2}\log_3 e = \dfrac{2}{x}\log_3 e$.

$\sim\!\!\!\!\checkmark$: Find the derivative of the following expressions.

1. $f(x) = e^{x^e}$, $\qquad f'(x) =$ _____ .
2. $f(x) = \ln x^e$, $\qquad f'(x) =$ _____ .

Answers

1. $f'(x) = e^{x^e} (\ln e)(ex^{e-1}) = (x^{e-1})(e^{x^e+1})$.

2. $f'(x) = \dfrac{ex^{e-1}}{x^e}\log_e e = \dfrac{e}{x}$.

11-4 PARTIAL DIFFERENTIATION*

This chapter has dealt with functions of a single variable up to this point. However, we know that in many cases the dependent variable is a function of several independent variables. Profits are a function of sales revenues and expenses. The extent of repair or service facilities required depends on the rate of demand for such service and the length of time required to accomplish it. Demand for a product may depend on consumer's disposable income, advertising, prices, credit, and perhaps other variables as well.

Such functions have appeared in this book several times. What we discuss here is the rate of change of the dependent variable with respect to a single one of the independent variables. When one variable is examined at a time, we ignore the other variables. More accurately, they are treated as constants. For example, suppose that profits can be written as a function of sales, s, and costs, c, as follows:

$$P \equiv f(s, c) = 3s - 2c - 1.$$

If the manager wishes to know the rate of change in profit for a unit change in sales, the answer is given by taking the derivative of the profit function with respect to sales while treating costs as a constant. This is done even though a change in costs may be expected if sales change. In order to indicate that the new derivative is taken with respect to only one of the inde-

* This section may be omitted without loss of continuity.

pendent variables, a new symbol is used. We write the derivative of profit with respect to sales as $\partial P/\partial s = 3$.

Symbol	*English Translation*
$\dfrac{\partial y}{\partial x}$	Take the derivative of the function y with respect to x, treating all other variables (letters) as constants.

This definition gives the *partial derivative* with respect to the variable x. For the example, $\partial P/\partial s$ is the partial derivative of profit with respect to sales. When taking partial derivatives, the independent variables with respect to which the derivative is not taken are treated as constants.

For the profit example there is also another partial derivative. The manager may be interested in the rate of change in profit with respect to cost. The partial derivative of profit with respect to cost is

$$\frac{\partial P}{\partial c} = -2.$$

The partial derivative of a function of several variables with respect to a particular independent variable is the rate of change of the function with respect to the particular independent variable. Other independent variables are treated as constants in the process of partial differentiation.

For the profit–sales–cost example, there are only three variables, and we could graph the result. Such a graph appears in Figure 11–1. Graphs of three-dimensional figures, a plane in this case, are typically difficult to visualize and our attempt is no exception. For this reason we have graphed the function as it would appear if one looked only at the P–s axis (Figure 11–2a) and as it would look if one could only see it from the P–c axis (Figure 11–2b). This is easily done by picking a value of one of the two independent variables and plugging it into the function. In each case the function is graphed for a single value of the omitted variable; for example, costs are set equal to zero in Figure 11–2a, and sales are set equal to 5 in Figure 11–2b. If some other value for costs were used in Figure 11–2a, lines parallel to, and hence with the same slope as, the one graphed would have been obtained. The slopes of the lines with respect to the variable of interest are indicated by the ratio of the rise to the run. They are identical to the partial derivatives obtained earlier.

Figure 11–2a shows that the partial derivative of profit with respect to sales (when cost = 0), $\partial P/\partial s$, is 3. In this case, but not in all cases, the partial derivative of profit with respect to sales is 3 for all values of cost. This is

FIGURE 11–1

Profit as a Function of Sales and Costs

$$P = 3s - 2c - 1$$

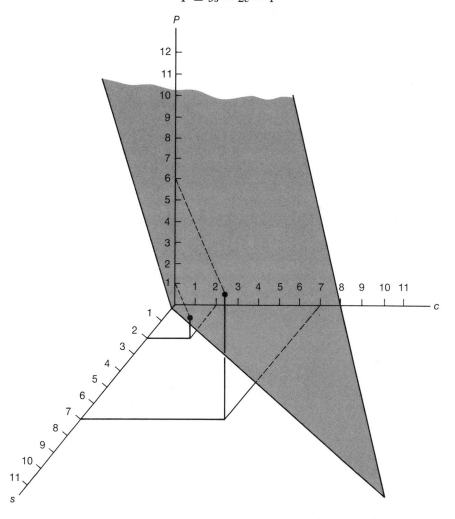

because the original function is a plane. If the original figure were not a plane, the partial derivative of profit with respect to sales could be different for different values of cost. In other words, in this case, the rate of change of profit with respect to sales could depend on the cost level. The rate of change of profits with changes in costs, $\partial P/\partial c$, is (-2) at a sales level of 5 (and at any sales level since, again, the original function is a plane). This is illustrated in Figure 11–2b.

FIGURE 11–2

Profit–Sales and Profit–Cost

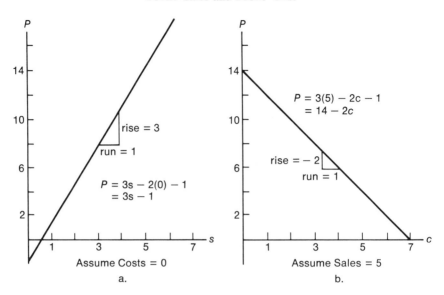

a.

b.

An additional and more complex example is given by the function with rule:

$$y \equiv f(x, z) = x^2 + xz + z^3.$$

Again the partial derivatives are obtained by treating the variables not involved in the differentiation as constants. Hence

$$\frac{\partial y}{\partial x} = 2x + z$$

and

$$\frac{\partial y}{\partial z} = x + 3z^2.$$

The partial derivatives are still functions of both variables.

As was true for simple derivatives, we can also take the second partial derivatives. Thus, for the last example, we obtain

$$\frac{\partial^2 y}{\partial x^2} = 2,$$

$$\frac{\partial^2 y}{\partial z^2} = 6z.$$

We can also take the second partial of y, first with respect to x and then with respect to z or vice versa,

$$\frac{\partial^2 y}{\partial x\, \partial z} = \frac{\partial}{\partial z}(2x + z) = 1$$

$$\frac{\partial^2 y}{\partial z\, \partial x} = \frac{\partial}{\partial x}(x + 3z^2) = 1.$$

The answer will be the same regardless of the order in which the differentiation is done. This last second partial derivative is called a *mixed partial derivative*.

Symbol	*English Translation*
$\dfrac{\partial^2 y}{\partial x^2}$	Take the second derivative of y with respect to x, treating all other variables (letters) as constants.
$\dfrac{\partial^2 y}{\partial x\, \partial z}$	Take the first derivative of y with respect to x, treating all variables except x as constants. Then take the derivative of this result with respect to z, treating all variables except z as constants.

: Find the partials required for the expression

$$y = e^x + x^m z^3 + \ln z.$$

1. $\dfrac{\partial y}{\partial x} = $ _____.

2. $\dfrac{\partial y}{\partial z} = $ _____.

3. $\dfrac{\partial^2 y}{\partial x^2} = $ _____.

4. $\dfrac{\partial^2 y}{\partial x\, \partial z} = $ _____.

Answers

1. $e^x + mx^{m-1}z^3$.

2. $3x^m z^2 + \dfrac{1}{z}$.

3. $e^x + m(m - 1)x^{m-2}z^3$.

4. $3mx^{m-1}z^2$.

11-5 SUMMARY

The rules for differentiation are needed to solve problems involving rates of change. The most important of these problems involve finding maximum and minimum values of functions describing costs, profits, and so on. This is the subject of Chapter 12.

This chapter develops the rules required for differentiation from the definition of the derivative as a limit. An intuitive approach is relied on to suggest each rule. In some cases a formal derivation using the delta method is relatively simple and the proof is also included.

The last portion of the chapter describes means of obtaining the rate of change of a function in more than one variable, with respect to one of these variables at a time. The results allow us to observe how changes in a single independent variable impact on the dependent variable.

RULES FOR DERIVATIVES

Rule 1: Powers

$$\frac{d}{dx}[x^n] = nx^{n-1}.$$

Rule 2: Constants

$$\frac{d}{dx}[k] = 0.$$

Rule 3: Sums

$$\frac{d}{dx}[f_1(x) + \ldots + f_n(x)] = \frac{d}{dx}f_1(x) + \ldots + \frac{d}{dx}f_n(x).$$

Rule 4: Products

$$\frac{d}{dx}[g(x) \cdot h(x)] = g(x) \cdot h'(x) + h(x) \cdot g'(x).$$

Rule 5: Quotients

$$\frac{d}{dx}\left[\frac{g(x)}{h(x)}\right] = \frac{h(x) \cdot g'(x) - g(x) \cdot h'(x)}{[h(x)]^2}.$$

Rule 6: The chain rule

$$\frac{dy}{dx} = \frac{dy}{du} \cdot \frac{du}{dx}.$$

Rule 7: Exponential functions

$$\frac{d}{dx}[a^{g(x)}] = a^{g(x)} (\ln a)(g'(x)).$$

Rule 8: Logarithmic functions

$$\frac{d}{dx}[\log_a g(x)] = \frac{g'(x)}{g(x) \ln a} = \frac{g'(x)}{g(x)} \log_a e.$$

NEW SYMBOLS

Symbol	English Translation
$\dfrac{\partial y}{\partial x}$	Take the derivative of the function y with respect to x, treating all other variables (letters) as constants.
$\dfrac{\partial^2 y}{\partial x^2}$	Take the second derivative of y with respect to x, treating all other variables (letters) as constants.
$\dfrac{\partial^2 y}{\partial x\, \partial z}$	Take the first derivative of y with respect to x, treating all variables except x as constants. Then take the derivative of this result with respect to z, treating all variables except z as constants.

PROBLEMS

Problems for Self-Study: 1b, 2b, 3f, 4f, 6a, 11c

11–1. Find the first and second derivatives of the following.
   a. $f(x) = 5x^3$
   b. $f(x) = 1/x$
   c. $f(x) = 6 + 4x^6$
   d. $f(x) = ax$
   e. $f(x) = b/x^a$
   f. $f(x) = x^{4a-1}$

11–2. Find the first and second derivatives of the following.
   a. $f(x) = 6x + 3x^2$
   b. $f(x) = \dfrac{1}{x} - \dfrac{2}{x^2}$

c. $f(x) = 7 + 2.7x^3$

d. $f(x) = x^{7/2} + (7/2)x^2$

e. $f(x) = ax^b + ax^{-b}$

f. $f(x) = x^3 + 3x^2 + 3x + 1$

11-3. Use rule 4 to find the first derivatives of the following.

a. $f(x) = x^3 \cdot (x + 1)$

b. $f(x) = x^a \cdot x^{b-c}$

c. $f(x) = 14x^0 \cdot dx^{-4}$

d. $f(x) = (26 - x)(x^2 + x)$

e. $g(y) = (3 + 2y)(1 + y)$

f. $f(x) = (a + x^b)(c + x^r)$

11-4. Find the first derivatives of the following.

a. $f(x) = \dfrac{x^2}{x - 1}$

b. $f(x) = \dfrac{x - 1}{x^2}$

c. $f(x) = \dfrac{x - 1}{x - 2}$

d. $f(x) = \dfrac{ax^b}{a + x^b}$

e. $g(y) = \dfrac{y - 4}{4 - y}$

f. $h(z) = \dfrac{z^2 - 3z + 2}{z - 3}$

11-5.* Find the first derivatives of each of the following.

a. $f(x) = (x^2 - 3x + 2)(x^3 + 2x^2 - 3)$

b. $f(x) = (x - 6)(x + 3)(x^2 - x + 7)$

c. $g(y) = \dfrac{(y^2 - 2)(3y + 5)}{y^3 + y^2}$

d. $h(z) = \dfrac{(z + 9)(7z - 10)}{(3z - 2)(z + 1)}$

e. $f(x) = \dfrac{x^2(x - 4)(3x + 8)}{17x^2 - 12}$

11-6. Using the chain rule, find the derivatives of the following.
    a. $f(x) = (x^2 + 3x - 1)^{20}$
    b. $f(x) = (x^2 + 4x)^{-1/2}$
    c. $g(y) = [(y + 12)(7y^2 - 3)]^3$
    d. $b(z) = (7z^6 + 4z^4 + 20z^3 + 6)^{2/3}$
    e. $f(x) = \left(\dfrac{x^2 + 3x - 2}{x^2 - 9}\right)^{7/6}$

11-7.* Find the first derivatives of the following. (*Hint:* Use substitution.)
    a. $y = (1 + 7x^3)^{25}$
    b. $f(x) = 24(2 + 5x + 3x^2)^7$

11-8.* Find the derivative of

$$y = 4[1 + (5 + x^4)^3]^6$$

using substitution and the chain rule.

11-9.* Let profit be defined as sales minus costs. Both sales and costs are functions of advertising.

$$\text{sales, } S = 100 + 12A^{1/2},$$
$$\text{costs, } C = 100 + 0.8(s) + A,$$

where S is dollar sales, C is dollar costs, and A is dollars of advertising. Define profit in terms of costs and sales and find the derivative of profit with respect to advertising. (*Hint:* Use substitution.)

11-10.* Find the first derivatives of the following.
    a. $f(x) = 6e^{-6x^2}$
    b. $f(x) = a^{ex}$
    c. $b(y) = e^{-1/2v^2} - e^{1/2v^2}$
    d. $g(z) = (ba)^{z^2}$
    e. $f(x) = e^{3z-2} \cdot a^{z^2}$

11-11. Find the first derivatives of the following.
    a. $f(x) = \ln x^2$
    b. $f(x) = \log_3 x^2$
    c. $f(x) = \log_{10} e^z$
    d. $f(x) = \ln (x^2 + 4x - 7)$
    e. $f(x) = \log_{10} (\ln (x^2 + 1))$

*11–12.** Find $\dfrac{\partial f}{\partial x}$, $\dfrac{\partial f}{\partial y}$, and $\dfrac{\partial^2 f}{\partial x\, \partial y}$ for the following.

    a. $f(x, y) = ax^2y + 3xy^2$

    b. $f(x, y) = (x + y)^3$

    c. $f(x, y) = x \ln y + e^{xy}$

    d. $f(x, y) = \dfrac{x^2 + y^2}{x^2 - y^2}$

11–13. The total receipts for y washing machines is given by

$$T = 140y \left(1 - \frac{y}{10,000} \right).$$

    Find the rate at which total receipts are changing when $y = 100$.

*11–14.** The weekly demand for phonographs is given by

$$f(p) = \ln (p + 1),$$

where $p \equiv$ price per unit in hundreds of dollars. Find the rate at which demand changes at a price of $100.

11–15. A company's profit at a point in time is given by $f(x) = 20 + 3x + x^2$, where x is the number of years the company has been in business ($x = 0$ in 1970) and $f(x)$ is in millions of dollars.

    a. At what rate are company profits growing after 3 years?

    b. Predict the level of profits when $x = 3$.

*11–16.** Suppose that a firm's profits are given by

$$f(x) = 260,000 + 3200x - 40x^2,$$

where x is the daily expenditure on advertising. Would it be profitable for the firm to increase advertising if their current advertising expenditures are

    a. $30 per day?

    b. $50 per day?

11–17. Demand for a consumer product is given by

$$f(x) = 200 - 100e^{-x},$$

where x is the number of years the product has been on the market.

    a. At what annual rate is demand growing after 2 years?

b. What is the actual change in demand between years 2 and 3?

c. What is the actual change in demand between years 1.5 and 2.5?

*11–18.** Cost and activity are related by the relationship

$$f(a) = (31 - 3a + a^2)^{1/2}.$$

Find the rate of change in cost at an activity level of $a = 6$.

11–19. The annual level of students in a given school system is given by

$$y = 20,000(1 + 50e^{-0.5x})^{-1}.$$

Find the annual rate at which the school is growing after 3 years.

*11–20,** A sales manager knows that the demand for his product, D, is a function of its price, p, advertising, A, and the average disposable income in his region, I.

$$D = 1000p^{-0.7} \cdot I^{0.6} + 350A^{0.83}.$$

Find the partial derivatives of D with respect to p, I, and A.

11–21. A cost control manager knows that the cost savings, S, in his area are a function of his budget, x, and that this function is a logistic function (described in Chapter 4). Suppose that

$$S = \frac{1}{k + ab^x},$$

where k, a, and b are constants. What is the derivative of S with respect to x?

*11–22.** Suppose that a company's electricity bill is a function of the electricity used, E, but that the electric company gives a "quantity discount" so that

$$C = a \cdot E^b, \qquad E \geq 0,$$

where $0 < b < 1$ and $a > 0$.

a. What is the shape of the C curve?

b. What is dC/dE, the incremental charge for another unit of electricity?

11–23. A production manager knows that liquid flows into an empty mixing vat at the rate of 500 cubic feet per minute. The vat is cylindrical with a base diameter d of 30 feet and a height h of 20 feet. What is the rate at which the liquid rises in the vat? (That is, find dh/dt.)

[*Hint:* The formula for the volume of a cylinder is $\pi(d/2)^2h$. Use the chain rule.]

11–24.* A company knows that the yearly interest, I, that it pays on its short-term borrowings, B, can be expressed as

$$I = 0.06\,B^{7/6}.$$

What is the incremental interest incurred by incremental borrowing? (That is, find dI/dB.)

11–25. Find dy/dx for the expression below, differentiating term by term where y is a function of x with derivative dy/dx, and then solving for

$$dy/dx.\ \left[\ Hint:\ \frac{d}{dx}\,(y^n) = ny^{n-1}\,\frac{dy}{dx}\,.\right]$$

$$x^2 + y^3 = 5x + 4y.$$

This is called implicit differentiation.

11–26.* It is a fact that $dy/dx = 1/(dx/dy)$.

    a. Check this formula using $y = 2x$.

    b. Use this formula to differentiate $y = \sqrt{x}$ for $x > 0$.

11–27. The cost of a product is given by

$$z = 110 + 10x + 30y^2 + 2xy,$$

where $z \equiv$ unit cost of producing a product in dollars, $x \equiv$ level of materials in pounds per unit, and $y \equiv$ amount of labor in hours per unit.

    a. Find the rate of increase in cost related to a unit increase in raw materials if labor is held constant at 2 hours per unit and the present level of material input is 3 pounds per unit.

    b. Find the rate of increase in cost related to a unit increase in per unit labor if material input is held constant at 3 pounds per unit and the present level of labor is 2 hours per unit.

12

Finding the Maximum or Minimum of a Function

Managers in many situations want to optimize some objective. A company president may want to *maximize* profits; a city manager wants to *minimize* the cost of providing certain services; a hospital manager wants to *maximize* the number of patient-contact hours; a job-shop manager wants to *minimize* the time a set of jobs spends waiting to be completed; a student wants to *maximize* learning or the number of correct answers on a test (or *minimize* the hours of study, subject to meeting a minimal standard on correct answers).

In Chapter 8, we briefly studied linear programming, a technique for optimizing a linear function subject to linear constraints. If a function (describing, say, the total cost of an inventory system) can be given by a differentiable function, differential calculus can be used to find its smallest (and largest) value. In fact, even though rates of change are useful in their own right, their greatest usefulness in managerial situations arises from finding the largest and smallest values of a function. In a sense, Chapter 9 was necessary for Chapter 10, which was needed before we could study Chapter 11. And now, in Chapter 12, we have reached the punch line.

The material in this chapter has extensive uses. It is used in inventory control and pricing strategy. It forms the basis for regression analysis, a branch of statistics used to relate one variable, such as sales of a product, to another, such as the amount of advertising. Economists use the concepts we will study in this chapter, sometimes called max–min theory, to derive a theory of the firm, and to study certain economic policy questions. Each of these areas will be discussed, along with examples, later. Still other examples are suggested by the problem material.

12-1 RELATIVE MAX–MIN POINTS

Finding Potential Relative Max–Min Points

In Chapter 5 the concept of relative max–min points was first introduced. The definition is repeated here.

A function given by $f(x)$ **has a relative maximum (minimum) at a point,** $x = a$, **if there is a small interval containing** $x = a$ **such that** $f(a)$ **is larger (smaller) than the value of the function at any other point in the interval.**

It may seem that a relative max or min is not a very useful concept and that what we need is a *global* max or min; that is, the value of x where the function takes on its largest (smallest) value for all x. However, relative max–min points are quite useful in identifying global max–min points, since global max–min points satisfy the definition of relative max–min points. Hence for now, we shall find it useful and realistic to confine ourselves to a discussion of relative maximum and minimum points.

To illustrate relative and global max–min points, consider the following set of examples. In Figure 12–1a there is a relative minimum at $x = +1$ (it also happens to be a global minimum). In Figure 12–1b there is a relative maximum at $x = 0$ (it also happens to be a global maximum). In Figure 12–1c the curve "flattens out" at $x = 0$, but the point is not a maximum or a minimum since the curve is lower to the left and higher to the right. In Figure 12–1d there is a relative maximum at $x = -1$ and a relative minimum at $x = \frac{2}{3}$. (There is no global maximum or minimum in Figure 12–1c or 12–1d.)

All the curves "flatten out" at the points indicated, but, as Figure 12–1c illustrates, that does not guarantee a relative maximum or relative minimum. On the other hand, the curve must "flatten out" for a relative maximum or relative minimum to exist.

Another (mathematically more precise) way to express the phrase "flatten out" is to say that the derivative of the function (its rate of change, its slope) must be equal to zero at the point where a relative maximum or minimum occurs. This is written in symbolic notation as

$$f'(x) = 0.$$

Thus $f'(x) = 0$ at some point implies that the function may have a maximum or a minimum at that point. And $f'(x) \neq 0$ implies that the function does not have a maximum or a minimum at that point. Mathematicians call a condition which is needed for a particular result, but which is not sufficient to guarantee it, a *necessary condition* for that result.

FIGURE 12–1

Examples of Relative Maxima and Minima

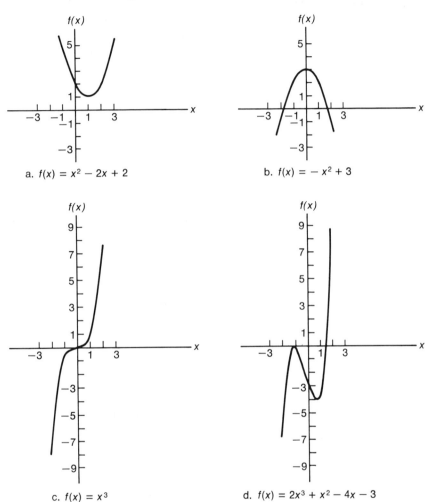

a. $f(x) = x^2 - 2x + 2$

b. $f(x) = -x^2 + 3$

c. $f(x) = x^3$

d. $f(x) = 2x^3 + x^2 - 4x - 3$

The *necessary condition*, **also called the first-order condition, for a function, given by** $f(x)$, **to have a relative maximum or minimum at a point,** a, **is that** $f'(a) = 0$.

Consider Figure 12–2. The derivative (slope) of the function at a point, b_1, is greater than zero, $f'(b_1) > 0$. This is illustrated by the positive slope of the tangent to the curve at b_1; the function is increasing at the point b_1. The function does not have a minimum or a maximum at b_1, since it is higher to the right of b_1 and lower to the left. Similarly, at b_3, $f'(b_3) < 0$, and the function does not have a minimum or maximum at b_3. Graphically the slope of the curve at b_3 is represented by the negative slope of the tangent to the curve at point b_3. Try these ideas on the relative minimum illustrated in Figure 12–3.

FIGURE 12–2

Relative (and Global) Maximum Illustrated

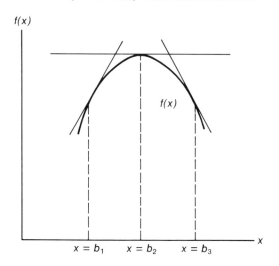

FIGURE 12–3

Relative (and Global) Minimum Illustrated

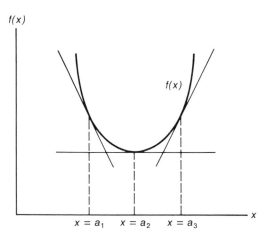

The reader will note that in the case of the relative maximum, illustrated in Figure 12–2, the slope of the tangent line is positive at $x = b_1, f'(b_1) > 0$, and this indicates that the function is increasing. This curve continues to increase until it reaches a maximum and the derivative is zero. For the relative maximum in Figure 12–2, this occurs at $x = b_2$; that is, $f'(b_2) = 0$. For values of $x > b_2$, the derivative, as indicated by the slope of the tangent line, is negative [$f'(x) < 0$]. For example, $f'(b_3) < 0$. A parallel development holds for the relative minimum illustrated in Figure 12–3. You should check your understanding by seeing if you can verbalize the characteristics of the derivative function around this relative minimum. [Whenever possible you should try to understand concepts on an intuitive level. The idea that $f'(x) = 0$ is necessary for a maximum or minimum is very intuitive—once you see it, of course. When you once see it intuitively and can explain it to someone else, it is quite unlikely that the concept will cause you further difficulty.]

To find potential max–min points of a function, given by $f(x)$, find the derivative function, $f'(x)$, and solve for any and all x values where $f'(x) = 0$.

Let's try an example. In Section 3–4 we graphically located an optimal level of advertising expenditure. We now see that we were merely finding a relative maximum point. Let's try our new approach on this type of problem. Suppose that the monthly change in sales revenues is related to changes in advertising expenditures by

$$f(x) = 3x - x^3 - 1, \qquad -2 \leq x < 5,$$

where x is in $1,000.

Taking the first derivative to locate any potential max–min points yields

$$f'(x) = 3 - 3x^2.$$

Setting this derivative equation equal to zero and solving gives

$$3 - 3x^2 = 0,$$
$$1 - x^2 = 0,$$
$$x^2 = 1,$$
$$x = \sqrt{1},$$
$$x = +1, -1.$$

Thus $x = +1$ and $x = -1$ represent possible maximum or minimum points. But which? We could graph the function to find out, but there are better ways.

One of these is the subject of the next subsection, but we can also use methods already at our disposal.

Recall from the discussion of Figure 12–2 that the derivative evaluated at a point to the left of a relative maximum is positive, indicating that the original function is increasing. To the right, the derivative is negative, indicating that the original function is decreasing. Picking a point in $f(x) = 3x - x^3 - 1$ to the left of $x = 1$ [but not so far to the left as the other point where $f'(x) = 0$], say $x = 0$, we obtain $f'(0) = 3$. This indicates that the original function is increasing to the left of the point $x = 1$. Picking a point to the right of $x = 1$, say $x = 2$, we obtain $f'(2) = -9$, indicating that the original function is decreasing. Thus we have a relative maximum at $x = 1$ and $f(1) = 3(1) - 1^3 - 1 = 2$. You are asked to check out $x = -1$ as an exercise.

1. Is the point $x = -1$ a relative maximum or minimum? Maximum_____ Minimum_____ How do you know? What monthly change in sales revenues is associated with a decrease of $1,000 in advertising?

2. Suppose that the change in sales revenues were given by

$$f(x) = e^{-x}, \qquad x \geq 0,$$

What potential relative max–min points can you find?

Answers

1. The point $x = -1$ is a relative minimum. Since $f'(-2)$ is negative and $f'(0)$ is positive, this case resembles the picture in Figure 12–3. At $x = -1$, $f(x) = -3$; hence, sales would decrease by $3,000.

2. The function given by e^{-x}, $x \geq 0$, has a value of 1 at $x = 0$ and gets continuously smaller, although remaining positive, as x gets larger. It therefore has no relative max–min points (such a function is called a *monotonically decreasing function*).

Checking the Potential Max–Min Points Using Second-Order Conditions

The second derivative, which was introduced in Section 10–1, can be used to identify a point where $f'(x) = 0$ as either a relative maximum or a relative minimum. Before proceeding we review the main points about the second derivative.

The second derivative is the derivative of the derivative.

That sounds simple enough. It means that if $f(x)$ defines a function and $f'(x)$ defines its derivative function, then the derivative of $f'(x)$ is the second derivative of $f(x)$, and so on for a third or fourth derivative (although we cannot think of a good reason for wanting to go this far). There are (as mentioned in Chapter 11) several ways of denoting a second derivative. We use $f''(x)$ or d^2y/dx^2.

Symbol	English Translation
$f''(x)$	The second derivative of $f(x)$.
$\dfrac{d^2y}{dx^2}$	The second derivative of y with respect to x, when an equation was written as $y = f(x)$.

For example,

$$f(x) = 4x^2 + 2x,$$
$$f'(x) = 8x + 2,$$
$$f''(x) = 8.$$

The second derivative, which is the rate of change of the derivative, gives us another and simpler way of determining whether we have a relative minimum or maximum when $f'(x) = 0$. If the point $x = a_2$ is a relative maximum (see Figure 12–2), the second derivative evaluated at that point will be negative, $f''(a_2) > 0$. This is true because the first derivative, as we have seen, is positive to the left of this point, zero at the point, and negative to the right of this point. It is decreasing and its slope is therefore negative. This is illustrated in Figure 12–4. Again a parallel argument can be made for a relative minimum point using Figure 12–5. Test your grasp of these ideas by doing so. (The reasoning is harder to grasp intuitively, but it can be done. You do not have to memorize the way to check second-order conditions.)

FIGURE 12–4

First Derivative Function for the Function in Figure 12–2

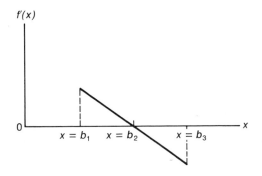

FIGURE 12–5

First Derivative Function for the Function in Figure 12–3

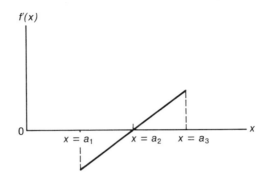

Notice that second derivative tests, called *second-order conditions*, involve evaluating a function, $f''(x)$, not solving any equation. We identify possible max–min points by solving $f'(x) = 0$. Second-order conditions are checked by evaluating $f''(x)$ at the x values where $f'(x) = 0$. This tells us which type of point we have.

Summary—Method of Identifying Relative Maximum and Minimum Points

1. For a differentiable function, given by $f(x)$, find $f'(x)$ and $f''(x)$.

2. Solve for all x values where $f'(x) = 0$.

3. For each of the points found in step 2, evaluate $f''(x)$. If

(*i*) $f''(x) > 0$, we have a relative minimum.
(*ii*) $f''(x) < 0$, we have a relative maximum.
(*iii*) $f''(x) = 0$, we probably have neither a relative maximum nor a minimum; the test is inconclusive.

(What we usually have in 3–(iii) is an "inflection point." An example of an inflection point is shown where $x = 0$ and $F(x) = 0$ in Figure 12–1c. An inflection point may occur when $f''(x) = 0$. This is discussed further in Section 12–3.)

For example, using Figures 12–1a and 12–1b:

$$f(x) = x^2 - 2x + 2 \qquad\qquad f(x) = -x^2 + 3$$

Step 1. $f'(x) = 2x - 2; f''(x) = 2$ $\qquad$ $f'(x) = -2x; f''(x) = -2$

Step 2. Solve $f'(x) = 2x - 2 = 0$ Solve $f'(x) = -2x = 0$

          $x = +1$ (only) $x = 0$ (only)

Step 3. $f''(x) = +2$, so $f''(1) = +2$. $f''(x) = -2$, so $f''(0) = -2$.

          Since $f''(x) > 0$, we have   Since $f''(x) < 0$, we have a

          a min.   max.

: Identify any relative max–min points in the following examples using first and second-order conditions, and evaluate $f(x)$ at any relative maximum or minimum point located.

1. $f(x) = 4x^3 + x + 1$ *2.* $f(x) = x^3 - 12x + 7$

3. $f(x) = 4x^2 - 2x + 3$ *4.* $f(x) = ax^2 + bx + c$

Answers

1. $f'(x) = 12x^2 + 1$. This derivative function is never zero. There are no relative maximum or minimum points.

2. $f'(x) = 3x^2 - 12$

   $f'(x) = 0$ at $x = +2$ and $x = -2$

   $f''(x) = 6x$. This is positive $(+12)$ for $x = +2$ and negative (-12) for $x = -2$. Thus $f(x)$ has a relative minimum at $x = +2$ and a relative maximum at $x = -2$.

To evaluate $f(x)$:

   $f(+2) = -9$,

   $f(-2) = +23$.

3. $f'(x) = 8x - 2$, and $f'(x) = 0$ at $x = \frac{1}{4}$; $f''(x) = 8$, so $f''(\frac{1}{4}) > 0$. Thus $f(x)$ has a relative minimum at $x = \frac{1}{4}$, and $f(\frac{1}{4}) = 2\frac{3}{4}$

4. $f'(x) = 2ax + b$

   $f'(x) = 0$ at $x = -b/2a$

   $f''(x) = 2a$. This function has a relative maximum at $x = -b/2a$ if $a < 0$ and a relative minimum if $a > 0$.

   You have just verified the formula given in Section 5–3 for finding the vertex of a parabola.

12–2 GLOBAL MAX–MIN POINTS

Most managers want to find the lowest cost (or highest profit), not just a cost lower (or a profit higher) than its neighbors. This section shows how to find the smallest (largest) value a function achieves. In many situations (both practical and contrived) the global maximum or minimum will also be a relative maximum or minimum. As we will see below, the relative max–min points should always be considered when searching for a global optimum. Thus, you will be happy to know, our time has not been wasted so far.

A function, given by $f(x)$, **has a global maximum (minimum) at a point,** $x = a$, **if** $f(x)$ **is at least as large (small) as it is for any other value of** x.

For example, in Figure 12–1a a global minimum occurs at $x = +1$, and in Figure 12–1b a global maximum occurs at $x = 0$. In both cases the relative max–min point was the global max–min point. You may wonder what other possibilities there are. A global maximum or minimum can occur only at a "critical point." A relative maximum or minimum is a critical point, but there are others.

Critical points **include all** x-**values where** $f(x)$ **might achieve its global maximum or minimum. The** *critical points* **are:**

1. All relative maximum or minimum points (within the allowable set of x values).
2. All x values where the derivative does not exist.
3. The end-point x values. That is, if x is constrained to a range of values $a \leq x \leq b$, then a and b are critical points. (A practical example is that inventory must always be ≥ 0, but it may also be constrained to fit in a warehouse.)

Most practical problems involve critical points of types 1 and 3. One situation in which a type 2 critical point occurs is when a manager considers how many units to order when there are price breaks at various order quantities, but it costs money to store extra items. Once we have identified all critical points, however, selecting the global optimum is a straightforward process.

Steps to find the global maximum (minimum) of a function given by $f(x)$:

1. Find all its critical points.
2. Evaluate $f(x)$ at all the critical points.
3. Choose the biggest (smallest) $f(x)$ value.

For example, Figure 3–5 depicts a curve representing income as a function of advertising expenditure. Suppose that another firm has a similar curve:

$$f(x) \equiv \text{dollar income (per day)},$$
$$x \equiv \text{dollar advertising expenditure (per day)},$$
$$f(x) = -10x^2 + 180x - 200, \quad 0 \leq x \leq 10.$$

How much should the firm spend on advertising in order to maximize income?

Step 1. Critical points:

$$f'(x) = -20x + 180,$$
$$f'(x) = 0 \quad \text{at } x = +9,$$
$$f''(9) = -20, \quad \text{so we have a relative maximum.}$$

The critical points are:

$$x = 0, 10 \quad \text{(the end points)},$$
$$x = 9 \quad \text{(the relative maximum)}.$$

There are no points within the allowable set of x values where the derivative does not exist.

Step 2.
$$f(0) = -200,$$
$$f(9) = +610,$$
$$f(10) = +600.$$

Step 3. $f(9) = 610$ is a global max.

The answer to the problem posed is that they should have an advertising expenditure of \$9 per day (if maximizing income is their objective).

: Find the global maximum and the global minimum of the following functions:

1. $f(x) = 4x^3 + x + 1$, for $0 \le x \le 2$.
2. $f(x) = x^3 - 3x^2 + 4$, for $0 \le x \le 4$.

Answers

1. As we learned earlier, this function has no relative max–min points. However, there is a global maximum and a global minimum. The only critical points are $x = 0$ and $x = 2$, the end points. $f(0) = +1$ is a global minimum; $f(2) = 35$ is a global maximum.

2.
$$f'(x) = 3x^2 - 6x,$$
$$f'(x) = 0 \quad \text{for } x = 0 \text{ and } x = 2.$$

The critical points are $x = 0, 2,$ and 4.

$$f(0) = 4, \quad f(2) = 0, \quad f(4) = 20.$$

$f(4) = 20$ is the global maximum; $f(2) = 0$ is the global minimum. [Note that we do not need to evaluate the second-order conditions if we evaluate $f(x)$ at all critical points.]

12–3   CURVE SKETCHING USING MAX–MIN THEORY

In earlier chapters, curve sketching was accomplished by first evaluating the equation at a number of values of the independent variable and then locating these points on a Cartesian coordinate system. Using the calculus, the graphing of most functions is made significantly easier. The critical points tell us a great deal about the graph of a function. However, knowledge of the location of one additional type of point, which can also be determined using the calculus, is helpful in graphing functions. These points are called *inflection points*.

An *inflection point* occurs where a curve changes from "facing down (up)" to "facing up (down)."

An example of an inflection point is given in Figure 12–1c. The inflection point occurs at the intersection of the x and $f(x)$ axes. Another example occurs in Figure 12–1d at $x = -\frac{1}{6}$.

A necessary condition for an inflection point at $x = a$ is that $f''(a) = 0$.

The reader can verify that both inflection points mentioned in the previous paragraph satisfy this necessary condition. Actually $f''(a) = 0$ does not always imply an inflection point at a value of $x = a$, but for nearly all managerial applications it is safe to assume that such points are inflection points.

Roots, critical points, and inflection points are very useful in curve sketching. They tell us when the curve crosses the x-axis, when it reaches its high and low points, and when it changes from "facing down" to "facing up," respectively. To sketch the curve, we simply plot those points and sketch around them.

For example, consider the function given by $f(x) = x^3 - 3x^2 - x + 3$. Factoring yields $f(x) = (x + 1)(x - 1)(x - 3)$. Hence the roots are $x = -1$, $x = +1$, and $x = +3$. Taking the first derivative gives $f'(x) = 3x^2 - 6x - 1$. Setting it equal to zero and solving,

$$f'(x) = 0 \qquad \text{at } x = \frac{+6 \pm \sqrt{36 + 12}}{6} = 1 \pm \frac{2}{\sqrt{3}}.$$

Since $f''(x) = 6x - 6$, there is a relative minimum at $x = 1 + 2/\sqrt{3} = 2.15$ and $f(2.15) = -3.1$, and there is a relative maximum at $x = 1 - 2/\sqrt{3} = -0.15$ and $f(-0.15) = +3.1$.

Finally, $f''(x) = 0$ when $x = +1$, so there is an inflection point at $x = +1$. (Note this is also, by coincidence, a root.) We shall use one other fact, not required but easily obtained: $f(0) = 3$. Now using all this information, we can sketch the curve. It is shown in Figure 12–6.

FIGURE 12–6

Graph of the Function Given by
$$f(x) = x^3 - 3x^2 - x + 3$$

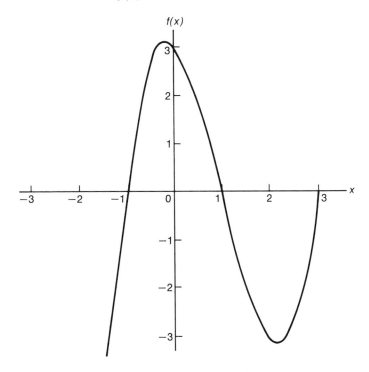

: Using the calculus where applicable, graph the function

$$f(x) = x^3 - x = 0.$$

Answer. The roots are $x = 0$, $x = -1$, and $x = +1$ since $f(x) = x(x - 1)(x + 1)$. $f'(x) = 3x^2 - 1 = 0$ at $x = 1/\sqrt{3}$ and $x = -1/\sqrt{3}$. $f''(x) = 6x$, hence $x = 1/\sqrt{3}$ is a relative minimum and $x = -1/\sqrt{3}$ is a relative maximum. $f(1/\sqrt{3}) = -2/3\sqrt{3} = -0.38$ and $f(-1/\sqrt{3}) = +0.38$. $f''(x) = 6x = 0$ at $x = 0$, an inflection point. The graph is shown in Figure 12-7.

FIGURE 12-7

Graph of the Function
$$f(x) = x^3 - x$$

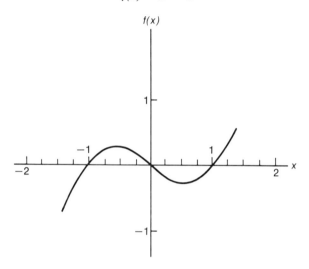

12-4 APPLICATIONS OF MAX–MIN THEORY: SOME EXAMPLES

Choosing an Optimal Price

If we can build a mathematical model of the objective, we can usually find a decision to maximize that objective. In this case if we can determine the objective of the manager, say it is profit maximization, and if we can relate profit to price, then it may be possible to find a price that will maximize profit. Suppose a manager knows that his demand function (units sold as a function of price) is given by $20 - p$. What price should he choose if he (inappropriately) elects to maximize *revenue*? (We consider the relation of revenue to price as a first step in the general solution.)

$$\text{revenue} = R(p) = \text{price times the number of units sold}$$
$$= p(20 - p) = 20p - p^2.$$

Symbolically

$$R(p) = 20p - p^2, \qquad p > 0.$$

Taking the first derivative,

$$R'(p) = 20 - 2p.$$

Setting the first derivative equal to zero, we find

$$R'(p) = 0 \qquad \text{at } p = 10.$$

The second derivative is

$$R''(p) = -2 \qquad \text{so } R''(10) < 0.$$

Thus we have a relative maximum at $p = 10$. The revenue at $p = 10$ is $R(10) = 100$. At $p = 0$, the only end point, $R(0) = 0$, hence at $p = 10$ there is a global maximum.

Suppose there is a \$3 cost per unit to produce each item. What price should the manager charge to maximize profit?

$$\begin{aligned}
\text{profit} = f(p) &= \text{revenue} - \text{cost} \\
&= R(p) - 3 \text{ (units sold)} \\
&= (20p - p^2) - 3(20 - p) = 23p - p^2 - 60, \qquad p > 0.
\end{aligned}$$

Hence

$$f'(p) = 23 - 2p.$$

Solving,

$$f'(p) = 0 \qquad \text{when } p = 11\tfrac{1}{2}.$$

(Note that this is higher than the price which maximizes revenue.)

$$f''(p) = -2 \qquad \text{and} \qquad R(0) = -60,$$

so this value of p yields a global maximum.

$$f(11\tfrac{1}{2}) = 72.25.$$

The manager should charge \$11.50 to maximize profits. It is important to observe that the optimal price to maximize profits differs from that which maximizes revenues.

The reader should be certain he understands how the $R(p)$ and $f(p)$ models were built, since building models is an important managerial responsibility. If the wrong model is constructed, it is likely that the wrong decision will be made, as has just been illustrated.

Choosing a Method of Taxation

Suppose that a state government is considering taxing the above firm, and the state wants to know what effect the tax will have on the firm's decisions. The state also wants to know whether the firm or the customer will bear the ultimate burden of the tax, that is, what the "incidence" of the tax will be. Three alternative taxation proposals are under consideration. (See if you can guess the effects of each on price and tax incidence in advance.)

Policy 1.   a percentage-of-profits tax.
Policy 2.   a sales tax per unit.
Policy 3.   a lump-sum tax (licensing tax).

Evaluation of tax policy 1:

$$\text{after-tax profit} = f_1(p) = af(p) = a(23p - p^2 - 60)$$

using the previous profit formula, where a is a constant (for example, if the tax rate is 20 percent, $a = 1 - 0.2 = 0.8$). Thus

$$f_1(p) = a(23p - p^2 - 60),$$

and the first derivative is

$$f_1'(p) = a(23 - 2p).$$

Solving,

$$f_1'(p) = 0 \qquad \text{at } p = 11\tfrac{1}{2}.$$

The tax has no effect on the optimal price charged. Furthermore, the company pays the entire tax.
Evaluation of tax policy 2:

$$\text{after-tax profit} = f_2(p) = f(p) - b \text{ (units sold)}$$
$$= f(p) - b(20 - p) = (23p - p^2 - 60) - b(20 - p),$$

where b is the sales tax per unit and equals a constant. Thus

$$f_2(p) = (23 + b)p - p^2 - 60 - 20b,$$

and the first derivative is

$$f_2'(p) = 23 + b - 2p.$$

Solving,

$$f_2'(p) = 0 \qquad \text{at } p = 11\tfrac{1}{2} + \frac{b}{2}.$$

In this case, the optimal selling price is higher; half the tax has been passed on to the consumer.

Evaluation of tax policy 3:

$$\text{after-tax profit} = f_3(p) = f(p) + c.$$

where c is the lump sum (license) tax. Taking the first derivative gives

$$f_3'(p) = f'(p) = 23 - 2p.$$

Solving,

$$f_3'(p) = 0 \qquad \text{at } p = 11\tfrac{1}{2}.$$

Again, as in tax 1, there is no effect on the price and the entire tax is paid by the firm.

We find that a lump-sum cost, such as a license tax, should not have an effect on a decision. Such costs are called "fixed costs," and a decision maker should pay no attention to them when he makes his decision. (This is one of the important ideas in an administrative education. Did you correctly figure this out before we did the mathematics?).

Solving a Problem in General Form

Sometimes it is advantageous to solve a problem in general form; that is, solve the problem putting arbitrary constants (a, b, c) in the formula instead of the numbers from a specific problem. $A = \pi r^2$ (the area of a circle equals the value π, 3.14, times the radius raised to the second power) is an example of a general formula. In the above problems, $20 - p$ uses 20 and 1 as specific numbers. We can replace those by unspecified constants and solve for an optimum price in general form.

Suppose that a firm has a linear demand function of the form

$$\text{demand} = a - bp.$$

Suppose further that each unit costs c ($c = \$3$ above). Then, using a, b, and c instead of 20, 1, and 3, a general formula for profit can be written as:

$$f(p) = p(a - bp) - c(a - bp).$$

The general first derivative is

$$f'(p) = a - 2bp + bc.$$

Solving gives

$$f'(p) = (a + bc) - p(2b) = 0$$

and

$$p = \frac{a + bc}{2b}$$

is the optimal price. $[f''(p) = -2b$, so we have a max if $b > 0.]$

The optimal price (to maximize profit) when the firm has a linear demand function has been found. To check this solution, substitute $20 = a$, $1 = b$, and $3 = c$ into the formula

$$p = \frac{a + bc}{2b} = \frac{20 + 1(3)}{2(1)} = 11\tfrac{1}{2}. \qquad \text{(It works!)}$$

An Inventory Problem

As a final example, consider a very common, and important, managerial decision problem, the problem of how many units of an item to order each time an order is placed. Suppose:

1. Demand per year = 1,000 units.
2. Each order costs $10 for paperwork, in addition to a $5 unit price for each item.
3. Each unit in inventory costs $1 per year to hold (cost of having capital tied up, storage, insurance, etc.).

The manager orders 500 units per order, and if inventories reach zero just as the next order arrives, there are $500/2 = 250$ units in inventory on the average. In general, if he orders Q units per order, the average inventory is $Q/2$.

If the manager orders 500 units per order, he orders $1,000/500 = 2$ times per year. If he orders Q units per order, he will order $1,000/Q$ times per year.

Total cost per year, $c(Q)$, as a function of the number of units ordered is

$$c(Q) = \frac{Q}{2}(\$1) + \frac{1,000}{Q}(\$10) + 1,000(\$5), \qquad Q > 0.$$

This cost represents the sum of annual inventory cost + annual ordering cost + total price paid annually for the units.

(At this point, the reader is advised to go back over the logic of the cost formula. If you think there are several implicit assumptions made, you are right! Do not worry about them for now.)

Suppose the manager wants to minimize the annual cost, $c(Q)$, by choosing the best order quantity, Q. The calculus, as you might have guessed, can be used to do this; $c'(Q)$ is set to zero.

$$c'(Q) = \frac{1}{2} - \frac{10,000}{Q^2}.$$

Setting the first derivative equal to zero and solving,

$$c'(Q) = 0 = \frac{1}{2} - \frac{10,000}{Q^2},$$

and

$$Q^2 = 20,000$$

Hence

$$Q = \sqrt{20,000} = 100\sqrt{2} = 141.4.$$

The optimal order quantity is 141.4 units, and $1000/141.4 = 7$ (roughly) orders will be placed per year. Notice that the annual cost of the items ($\$5 \times 1,000 = \$5,000$) is a fixed cost and plays no part in the optimal answer.

Just to be sure the result is a relative minimum, we can check the second-order conditions:

$$c''(Q) = \frac{60,000}{Q^3}.$$

This is greater than zero since $Q > 0$, and we have a relative minimum. (Since $c(Q)$ increases below Q and above Q it is also the global minimum.)

1. Evaluate $c(Q)$ for $Q = 100$, $100\sqrt{2}$, and 200 to see that the calculus has not played a trick on us.
2. Substitute unspecified constants for annual demand, ordering cost, and inventory cost, and solve the inventory problem in general. Check your final formula against the above example. Use a, b, and c for 1,000, 10, and 1, respectively, and drop the annual cost of the units from the formula since it can be ignored in making the decision, as shown above.

Answers

1. $c(100) = \dfrac{100}{2}\,(1) + \dfrac{1,000}{100}\,(10) + 5,000 = 5,150,$

   $c(200) = \dfrac{200}{2}\,(1) + \dfrac{1,000}{200}\,(10) + 5,000 = 5,150,$

   $c(100\sqrt{2}) = \dfrac{100\sqrt{2}}{2}\,(1) + \dfrac{1,000}{100\sqrt{2}}\,10 + 5,000 = 5,141.4.$

The answer is verified. Observe also that, at the optimal value of Q, the first two cost terms are equal (both are $50\sqrt{2}$). This is not a coincidence but will always be true at the minimum point of this particular cost function, containing one term of Q^1 and one of Q^{-1}. If inventory holding costs are higher than ordering costs, Q should be reduced until the two are equal. If ordering cost is higher, Q should be increased until the two are equal. The calculus automatically balances the two costs.

2. $c(Q) = \dfrac{Q}{2} c + \dfrac{a}{Q} b,$

$c'(Q) = \dfrac{c}{2} - \dfrac{ab}{Q^2}.$

Solving,

$$c'(Q) = 0 = \frac{c}{2} - \frac{ab}{Q^2},$$

$$Q^2 = \frac{2ab}{c},$$

$$Q = \sqrt{\frac{2ab}{c}},$$

where a is the yearly demand, c is the yearly holding cost per unit, and b is the cost of placing an order. [If $\sqrt{2ab/c}$ is substituted into $c(Q)$, we see that each of the two terms equals $\sqrt{abc/2}$.]

This is called the "economic order quantity" formula. It says, among other things, that optimal order size varies as the square root of demand. Many organizations still use inventory rules such as: order an amount equal to 6 months' demand of each item. This rule makes order size vary linearly with demand. Many organizations could save money by using the square-root formula.

*12–5 MAX–MIN THEORY FOR FUNCTIONS OF TWO VARIABLES

As we have seen earlier, some functions involve more than one independent variable. An example is

$$f(x, y) = x^2 + xy + 2y^2 - 7y.$$

---

* This section may be skipped without loss of continuity. It is somewhat more difficult than the other portions of the chapter.

Also, we know that we can take partial derivatives, which give the rate of change of the function with respect to each one of the variables. For example,

$$\frac{\partial f}{\partial x} \equiv \text{partial derivative of } f \text{ with respect to } x,$$

$$\frac{\partial f}{\partial y} \equiv \text{partial derivative of } f \text{ with respect to } y.$$

The partial derivative of f with respect to x is found, as is discussed in Chapter 11, by assuming that y is a constant. For $\partial f/\partial y$ it is assumed that x is a constant. Thus

$$\frac{\partial f}{\partial x} = 2x + y \quad \text{and} \quad \frac{\partial f}{\partial y} = x + 4y - 7.$$

As in the case of a function of one variable, a function of two variables must "flatten out" if it is to have a relative maximum or a minimum. In fact, it must "flatten out" in both the x and y directions at once; otherwise at this point there would be both a direction of increase and a direction of decrease. Examine Figure 12–8.

The function $f(x, y)$ shown in Figure 12–8 has a relative (and global) maximum. At the maximum point, both $\partial f/\partial x$ and $\partial f/\partial y$ are zero. This is

FIGURE 12–8

**Relative Maximum for a Function
in Two Variables**

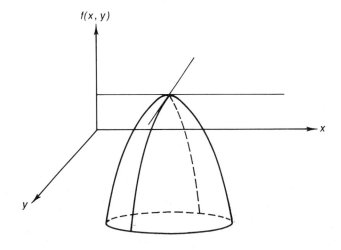

illustrated by the "flat" or horizontal tangents to the figure at its maximum point. Imagine the figure to be half a cucumber sitting on a table (the *xy* plane); then a plate balanced on the top of the cucumber would be parallel to the table top.

To find potential max–min points for a function of two variables, given by $f(x, y)$, **solve for all points where** $\partial f/\partial x = 0$ **and** $\partial f/\partial y = 0$ **are simultaneously satisfied.**

The second-order conditions for a function of two variables to have a relative maximum (or a relative minimum) are complicated. We will not discuss them here. (Presumably in an application, a decision maker would know whether a decision was minimizing cost or maximizing cost.) For functions of three or more variables, potential relative max–min points are identified in the same way; candidates are identified by finding points where the partial derivatives of the function with respect to each of the three or more variables are all (simultaneously) zero.

For example, still using the same function,

$$f(x, y) = x^2 + xy + 2y^2 - 7y,$$

$$\frac{\partial f}{\partial x} = 2x + y = 0,$$

$$\frac{\partial f}{\partial y} = x + 4y - 7 = 0.$$

Hence we want to solve for *x* and *y*, where

$$2x + y = 0,$$
$$x + 4y - 7 = 0.$$

Solving, we obtain

$$x = -1, \qquad y = 2.$$

This point ($x = -1, y = 2$) is a relative minimum point. This can be verified by trying some points close to it; you will see that $f(x, y)$ is lower at $x = -1, y = 2$ than at any neighboring point. When three or more independent variables are involved, it is no longer possible to draw pictures or build replicas of the situation. One is forced to think abstractly about such situations; that is, one is forced to model and solve them mathematically.

*Simple Linear Regression

In Figure 3–9 a linear relationship was estimated using some data. In practical problems, the manager often wants to relate one variable to another—demand to advertising expenditure, yield of corn per acre to amount of fertilizer used per acre, or the number of serious cases of influenza to public health expenditure on a vaccination program. Rather than drawing a line through the data by eye, he may prefer to find a "best" line mathematically. Luckily, he can use his trusty partial derivatives to accomplish this task.

Suppose that

$y_i \equiv$ values of the variable we want to explain, says cases of influenza (last year) in each of 100 areas,

$x_i \equiv$ values of the controllable variable, public health expenditures, for example.

Suppose that the manager wants to relate y to x by finding the "best" straight line:

$$y = a + bx.$$

He wants to specify the constants a and b that do the "best" job. But what does "best" mean in such a problem? Luckily, there is an (arbitrary) answer. The "best" line is defined to be the one with the minimum squared error. It is the one such that when the vertical distance of each point from the fitted line (the error) is squared, and all squared errors are summed, the total is less than from any other line. For a point x_i, $a + bx_i$ is the value given by the fitted line, and y_i is the actual (the observed) value of y for that x. The error term in the prediction, then, is given by:

$$y_i - (a + bx_i).$$

This is how wrong the line is for the single point x_i. The sum of the errors for all points is

$$\sum_{i=1}^{n} [y_i - (a + bx_i)],$$

where $n \equiv$ the number of data points, 100 in our example.

But this sum of errors cannot be used as a criterion for selecting the "best" line since any number of lines can be found, most of which do not fit the data at all well, for which this sum is zero. We do not have the space

---

* This subsection may be skipped even if the rest of Section 12-5 is read.

here to justify just why squaring these errors is the technique used. You can learn about the reasons in a statistics course. We simply state that the accepted technique minimizes the sum of the squared errors:

$$\sum_{i=1}^{n} [y_i - (a + bx_i)]^2.$$

Finally the problem originally posed is ready for solution. Given

$$f(a, b) = \sum_{i=1}^{n} [y_i - (a + bx_i)]^2.$$

find *a* and *b* such that $f(a, b)$ is minimized. (Notice that *a* and *b* are not constants here but are the *decision variables*). Partial derivatives are necessary to accomplish the minimization, since two independent variables are involved.

$$\frac{\partial f}{\partial a} = 0 = \sum_{i=1}^{n} (-2)[y_i - (a + bx_i)],$$

$$\frac{\partial f}{\partial b} = 0 = \sum_{i=1}^{n} (-2x_i)[y_i - (a - bx_i)].$$

It is very tedious to solve these two equations simultaneously, so, probably for the only time, we give you the answer. If $\bar{x}$ and $\bar{y}$ (the averages of the *x* and *y* values) are defined as

$$\bar{x} = \sum_{i=1}^{n} \frac{x_i}{n} \quad \text{and} \quad \bar{y} = \sum_{i=1}^{n} \frac{y_i}{n},$$

then

$$b = \frac{\sum\limits_{i=1}^{n} x_i y_i - n\bar{x}\bar{y}}{\sum\limits_{i=1}^{n} (x_i)^2 - n(\bar{x})^2}$$

$$a = \bar{y} - b\bar{x}.$$

These are the optimal constants for the straight line. All items are known except *a* and *b*. You can (if you really want to) verify these equations by plugging them back into the partial derivative equations above. Using these values, we might find that, for a given set of data:

> The number of serious cases of influenza in one area =
> 1,000 − 0.03 (dollars spent on a vaccination program).

Then it can be estimated that if $10,000 is spent on the program, we will have

$$1{,}000 - 0.03\ (10{,}000) = 700 \text{ cases of influenza.}$$

If $20,000 is spent, on the other hand, we can expect 400 cases. Using such data, we can decide how much to spend.

Price–Advertising

Suppose that a manager, wishing to maximize profits, knows his firm has a demand function of the form

$(20 - p + A)$, where p = price and A = units of demand added by advertising.

Also, the units of demand added by advertising cost increasingly more, such that the cost of increasing demand by A units is A^2. Each unit costs $3 to produce, so

$$\text{profit} = f(p, A) = p(20 - p + A) - 3(20 - p + A) - A^2.$$

To proceed to find the optimal p and A, it is necessary to take the first partial derivatives with respect to A and p and solve. This gives

$$\frac{\partial f}{\partial A} = p - 3 - 2A = 0,$$

$$\frac{\partial f}{\partial p} = 2p + 23 + A = 0.$$

Solving,

$$A = 5\tfrac{2}{3},$$
$$p = 14\tfrac{1}{3}.$$

This pair of values does give a relative and, in this case, a global maximum. Notice that the optimal price is higher when advertising is included, and since $f(14\tfrac{1}{3}, 5\tfrac{2}{3}) = 96\tfrac{1}{3}$, profits are also higher than in Section 12–4, where advertising was not considered.

✓ : Find potential max–min points for:

1. $f(x, y) = 3x^2 - 2x - 6xy + 4y^2 - y.$
2. $f(x, y) = -2x^2 - 3x - y^2.$

Do you think you have a relative maximum, a relative minimum, or neither?

Answers

1. $\partial f/\partial x = 6x - 2 - 6y = 0$,
   $\partial f/\partial y = -6x + 8y - 1 = 0$. Solving we obtain $y = \frac{3}{2}$ and $x = \frac{11}{6}$.

We have found a relative minimum.

2. $\partial f/\partial x = -4x - 3 = 0$ and $\partial f/\partial y = -2y = 0$.

Solving, $x = -\frac{3}{4}$ and $y = 0$. We have found a relative maximum in this case.

12–6 SUMMARY

Calculus can be used to locate maxima and minima of a function. Since many managerial problems can be expressed in mathematical form, and since minimizing cost or maximizing profit is a common objective, this chapter is of primary importance.

A relative maximum or minimum is found by finding points where the first derivative is zero. The second derivative is evaluated at those points to see whether a relative maximum or minimum has been found. If it is positive, a minimum has been found. If negative, a maximum has been found. A global maximum or minimum is found by evaluating the function at all relative max–min points, end points, and points where $f'(x)$ does not exist. These points are called *critical points*. Establishing how to identify a global maximum or minimum is the main purpose of this chapter. Often, a relative maximum or minimum is the only point we need to consider. This was true, for example, in the illustrations given on inventory control and pricing strategy.

PROBLEMS

Problems for Self-Study: 1, 3, 5, 9, 10, 22

12–1.   Identify all relative max–min points of the following.
  a. $f(x) = x^3 + 3x^2 - 9x$
  b. $f(x) = x^2 + 4x + 1$

12–2.   Identify all relative maximum or minimum points in the following.
  a. $f(x) = x^2 e^{-x}$
  b. $f(x) = 2x + 3x^{-1} + 4$

12–3.   Find the global max–min points of the following. Begin by identify-fying all critical points.
  a. $f(x) = 2x^2 - x, 0 \le x \le 10$

b. $f(x) = -x^2 + 4x - 5$

c. $f(x) = 3x - 5, 0 \le x \le 4$

12-4.* Given $f(x) = 2x^3 - 5x^2 + 4x - 1$, find all relative max–min points, factor to find x values where $f(x) = 0$, and use this information to sketch the curve. Assuming that $0 \le x \le 2$ is required, find the global max and min points.

12-5. Given $f(x) = x^3 - 4x$, find all relative max–min points, factor to find x values where $f(x) = 0$, and use this information to sketch the curve. Assuming that $-2 \le x \le +2$, find the global maximum and minimum points.

12-6.* The number of people, Y, who can use a recreation facility depends on the amount spent for equipment, x, according to the formula

$$Y = -x^3 + 10,000x^2 \qquad \text{for } x \ge 0.$$

Suppose that the city fathers wish to spend enough money so that the number of people accommodated per dollar is maximized. What is the appropriate level of expenditure?

12-7. The average waiting time, T, in a hospital emergency room depends on the number of people on the staff, x. The form of the relationship is

$$T = x^2 - 30x + 240 \qquad \text{for } x \ge 1.$$

Find the level of staff that will minimize the average waiting time.

12-8.* The cost of providing a single customer with replacement parts for a consumer durable is currently $40 and is increasing linearly with time so that the cost equals $40 + 10t$, where t is time in years. The demand for parts is decreasing exponentially (from a current level of 100), so that demand equals $100e^{-t}$. When will the total cost of service for this machine reach a maximum?

12-9. A manager has a linear demand function in units of the form demand $= 50 - 4p$. Each unit costs $5, and the company has a long-standing policy that requires $p \le 10$. How much should they charge to maximize profit? If $p \le 8$ is required, what price should they charge?

12-10. An inventory manager knows that he has an ordering cost of $40 per order, an inventory cost of $2 per item per year, and an annual demand of 4000 per year. However, his warehouse allows a maximum order size of 100. How many should he order? How much does he lose because of the constraint?

12-11.* The manager of a hospital pharmacy is in charge of ordering medicine for his inventory. A particular drug has an ordering cost of $20 per order, an inventory cost of $0.50 per item per year, and an annual demand of 6000 items per year. How many items should be ordered each time?

12–12. The average service time, T, at a fast-food counter depends on the number of items ordered, x. If $T = x^3 - 10x^2 + 20$, and a person must order 20 items, how many trips should he make to minimize his total waiting time?

12–13. * A wine manufacturing company believes that its wine increases in value according to

$$\text{value} = \tfrac{1}{2} \, (\log_e t).$$

If they want to maximize the value of the wine, they will hold it forever. Suppose, instead, that they want to maximize the profit per year spent in their cellars, that is, maximize $\tfrac{1}{2}(\log_e t)/t$. How long should they hold the wine?

12–14. The Sudsy Soap Company continually markets new soap products. They have found that their sales increase initially, then decrease. In particular:

$$S(t) \equiv \text{rate of sales as a function of time} = a(t + t^2/2 - t^3/10),$$

where t is in years, sales are in thousands of cases, and a is a constant.
a. When do sales achieve their global maximum (for $t > 0$)?
b. If the rate of sales is equal to 7 (thousand) when $t = 1$, what is the value of the constant a?

12–15. * A manager has estimated his demand function, and he believes it is given by

$$\text{demand} = 100 + 3p - p^2.$$

His cost is $3 per unit.
a. What price should he charge to maximize profit? (Leave the answer in square-root form.)
b. Obtain the second derivative and state how you would check to see if you have a maximum.
c. If the demand function were to change to

$$\text{demand} = 100 + 3p - 2p^2,$$

would the new answer be higher or lower than before? Why? (An intuitive answer is acceptable.)

*12–16.** The city of Mythaca is considering the construction of a housing project for its senior citizens. Two proposals are before the city fathers. The first involves separate dwelling units in clusters with a common dining and recreational facility. An alternative proposal involves one high-rise structure. The cost of either facility is a function of the number of dwelling units, construction requirements, and associated costs. The builder has estimated the average-cost functions under the blueprint restrictions to be of the form

$$Proposal\ 1: AC_1 = x^2 - 4x + 6,$$

$$Proposal\ 2: AC_2 = \frac{x^3}{3} - 3x^2 + 8x + 2,$$

where x is measured in hundreds of units and AC in thousands of dollars. Thus if $x = 2$, the average cost per unit under proposal 1 is $(2^2 - 4(2) + 6)1000 = \$2000.]$

It is important that average cost per dwelling unit be minimized, since the necessary rent requirement will be determined in part thereby. If the city fathers insist on producing at least 400 dwelling units, but they can spend no more than \$3,000,000:

a. What is the optimal proposal?

b. How many units should be constructed?

c. What is the total cost to the city?

Use the differential calculus to obtain your solution. [*Remember* that the solution involves building the number of units for which the average cost is minimized, subject to (1) a requirement that at least 400 units be built, and (2) a constraint on the total spending.]

*12–17.** An eastern business school is interested in reducing its deficit by raising tuition, but they know there is some limit on how much people will pay. In particular, they have done a market study which shows that they can "maintain quality" and obtain $(1000 - 0.2T)$ students, where T is the tuition charged.

The cost is, of course, an increasing function of the number of students, since more faculty must be hired. There is a fixed cost of \$300,000 to operate such a school, and there must be one faculty member for every 10 students. Faculty earn \$10,000 each at this school.

a. What tuition should they charge (to make the most "profit")? How many students and faculty will they have? How much "profit" will they make?

b. If they are constrained by university policy to have tuition be less than or equal to $2750, how much tuition should they charge? Justify your answer.

12–18.* A university community is considering expanding its detention center downtown. Being short of funds the city wishes to use a 100,000-foot length of wire fencing that it already owns to make two separate enclosures. City ordnances require a square enclosure for men and a circular enclosure for women, but they state no minimum area requirement. To provide the fencing for both enclosures the wire fence will be cut once and all of it will be used. What is the maximum total area for the two enclosures that can be obtained and how do you know it is the maximum? (This is a hard problem.)
Formulas you may want to use are:

1. Area of a circle $= \pi r^2$ $r \equiv$ radius
2. Area of a square $= s^2$ $s \equiv$ side
3. Perimeter of a circle $= 2\pi r$
4. Perimeter of a square $= 4s$

12–19. A city has enough money to buy 60,000 square yards of land to build a rectangular stadium. Given this, is it possible to find a set of dimensions such that the stadium's perimeter (and therefore seating capacity) is maximized?

12–20.* The inventory manager of a large retail store faces an inventory problem different from that of Problem 12–10. In particular, if more than 100 units of a particular item is ordered, the purchase price is reduced 5 percent (and inventory cost also decreases 5 percent). (You must now include purchase cost in the annual cost, since it is not constant for all purchase quantities.) The necessary data are:

$$\text{ordering cost} \quad = \quad 10$$
$$\text{annual demand} = 250$$

For quantities below 100: inventory cost $=$ \$2.00 per unit per year
purchase cost $=$ \$20 per unit
For quantities above 100: inventory cost $=$ \$1.90 per unit per year
purchase cost $=$ \$19 per unit

Thus total annual cost is

$$TC[Q] = \begin{cases} \dfrac{250}{Q}\,10 + \dfrac{Q}{2}\,(2.0) + 20(250), & 0 \le Q < 100, \\[2ex] \dfrac{250}{Q}\,10 + \dfrac{Q}{2}\,(1.9) + 19(250), & 100 \le Q \le 200. \end{cases}$$

To solve this problem for the optimal Q, you must find any relative max–min points of both segments, and evaluate the function at $Q = 100$, since that is a critical point where the derivative does not exist. You are to tell the manager what order size (Q) to use, to minimize cost.

12–21.* The inventory in Problem 12–20 has a cost function of the general form shown. That is, it has a discontinuity at the quantity discount value.

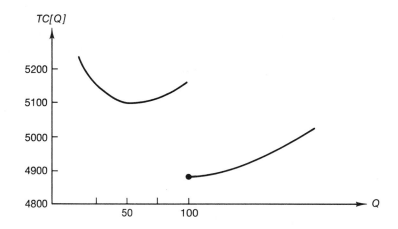

a. What would the shape of the curve be (in general) if there were several quantity discount levels? (That is, the price is p up to level 1, $0.95p$ up to level 2, $0.92p$ up to level 3, and so on.)

b. A general method of solving this type of problem is:

(1) Solve for the economic order quantity using the square-root formula and using each price. If the value of Q found is in the range corresponding to that price, compute $TC[Q]$, including the variable cost of purchasing the items. Otherwise, eliminate that quantity from contention.

(2) Evaluate $TC[Q]$ at each quantity discount point.

(3) Choose the Q with the smallest $TC[Q]$. Very simply, why does this method work?

12–22. Find potential max–min points of the following. Do you think you have found a maximum, a minimum, or neither?

a. $f(x, y) = x^2 + y^2$

b. $f(x, y) = x^2 - y^2 + xy$

12–23.* Find potential max–min points for the following. If you cannot complete one of the cases, say why. (*Hint:* Part *a* is a review of your algebra.)

a. $f(x, y) = 4x^3 + 2x^2 + 3xy - \frac{1}{2}y^2 + x$

b. $f(x, y) = x^3y^2 + y^4x + x^3 + 4x$

c. $f(x, y) = 7x + 4y$

12–24.* In the price–advertising example in Section 12.5, what are the optimal values if the demand relationship changes to $30 - p + A$?

12–25. In Problem 12–24, suppose that the company had a long-standing policy of never charging more than $20. How much should they charge? How much should they advertise? Will the profit be higher or lower after the constraint is added?

13

Introduction to Integration

The Aluminum Salvage Corporation reclaims aluminum from used beer and soda cans. Because the use of aluminum cans is increasing and since more people are saving the cans for ecological reasons, their production is increasing at a rate of 200 tons per month. Their current production rate is 2,500 tons per month. The president has just received an inquiry concerning a potential larger order for 60,000 tons and would like to know how long it will take them to produce it. The delivery date is critical to their getting the contract, so he will turn the entire plant over to meeting the order. The current inventory is already promised to other customers. The president also wants to know how much the company can produce during the next 12 months.

This problem is one of summing up production over different periods of time. However, because the growth in production is going on continuously, we cannot simply add monthly production as we would do if monthly production were at a constant level. In a sense we want to "sum up" production in continuous time, adding one second's production plus the next second's production, and so on. Since adding production second by second is tedious, we would like to have an easier way. Integral calculus (integration) is a method of "summing up" continuously. Before solving the Aluminum Salvage Company's problem, we need a better understanding of just what integration is and how it works.

13–1 THE INTEGRAL AS AN AREA

If a distillation tower is producing gasoline at a rate of 50 gallons per hour, how many gallons will it produce in 2 hours? (That's easy, you say,

325

100 gallons. But integration gives us a harder, but insightful, way of solving the problem.)

To solve the problem, you probably multiplied 2 by 50. But you could also multiply 4 (half-hour segments) by 25 (gallons per half-hour) or 8 (quarter-hour segments) by $12\frac{1}{2}$ (gallons per quarter-hour), and so on. Each of these solutions gives the same answer. The rate of production is pictured in Figure 13–1. In general, for any amount of time, the total production equals $50t$, where t is time measured in hours. (If the Aluminum Salvage Company's production were constant over time, this method would work for it, too. Unfortunately, the rate is not constant.)

FIGURE 13–1

A Constant Production Rate

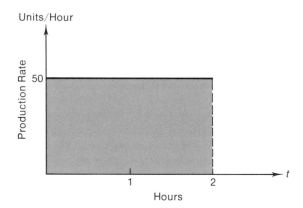

Hours

The total production also happens to be the area under the curve giving the production rate. As you may remember from plane geometry, the area of a rectangle equals the base times the height. For an aribtrary value of time, t, the area is $50t$. In our example, t goes from 0 to 2, and the area is 100. This leads us to the first intuitive definition of integration.

Integration gives the area under a curve. The area is called the *integral* **when the interval is left arbitrary. When the interval is specified, the area is called the** *definite integral.* **(In the above example, $50t$ is the integral, and 100 is the definite integral.)**

Integration "sums up continuously," and the result is the area under the curve. If the rate of 50 gallons per hour were replaced with a general rate of b gallons per hour, the total production would be bt gallons for t units of time. If c units were already stockpiled at time zero, total gallons available after t hours would be $bt + c$.

Suppose that we wanted to find the total production in 5 hours if the tower was just started (at time zero), but the rate of production increases 20 gallons per hour for the first 5 hours. That is, its rate of production equals $20t$, $0 < t < 5$. This rate is pictured in Figure 13–2.

FIGURE 13–2

An Increasing Production Rate

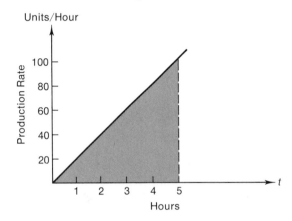

As you may remember from your plane geometry, the area of a triangle is one-half the base times the height. In Figure 13–2 the height always equals $20t$, and the base equals t. The area, then, is $\frac{1}{2}(20t)(t) = 10t^2$. The area from 0 to 5 is $\frac{1}{2}(20 \cdot 5)(5) = 250$. Integrating the rate of production, $20t$, gives $10t^2$; $F(t) = 10t^2$ is the integral. The definite integral from 0 to 5 is 250.

About this time you are wondering: "There must be something more to this integration stuff. When does it get hard?" Well, here it comes.

Suppose we have a curve that is not composed of straight lines (see Figure 13–3). Integrating still gives the area under the curve, but plane geometry will no longer give us the precise answer.

Suppose, for example, that we want the area under $f(x) = (x^2/4) + 1$ from $x =$ zero to $x = 3$. Even though plane geometry does not give us the precise answer, it can be used to approximate that area. One approximation is accomplished by summing the area of three rectangles, each with a base equal to 1 and a height equal to the value of the curve in the middle of the base. The three rectangles are illustrated in Figure 13–3.

FIGURE 13–3

Graph of $f(x) = (x^2/4) + 1$

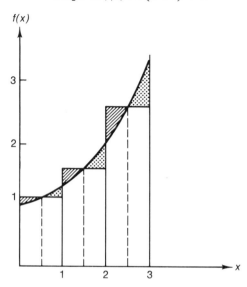

They have heights of $f(\frac{1}{2}) = 1\frac{1}{16}$, $f(1\frac{1}{2}) = 1\frac{9}{16}$, and $f(2\frac{1}{2}) = 2\frac{9}{16}$, respectively. We estimate the area under the curve by adding the areas of the three rectangles. These areas are given by the product of their heights by their bases, or simply by the heights here, since the base equals 1 in each case. We obtain

$$\text{area} = f(\tfrac{1}{2}) + f(1\tfrac{1}{2}) + f(2\tfrac{1}{2}) = 1\tfrac{1}{16} + 1\tfrac{9}{16} + 2\tfrac{9}{16} = 5\tfrac{3}{16} = 5.19.$$

The answer is only approximate since, as you can see from Figure 13–3, these rectangles have added some extra area (the darkened portions of Figure 13–3), and left other areas out of the sum (the dotted portions of Figure 13–3). These areas do not precisely offset one another. We wonder, then, how close our approximation is and how we can improve it. We will find out how good the approximation is when we discover how to obtain the exact answer. But we see immediately that a closer approximation can be obtained simply by using more rectangles. For example, the approximation obtained using six rectangles, each with a base of $\frac{1}{2}$, is shown in Figure 13–4. The resulting approximation is

$$\tfrac{1}{2}f(\tfrac{1}{4}) + \tfrac{1}{2}f(\tfrac{3}{4}) + \tfrac{1}{2}f(1\tfrac{1}{4}) + \tfrac{1}{2}f(1\tfrac{3}{4}) + \tfrac{1}{2}f(2\tfrac{1}{4}) + \tfrac{1}{2}f(2\tfrac{3}{4})$$
$$= \tfrac{1}{2}(\tfrac{65}{64}) + \ldots + \tfrac{1}{2}(\tfrac{185}{64}) = 5.23.$$

FIGURE 13–4

Finding the Area under $f(x) = (x^2/4) + 1$
Using Six Rectangles

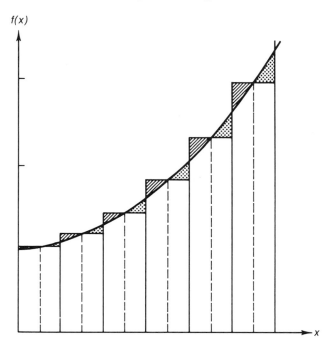

The estimate is slightly larger than before. Using a base of 1 we were throwing away more dotted area than we were adding darkened area. An even closer approximation is possible if more rectangles are used. As we add more and more rectangles we will get closer and closer to the exact area of $5\frac{1}{4}$. (This figure is derived in Section 13–2.) In the limit, when an infinite number of rectangles are used, the exact area of $5\frac{1}{4}$ is obtained. Thus the definite integral can be defined as a limit.

Given $f(x)$, **continuous over the interval** $a < x < b$, **the definite integral of** $f(x)$ **from** a **to** b **gives the area under the curve from** a **to** b, **and it is defined as**

$$\lim_{\substack{n \to \infty \\ \Delta x \to 0}} \sum_{i=1}^{n} f(x_i)\Delta x, \qquad \text{if it exists.}$$

The limit is taken as the number of rectangles, *n*, gets very large and as the width of each rectangle, Δx, gets very small. The $f(x_i) \cdot \Delta x$ is the area of one small rectangle, and we sum over all the rectangles.

$$\int_a^b f(x)\, dx = \lim_{\substack{n \to \infty \\ \Delta x \to 0}} \sum_{i=1}^n f(x_i)\, \Delta x.$$

The values *a* and *b* are called the limits of integration. The value *b* is the upper limit of integration, and *a* is the lower limit.

The definition is illustrated in Figure 13–5.

FIGURE 13–5

The Definite Integral — The Area under the Curve from *a* to *b*

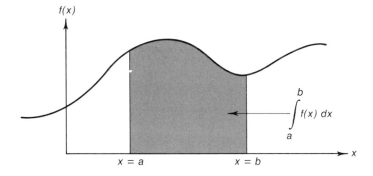

The definition looks complicated, but it simply says that we take more and more rectangles, of smaller and smaller width. In the limit we take infinitely many rectangles each with nearly zero width, and there is no longer any approximation, but an exact answer. The integral sign says: "Continuously sum rectangles of width *dx* (a positive width as close to zero as possible) from values of $x = a$ to $x = b$."

New Symbol	*English Translation*
$\int_a^b f(x)\, dx$	Find the area under the curve, $f(x)$, from $x = a$ to $x = b$; sum continuously, from $x = a$ to $x = b$. This is the definite integral of $f(x)$ from $x = a$ to $x = b$.

The definite integral gives a number, an area. Examples are given below, based on the earlier gasoline production example.

If $\qquad f(t) = 50: \displaystyle\int_0^2 50dt = 100, \qquad \int_0^{t_0} 50dt = 50t_0.$

If $\qquad f(t) = 20t: \displaystyle\int_0^5 20t\,dt = 10t^2 = 250.$

The integral is called a definite integral because it gives a single numerical answer in the form of a real number that depends on the interval, a to b, considered. (Notice that we can use t, x, or any letter in the function. The name we give to the variable does not, and should not, affect the answer.)

Finding Values for the Definite Integral Graphically

The definite integral of any continuous function exists and can be approximated graphically (if need be). This is important since when we introduce general rules for finding definite integrals, we will see that the rules do not work in all cases. Graphical integration can be accomplished in several ways, and the accuracy of the techniques vary. Two relatively easy ways of accomplishing graphical integration are examined next. Both give only approximate answers.

Following are two methods for graphical integration of a continuous function given by $f(x)$ from $x = a$ to $x = b$:

1. (a) Choose a small value, Δx, to use as the base of a rectangle as in the definition. Divide the interval ($a < x < b$) into subintervals of size Δx.
   (b) Evaluate $f(x)$ at the midpoint of each of these subintervals. The value of $f(x)$ in the middle of the ith subinterval is $f(x_i)$.
   (c) Compute $\Delta x \cdot f(x_i)$ for each of these subintervals, and sum these areas to obtain an approximate value of the definite integral. (The smaller Δx is, the closer the approximation will be, and the more calculations you will have to make.)

2. (a) Plot $f(x)$ on graph paper that is divided into small squares.
   (b) Count the number of small squares under the curve. Include a guess as to the total contributed by partial squares.
   (c) Determine the area of each square, and multiply the number of squares by the area of each square. (The accuracy of the approximation will be better and you will have more work to do as you choose paper with smaller and smaller squares.)

For an example, we return to the Aluminum Salvage Company's problem. Assume that they can produce aluminum at a rate given by $f(t)$ below, where t is time, measured in months.

$$f(t) = 2,500 + 200t \qquad (t = 0 \text{ is "now"}).$$

Recall that the president of the firm wants to know how long it will take them to produce 60,000 tons and how much they can produce in the next 12 months.

Symbolically, he wants to know the value of

$$\int_0^{12} (2{,}500 + 200t)\, dt$$

and to find b such that

$$\int_0^b (2{,}500 + 200t)\, dt = 60{,}000.$$

The function, $f(t) = 2{,}500 + 200t$, is graphed in Figure 13–6. Each square has an area of $1 \times 400 = 400$ tons. The two methods of graphical integration are shown below.

Method 1	*Method 2*

Method 1

Use $\Delta t = 2$ months

$$\int_0^{12} f(t)\, dt = 2f(1)$$

$$+\, 2f(3) + 2f(5) + 2f(7)$$
$$+\, 2f(9) + 2f(11) = 44{,}400 \text{ (tons)}$$

Method 2

Counting squares, we estimate 111 squares. Thus the area is 111×400.

$$= 44{,}400 \text{ (tons)}$$

FIGURE 13–6

Rate of Aluminum Production

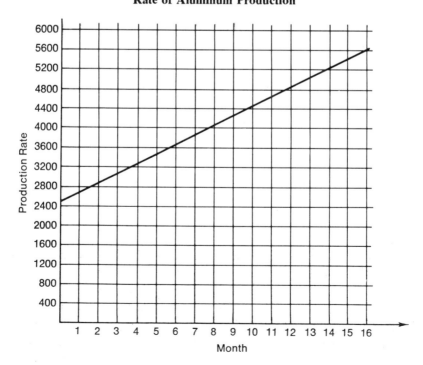

Month

For this problem both approximations give the same answer. Furthermore, this is the exact answer. That is not usually the case.

The president still needs to find b such that total production to month b is 60,000 tons. The value of b is more than 12 since we have just seen that the firm produces only 44,400 tons in 12 months. To find b, continue to increase b (past 12) until 60,000 is reached.

Trying $b = 14$, we add: $2f(13) = 10,200$.

$$\int_0^{14} f(t)\, dt = 44,400 + 10,200 = 54,600.$$

For $b = 16$, the area from 14 to 16 is added. This gives $2f(15)$, or 10,800, for a total of 65,400, which is too much. Trying $b = 15$, we add $1f(14\frac{1}{2}) = 4,400$. The total is now exactly 60,000. It will take the company 15 months to meet an order for 60,000 tons of aluminum.

⌐⌐ : Given $f(x) = 1 - x^2$, find $\int_0^1 f(x)\, dx$, using both methods of graphical integration. Use Figure 13–7 for method 2 and $\Delta x = 0.2$ for method 1. This problem does not work out exactly; what do you think the exact answer is? (Make a guess.)

Answers

FIGURE 13–7

Graph of $f(x) = 1 - x^2$

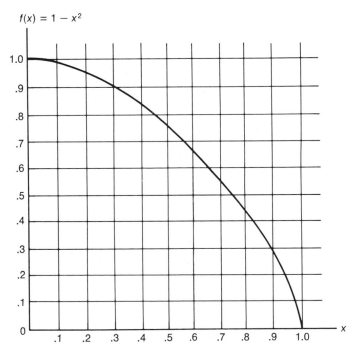

$f(x) = 1 - x^2$

<table>
<tr><td>

Method 1

Use $\Delta x = 0.2$.

$\int_0^1 (1 - x^2)\, dx = 0.2[f(0.1)$
$+ f(0.3) + f(0.5)$
$+ f(0.7) + f(0.9)] = 0.67$.

</td><td>

Method 2

Each square has an area $= (0.1)(0.1) = 0.01$.
We count (approximately) 67 squares.
The area is, then, approximately 0.67:

$\int_0^1 (1 - x^2)\, dx = 0.67$.

</td></tr>
</table>

A good guess as to the exact value (especially since it is correct) is that
$\int_0^1 (1 - x^2)\, dx = \frac{2}{3} = 0.666 \ldots$.

13–2 THE INDEFINITE INTEGRAL AND THE FUNDAMENTAL THEOREM OF CALCULUS

Integration is the *inverse process* of differentiation. That is, if we integrate $f(x)$, then take the derivative of the result, we obtain $f(x)$ again. If we add 3 to and subtract 3 from a function, we get the original function. Subtraction is the inverse process to addition. Integration is the inverse process to differentiation. This is the basis for the definition of the indefinite integral, given below.

The *indefinite integral* of $f(x)$ [called the *antiderivative* of $f(x)$ in some texts] is a function given by $F(x)$ whose derivative is $f(x)$. **Symbolically:**
The *indefinite integral* of $f(x)$ is

$$\int f(x)\, dx = F(x),$$

where $F'(x) = f(x)$. $F(x)$ contains an arbitrary added constant since the derivative of any constant is zero.

For example,

$\int 20dt = 10t^2 + c$, where c is an arbitrary constant. We found this result in Section 13–1. To check that formula:

$$\frac{d}{dt}(10t^2 + c) = 20t.$$

For another example, $\qquad \int x^2\, dx = \frac{x^3}{3} + c$.

To check:

$$\frac{d}{dx}\left(\frac{x^3}{3} + c\right) = \frac{3x^2}{3} = x^2.$$

Indefinite integrals are always written with $+c$ (plus an arbitrary constant) at the end. Since the derivative of any constant is zero, any constant could be used and we still would satisfy the definition. The term indefinite is used since integrating here does not give a single real number but rather a function whose value depends on x (or t or another variable name). No limits of integration are included with the integration symbol, $\int$, when an indefinite integral is sought.

New Symbols	*English Translation*
$\int f(x)\,dx = F(x)$	Find a function whose derivative with respect to x is $f(x)$. This function is called the indefinite integral and is written as $F(x)$.

For example, if $f(x) = 6x^2 + 4$, then $\int (6x^2 + 4)\,dx = 2x^3 + 4x + c$ because the derivative with respect to x of $2x^3 + 4x + 6$ is $6x^2 + 4$:

$$\frac{d}{dx}(2x^3 + 4x + c) = 6x^2 + 4.$$

There are, of course, many other terms that can be used in discussing indefinite integrals and related topics. We will avoid their use here, to keep the exposition as simple as possible.

We now have two types of integrals, definite and indefinite. With any luck at all, there should be some connection. A connection is provided by the Fundamental Theorem of Calculus, which says that the inverse of differentiation (the indefinite integral) can be used to evaluate the definite integral. This is important since, as you saw, graphical integration can be tedious.

The Fundamental Theorem of Calculus

Given a function and its indefinite integral, given by $f(x)$ and $F(x)$, then

$$\int_a^b f(x)\,dx = F(b) - F(a).$$

This is denoted by

$$\int_a^b f(x)\,dx = F(x)\Big|_a^b = F(b) - F(a).$$

Somehow, you expected that the Fundamental Theorem of Calculus would be a bit more grandiose. Sorry, but this is all there is to it. Moreover, you have to accept it on faith, since a proof is beyond our purpose in this book. Notice that since the indefinite integral is both added and subtracted, any constant included in the indefinite integral would cancel. Thus the constant term can be forgotten in evaluating definite integrals!

For example, we can find the integral for the gasoline example in Section 13–1.

$$\int_0^2 50\,dt = 50t\Big|_0^2 = 50(2) - 50(0) = 100$$

and

$$\int_1^3 x^2\,dx = \frac{x^3}{3}\Big|_1^3 = \frac{3^3}{3} - \frac{1^3}{3} = \frac{26}{3}.$$

New Symbol	*English Translation*
$F(x)\Big|_a^b = F(b) - F(a)$	The indefinite integral evaluated from a to b; this value equals the indefinite integral evaluated at b minus the indefinite integral evaluated at a.

The second version of the gasoline production example from the beginning of Section 13–1 can now be verified. The production rate is $f(t) = 20t$. The indefinite integral is

$$\int 20t\,dt = 10t^2 + c$$

To check this formula:

$$\frac{d}{dt}(10t^2 + c) = 20t.$$

If we wanted, in addition, to evaluate this function, say from 0 to 3, we would obtain

$$\int_0^3 20t\,dt = 10t^2\Big|_0^3 = 90.$$

Finally, let's verify the integral we approximated graphically in Section 13–1.

$$\int_0^3\left(\frac{x^2}{4} + 1\right)dx = \left(\frac{x^3}{12} + x\right)\Big|_0^3 = \frac{27}{12} + 3 = 5.25$$

It seems that we have eliminated the need for graphical integration as long as the indefinite integral in question can be found. But at the moment all we can do is make a guess as to what the indefinite integral required is and then check it by differentiation. If we get the original function back, our choice for the indefinite integral was correct. Unfortunately we have no procedures that help us to get the required integral, other than the biblical method of seek and ye *may* find. Chapter 14 gives a set of rules that will help us find most integrals without guessing.

Using only what we know now, several additional facts can be established. For example,

$$\int_a^a f(x)\, dx = F(a) - F(a) = 0,$$

$$\int_a^b f(x)\, dx = F(b) - F(a) = -\int_b^a f(x)\, dx = -F(a) + F(b).$$

The first fact will be revisited if the reader studies probability and statistics.

Sometimes integration is needed to find the area between two curves. This poses no additional difficulties. For example, suppose that a new firm is receiving revenue at an (increasing) rate of $f(x) = x^2$, but its costs are growing linearly at a rate of $g(x) = x$. How much does it lose during its first year of operation? How much does it make during the second year of operation? (All values are in units of $1,000.)

$$\text{first year total profit} = \text{total revenue} - \text{total cost}$$

$$= \int_0^1 (x^2 - x)\, dx = \left(\frac{x^3}{3} - \frac{x^2}{2}\right)\Big|_0^1$$

$$= -\tfrac{1}{6} \text{ (thousand).}$$

$$\text{second year total profit} = \int_1^2 (x^2 - x)\, dx = \left(\frac{x^3}{3} - \frac{x^2}{2}\right)\Big|_1^2$$

$$= +\tfrac{2}{3} - (-\tfrac{1}{6}) = \tfrac{5}{6} \text{ (thousand).}$$

$$\text{total profit during the 2-year period} = \int_0^2 (x^2 - x)\, dx = \left(\frac{x^3}{3} - \frac{x^2}{2}\right)\Big|_0^2$$

$$= +\tfrac{2}{3} \text{ (thousand).}$$

(Note that the definite integral from 0 to 2 equals the sum of the definite integrals from 0 to 1 and 1 to 2.)

To check the indefinite integral used, we differentiate and find

$$\frac{d}{dx}\left(\frac{x^3}{3} - \frac{x^2}{2}\right) = x^2 - x.$$

The areas in question are shown as the area between two curves in Figure 13–8. In general, do not worry about the area between two curves. Total revenue minus total cost is easier to think about than the area between two curves, and it leads to the same result.

FIGURE 13–8

Total Revenue–Total Cost: The Area between Two Curves

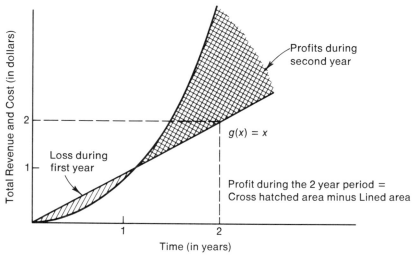

~~~

1. Find an indefinite integral for the following. Verify your answer by differentiation.

    (a) $f(x) = x/3$.   (c) $f(x) = 4 + x$.

    (b) $f(x) = e^x$.   (d) $f(x) = 3x^4$.

2. Find the definite integral of each of the four functions described in Problem 1, from $x = 0$ to $x = 1$.

3. Find the area between the curve in part (c), Problem 1, and the curve in part (a), Problem 1, from $x = 1$ to $x = 2$.

Answers

1. (a) $F(x) = x^2/6 + c$; $F'(x) = x/3$.

   (b) $F(x) - e^x + c$; $F'(x) = e^x$.

   (c) $F(x) = 4x + x^2/2 + c$; $F'(x) = 4 + x$.

   (d) $F(x) = 3x^5/5 + c$; $F'(x) = 3x^4$.

2. (a) $F(1) - F(0) = \frac{1}{6}$.

   (b) $F(1) - F(0) - e - 1$.

   (c) $F(1) - F(0) = 4\frac{1}{2}$.

   (d) $F(1) - F(0) = \frac{3}{5}$.

3. $\int_1^2 (4 + x - x/3)\, dx = (4x + x^2/2 - x^2/6) \Big|_1^2 = (4x + x^2/3) \Big|_1^2$
$$= 9\tfrac{1}{3} - 4\tfrac{1}{3} = 5.$$

13–3 SUMMARY

Integration finds the area under a curve; integration sums up continuously. The definite integral, which is defined as a limit, gives a value for an area or a sum. In the early part of this chapter, we found that we might be given a rate (of production, for example) and want to find total production over some interval. The definite integral gives this total or sum, and it can be found graphically for any continuous function. Luckily we do not have to do so.

The indefinite integral is the inverse of the derivative. An indefinite integral of $f(x)$, written $\int f(x)\, dx = F(x)$, is a function whose derivative equals $f(x)$. That is, $F'(x) = f(x)$. The definite integral and the indefinite integral are related by the Fundamental Theorem of Calculus:

$$\int_a^b f(x)\, dx = F(b) - F(a).$$

This theorem says that the definite integral of $f(x)$ from a to b equals the indefinite integral (the antiderivative) evaluated at b minus the indefinite integral evaluated at a. This allows us to obtain values for the definite integral (such as the total production of aluminum over some period of time) without using the graphical technique.

At this point we still can find indefinite integrals only by trial and error, and then we can check the result by differentiation. Chapter 14 will give rules of integration for most functions of interest in management problems.

NEW SYMBOLS

Symbol	English Translation
$\int_a^b f(x)\, dx$ [the definite integral of $f(x)$ from a to b]	Find the area under the curve $f(x)$, from $x = a$ to $x = b$; sum the $f(x)$ values continuously from $x = a$ to $x = b$.
$\int f(x)\, dx = F(x)$	Find a function whose derivative with respect to x is $f(x)$. This function is called the indefinite integral of $f(x)$, and it is written as $F(x)$.
$F(x) \Big|_a^b = F(b) - F(a)$	Evaluate $F(x)$ at $x = b$ and subtract from that $F(x)$ evaluated at $x = a$.

PROBLEMS

Problems for Self-Study: 2, 4, 8, 10, 11

13–1.* Find the area contained in each of the regions below using plane geometry. (All inequalities must be satisfied simultaneously.)

    a. $y \geq 0,\ x \geq 0,\ x \leq 4,\ y \leq 6$

    b. $y \geq 0,\ x \geq 0,\ x \leq 3,\ y \leq 2x$

    c. $y \geq 0,\ x \geq 0,\ x \leq 6,\ y \leq 6 - x$

    d. $y \geq 0,\ x \geq 0,\ x \leq 4,\ y \leq \begin{cases} 2 & \text{for } 0 \leq x \leq 2 \\ 3 & \text{for } 2 < x \leq 4 \end{cases}$

13–2. Using method 1 described in the text and rectangles of width 0.2, approximate the area A under each curve from $x = 0$ to $x = 1$.

    a. $f(x) = 3 + x$

    b. $f(x) = 2x$

    c. $f(x) = x^2$

    d. $f(x) = x^3$

    e. $f(x) = x^2 - x^3$

13–3. Using method 2 (counting the squares) with a grid of width 0.1, approximate the areas described in Problem *13–2*.

13–4. Find an indefinite integral for each of the following. Verify your answer by differentiation. (Part *d* is difficult. Check the answer if it takes too much time.)

    a. $f(x) = ax/b$

    b. $f(x) = \dfrac{x^2}{2} - x$

    c. $g(y) = (a - y)^2$

    d. $f(x) = \dfrac{1}{(x + 1)^2}$

13–5.* The derivative of $\log_e x = 1/x$. Using this information, find

    a. $\displaystyle\int \frac{1}{x}\,dx$ *c.* $\displaystyle\int \frac{a}{bx}\,dx$ *e.* $\displaystyle\int \frac{1}{x + a}\,dx$

    b. $\displaystyle\int \frac{a}{x}\,dx$ *d.* $\displaystyle\int \frac{1}{x^2}\,dx$

13–6. Using one of the graphical techniques, find $\int_0^1 f(x)\,dx$ for

a. $f(x) = \begin{cases} 2x, & x < \frac{1}{2} \\ 4x^2, & x \geq \frac{1}{2} \end{cases}$

b. $f(x) = \begin{cases} 2x, & x < 2 \\ x^2, & x \geq 2 \end{cases}$

c. $f(x) = \begin{cases} 1, & x < \frac{1}{4} \\ 2, & x \geq \frac{1}{4} \end{cases}$

13–7.* Find each of the definite integrals below.

a. $\int_a^b \dfrac{ax}{b}\,dx$

b. $\int_0^1 \left(\dfrac{x^2}{2} - x\right) dx$

c. $\int_2^3 (a - y)^2\,dy$

d. $\int_0^1 \dfrac{1}{(x + 1)^2}\,dx$

13–8. Use the definite integral to find the exact areas in Problems 13–2 and 13–3. How close were the approximations?

13–9.* a. Using both graphical methods, find the area between $f(x) = 2x$ and $g(x) = x^2$ from $x = 0$ to $x = 2$.

b. Find $\int_0^2 (2x - x^2)\,dx$ to obtain the exact answer to the question in part a.

13–10. Using plane geometry, one of the graphical methods, and integration, find the area between $f(x) = 3x$ and $g(x) = x$, from $x = 1$ to $x = 3$.

13–11. The Aluminum Salvage Company's president wants to find b such that

$$\int_0^b (2500 + 200t)\,dt = 60{,}000.$$

Solve the definite integral in terms of b, and then solve for b.

13–12. A firm that manufactures fad items (Fadite, Inc.) believes that sales for each item follow a pattern of quick growth, then quick decay. In particular:

sales $= at - bt^2, \quad 0 < t < a/b, \quad$ where t is in months.

a. Why is the function described only valid for $0 < t < a/b$?

b. Find the definite integral that would give sales over the life of the item.

c. If $a = 10$ and $b = 1$, how many sales do they obtain over the item's life? Find the answer graphically and using integration.

*13–13.** Suppose that the Fadite company believes it has a new product line that will not lose its sales immediately. In particular, they think that sales $= at - bt^2$ until peak sales are reached and that the peak sales are then maintained for 12 months. Following that, sales decline until they reach zero at $(a/b) + 12$. Thus sales are given by

$$
\text{sales} = \begin{cases} at - bt^2, & 0 < t < \dfrac{a}{2b}, \\[2mm] a^2/4b, & \dfrac{a}{2b} < t < \dfrac{a}{2b} + 12, \\[2mm] a(t - 12) - b(t - 12)^2, & \dfrac{a}{2b} + 12 < t < \dfrac{a}{b} + 12. \end{cases}
$$

a. Where did $(a/2b)$, $(a^2/4b)$, and $(t - 12)$ come from?

b. Draw the sales curve for $a = 10$, $b = 1$.

c. Integrate or find graphically, to obtain total sales over the product's life.

*13–14.** The Fadite company in Problems 13–12 and 13–13 has a competitor, the Junkite Corporation. Junkite believes that through advertising properly, it can avoid the sharp decline at the end of a product's life. They believe that their products exactly follow Fadite's pattern in Problem 13–13 for the first two time segments (0 to $a/2b$ and $a/2b$ to $(a/2b) + 12$). Then they believe that sales decline linearly over a 6-month period. That is,

$$
\text{sales} = \begin{cases} at - bt^2, & 0 < t < a/2b, \\ a^2/4b, & a/2b < t < a/2b + 12, \\ (a^2/4b)(a/2b + 18 - t)/6, & a/2b + 12 < t < a/2b + 18. \end{cases}
$$

a. Draw the sales function.

b. If $a = 10$ and $b = 1$, how many sales above the Fadite sales does Junkite obtain? (Fadite's total sales figure was $466\frac{2}{3}$.)

13–15.* The ABC firm estimates that its short-term bank borrowings, *B*, will vary over the next 12 months according to

$$B = 3 + \frac{1}{12}(t - 6)^2, \qquad 0 \le t \le 12,$$

where *B* is borrowings in millions of dollars and *t* is time, measured in months. Suppose that the monthly interest rate is 0.5 percent. Find the total interest payments *I* over the next 12 months.

13–16. A particular machine used in production must be started and stopped gradually so that over a 16-hour work shift, its rate of output *X* is

$$X = f(t) = 8 - \frac{1}{8}(t - 8)^2,$$

where *t* is time measured in hours and *X* is measured in 100s of units produced. Find the total production *P* during the day

a. Using method 1 with rectangles of width 2.

b. By integration.

13–17.* The machine in Problem 13–16 can be operated on a 24-hour shift. It must be shut down once per day to be cleaned, but, since cleaning takes essentially no time, it can be operated a full 24 hours. The performance during the first 8 hours and last 8 hours are exactly as it was when a 16-hour shift was used. During the middle 8 hours, it operates at its maximum rate of output, 8 per hour. That is,

$$\text{rate of output} = \begin{cases} 8 - \frac{1}{8}(t - 8)^2, & 0 < t < 8, \\ 8, & 8 \le t \le 16, \\ 8 - \frac{1}{8}(t - 16)^2, & 16 < t \le 24. \end{cases}$$

a. Draw the curve showing the rate of output.

b. Find the total production during the 24-hour day.

c. The average rate of output equals total output divided by hours of operation. How much is the average rate of output increased by operating 24 hours per day?

13–18.* The cost of producing the *x*th unit at the ABC plant is

$$f(x) = 50 - \frac{x}{2} \qquad \text{for } 0 \le x \le 75.$$

Find the cost of producing 50 units

a. Using plane geometry.

b. By integration.

13–19.* The cost of producing the xth unit at the DEF plant is

$$f(x) = 10 + \frac{20}{x+1}.$$

What is the cost of producing the first 100 units?

13–20. The exponential function, $f(x) = e^{ax}$, has a derivative of ae^{ax}. Thus the indefinite integral of ae^{ax} is $\frac{1}{a}e^{ax} + c$. Using this basic idea, find (and verify by differentiation)

a. $\int e^x\, dx$

b. $\int ae^{bx}\, dx$

13–21. Sales at any point in time over the next year $(0 \le t \le 1)$ may be described by an exponential growth curve

$$f(t) = S_0 e^{at},$$

where S_0 is the current sales level and a is the continuous growth rate. (See Problem 13–20 for the necessary indefinite integral.)

a. Find the total sales, S, over the next year in terms of S_0 and a.

b. Find total sales over the next year when $S_0 = \$1,000,000$ and $a = 0.2$, by substituting into the answer from part a.

13–22.* a. A liquid chemical flows into a mixing vat at the rate of 6 gallons per minute. It takes 100 minutes for the vat to fill. Use integration to find the volume of the vat.

b. Suppose the vat held 840 gallons. Use integration to find the length of time needed to fill the vat.

13–23.* Find the indefinite integrals of the sums of the following.

a. $f_1(x) = x^2, f_2(x) = x$

b. $f_1(x) = (a + x)^2, f_2(x) = (a - x)^2$

c. $f_1(x) = x^2 - x, f_2(x) = x + x^2$

13–24. Sales are expected to grow continuously at an annual rate of 0.20 while costs are expected to grow at 0.15. Presently sales are 1000 and costs are 900. Find total profit over the next year ($0 \leq t \leq 1$). Remember that e^{at} represents continuous growth at a rate a for t years. Also, the necessary indefinite integrals can be found from Problem 13–20.

13–25. * The manager of a cost control center knows that the amount of cost saving is a function of the amount spent in cost investigations, x. The incremental savings attributed to the xth dollar is

$$C' = f(x) = 100e^{-x/100}.$$

a. Find the total cost savings as a function of the budget for investigation, B. Refer to Problem 13–20 for the necessary indefinite integrals.

b. Find the total cost savings when $B = 1000$.

14

Rules of Integration

Now that we know the inner workings of calculus (the Fundamental Theorem) and the theory of integration, it is time to learn how to find an integral. We know how to check a potential answer (take the derivative and see if you get the original function), but coming up with candidates can be tedious.

Integration is more difficult than differentiation in that there is not a "delta-process" to fall back on; worse yet, some continuous functions do not have indefinite integrals. Every single equation function composed of x^n, e^x, or $\log x$ (combined with constants) can be differentiated. But an indefinite integral does not exist for every such function. This complicates our life. [An important example for which it is impossible to find an indefinite integral is e^{x^2}.]

Given the difficulties involved in trial-and-error integration, it is important to have large classes of functions for which rules of integration exist. This chapter is devoted to finding such rules, and to introducing a few sneaky tricks that will allow us to integrate some difficult functions. As in differentiation, we will first learn how to deal with polynomials; later sections deal with special functions and trickery.

Before beginning, it is worthwhile to emphasize that any definite integral can be found graphically. It is not any fun, but it can always be done. Precisely how to do a graphical integration was discussed in Chapter 13. The purpose of Chapter 14 is to save us from such tedious calculations.

346

14–1 INTEGRATING POLYNOMIALS

In this section we will develop three rules which will suffice for integrating polynomial functions common to managerial problems. The first of these rules is suggested by the integral of $f(x) = x$.

$$\int x \, dx = \frac{x^2}{2} + c, \text{ since } \frac{d}{dx}(x^2/2 + c) = x.$$

The procedure for finding the integral here can be described as follows: raise the power of x by 1 and divide the constant multiplier by the new power. Finally, add a general constant, c. This procedure is generalizable and leads to the first rule for integration.

Rule 1 for Integration: POWERS

$$\int x^n \, dx = \left(\frac{x^{n+1}}{n+1}\right) + c, \quad \text{when } n \neq -1.$$

An example using this rule is

$$\int x^5 \, dx = \frac{x^6}{6} + c.$$

If the definite integral from zero to 1 is desired, we have

$$\int_0^1 x^5 \, dx = \frac{x^6}{6} \bigg|_0^1 = \frac{1}{6} - 0 = \frac{1}{6}.$$

This rule is most easily justified by taking the derivative of the answer.

$$\frac{d}{dx}\left(\frac{x^{n+1}}{n+1} + c\right) = x^n.$$

The power rule is true for fractional exponents, all negative exponents except -1, and for zero. (x^{-1} will be covered in the special functions section.) For example,

$$\int_0^4 x^{3/2} \, dx = \frac{x^{5/2}}{5/2} \bigg|_0^4 = \frac{32}{5/2} - 0 = \frac{64}{5}$$

and

$$\int_2^4 7dx = \int_2^4 7(x^0)\, dx = \frac{7x^1}{1}\bigg|_2^4 = 7x\bigg|_2^4 = 14.$$

We could write the $n = 0$ case as a separate rule for constants, but that is not necessary. As another example, we can use rule 1 for

$$\int a\, dx = ax + c, \qquad \text{where } a \text{ and } c \text{ are constants.}$$

The function $f(x) = 2x$ with integral

$$\int 2x\, dx = x^2 + c_1, \qquad \text{since } \frac{d}{dx}(x^2 + c_1) = 2x,$$

can be used to suggest the second rule for integration. We may write

$$f(x) = 2(x).$$

Now using rule 1 for integration we know that

$$\int x\, dx = \frac{x^2}{2} + c_2.$$

Multiplying both sides of this equation by 2 and letting $c_3 = 2c_2$ gives

$$2\int x\, dx = x^2 + c_3,$$

but this is the integral of the original function $f(x) = 2x$ (with the general constant c_1 replaced by c_3). Hence we may write

$$\int 2x\, dx = 2\int x\, dx.$$

This suggests the second rule for integration.

Rule 2 for Integration: CONSTANT TIMES A FUNCTION

$$\int af(x)\, dx = a\int f(x)\, dx, \textbf{ where } a \textbf{ is a constant.}$$

For an example, consider

$$\int 3x^2 \, dx = 3 \int x^2 \, dx = \frac{3x^3}{3} + c = x^3 + c.$$

To check the answer, we take the derivative of $(x^3 + c)$:

$$\frac{d}{dx}(x^3 + c) = 3x^2.$$

The definite integral from, say, 0 to 3 is

$$\int_0^3 3x^2 \, dx = 3 \int_0^3 x^2 \, dx = 3\left(\frac{x^3}{3}\right)\Big|_0^3 = 27 - 0 = 27.$$

Rule 2 can be validated by taking the derivative of the answer. In particular, $\frac{d}{dx}[a \int f(x) \, dx] = af(x)$, and the rule is validated.

The third rule for integration can again be suggested by an example. Suppose that we wish to integrate $h(x) = 2x + 4x$. We know already that

$$f(x) = 2x \text{ has the integral } \int 2x \, dx = x^2 + c_1$$

and using rules 1 and 2,

$$g(x) = 4x \quad \text{has the integral } \int 4x \, dx = 2x^2 + c_2.$$

Further, using rules 1 and 2 again,

$$h(x) = 2x + 4x = 6x \quad \text{has the integral } \int 6x \, dx = 3x^2 + c_3$$
$$= 2x^2 + x^2 + c_3.$$

Letting the general constant $c_3 = c_1 + c_2$ we see that

$$\int 6x \, dx = \int 2x \, dx + \int 4x \, dx.$$

In words, rule 3 is that a sum may be integrated by working on its terms one at a time.

Rule 3 for Integration: SUM OR DIFFERENCE

$$\int [f(x) \pm g(x)] \, dx = \int f(x) \, dx \pm \int g(x) \, dx.$$

For an example consider

$$\int (x^2 + x)\, dx = \int x^2\, dx + \int x\, dx = \frac{x^3}{3} + \frac{x^2}{2} + c, \quad \text{where } c \text{ is a constant.}$$

The above is an indefinite integral. To check the answer, we take the derivative of

$$\frac{x^3}{3} + \frac{x^2}{2} + c; \quad \frac{d}{dx}\left(\frac{x^3}{3} + \frac{x^2}{2} + c\right) = x^2 + x.$$

It works! If we wanted the definite integral from, say, 2 to 3:

$$\int_2^3 (x^2 + x)\, dx = \int_2^3 x^2\, dx + \int_2^3 x\, dx = \frac{x^3}{3}\bigg|_2^3 + \frac{x^2}{2}\bigg|_2^3$$

$$= \left(\frac{27}{3} - \frac{8}{3}\right) + \left(\frac{9}{2} - \frac{4}{2}\right) = \frac{53}{6}.$$

When the integral is separated the same limits of integration apply to both (all) portions of the integral.

Rule 3 can be justified by taking the derivative of the answer to see if we obtain the original function.

$$\frac{d}{dx}\left[\int f(x)\, dx\right] \pm \frac{d}{dx}\left[\int g(x)\, dx\right] = f(x) \pm g(x),$$

and the rule is validated. [We caution the reader that this chapter has continued our policy of intuitive justifications (sloppy proofs) for the procedures we wish you to master.]

Rule 3 allows us to decompose complicated problems involving integrals into several smaller problems which are easier to solve. For example, since we can integrate the first two parts of a three-term function and then combine the result with the integral for the third term, we can use rule 3 to integrate a sum or difference of 3, 4, 17, or any number of terms. For example,

$$\int (x^2 + x + 1)\, dx = \frac{x^3}{3} + \frac{x^2}{2} + x + c.$$

More generally, rule 3 allows us to attack an integral term by term, and rule 2 allows us to remove multiplicative constants to get down to the basic components.

Rules 1, 2, and 3 enable us to integrate all polynomials, as well as functions involving negative and fractional exponents. For example, we can now integrate the general polynomial

$$\int (a_n x^n + a_{n-1} x^{n-1} + \ldots + a_1 x^1 + a_0)\, dx$$

$$= \frac{a_n}{n+1} x^{n+1} + \frac{a_{n-1}}{n} x^n + \ldots + \frac{a_1}{2} x^2 + a_0 x + c.$$

Specific examples include

$$\int \left(17x^4 + \frac{1}{2} x^{-3} + 2x^{3/4} \right) dx = \frac{17}{5} x^5 - \frac{1}{4} x^{-2} + \frac{8}{7} x^{7/4} + c$$

$$\int_1^3 x^{-2}\, dx = -1(x^{-1}) \Big|_1^3 = -\frac{1}{3} - (-1) = +\frac{2}{3}.$$

As a practical illustration, suppose that a manager of a manufacturing division knows his labor costs are currently $100 per day, and they are increasing at the rate of $0.20 per day. Since he is being evaluated as the manager of a cost center, his main concern is staying within his present and future expenditure budgets. Suppose he wants to know how much he will spend, if he operates at the present scale of operation, over the next 2 years (500 working days). His cost function is given by

$$c(t) = 100 + 0.2t.$$

Total cost over the 2-year period is equal to

$$\int_0^{500} c(t)\, dt = \int_0^{500} (100 + 0.2t)\, dt = 100t + 0.1t^2 \Big|_0^{500}$$
$$= 50,000 + 25,000 = \$75,000$$

The 20-cent-per-day increase may seem small but it accounts for fully $\frac{1}{3}$ of the total cost $(25,000/75,000)$ over the 2 years.

Another example is given by the demand forecasting techniques used by many firms; some firms find it reasonable to assume that demand is growing linearly with time. Other firms find it more reasonable to assume that the relation of demand with time is quadratic. Both types of firms may want to make a forecast of total sales for the next few years, for the purpose of long-range financial planning. If the quadratic form is appropriate, then demand as a function of time is given by

$$\text{demand} = a + bt + ct^2, \qquad 0 < t,$$

where a is the current rate of sales, t is measured treating "now" as zero, and b and c are constants we assume are either known or can be estimated for the firm. If, on the other hand, the firm thinks that growth is linear, c is set equal to zero, and a and b are estimated. The methods of regression analysis, to which we referred in Section 12–5 and which you may study in a statistics course, provide one means of estimating the constants a, b, and c.

To illustrate how total sales might be useful in planning, suppose that a firm wants to eliminate (in easy stages) all product lines that will not gross at least \$10 million over the next five years. It could proceed as follows, using the quadratic demand relationship.

$$\text{Total sales expected in the next 5 years} = \int_0^5 (a + bt + ct^2)\, dt$$

$$= \left(at + \frac{bt^2}{2} + \frac{ct^3}{3} \right) \Bigg|_0^5$$

$$= \left(5a + \frac{25}{2} b + \frac{125}{3} c \right).$$

They have five products, and the estimates of a, b, and c, obtained from a statistical analysis, for each product are:

	Product 1	Product 2	Product 3	Product 4	Product 5
a	2,000,000	1,600,000	1,500,000	1,200,000	1,000,000
b	0	100,000	100,000	200,000	100,000
c	0	0	30,000	90,000	60,000

Expected sales are $5a + \frac{25}{2} b + \frac{125}{3} c$. Thus expected sales for each product are:

Product 1: 10,000,000
Product 2: 9,250,000
Product 3: 10,000,000
Product 4: 11,250,000
Product 5: 8,750,000

Products 2 and 5 should be eliminated (assuming they really want to eliminate all items that will not gross \$10 million). The company should be sure that it is not considering fixed costs in the decision and that the abandonment decision will not adversely affect customer relations.

Derive the formulas for the following indefinite integrals and evaluate part (b) from $x = 2$ to $x = 4$ and part (d) from $x = 1$ to $x = 2$.

(a) $\int (x^{7/3} + 2)\, dx$.

(b) $\int 0.7x^2\, dx$.

(c) $\int (x^{-1} + x^{2/7})\, dx$.

(d) $\int (3x^{-4} + 4x^{-3})\, dx$.

Answers

(a) $\frac{3}{10}x^{10/3} + 2x + c.$

(b) $0.233x^3 + c.$

(c) Cannot be done (yet) since $\int x^{-1}\,dx$ has not been discussed.

(d) $-1x^{-3} - 2x^{-2} + c.$

Evaluating,

(b) $\dfrac{0.7}{3}\,x^3\,\Big|_2^4 = \dfrac{0.7}{3}\,(56) = 13.1$

(d) $(-x^{-3} - 2x^{-2})\,\Big|_1^2 = \left(-\dfrac{1}{8} - \dfrac{1}{2}\right) - (-1 - 2) = 2\dfrac{3}{8}.$

14–2 INTEGRATING SOME SPECIAL FUNCTIONS

In the previous section we discussed the power rule for integration, but x^{-1} was excluded. This section treats this special case. In addition, rules for integrating exponential and logarithmic functions are given. The exponential function has special importance in managerial problems since it represents continuous compounding (that is, day-by-day or minute-by-minute compounding of interest).

There is no simple intuitive way of introducing the rule for integrating x^{-1}. We might call it our biblical rule since we must ask you to accept it on faith.

Rule 4 for Integration: x^{-1}

$$\int \frac{1}{x}\,dx = \int x^{-1}\,dx = \log_e x + c.$$

For examples consider

$$\int_1^e (3x^{-1} + 2)\,dx = (3\log_e x + 2x)\,\Big|_1^e = 3 + 2e - 2 = 1 + 2e$$

and

$$\int 2x^{-1}\,dx = 2\log_e x + c.$$

To check rule 4 we take the derivative of $\log_e x$.

$$\frac{d}{dx}(\log_e x) = \frac{1}{x} = x^{-1}.$$

This may appear to be a circular argument, since we also stated the differentiation rule in Chapter 11 without proof. However, as discussed in Chapter 11, the differentiation rule can be validated using the limit definition of e (another act of faith is required on the reader's part for this result) and the limit definition of the derivative.

You may have wondered what was natural about natural logarithms to the base $e = 2.718 \ldots$. Now we can tell you that the area under the curve x^{-1} will give the values of $\log_e x$; that is, its indefinite integral is $\log_e x + c$. (Still does not sound natural to you?) To make the above constant zero, the definite integral (area) is taken from $x = 1$ up to any value. Thus

$$\int_1^a x^{-1}\,dx = \log_e x \bigg|_1^a = \log_e a - \log_e 1 = \log_e a - 0 = \log_e a,$$

where a is any constant.

If you felt the urge you could make your own table of natural logarithms by numerically integrating x^{-1} from 1 up to the values in question. The shaded area in Figure 14–1 gives the integral of x^{-1} from 1 to 2. That area would equal $\log_e 2$. (If this does not impress you, nothing will.)

FIGURE 14–1

Graph of x^{-1}

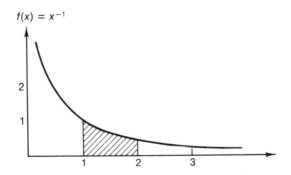

More frequently, of course, we will use someone else's logarithm tables. An example is given by Table II at the back of the book. We find from Table II that the definite integral of $1/x$ from 1 to 2 is $\log_e 2 = 0.69315$.

This follows since $\log_e a = (\log_e 10) \log_{10} a = 2.3026 \log_{10} a$, so we can find $\log_e a$ for any a value using Table II, which gives $\log_{10} a$.

$$\int_2^3 \frac{2}{x} \, dx = 2 \log_e x \Big|_2^3$$
$$= 2 \, (\log_e 3 - \log_e 2)$$
$$= 2 \log_e \left(\frac{3}{2}\right)$$
$$= 2 \log_e (1.5)$$
$$= 2(0.40547)$$
$$= 0.81094, \qquad \text{using Table II to find } \log_e 1.5.$$

The definition of logarithms by an area (integral) can help you to understand some of the rules for operating with logarithms. For example, the integral of x^{-1} from 3 to 4 represents natural logarithm of $\frac{4}{3}$. You can see in Figure 14–2 that it is equal to the area from 1 to 4 ($\log_e 4$) minus the area from 1 to 3 ($\log_e 3$). Thus $\log_e \frac{4}{3} = \log_e 4 - \log_e 3$. Similarly, $\log_e 4 = \log_e 3 + \log_e 4 - \log_e 3 = \log_e 3 + \log_e \frac{4}{3} = $ area from $x = 1$ to $x = 3$ plus the area from 3 to 4.

FIGURE 14–2

Logarithms of 4/3 and 3 Illustrated on a Graph of x^{-1}

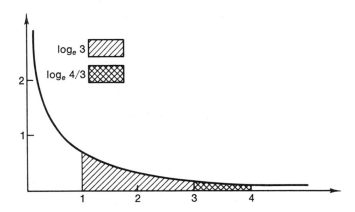

Having studied the function whose integral gives the natural logarithms, we turn to an investigation of the integral of the logarithmic function itself. Again no intuitive example is available, and we pursue the biblical method of introducing the rule.

Rule 5 for Integration: $\log_a bx$

$$\int \log_a bx \, dx = (x \log_a bx - x \log_a e) + c.$$

You'd never guess that one, would you? In a freshman calculus class, one instructor was asked how someone came up with that formula. He said: "Someone chose it because it worked." That answer does not satisfy us either, but we do not know a better one. Let us see if it really does work, by differentiating the answer (using rules 4 and 8 for differentiation).

$$\frac{d}{dx}(x \log_a bx - x \log_a e) + c = x\left(\frac{b}{bx} \log_a e\right) + \log_a bx - \log_a e$$

$$= \log_a e + \log_a bx - \log_a e = \log_a bx,$$

and it works. Now for an example:

$$\int_3^9 \log_3 x \, dx = (x \log_3 x - x \log_3 e) \Big|_3^9$$

$$= [9(2) - 9 \log_3 e] - (3 - 3 \log_3 e)$$

$$= 15 - 6 \log_3 e.$$

A logarithmic function can be used (beginning with $x = 1$, but not $x = 0$) to depict a relationship that is growing and continues to grow but at a decreasing rate. The demand for a relatively new product might be modeled in this manner if demand is considered over a fairly long period of time.

Suppose, for example, that at $t = 1$ a firm has zero sales but that sales growth over time is described by the function

$$\text{sales} = 5{,}000 \log_e t, \quad \text{with } t \text{ measured in years.}$$

Two dollars is made (above cost) on each item. Suppose we ask how long it will take to recover a \$10,000 initial investment. The profit at any time t is $2(5{,}000) \log_e t$.

We must find t such that

$$\int_1^b 2(5{,}000) \log_e t \, dt = 10{,}000.$$

Integrating,

$$10{,}000t \, (\log_e t - \log_e e) \Big|_1^b = 10{,}000$$

or

$$t \left(\log_e t - 1\right)\Big|_1^b = 1,$$

$$b \left(\log_e b - 1\right) - 0 + 1 = 1.$$

Thus we want to find b such that

$$b(\log_e b - 1) = 0$$

or

$$\log_e b = 1 \quad \text{and} \quad b = e = 2.7 \text{ years.}$$

The "payback period," the time it will take to recover the $10,000 investment, if sales grow according to the forecast, is 2.7 years. A payback period is a commonly used criterion for investment decisions (although it has some faults, as you may discover in other courses), and 2.7 years is a reasonably good (in that it is short) payback period.

The inverse of the logarithmic function (written again with x as the independent variable) is $f(x) = a^x$. Once again intuitive examples evade our grasp and we are forced to merely state the rule for integrating this function.

Rule 6 for Integration: a^{bx}

$$\int a^{bx} \, dx = \frac{a^{bx}}{b \log_e a} + c.$$

The result is not intuitive, so we press on with several examples:

$$\int_0^1 e^x \, dx = e^x \Big|_0^1 = e - 1 = 1.7.$$

$$\int (4^x + 1) \, dx = \frac{4^x}{\log_e 4} + x + c.$$

$$\int e^{ax} \, dx = \int (e^a)^x \quad \frac{e^{ax}}{\log_e e^a} + c = \frac{e^{ax}}{a} + c.$$

To validate rule 6, take the derivative (using rule 7 for differentiation).

$$\frac{d}{dx} \left(\frac{a^{bx}}{b \log_e a} + c \right) = \frac{1}{b \log_e a} \left[a^{bx}(\log_e a)b \right] = a^{bx}.$$

The last example is an important special case. It points out the case of dealing with e^x. We now know that

$$\frac{d}{dx}(e^{ax}) = ae^{ax} \quad \text{and} \quad \int e^{ax}\, dx = \frac{1}{a}e^{ax} + c.$$

Exponential functions are applied to many real managerial situations. Continuous compounding has been mentioned and is discussed further in Chapter 15. In addition, a negative exponential function, e^{-x}, can be used to describe the decay function of advertising effectiveness. It also has several scientific uses as well as other administrative applications. The exponential function, on the other hand, is used to describe the spread of epidemics, and some costs (such as college tuition) have been described as "rising exponentially." Sales for a new product can be described by some complex functions that involve exponential terms; they typically have an increasing initial rate of growth, followed by slower growth, and, eventually, no growth in demand. (The reader is referred to the discussion in Section 4-3 on growth functions.) An example, using integration, is given below.

The Department of Agriculture has funds to expend on pest control. They are evaluating the harm caused by several pests, including the gypsy moth. The gypsy moth devours tree leaves, eventually killing the tree. If unchecked, their numbers (and thus the acreage they can destroy) grow exponentially. In particular, suppose they are currently destroying the woodlands at a rate of 1,000 square miles per year, and their rate of increase is e^{2t} per year. If unchecked, how many square miles will they destroy in the next 5 years? This destruction goes on continuously and thus

$$\text{total destruction} = \int_0^5 1,000e^{2t}\, dt$$

$$= \frac{1,000}{2}e^{2t}\Big|_0^5 = 500e^{10} - 500.$$

or over 10 million square miles. The current destruction level of 1,000 is represented by the constant 1,000, and the integration begins at $t = 0$. Since $e^0 = 1$, the rate of destruction at any point in time is e^{2t} times the initial rate. The total amount of destruction in 5 years is, you'll agree, fantastic.

Exponential growth occurs any time the rate of growth of a population is proportional to the number presently in the population. This occurs, as above, when a species reproduces without being checked by any natural enemy. It also occurs when, for example, an amount of interest is proportional to the principal, and we continuously compute interest and add it to the principal. If a new product's major form of advertising is "word of mouth" advertising, then new sales may be proportional to the current amount of sales, and the growth in sales of the product would be exponential. (This can only go on for a short time, however.)

In the gypsy moth example, the Department of Agriculture might be interested in trying to arrest the spread of the moth. The effect of different control techniques can be studied mathematically, and this is important to do since different control methods will have different costs. Suppose (in a somewhat simplified example) that one control plan sprays 20,000 square miles per year but leaves the growth rate unchanged (that is the simplification). When as many acres have been sprayed as are destroyed, the gypsy moth will have been stopped. How many square miles will be destroyed in total, assuming the moth has a 20,000-square-mile head start?

We want to find T such that

$$20,000 + \int_0^T 1,000e^{2t}\, dt = 20,000T,$$

or, integrating:

$$20,000 + \int_0^T 1,000e^{2t}\, dt = 20,000 + 500e^{2t}\Big|_0^T = 20,000 + 500(e^{2T} - 1)$$
$$= 20,000T.$$

Simplifying we obtain

$$e^{2T} = 40T - 39.$$

Solving this equation by trial and error, that is, by trying different values of T, and using Table I, until we find one that works, we obtain

$$T = 1.34.$$

The moth will have devoured

$$20,000 + \int_0^{1.34} 1,000e^{2t}\, dt$$

or about 27,000 square miles before being stopped. The danger of exponential growth is striking. If the control plan called for spraying only 10,000 square miles per year (an apparently safe number in that the current destruction rate is only 1,000 square miles per year), the moth would win. In this case the moth would soon be expanding faster than the spray plan, and the moth would never be brought under control. This is examined further in one of the problems at the end of this chapter.

⌒ : Evaluate the following integrals:

1. $\int_1^2 (x^2 + 2x^{-1})\, dx.$

2. $\int 4^x\, dx.$

3. $\int_0^1 2^{2x}\, dx.$

4. $\int_4^{16} \log_4 x\, dx.$

Answers

1. $\dfrac{x^3}{3} + 2 \log_e x \Big|_1^2 = \dfrac{7}{3} + 2 \ (\log_e 2)$

2. $\displaystyle\int 4^x \, dx = \dfrac{4^x}{\log_e 4} + c$

3. This case has the same indefinite integral as 2 since $2^{2x} = 4^x$. Thus

$$\int_0^1 2^{2x} \, dx = \dfrac{3}{\log_e 4}$$

4. $\displaystyle\int_4^{16} \log_4 x \, dx = (x \log_4 x - x \log_4 e) \Big|_4^{16}$

$$= (32 - 16 \log_4 e) - (4 - 4 \log_4 e)$$

$$= 28 - 12 \log_4 e$$

14–3 INTEGRATION BY TRICKERY

Several functions that cannot be integrated by the methods of Sections 14–1 and 14–2 can be dealt with by methods we call trickery. This section examines three such methods: (1) substitution, (2) parts, and (3) the "Best Method of Integration." There are other methods, but the ones in this section in conjunction with those in Sections 14–1 and 14–2 provide all the integration techniques necessary to master the calculus needed for most managerial problems. Section 14–3 is important, but it is difficult. It should be attempted after you have a thorough grasp of Sections 14–1 and 14–2. (However, if the first two methods in this section are too tough, at least master the "Best Method of Integration.")

Integration by Substitution

Integration by substitution is similar to differentiation using the chain rule. Recall, from Chapter 11, that we can differentiate a function, given by $f(x)$, as follows:

$$y \equiv f(x) = (2x + 3)^4.$$

Let $u = 2x + 3$; then $du/dx = 2$. Also $y = u^4$, and $dy/du = 4u^3$. Hence

$$\dfrac{dy}{dx} = \dfrac{dy}{du}\dfrac{du}{dx} = f'(x) = 4u^3\dfrac{du}{dx} = 4(2x + 3)^3 2 = 8(2x + 3)^3.$$

What we did in the above problem was make an ugly problem prettier by judiciously substituting $u = 2x + 3$. Next we'll pull the same sort of trick in an integration problem.

$$\int_0^1 (2x + 3)^4 \, dx.$$

Let

$$u = 2x + 3$$

$$\frac{du}{dx} = 2, \quad \text{so } \frac{du}{2} = dx.$$

(This is an important step. Treating du and dx as separate entities is legitimate, although we do not discuss "differentials" (du and dx) in this book. However, we will not let that stop us, since the method does work.)

Then

$$\int_0^1 (2x + 3)^4 \, dx = \int_{x=0}^{x=1} u^4 \left(\frac{du}{2}\right) = \frac{1}{2} \int_{x=0}^{x=1} u^4 \, du.$$

Now this function in u is easy to integrate. We get

$$= \frac{1}{10} u^5 \Big|_{x=0}^{x=1}$$

but the limits of integration are still in terms of x. Substituting $u = 2x + 3$ gives

$$\frac{1}{10} (2x + 3)^5 \Big|_0^1 = \frac{3{,}125}{10} - \frac{243}{10}.$$

The only method or set of steps that can be specified for integration by substitution is given below.

Method for Integration by Substitution

Step 1. Make a substitution that makes the problem easy. [Set u equal to the part that is causing you trouble, the ugly part. Remember to substitute for dx as well as $f(x)$.] Cleverness in choosing the substitution is necessary, but unfortunately, it only comes with practice.

Step 2. Perform the integration using the new variable.

Step 3. Reverse the substitution to get the answer.

For another example, consider

$$\int (x^2 + 19)^{1/3} x \, dx.$$

Let $u = x^2 + 19$:

$$\frac{du}{dx} = 2x, \quad \text{so } x \, dx = \frac{du}{2}.$$

Then

$$\int (x^2 + 19)^{1/3} x\, dx = \frac{1}{2} \int u^{1/3}\, du = \left(\frac{1}{2}\right) \frac{u^{4/3}}{4/3} + c$$

$$= \frac{3}{8} u^{4/3} + c = \frac{3}{8} (x^2 + 19)^{4/3} + c.$$

A very important application of this technique involves predicting expected sales and the number of units of "lost sales." A full explanation of this problem is beyond this text, but under certain assumptions about the likelihood of different numbers of customers, both questions involve an integral of the form shown below.

$$a \int xe^{-x^2}\, dx, \qquad \text{where } a \text{ is a constant.}$$

As you may recall (see Figure 4–11 and the related discussion), e^{-x^2} is the basic form of the normal distribution, a commonly used method of describing uncertainty in statistics. It cannot be integrated exactly, only numerically. However, xe^{-x^2} can be integrated, and this is useful to know.

To integrate $a \int xe^{-x^2}\, dx$, let $u = x^2$. (The substitution is not an obvious one, but it will work. In practice, we are often forced to try several alternatives before stumbling on one that works. Sometimes none works.) Then $du = 2x\, dx$, and

$$a \int xe^{-x^2}\, dx = a(\tfrac{1}{2}) \int e^{-u}\, du = a(-\tfrac{1}{2})e^{-u} + c = -\frac{a}{2} e^{-x^2} + c.$$

Suppose that we wanted to evaluate the integral from 0 to ∞. Then

$$a \int_0^\infty xe^{-x^2}\, dx = -\frac{a}{2} e^{-x^2} \Big|_0^\infty = -\frac{a}{2}(0 - 1) = \frac{a}{2} \qquad (e^{-\infty} = 0).$$

Integration by Parts

Integration by parts requires (unfortunately) even more cleverness than integration by substitution. If you have difficulty with it at first, do not worry; cleverness comes with practice (and the Best Method is still available). Integration by parts is based on a formula.

Formula for Integration by Parts

$$\int u\, dv = uv - \int v\, du.$$

A few examples may help you see how this method works. Consider the following integral.

$$\int xe^x \, dx.$$

Suppose we try $u = x$; then $dv = e^x \, dx$. We must find du and v. $du/dx = 1$, so $du = dx$. Integrating, $dv = e^x \, dx$ gives

$$\int dv = \int e^x \, dx \qquad \text{and} \qquad v = e^x.$$

Substituting into the formula,

$$\int xe^x \, dx = \int u \, dv = uv - \int v \, du = xe^x - \int e^x \, dx = xe^x - e^x + c.$$

Once the proper choices for u and dv are made, the formula may significantly simplify a difficult problem. For a second example consider $\int x \log_e x \, dx$.

$$\int x \log_e x \, dx$$

Let $u = \log_e x$, so that $dv = x \, dx$. Now we compute $du = (1/x) \, dx$ and $v = \frac{1}{2}x^2$. Then

$$\int x \log_e x \, dx = \int u \, dv = uv - \int v \, du$$

$$= \frac{1}{2}x^2 \log_e x - \frac{1}{2} \int x^2(1/x) \, dx$$

$$= \frac{1}{2}x^2 \log_e x - \frac{1}{2} \int x \, dx = \frac{1}{2}x^2 \log_e x - \frac{1}{4}x^2 + c.$$

The method or set of steps for integration by parts is given next.

Method for Integration by Parts

Step 1. Very cleverly select u and dv from the function to be integrated.

Step 2. Solve for du and v.

Step 3. Apply the formula for integration by parts, writing $uv - \int v \, du$.

Step 4. Complete the integration.

Integration by parts is difficult compared to the other techniques of integration. The reader should go back over the two examples to see that he understands what was done. Do not expect to be able to do new problems using this method without difficulty. (We do not expect that, as will be clear when you read about the Best Method.) The proper selection of u and dv is seldom obvious.

Integration by parts can be used to determine the present value of an income stream. For example, suppose that a firm now makes $1,000 profit per year and that the amount is increasing at a rate of $100 per year, and the money comes in continuously (or nearly so). Then an owner receives income at any point in time at a rate of $1,000 + 100t$, where t is time measured in years. If an investor is considering buying this firm, he would be interested in the present value of this income stream. This type of problem is discussed further in Chapter 15. For now, we will say that this problem involves an integral of the form $\int xe^x\, dx$, a problem we solved above using integration by parts. The problem of finding the wealth of someone who is continuously adding to his bank account after some time is also of this form. Chapter 15 investigates both of these problems extensively.

The Best Method of Integration

Having just suffered through integration by substitution and parts you are undoubtedly ready for this. Our main purpose in this book is to learn mathematics so that it can be used to solve problems—not to learn it for its own sake. To use mathematics intelligently requires an understanding of what is going on—even in integration techniques. However, for the most part you will want to obtain an answer, by any feasible method.

The Best Method of Integration

Step 1. Remove a table of integrals from the bookshelf.
Step 2. Look up the integral of the function in question.

There are many tables of integrals. Your library probably has one or two. One such table is found in E. J. Cogan, and R. Z. Norman, *Handbook of Calculus, Difference, and Differential Equations*, Englewood Cliffs, N.J., Prentice-Hall, Inc., 1958, Chap. 10.

For example, on page 191 of the above reference we find

$$\int x\sqrt{(a^2 - x^2)^3}\, dx = -\frac{1}{5}\sqrt{(a^2 - x^2)^5} + c,$$

where a is a constant.

The above integral is not (to our knowledge) of any particular use in management applications. The point is only that there are books where difficult integrals can be found (and "difficult" may have different meanings to different people).

$\sim\!\!\!\swarrow$: Perform the following integrations. Do not complete the arithmetic.

1. $\int_0^1 (3x + 5)^6 \, dx$ (substitution will work)

2. $\int_1^3 \dfrac{2x + 3}{x^2 + 3x + 8} \, dx$ (substitution will work)

3. $\int bxe^{ax} \, dx$ (integration by parts will work)

Answers

1. Let $u = 3x + 5$, then $du = 3dx$.

$$\int_0^1 (3x + 5)^6 \, dx = \int_0^1 \tfrac{1}{3}u^6 \, du$$

$$= \frac{1}{21} u^7 \Big|_{x=0}^{x=1} = \frac{1}{21} (3x + 5)^7 \Big|_0^1$$

$$= \frac{1}{21} (8^7 - 5^7)$$

2. Let $u = x^2 + 3x + 8$; then

$$du = 2x + 3.$$

$$\int_1^3 \frac{2x + 3}{x^2 + 3x + 8} = \int_1^3 \frac{1}{u} \, du$$

$$= \log_e u = \log_e(x^2 + 3x + 8) \Big|_1^3$$

$$= \log_e 26 - \log_e 12$$

3. Let $u = x$ and $dv = e^{ax} \, dx$; then $du = dx$ and $v = (1/a)e^{ax}$.

$$\int bxe^{ax} = b \int u \, dv = b[uv - \int v \, du]$$

$$= \frac{b}{a} xe^{ax} - \frac{b}{a} \int e^{ax} \, dx$$

$$= \frac{b}{a} (xe^{ax} - \frac{1}{a} e^{ax})$$

$$= \frac{b}{a} e^{ax} \left(x - \frac{1}{a} \right)$$

(This formula will be helpful in Chapter 15.)

14–4 SUMMARY

Integration is the continuous form of summation. In this chapter we see that integration is useful to find the expected number of units out of stock, the total sales of a new product, or the present value of an income stream. In Chapter 15 these examples are expanded and several other applications are discussed.

The rules of integration for polynomials are simple. Methods of integration for special functions and integration by trickery get increasingly difficult until the Best Method is introduced. Knowing how to integrate complex functions is not important for managerial applications. Understanding integration, the type of problem it applies to, and knowing how to use it are important. Understanding is best gained by actually setting up problems and integrating them to obtain the answers. The problems give you an opportunity to do that. In Chapter 15 we will discuss several more applications at length, and again you will get a chance to practice on some problems.

RULES FOR INTEGRATION

Rule 1: $\displaystyle\int x^n dx = \frac{x^{n+1}}{n+1} + c.$

Rule 2: $\displaystyle\int af(x)\,dx = a\int f(x)\,dx,$ where a is a constant.

Rule 3: $\displaystyle\int [f(x) \pm g(x)]\,dx = \int f(x)\,dx \pm \int g(x)\,dx.$

Rule 4: $\displaystyle\int \frac{1}{x}\,dx = \int x^{-1}\,dx = \log_e x + c.$

Rule 5: $\displaystyle\int \log_{ba} x\,dx = x\log_a bx - x\log_a e + c.$

Rule 6: $\displaystyle\int a^x\,dx = \frac{a^{bx}}{b\log_e a} + c.$

In addition to these rules, we have the three methods of integration by trickery given in Section 14–3. The reader is referred to that section for statements of the methods. The only formula is one for integration by parts:

$$\int u\,dv = uv - \int v\,du.$$

PROBLEMS

Problems for Self-Study: 1, 7, 12, 19, 20

14-1.   Perform the following integrations.

a. $\displaystyle\int_0^2 (x^{3/2} + x)\,dx$

b. $\displaystyle\int_0^1 (x^4 + \tfrac{3}{2}x^3)\,dx$

c. $\displaystyle\int (2x^{-3} - 4x^3)\,dx$

14-2.* Perform the following integrations.

a. $\int_2^3 (\tfrac{1}{2}x^3 + x)\,dx$

b. $\int_{-1}^1 (x^2 - 4)\,dx$

c. $\int x^{19}\,dx$

14-3. A sales manager believes that sales of one of the firm's products is growing linearly with time, at a rate of 150 units per year. They currently are selling at a rate of 1000 units per year.

a. How many units will they sell in the next 5 years?

b. If, instead of $1000 + 150t$, they believed they could cause an increasing rate of growth by advertising so that the demand-time equation becomes

$$1000 + 150t + at^2, \qquad \text{where } a \text{ is a constant,}$$

what value does a have to take on to meet an 8000 units sales goal for the next 5 years?

14-4.* A local government's rate of expenditure is a quadratic function of time:

$$E(t) = 1,000,000 + 100,000t + 10,000t^2.$$

Their revenues, largely from property taxes, are a linear function of time:

$$R(t) = 1,200,000 + 50,000t.$$

Time, t, is measured in years.

a. When will the rate of expenditure equal the rate of revenue acquisition?

b. Assuming they save excess revenues when they are able, how long will it be before total expenditures exceed total revenues? Assume that they have no excess revenue currently.

14-5. Find $f(x)$, as best you can, in each of the following cases.

a. $f'(x) = 3x + 12x^2$

b. $f''(x) = 7 + 4x^3$

c. $f''(x) = 1 + x + x^4$

If $f(x) = 0$ when $x = 0$ in all three cases and $f'(x) = 0$ when $x = 0$
in all three cases, what values do the unspecified constants have?

14–6.   Integrate the following. Verify the integration by differentiation.

a. $\displaystyle\int_1^e (x^{-2} + x^{-1} + x^0)\,dx$

b. $\displaystyle\int \left(\frac{4}{x} + \frac{6}{x} + x^2\right) dx$

14–7.   Integrate the following. Verify the integration by differentiation.

a. $\displaystyle\int_4^{16} (\log_4 x + x^{-3/2})\,dx$

b. $\displaystyle\int (e^{2x} + 1 - x^{-2} - x^{-1})\,dx$

14–8.   Graphically show (with a shaded area) the following values.

a. $\log_e e$

b. $\log_e(\tfrac{5}{3})$

c. $\log_e 4$

14–9.   Perform the following integrations. If a difficulty arises, indicate
what it is.

a. $\displaystyle\int_{10}^{100} (\log_{10} x + x^{-1})\,dx$

b. $\displaystyle\int_2^8 \log_2 x\,dx$

c. $\displaystyle\int_0^1 \log_e x\,dx$

14–10. In Section 14–2 we studied a firm whose sales grew with time according to

$$\text{total sales up to year } a = S(a) = \int_1^a 5000 \log_e(t).$$

If, instead of obtaining \$2 per item, the firm received only \$1 per
item, how long would it take to recover a \$10,000 initial investment?
The final answer will require trial and error; when you get to that
stage, quit. Do not compute a final answer.

14–11.* A firm producing several products has one product whose sales per period are declining according to

$$S(t) = 4 - 2t, \qquad 0 \le t \le 2,$$

where S is in thousands. The contribution per unit (selling price less variable cost) is $5, and the firm has fixed costs related to this product of $10,000 per year.

a. If they want to maximize profit they will stop producing the item at a point in time when it no longer yields a contribution sufficient to cover the fixed costs. When is that?

b. For company identification reasons they want to continue to market the product until total contribution (from this point in time on) equals total fixed cost. When is that?

14–12. A university knows that its cost per student is rising as follows:

$$C(t) = 5 + 0.1t + 0.01t^2, \qquad \text{where } C \text{ is in thousands of dollars.}$$

At the same time, the fraction of the cost that must be paid by a middle-income student is rising as follows:

$$f(t) = 0.4 + 0.05t.$$

How much will be paid by a middle-income student who will study for the next 8 years? (Assume that the functions are continuous so that integration can be used.) The student must pay $f(t) \cdot C(t)$.

14–13. Perform the following integrations.

a. $\displaystyle\int_{2}^{1} \frac{1}{2} e^{4x}\, dx$

b. $\displaystyle\int_{a}^{b} 2^x\, dx$

c. $\displaystyle\int (e^{(x+2)} + x^2)\, dx$

14–14.* In the gypsy moth example of Section 14–2, we found that it will take 1.34 years to catch up with the moth if spraying is done at a rate of 20,000 square miles per year.

a. Graphically depict the intersection of sprayed area and destroyed area that we solved for.

b. Perform the analysis up to the final trial-and-error solution assuming 10,000 square miles of spraying per year. Convince yourself that the moth will win, and display this situation graphically.

14–15.   In the gypsy moth example of Section 14–2 and in Problem 14–14
we investigated various rates of spraying and their effect on the spread
of the gypsy moth. The minimum rate of control (spray) that will stop
an epidemic (moth) that has a head start is one that has a control line
tangent to the spread of the epidemic. That is,

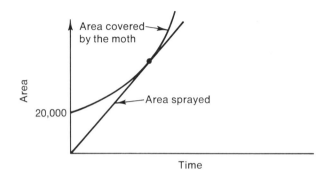

a. Using the gypsy moth example, describe this solution using
calculus. Use a for the rate of spray, and remember that the moth
has covered $20{,}000 + \displaystyle\int_0^T 1000e^{2t}\, dt$ at time T.

b. How would you solve for a?

14–16.* Suppose that a pest was spreading, not exponentially, but according
to a rate of destruction $= 6t$, and the pest has a head start of 12. In
Problem 14–15, the minimum rate of control was discussed. Using
the definition of minimum control given there, find the minimum
rate of control in this case. (When control is achieved, the rate of
destruction equals the rate of spray and the total destruction equals
the total area sprayed.)

14–17.   A government agency is sponsoring an inoculation program in a
rural area. The total population is P persons. The rate of attracting
new persons for the program is a constant fraction of those that have
not been reached. This is due to a media advertising campaign which,
they feel, convinces a given fraction of the potential users of the
value of the program each time the advertising campaign is run. Let
$N \equiv$ number of persons contacted (in total), and $P \equiv$ number of
persons in the population.

a. $\dfrac{dN}{dt} = K\,(\underline{\hspace{3cm}})$; fill in the blank.

b. Show how you would find the form for $N(t)$. You need not obtain a final answer.

14–18.* Suppose (see Problem 14–17) that $N(t) = P - e^{-Kt-c}$ describes the number of persons reached by an inoculation program when new users arrive at a rate equal to a constant times the number of persons not yet innoculated. ($P = 100,000 =$ number in the population, N is the number inoculated, K and c are constants.)

a. If no one has been reached at time zero, what value does the constant c assume?

b. If $K = 0.5$, when has the program reached 80 percent of the potential users of the program? Assume that time is measured in months. (This problem is easier to set up than to complete.)

14–19. Perform the following integrations.

a. $\int 3xe^{(x^2 + 4)} dx$

b. $\int_0^1 (1 + x)^{7/2} dx$

c. $\int (a + bx)^d dx$, where a, b, and d are constants, and $d \neq -1$.

14–20. Perform the following integrations by parts.

a. $\int x(x + 2)^2 dx$

b. $\int x^2 e^x dx$

14–21.* Perform the following integrations. Verify the solution by differentiation.

a. $\int [(3 + \pi)x^4 - 17x^{-2}] dx$

b. $\int ex^{2/3} dx$

c. $\int 0.241x^{0.352} dx$

14–22.* In Problem 14–3 suppose that our sales manager thinks sales are $1000 + 150t + at^2$ but that a is negative?

a. What value does a have to take on if the firm is to have zero cumulative sales after 5 years?

 b. What is wrong with the answer to part *a*? What is the maximum
    amount of time sales can be governed by the sales pattern given?

14–23. Find the values of the constants that are unspecified.

 a. $\displaystyle\int_0^a (x + 1)\, dx = 4$; find *a*.

 b. $\displaystyle\int_1^2 b(x + 5)\, dx = 10$; find *b*.

 c. $\displaystyle\int_a^b x\, dx = 4$; find *a* and *b*.

14–24.* Find the values for the unspecified constants in the integrals.

 a. $\displaystyle\int_1^2 e^{(x + a)}\, dx = e^3(e - 1)$; find *a*.

 b. $\displaystyle\int_0^1 e^{bx}\, dx = e - 1$; find *b*.

 c. $\displaystyle\int_1^e \log_a x\, dx = 1/2$; find *a*.

14–25.* Perform the following integrations. (Part *a* requires integration by
       substitution, and part *b* requires integration by parts.)

 a. $\displaystyle\int x^2 \log_e x^3\, dx$

 b. $\displaystyle\int x^2 \log_e x^2\, dx$

15

Applications of Integration

The major application of differentiation is in finding the maximum or minimum of a function (and max–min theory is applicable to many managerial problems). There is no analogous major application of integration. Integration is used to perform its general function, sum up continuously, in several different areas of application. This chapter examines a few applications (in addition to those mentioned in Chapter 14) of integration, trying to discuss the more important ones, but in no sense is it an exhaustive discussion.

The three general areas that are examined here are continuous compounding and discounting, models of new product sales, and measuring advertising effectiveness. Continuous compounding and discounting is very important in that daily compounding (for example) is most easily dealt with as continuous compounding. Continuous compounding yields results that are indistinguishable from daily compounding for all practical purposes. Continuous compounding and discounting were introduced in Section 4–1, and it is discussed more fully in Section 15–1. Predicting the sales of a new product is important, and the prediction process may use integration since the rate of change of sales may be available early in a product's life cycle, before a guess as to next year's sales can be made. The integral of a rate gives a total sales figure, so integration may help us, as is shown in Section 15–2.

Section 15–3 discusses applications of integration to measuring advertising effectiveness. Frequently the rate of change of sales with respect to a change in advertising is known, and we can use integration to obtain sales as a function of advertising. A simple example of this application is given in Section 15–3.

One general characteristic of integration problems is worth noting. If integration is to be useful, we must be given a rate, and need to know the total (sum). For example, if we are given a rate of speed of 40 miles per hour, we

373

can find the total mileage covered in (say) 5 hours, and we can find it using integration (or in easier ways). If we know the rate at which someone adds to their bank account, with interest compounded continuously, integration gives the total dollars in the bank account after a certain time. If we know the rate of change, the original function (total) is found by integration (a summing-up process).

15–1 CONTINUOUS COMPOUNDING AND DISCOUNTING

As we learned in Section 4–1, e^{rt} and e^{-rt} are used in continuous compounding and discounting, respectively. That is, if a person puts $1 in a bank account with daily compounding at a rate of 5 percent per year, $e^{0.05t}$ represents the amount of money he has after t years. (Daily compounding is essentially continuous, and $e^{0.05t}$ is easier to work with than the formulas for daily compounding.)

In Section 14–3 a problem of a firm with growing profits is introduced. In particular, the firm is currently making profits at a rate of $1,000 per year, but this rate will increase at the rate of $100 per year. Thus the firm at any point in time is earning at a rate of $1,000 + 100t$. The firm will be worthless after 10 years, since its patent will run out and larger companies will be able to produce their product more cheaply. How much will the firm make in 10 years?

$$\text{total profit} = \int_0^{10} (1{,}000 + 100t)\, dt = 1{,}000t + 50t^2 \Big|_0^{10} = \$15{,}000.$$

Integration performed the summing process (continuously) to find the firm's total profits.

Suppose a potential buyer for the firm has a personal discount rate of 10 percent. (He could earn 6 percent in the bank, and he feels he should earn more, 4 percent more, because of the risk associated with owning a firm.) The present owners are asking $12,000. They say that, since the firm will make $15,000 over the 10-year period, this is a good deal. Is it?

Each dollar must now be discounted, at a continuous discounting rate It is incorrect to simply discount $15,000 for an average of 5 years. Thus we obtain

$$\text{total discounted value} = \int_0^{10} (1{,}000 + 100t)e^{-0.1t}\, dt,$$

where the 0.1 in the exponent is the buyer's discount rate. So

$$\text{total discounted value} = \int_0^{10} 1{,}000e^{-0.1t}\, dt + \int_0^{10} 100te^{-0.1t}\, dt$$

$$= -10{,}000e^{-0.1t} \Big|_0^{10} + \int_0^{10} 100te^{-0.1t}\, dt.$$

The first integral is easy to find, and it represents the present value obtained in 10 years, when money comes in at a rate of $1,000 per year. This can be used to compute the value of rental properties by itself. In this problem it is only part of the answer. The second part requires integration by parts. Let's examine it separately.

We want to find

$$100 \int_0^{10} te^{-0.1t} \, dt.$$

This problem was solved in general form in the exercises after Section 14–3. We will repeat it here to refresh our memories.

Let $u = t$ and $dv = e^{-0.1t} \, dt$. Then $du/dt = 1$, so $du = dt$ and $\int dv = \int e^{-0.1t} \, dt$, so $v = -10e^{-0.1t}$. Then

$$100 \int_0^{10} te^{-0.1t} \, dt = 100 \int_0^{10} u \, dv.$$

Applying the formula for integration by parts we obtain

$$100uv \Big|_0^{10} + 100 \int_{t=0}^{10} v \, du = -1,000te^{-0.1t} \Big|_0^{10} + 1,000 \int_0^{10} e^{-0.1t} \, dt$$

$$= [-1,000te^{-0.1t} - 10,000e^{-0.1t} \, dt] \Big|_0^{10}.$$

The reader should check the above steps to be sure he understands them. Next, we return to the original problem, having now integrated both parts. The integral is put together below, then evaluated from zero to 10 using Table I, at the back of the book, for powers of e.

$$\int_0^{10} (1,000 + 100t)e^{-0.1t} \, dt = -10,000e^{-0.1t} \Big|_0^{10} - 1,000te^{-0.1t} \Big|_0^{10}$$

$$- 10,000e^{-0.1t} \Big|_0^{10}$$

$$= 20,000 - 30,000e^{-1} \approx \$8,900.$$

The potential buyer should not buy! Even if the asking price is lowered to $10,000.

If you have trouble following the example, it may please you to know that the Best Method can be used here. On page 200 of the integral table previously referenced we find

$$\int xe^{ax} = \frac{e^{ax}}{a^2} (ax - 1).$$

Substitute $a = -0.1$ to see that it works on the second part of the integral.

In addition to the Best Method, the hard part of the problem was solved at the end of the previous section as an exercise. The reader should be certain he knows how to write the discounted profit equation, and how to apply the integration formula. If you feel that you could not duplicate the integration technique without help do not worry. If you feel you could not get the answer as to whether or not to buy the firm, do worry.

The above problem really contained a subproblem: What is the present value of an income stream that comes in at a constant rate? That was the first integral. The entire problem is: What is the present value of an income stream that is growing at a constant rate?

The subproblem is faced by a landlord who receives rent at a constant rate (even monthly discounting gives practically the same answer as continuous discounting), by an individual who saves a given amount out of each paycheck or even by an individual wanting to know the present value of a constant salary for some number of years. Any individual or firm that receives rent, royalties, or income at a constant rate should be interested in the present value of that stream of income. Let's solve this problem in general.

The present value of an income stream arriving at a constant rate is given by

$$\text{present value} = \int_0^T Ae^{-rt}\, dt,$$

where

$T \equiv$ length of time under investigation, 10 years in the above example,

$A \equiv$ constant rate at which the firm or individual receives income,

$r \equiv$ discount rate of the individual or firm, 10 percent in the above example.

$$\int_0^T Ae^{-rt}\, dt = -\left(\frac{A}{r}\right)e^{-rt}\Big|_0^T = -\left(\frac{A}{r}\right)(e^{-rT} - 1)$$

$$= \left(\frac{A}{r}\right)(1 - e^{-rT}).$$

For example, if a pipeline company receives royalties at a rate of \$10,000,000 per year for 5 years, and if the firm has a discount rate of 0.10, then the present value is

$$\frac{10,000,000}{0.1}(1 - e^{-0.5}) \approx \$39,000,000.$$

If they were to receive the same royalties for 10 years, the present value would be

$$(100,000,000)(1 - e^{-1}) \approx \$63,000,000.$$

Looking forward from right now, the income for the second 5 years is not worth as much to them as the income for the first 5 years (only $24,000,000). If the royalties were to go on forever, that is, $T = \infty$, the discounted present value only increases by $37,000,000 over the figure for 10 years, even though an infinite amount of royalties is received during that period. (The numbers in the answer depend on the discount rate; ask your financial expert to determine an appropriate rate.)

The second problem mentioned above has a growing stream of income; that problem is solved for the example. We can also solve it in general, as follows: At any point in time, the rate of income is $A + Bt$. Other variables are as given for the constant rate case. The present value of a linearly increasing income stream is given by

$$\text{present value} = \int_0^T (A + Bt)(e^{-rt})\, dt$$
$$= \left(\frac{A}{r}\right)(1 - e^{-rT}) + B \int_0^T te^{-rt}\, dt.$$

Now using the Best Method of Integration we obtain

$$\left(\frac{A}{r}\right)(1 - e^{-rT}) + \left[\frac{Be^{-rt}}{r^2}(-rt - 1)\right]\Big|_0^T$$
$$= \left(\frac{A}{r}\right)(1 - e^{-rT}) - \frac{B}{r^2}[e^{-rT}(rT + 1) - 1].$$

The formula was derived using the Best Method, with the integral formula shown earlier in this section. (It can be derived using integration by parts.) The formula can be verified by substituting $A = 1{,}000$, $B = 100$, $r = 0.1$, and $T = 10$. The value using the previous formula is

$$\text{present value} = \frac{1{,}000}{0.1}(1 - e^{-1}) - \frac{100}{(0.1)^2}[e^{-1}(2) - 1]$$
$$= 10{,}000 - 10{,}000e^{-1} - 20{,}000e^{-1} + 10{,}000$$
$$= 20{,}000 - 30{,}000e^{-1}.$$

This is the same answer as found above. In case you are wondering why it always works for us but not for you, the first time we solved for this formula a sign was wrong. Trying the numbers allowed us to find the error.

The two formulas given so far in this section deal with continuous discounting. Continuous compounding is also of interest. For example, a company may put receipts into a bank account at a constant rate, and remove the receipts every 6 months (say) to invest in other activities of the firm. An individual may have a salary, a fraction of which he banks at a constant rate.

He may want to know how long it will take to save enough for a down payment on a house. If, in both cases, the bank uses daily (continuous) compounding, the problem is one that can be solved using integration.

For example, a motel makes $1,000 per month above costs (living expenses for the owners are included in the costs). The receipts are placed in a continuously compounded bank account at $\frac{1}{2}$ percent per month. A prospective owner will buy the motel if he can build up $25,000 in the bank account in 2 years. Will he be able to buy the motel?

Each dollar received earns interest from the time the money is deposited until $t = 2$ years $= 24$ months. That is, each dollar is worth $e^{r(24-t)} = e^{0.005(24-t)}$ at the end of 24 months, if it is earned at time t. This statement is important; be sure you understand it. It is true since e^{rt} accomplishes continuous compounding for t periods, and since each dollar earns interest for $24 - t$ months. After 24 months, the bank account will contain

$$\int_0^{24} 1{,}000 e^{0.005(24-t)}\, dt = \int_0^{24} 1{,}000 e^{0.12} e^{-0.005t}\, dt = \frac{1{,}000 e^{0.12}}{-0.005} e^{-0.005t} \Big|_0^{24}$$

$$= (200{,}000 e^{0.12})(-e^{-0.12} + 1)$$

$$= 200{,}000(-1 + e^{0.12}) \approx \$25{,}500.$$

He should purchase the motel. He will reach his goal.

Since interest rates change (among other things), it would be useful to solve this problem in general. Namely, if a firm or individual adds at a constant rate to a bank account with continuous compounding, how much money will be in the account after some period of time? This is the future (compounded) value of an income stream arriving at a constant rate. Let:

$T \equiv$ length of time under investigation (sometimes called the time horizon),

$r \equiv$ rate of interest that the bank pays,

$A \equiv$ rate at which the firm or individual adds to the account (T, r, and A must be in the same unit of time).

Then

value of the bank account after T years

$$= \int_0^T A e^{r(T-t)}\, dt = \frac{A e^{r(T-t)}}{-r} \Big|_0^T$$

$$= \frac{A e^{rT}}{-r}(e^{-rT} - 1) = \frac{A}{r}(e^{rT} - 1) = e^{rT}\left[\frac{A}{r}(1 - e^{-rT})\right].$$

The last form shows that the future value is e^{rT} times the present value.

The formula can be validated by checking the numbers from the above example. One comment worth making is that as T goes to infinity, the value of the account also goes to infinity. That was not true for discounting; the reader should try to see if he can explain the reason for this difference.

A major application of formulas of this type is in retirement plans. If an individual and/or his firm pay at a rate of A dollars per year for 40 years, how large a retirement benefit will be accumulated? Given a particular life expectancy, how much per year can he receive while using only his own retirement fund (remember that the money remaining continues to earn interest)? If his salary grows at a rate of B dollars per year, how large a benefit will he have? This last problem is exactly analogous to the discounting of a growing income stream. The derivation of the formula is left as one of the problems at the end of the chapter.

1. (a) If an individual has a personal discount rate of 10 percent per year, how much is an annual salary of $20,000 for 20 years worth to him (what is its present value)? Value = _____.
   (b) If another person has a discount rate of 5 percent per year, how much is it worth to him? Explain the difference in the two answers.
      Value = _____.
2. If the individual making $20,000 per year saves $2,000 of it toward retirement, how much interest does he earn in 40 years if his bank account pays 5 percent per year? Interest = _____.

Answers

1. (a) Value $= \int_0^{20} 20{,}000e^{-0.1t}\, dt$

   $$= -200{,}000e^{-0.1t}\Big|_0^{20} = 200{,}000\,(-e^{-2} + 1) \approx \$172{,}000$$

   (b) Value $= 400{,}000\,(-e^{-1} + 1) \approx \$252{,}000$

   The same salary is worth more to the individual whose discount rate is smaller since he values future money almost as much as current dollars.

2. Value $= \int_0^{40} 2{,}000e^{0.05(40-t)}\, dt\,;$

   Interest $=$ value $-$ (40)(2,000).

   Applying the formula,

   $$\text{value} = \frac{2{,}000}{0.05}\,(e^2 - 1) \approx 250{,}000.$$

   He earns approximately $170,000 interest during the 40 years.

15–2 A NEW PRODUCT APPLICATION

In some situations it is easier to estimate the rate of change of demand for a new product than to estimate the demand pattern itself. This situation can occur when a product is very new (early in its "life cycle"), since we can observe how fast the demand is increasing. Suppose we believe that for all new products of a certain type, sales follow an S-shaped curve with time, as shown in Figure 15–1.

FIGURE 15–1

Demand vs. Time for a New Product

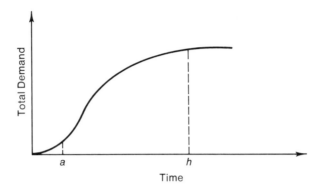

The firm may observe data up to point *a*, then try to guess what the demand up to point *h* will be. For example, suppose that a firm, after market testing and observing the early returns, believes that they are marketing a product that has an S-shaped curve. The curve, $S(t)$, is S-shaped since dS/dt is known to them to be

$$\frac{dS}{dt} = b + ct - dt^2,$$

where t is time and sales are in thousands. Their research group has estimated that

$$b = 0, \qquad c = 10, \qquad d = 1.$$

Thus

$$\frac{dS}{dt} = 10t - t^2.$$

How many units do they expect to sell during the first 10 years if they have sold $4\frac{2}{3}$ (thousand) to date and $t = 1$ currently?

$$S(10) = \int_{1}^{10} (10t - t^2)\, dt + 4\tfrac{2}{3}$$

$$= \left(5t^2 - \frac{t^3}{3} \right)\Bigg|_{1}^{10} + 4\tfrac{2}{3} = 166\tfrac{2}{3} \text{ (thousand)}.$$

They expect to sell $166\frac{2}{3}$ (thousand) units over the first 10 years of the product. In addition, they can use $S(t) = 5t^2 - (t^3/3) + 4\frac{2}{3}$ as a guideline to check their progress. Every so often they can examine total demand to date and revise the estimate of the 10-year total if they are running high or low. As you might expect, a small error in estimating the coefficients at an early stage can cause very large errors in the 10-year prediction.

Another interesting example occurs when a product is advertised largely by "word-of-mouth advertising." When that is true, in the early stages of a product, the rate of change of sales may be proportional to the number of sales made so far. (This pattern cannot be followed once the product starts to saturate the market.) Let's put these statements into symbols.

The rate of change of sales $= dS/dt$ is proportional to the number of sales to date. Thus $dS/dt = aS$. Rearranging we can write

$$\frac{dS}{S} = a\, dt.$$

Now we can integrate both sides.

$$\int \frac{dS}{S} = \int a\, dt,$$

so that

$$\log_e S = at + c;$$

or this can be written as

$$S(t) = e^{at+c} = be^{at} \qquad \text{(where } b = e^c \text{ is a constant).}$$

We first met this function in Section 4–3 in the material on growth curves.

An important idea in applied mathematics is that if a function has a growth (or decay) rate that varies as its current value, the function is an exponential function.

Suppose that we have data on monthly sales for a new product for 4 months. Looking at the data, we see that the monthly change in sales is approximately $0.4S$, where S is the total sales to date. Thus

$$\frac{dS}{dt} = 0.4S \qquad \text{(0.4 is our estimate of } a\text{).}$$

Using the above formula for $S(t)$,

$$S(T) = be^{0.4t}.$$

Suppose that the firm estimates that $b = 6.0$ [this implies that $S(0) = 6$, which may be unrealistic]. They think this pattern will last for 12 months.

How many units will they sell during the first 12 months (that is, the first 4 plus the next 8 months)?

$$S(12) = 6e^{0.4(12)} = 6e^{4.8} \approx 725.$$

They expect to sell about 725 units during the first year. This is true even though the function gives the following predictions for the first few months.

	Total Sales	*Monthly Sales*
$t = 1$	$6e^{0.4} = 9$	$9 - 6 = 3$
$t = 2$	$6e^{0.8} = 13.5$	$13.5 - 9 = 4.5$
$t = 3$	$6e^{1.2} = 20.2$	$20.2 - 13.5 = 6.7$
$t = 6$	$6e^{2.4} = 66$	

Imagine the growth that occurs to get the 12-month total up to 725. It would appear that either the product is really "taking off," or the marketing research department is optimistic about this pattern lasting for 12 months. (If it lasts for 6 months, they expect total sales of only 66 during those first 6 months.)

In the above two examples, you have been introduced to the first ideas of differential equations. (Have no fear, we will not introduce any more such ideas.) The problems were: knowing the rate, find the original function. In the latter example we solved an important differential equation. We provided a "proof," using integration, of the statement made in Section 14–2 that, if the rate of change of a function varies as its current value, the function is exponential.

⌐√   :   In the first example $dS/dt = b + ct - dt^2$ is used, and it is used for the following questions.

   1. Find $S(t)$ using b, c, and d.
   2. Using $b = 10$, $c = 10$, and $d = 1$, plot the curve to see if it is S-shaped. Assume that no sales have occurred by time zero.

Answers

   1. $\dfrac{ds}{dt} = b + ct - dt^2$

   $S(t) = \displaystyle\int (b + ct - dt^2)\, dt$

   $= bt + \dfrac{ct^2}{2} - \dfrac{dt^3}{3} + \text{a constant}$

   (The constant will be equal to the sales that have already occurred by time zero. Assume that it is zero here.)

2.

t	$S(t)$
0	0
1	$14\frac{2}{3}$
2	$37\frac{1}{3}$
3	66
4	$98\frac{2}{3}$
5	$133\frac{1}{3}$
6	168
10	$266\frac{2}{3}$

The rate of change of sales reaches its peak (at an inflection point) at $t = 5$. The curve is S-shaped.

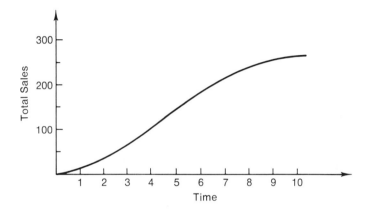

15–3 ADVERTISING EFFECTIVENESS

Another application of integration to what can be called "marketing" problems is in determining the effect of advertising on sales. In many such situations the rate of change of sales with respect to a change in advertising is known. From that we can obtain sales as a function of advertising expenditure, and this function can be used to make advertising (as well as other) decisions.

The dollar effect of advertising on sales usually decreases as more and more is spent. That is, the first dollar of advertising adds more to demand than the one-thousandth dollar. In fact, the effect of additional advertising may even become negative at some point; that is, the dollar expenditure may even cause sales revenues to decline. (How do you react, as a buyer, to the same terrible TV commercial when you see it for the tenth time?)

Several functions can be used to describe the suggested relationship between advertising and sales. Some examples are:

(i) $\dfrac{dS}{dA} = a - bA,$ $\qquad$ (iii) $\dfrac{dS}{dA} = bA\left(\dfrac{a - S}{a}\right).$

(ii) $\dfrac{dS}{dA} = \dfrac{a}{bA},$ $\qquad$ (iv) $be^{-aA},$

where a and b are constants. All of these imply some decreasing returns to scale. In number (iii), advertising has a decreasing effect as the amount of sales, S, approaches a. This assumes that at some point the firm has reached most of the customers and further advertising has less value than earlier advertising expenditures.

In numbers (ii) and (iv), sales never turn negative for $A > 0$. In case (i), sales can be negative for $A > 0$. Numbers (ii) and (iv) can be made to decrease slowly or rapidly by choosing a and b properly.

Suppose, as an example, that a small manufacturing firm wants to expand its market and is considering an increase in advertising as one possible means. Let $S \equiv$ total sales in a given month (in thousands of units) and $A \equiv$ advertising expenditure per month (in thousands of dollars). The current level of advertising is \$1,000 per month and current sales are 10,000 units per month. During the last 2 years, the firm has tried several levels of advertising. The firm's market research group has examined the data (consisting of advertising expenditures, sales, and the change in sales from the previous month) for the different periods and believes that

$$\frac{dS}{dA} = \frac{a}{A^b}$$

best fits their situation. They ran some statistical routines (called regressions) to estimate a and b using several years of data for ΔS, ΔA, and A, and they have estimated $a = 2$ and $b = 1$. Thus the firm believes that the rate of change of sales with respect to a change in advertising varies inversely with advertising expenditure. The reader should satisfy himself that this form is consistent with a decreasing effect of additional advertising dollars, but that each dollar always helps, at least a little. In particular, the firm estimates that

$$\frac{dS}{dA} = \frac{2}{A}.$$

The firm wants to know the answers to three questions.

1. They are considering raising their advertising expenditure to \$2,700. What will their sales be then?

2. The president wants to have total sales of 14,000 per month. How much advertising is needed to reach that goal? The president believes that goal is necessary to the long-run strength of the firm.

3. If they sell the item for $3, and it costs $1 to produce, what is the optimal (short-run) advertising expenditure?

First we must find sales as a function of advertising. We know that

$$\frac{dS}{dA} = \frac{2}{A}.$$

Rearranging we obtain

$$dS = 2\left(\frac{dA}{A}\right) \quad \text{so that} \quad \int dS = \int \frac{2}{A}\, dA.$$

Integrating,

$$S(A) = 2 \log_e A + c.$$

Before this expression can be used, we need to evaluate c. We know, however, that $S(A) = 10$ when $A = 1$. Thus

$$10 = 2(0) + c \quad \text{and} \quad c = 10.$$

(Solving for the arbitrary constant, using current conditions, is an important step in this type of problem.) Finally,

$$S(A) = 2 \log_e A + 10.$$

This relationship can be used by the firm to estimate the effect of advertising on sales. To answer question 1, if the firm increases its advertising expenditure to 2.7 thousand, then sales will increase to 12,000 units. That is,

$$S(2.7) = 2 \log_e(2.7) + 10 = 12.$$

To answer question 2, we need to find A such that

$$14 = 2 \log_e A + 10 \quad \text{or} \quad 2 = \log_e A$$

and

$$A = e^2 = 7.3.$$

The firm must expend 7.3 thousand dollars to reach the president's goal.

Question 3 is more complex, but its solution shows that integration and differentiation can be used together. We integrated to obtain $S(A)$, which was used to answer questions 1 and 2. $S(A)$ is also part of the solution to question 3. We must write a total profit function, given by $f(A)$, using a selling price of \$3, a cost of \$1, and $S(A)$.

$$f(A) = (3 - 1)S(A) - A$$
$$= (2)2 \log_e A - A = 4 \log_e A - A.$$

To maximize $f(A)$ we take the first derivative, set it equal to zero, and solve.

$$f'(A) = 0 = \frac{4}{A} - 1 = 0.$$

Solving for A, we obtain $A = 4$. The optimal level of advertising, to maximize the short-run total profit, is 4 thousand dollars.

1. (a) If $dS/dA = 2e^{-A}$ and if $S(0) = 2$, find $S(A)$.
    (b) What is the largest value sales can ever reach?
2. (a) In the example in this section, how much difference in profit is there between the president's level of advertising of 7.3 thousand and the "optimal" 4 thousand?
    (b) If $dS/dA = 3/A$, how large does A have to be to reach 14,000 sales?

Answers

1. (a) $dS = 2e^{-A} dA$, so $S(A) = -2e^{-A} + c$; when $A = 0$, $S(0) = 2$, so $c = 4$.
    (b) If $A = \infty$, $S(A) = c = 4$.
2. (a) $f(4) = 2(2)(1.4) + 10 - 4 = 11.6$ thousand
    $f(7.3) = 2(2)2 + 10 - 7.3 = 10.7$ thousand
    (b) If $dS/dA = 3/A$, then $\int dS = \int \frac{3}{A} dA$, and $S(A) = 3 \log_e A + c$,
    where $c = 10$ still holds.
    Then, if $S(A) = 14$, $\log_e A = \frac{4}{3}$, so $A = e^{4/3} \approx 3.8$.

15–4 SUMMARY

This chapter examines applications of integration. In each of the applications, we have a rate (or something analogous), and we want to sum over a range of values to obtain a total. The totals dealt with include a present value of an income stream, either with a constant rate or a growing rate, and a total ending amount in a bank account or retirement fund when the account is paid into continuously. Both of these are of interest to firms and individuals.

Applications of integration to new product models are also given. Integration is often used in investigating advertising effectiveness so that we can study the impact of changing advertising levels. Even though there are many other applications of integration to managerial problems, the ones given in this chapter are among the most common and most important. Understanding these applications will stand the reader in good stead.

PROBLEMS

Problems for Self-Study: 3, 6, 7, 8, 23

15–1. A firm has two potential investments, each of which costs $1,000,000 initially, and nothing thereafter. They only have funds to invest in one of them. The data on the two investments are shown below:

Investment A	*Investment B*
Earns money at a rate of $150,000 per year for 10 years, and nothing thereafter	Earns money at a rate of $270,000 per year for 5 years, and nothing thereafter

    a. If the firm has a discount rate of 0.10, which, if either, investment should they choose?

    b. If the firm has a discount rate of zero, which should they choose?

15–2.* *a.* An individual has a rate of salary described by $A + Bt$, where A and B are constants and t is time in years. He currently, $t = 0$, earns at a rate of A per year, and he will work for T years. If he puts a fraction, f, of his money into a bank account earning r per year, continuously compounded, how much will he have after T years?

    b. As an example, use the following values and determine how much he will have after T years.

$$A = 10,000$$
$$B = 1,000$$
$$T = 40$$
$$r = 0.05$$
$$f = 0.10$$

15–3.   A firm has a new product for which it is certain the new product will
         follow a known pattern of sales growth. (They have observed many
         products of this type before.) The pattern, for the first 2 years, is:
         annual rate of sales at a time t, where sales are in thousands and t is
         measured in years, is equal to

$$ARS = a\left(2t - \frac{t^2}{2} + \frac{t^3}{6}\right),$$

where a is a constant that depends on how well the product "catches
on." You also know:

   (1) The constant a can be estimated very early in the 2-year period.

   (2) A product is considered a success only if the total sales volume
         for 2 years is at least 10,000. If they expect less than that, they
         will abort the product.

   (3) There have not been any sales of the product before time zero.

   a. What value of a will make them abort the product?

   b. If a equals 6, what is their expected first year's sales?

15–4.   The Ace Hot Dog Company believes that their sales are growing
         exponentially, while their costs are growing linearly. In particular:

sales (in tons) $= 1,000e^{0.05t}\,dt,$ $0 < t < 10$ (t is in years),
cost (in dollars) $= 500,000 + 50,000t,$ $0 < t < 10.$

They sell hot dogs for $1000 per ton, so profit is equal to sales times
$1000 minus cost.

   a. How much profit will they make in the next 10 years?

   b. What is the present value of the revenue stream if the firm's
        discount rate is 10 percent? That is, what is the present value of the
        $1000 times the sales stream of revenue?

   c. In part *b*, what is the answer if the discount rate is 5 percent?

15–5.*   In Problem 15–4 we see that the Ace Hot Dog Company will receive
         revenues with a discounted present value of $7,880,000 with a dis-
         count rate of 10 percent and $10,000,000 with a discount rate of
         5 percent. The firm's cost function is given by

$$\text{cost} = 500,000 + 50,000t, \qquad 0 < t < 10.$$

   a. Use the formula in the text for the present value of a linearly in-
        creasing income stream to find the present value of the cost stream,
        at a discount rate of 5 percent.

b. Discounted profit = discounted revenue minus discounted cost. Also, the future value of a present sum (such as a present value) can be found by multiplying the sum by e^{rT}, where r is the rate of interest and T is the time horizon. If the firm puts all profits into a bank account at 5 percent, continuously compounded, will they have enough to buy a new plant costing $10,000,000 10 years from now?

15-6. A firm is considering two investments, which generate revenues at the following rates:

Investment A	Investment B
$100,000 + 10,000t, \ 0 < t < 5$	$120,000, \ 0 < t < 5$

Time, t, is measured in years.

a. Which investment generates the most total revenue over the first 3 years?

b. Which investment generates the most total revenue over the first 5 years?

c. Which investment is the preferable investment?

15-7. *a.* If the firm that is considering the two investments described in Problem 15–6 has a discount rate of 0.10, which investment do they prefer over a 5 year period?

b. If investment B (only) returned $120,000 each year for 6 years instead of 5, would the answer to part *a* change?

15-8. The theory of probability is one where integration is applied. Probability is extremely useful in management decision making. The next several problems will investigate some applications of integration to probability, as well as an application of probability to management. A probability density function gives the relative likelihood of different occurrences (such as how many units of demand there will be) when the occurrence is uncertain and may take on any value in some interval. A probability density function is always a continuous function on the range in question. In addition, there are two other requirements. For a probability density function given by $f(x)$, $a < x < b$, these are:

(*1*) $f(x) \geq 0$ for all x (negative probability is impossible)

(*2*) $\int_a^b f(x) \, dx = 1$ (the probabilities "sum" to 1)

Which of the following are probability density functions? Verify your answer.

a. $f(x) = 2x, 0 \leq x \leq 1$ b. $f(x) = 2x, 0 < x < 1$

c. $f(x) = \frac{1}{3}x, -1 \leq x \leq 2$ d. $f(x) = 1, 0 < x < 1$

e. $f(x) = \frac{1}{2}, -1 \leq x \leq 1$ f. $f(x) = e^{-x}, 0 \leq x < \infty$

g. $f(x) = 3e^{-3x}, 0 \leq x < \infty$.   h. $f(x) = x^2, 0 \leq x \leq \frac{1}{2}$

15–9.* Find the value for a that makes each of the following functions a probability density function. Refer to Problem 15–8 for a definition of a probability density function.

a. $f(x) = 4x + 3, 0 \leq x \leq a$

b. $f(x) = a + 1, 1 \leq x \leq 3$

c. $ae^{-2x} dx, 0 \leq x \leq \infty$

15–10.* For a particular service station, the probability density function for the length of time in minutes it takes to service a car is given by

$$f(x) = 2e^{-2x}, \qquad 0 < x < \infty.$$

This is an example of the "exponential probability distribution" which is widely used in describing service times and arrival patterns in waiting-line situations.

a. Is $f(x)$ a legitimate probability density function?

b. What is the probability that service is complete in 1 minute?
[This is found by $\int_0^1 f(x) dx$.]

c. What is the probability that service will take 1 minute or more?
[This is found by $\int_1^\infty f(x) dx$.]

15–11.* A balloon manufacturing company believes that they will sell at least 1 million balloons and at most 2 million balloons this year. They say that the following probability density function describes the relative probability of the numbers in between.

$$f(x) = -\frac{7}{6} + 3x - x^2, \qquad 1 < x < 2 \ (x \text{ is in millions}).$$

a. Is this a probability density function? That is, is the area under the function equal to 1, and is the function ≥ 0 at all points?

b. The company makes a profit if they sell more than 1.4 million balloons. [The probability of this event is found by $\int_{1.4}^{2.0} f(x)\,dx$.] What is the probability that they will make a profit?

c. Sketch the probability density function and shade the area that gives the probability asked for in part b.

15–12. Another concept used in probability is the *expected value* of a random variable. On an intuitive level, the expected value of a random variable x, call it $E(x)$, may be thought of as the weighted average of the outcomes. Formally, the expected value of a continuous random variable with probability density function $f(x)$, $a \leq x \leq b$, is defined as

$$E(x) = \int_a^b x \cdot f(x)\,dx.$$

Find the expected value of the functions in Problem *15–8*, for parts a, b, d, and e.

15–13.* The exponential distribution is referred to several times in the problems for this chapter. The general form of the exponential probability density function is given by

$$f(x) = ae^{-ax}, \qquad 0 < x < \infty,$$

where a is a constant, $a > 0$.

a. Show that ae^{-ax} is a legitimate probability density function. That is, show that

$$\int_0^\infty f(x)\,dx = 1 \qquad \text{and} \qquad f(x) \geq 0 \qquad \text{for all } x \text{ values}.$$

b. Find the expected value of the general form of the exponential probability distribution. This is found by obtaining $\int_0^\infty xf(x)\,dx$. (You may take it on faith that $\infty \cdot e^{-\infty} = 0$.)

15–14. What is the *expected value* of the service time in Problem 15–10? (You may take it on faith that $\infty \cdot e^{-\infty} = 0$.)

15–15.* What is the expected number of balloons sold by the firm discussed in Problem 15–11? The expectation is given by

$$\int_1^2 xf(x)\,dx.$$

*15–16.** A dust-resistant chemical must be applied to a surface of somewhat unusual shape (the lined area in the figure). It may be described by the following functions:

Top border: $f(x) = 70 - \frac{1}{10}x^2$;

Left side: $x \geq 0$;

Bottom border: $f(x) = \frac{1}{5}(x - 10)^2$;

Right side: $x \leq 20$.

Find the area to be covered.

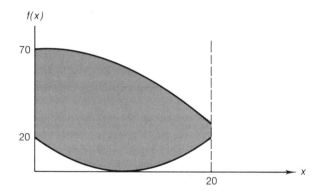

*15–17.** The Bentwood Corporation has a sales pattern that is highly seasonal. The sales level at any point in time over a year ($0 \leq t \leq 12$) may be given by

$$S(t) = 300 + 100\left[-\frac{1}{6}(t - 6)\right]^3 + \frac{100}{3}(t - 6)$$

a. Sketch the curve.

b. What will the total yearly sales be?

*15–18.** Suppose that the rate of change of sales with respect to time is

$$\frac{\partial S}{\partial t} = bS$$

and that the rate of change of sales with respect to advertising is

$$\frac{\partial S}{\partial A} = cS$$

Find the expression for S as a function of A. (*Hint:* The desired expression is exponential in form, $e^{f(t)}$. This problem is relatively more difficult than the other problems.)

15-19. Suppose that the rate of change of sales with respect to time is

$$\frac{dS}{dt} = (b + ct)S$$

What function describes S?

15-20. A firm knows that sales for their new products follows the following form: sales $= e^{a + bt + ct^2/2}$. They want to determine the values of the constants as quickly as possible. They know:

$$t = 0, \qquad S(0) = 1,$$
$$t = 1, \qquad S(1) = 2.7 \qquad (e^1 \approx 2.7),$$
$$t = 2, \qquad S(2) = 7.3 \qquad (e^2 \approx 7.3).$$

a. Find a, b, and c.

b. When will sales reach 20?

15-21.* The president of the LMN Company knows that his product sells at $\$p$, but the costs of production vary with the amount produced. The cost of producing the xth unit is given by $c(x) = b + cx^d$, where $d > 0$, $c > 0$, and $p > b$.

a. Find LMN's profit as a function of the number of units produced and sold, S.

b. Maximize profit with respect to S.

15-22. Suppose that the rate of change of sales with respect to advertising is given by

$$\frac{dS}{dA} = a - bA$$

where S is measured in units, $b > 0$, and A is measured in dollars.

a. At what point are sales maximized? How do you know?

b. At what point does an increase in advertising lead to a decrease in sales?

c. If the profit margin on each sale is $\$c$, at what advertising level is profit maximized?

15–23. A marketing manager knows that his rate of change of sales with respect to advertising is a decreasing function, as follows:

$$\frac{dS}{dA} = \frac{4}{A}, \qquad A > 0,$$

where $A \equiv$ advertising in thousands of dollars and $S \equiv$ sales in hundreds.

  a. Find $S(A)$, sales as a function of advertising, if the manager knows that he can sell 5 (hundred) when $A = 1$.

  b. If each unit sells for p dollars above variable cost, find the function for profit (sales revenues minus advertising cost).

  c. Find the optimal level of advertising for a price of p dollars above variable cost.

15–24.* Suppose that a person deposits money into a savings account at the rate of $2000 per year for 5 years and $3000 per year for the following 5 years. The bank pays interest at the rate of 5 percent per year. What is the value of the account after 10 years? (Leave the answer in terms of e to a power.)

15–25.* Suppose that an income stream can be given by

$$I = \begin{cases} 100 + 10t & \text{for } 0 \le t \le 5, \\ 150 & \text{for } 5 < t \le 10. \end{cases}$$

What is the present value of this stream using a discount rate of 10 percent? (Leave the answer in terms of powers of e.)

16

Sets

We have relied heavily on intuition in reviewing and, in some cases extending, our knowledge of mathematics. A relatively new branch of mathematics based on one very simple concept, the concept of a set, can be used to tighten our understanding of some of the important fundamental ideas we have studied earlier in this book.

But that is not our only reason for adding this chapter. From the simple concept of a set, many of the ideas of mathematics can be developed. Indeed the essential ideas in some areas, including those in probability and statistics, are substantially easier to comprehend using this "new math." Because of its simplicity and generality, most of mathematics, including even that at the grammar school level is now being taught this way. This chapter introduces the basics of set theory. We will rely heavily on definitions.

16–1 THE CONCEPT OF A SET

The basic notion of a set is intuitive, but it is left undefined. Examples include the 92nd Congress, the set of items you are wearing now, the currently outstanding stock certificates of a particular company, the positive integers less than 5, the countries belonging to the United Nations at a point in time, the assets of a given organization, and so on. Although the concept of a set is not defined, a set must have two important characteristics or properties to be useful to us.

Required properties of a set

1. The set must be "well defined." (We must be able to identify each element.)
2. The members (elements) in the set must be distinct. (We must be able to tell them apart.)

For the present, a set will be denoted by any of three methods:

1. The use of a capital letter.
(Example: Let *S* be the set of positive integers less than 5.)
2. Writing out the elements within braces, { }.
(Example: $S = \{1, 2, 3, 4\}$.)
3. Using a defining property together with a lower case letter to stand for the elements in the set.
(Example: $S = \{x : x$ is a positive integer less than 5$\}$.)

This last method is read, "*S* is the set of all elements *x* such that *x* is a positive integer less than 5." The meaning of the symbols is indicated again as follows:

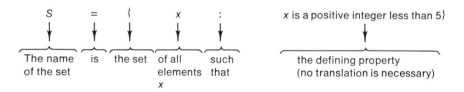

The letter *x* is called a *variable* over the set *S* since it can stand for any of the elements in *S*. Commas are used to separate the several elements in the set when it is written out as in the second method of denoting a set. Note that the order of listing the elements is irrelevant. The sets $\{1, 2, 3, 4\}$ and $\{4, 3, 2, 1\}$ are identical.

The choice of a method to specify a set depends on the ease and precision desired. For example, when specifying the assets of a firm, say for consideration in a purchase contract, it may be adequate and easiest to use method 1. However, if there is the possibility of some disagreement, it would be better to list each separate element in the set as method 2 would do.

We specified above that one property a set must have is that its elements are well defined. This means that if any object is considered, it must be clear to all parties concerned whether the object is an element in the set under consideration or not. This is relevant, for example, to purchasing the assets of a firm. It must be clear whether an item under discussion is or is not an element in the set of the firm's assets. More precisely, we must be able to say unequivocally for any object (element), call it x, either:

1. The element belongs to the set (and we write $x \in S$, which is read "x is an element of the set S")

or

2. The element does not belong to the set (and we write $x \notin S$, which is read "x is not an element of the set S").

Symbol	English Translation
$\in$	is an element of
$\notin$	is not an element of

The set S of positive integers less than 5 is a well-defined set. For any element it is possible to determine which of the above two statements applies. For example, 3 is an element of S, $3 \in S$; while 5 is not an element of S, $5 \notin S$.

It is less clear whether the assets of a particular firm constitute a well-defined set. It may be clear that the main factory building belongs to the set. But what about the company's "loyal and enthusiastic workforce"? If there is some question among the discussants concerning the membership of this element in the set, then the term "asset" must be more precisely specified to avoid this issue or the members of the set should be listed. Once all the elements are listed a well-defined set is obtained.

The importance of the property of being well defined is further illustrated by applying it to the set of qualities needed for success in learning mathematics. There is probably some, but not complete, agreement on the qualities which, if possessed, would lead to success. Different elements would be suggested by different persons, and it would not be possible to say for most elements suggested that one of them does or does not belong to the set. Hence, although abstractly such a set of qualities may exist, the set probably cannot be specified operationally.

The second characteristic of a set, distinctness, means that no two elements in a set can be identical. We cannot include both 4 and 2^2 as separate elements in the set of positive integers less than 5. The Senior Senator from New York and Jacob B. Javits cannot be treated as two separate elements in the set called the Ninety-Second Congress of the United States.

Distinction Between an Element and a Set

It is important not to confuse the concept of an element and the concept of a set. An element belongs to a set. It is not the same thing as the set even if it is the only element in the set. Consider the set S_1 which we define to be the

Chamber of Commerce of Barnesville, Ohio (a small community 10 miles northwest of Stumptown). Suppose that Barnesville's Chamber of Commerce consists of three members: B. Stone, N. Lyons, and J. Haas. Then we can write

$$S_1 = \{\text{B. Stone, N. Lyons, J. Haas}\}.$$

The Barnesville Chamber of Commerce is a different notion than the elements that comprise it. Suppose that in a dispute over policy, the last two members listed resign. The set S_1 now consists of a single member, B. Stone. But the idea "B. Stone" and the idea "Barnesville Chamber of Commerce" are different. It may be true that in speaking about the Barnesville Chamber of Commerce, interest centers on B. Stone, but the notions are by no means identical. Stone is a person and in most respects has no connection with the Chamber of Commerce. The Chamber of Commerce in turn is inanimate and connotes the members, the properties, and the objectives of the organization, among other things. The difference is highlighted by the right of Stone to resign and thereby disassociate himself from the set. The Barnesville Chamber of Commerce still exists as a concept even though it has no members; it is an empty set. To emphasize the difference between an element and a set, we can write

$$\text{B. Stone} \neq \{\text{B. Stone}\}.$$

As another example, consider the set of companies in which Mr. Smith owns stock. If Mr. Smith owns only one stock, say Avon, the set of stocks held by Smith is written {Avon}. This set has only one element and that element, the Avon Company, is certainly a different idea than the set of stocks held by Mr. Smith.

The elements of a set may themselves be sets. Suppose that Mrs. Smith holds two stocks, Xerox and Merck. Then the set of stocks held by Mrs. Smith is written {Xerox, Merck} $= P_1$. We might call this set her portfolio. Mr. Smith's portfolio is {Avon} $= P_2$. The set of portfolios held by the Smiths is written

$$\{P_1, P_2\} = \{\{\text{Xerox, Merck}\}, \{\text{Avon}\}\}.$$

Again, the element Avon is different from the portfolio {Avon}, and the portfolio, also a set, {Avon}, is different from the set of portfolios even if Mrs. Smith sold her holdings and we wrote {{Avon}}. Admittedly, {{Avon}} is a heady concept.

: Answer the following questions concerning the set $\{2, 4, \{6, 8\}\}$.

1. How many elements are in this set? _____

2. Could this be called the set of even positive
integers less than 10? _____

Answers.   There are three elements. They are 2, 4, and the set {6, 8}. The set is not the set of even positive integers less than 10. Such a set contains four elements rather than three. It is written {2, 4, 6, 8}.

Set Equality

Two sets are said to be equal if they have the same elements.

Order is not a required or relevant property of sets written in braces. Thus the set $S = \{1, 2, 3, 4\}$ and the set $\{3, 4, 1, 2\}$ are equal. The sets $L_1 = \{2, -8\}$ and $L_2 = \{1 + 1, (-2)^3\}$ are equal since $1 + 1 = 2$ and $(-2)^3 = -8$. One fact related to the idea of set equality is that it is necessary for two equal sets to have the same number of elements.

$\sim\!\!\!\checkmark$:   If two sets have the same number of elements, are they equal?

Yes _____.
No _____.
Maybe_____.

Answer.   An equal number of elements is necessary, but it is not sufficient to assure set equality. The sets $L_1 = \{2, -8\}$ and $P_1 = \{\text{Xerox, Merck}\}$ have the same number of elements, but they are not equal since the elements are not the same.

Ordered Sets

Sets do not normally involve order. If we want to explicitly include order as a special characteristic of a set, we will always write the set using parentheses. Hence (1, 2, 3, 4) is the *ordered* set of positive integers less than 5. Order sets written using parentheses are equal only if they include the same elements in the same order. In an ordered set, an element may appear twice, since, for example, a number 2 in the first position is not the same as a number 2 appearing in the third position.

Symbol	*English Translation*
( )	The *ordered* set of elements appears within the parentheses separated by commas.

As an example consider five separate measurements on the number of vitamin pills in five separate bottles leaving a filling machine. This ordered set might be $A_1 = (100, 99, 100, 98, 97)$. Although the first and third observations are the same, this does not violate the distinctness characteristic of a set, because the members of this ordered set represent observations on distinct bottles. We could have written $A_1 =$ (number of pills in bottle 1 = 100, number of pills in bottle 2 = 99, number of pills in bottle 3 = 100, . . .). Since the context of the discussion is clear, the extra words are omitted.

Usually order is retained in writing a set if it is relevant to the question for which the observations are obtained. Here order may signify a change in the filling characteristics of the machine. Further observations may indicate the likelihood of a trend and cause the machine operator to stop the process and search for trouble.

$\sqrt{}$: Are the following true or false?

1. $(1, 2) = \{2, 1\}$?	True_____	False_____
2. $(1, 2) = (1, \{2\})$?	True_____	False_____
3. $\{(1, 2), (2, 1)\} = \{(2, 1), (1, 2)\}$?	True_____	False_____
4. $(1) = \{(1)\}$?	True_____	False_____
5. $(1, 2) = (2, 1)$?	True_____	False_____

Answers. The ordered set $(1, 2)$ in case 1 is not the same as an unordered set $\{1, 2\}$. Case 3 is true. In cases 2 and 4, the elements are not the same so the sets are not equal. In case 5, ordered sets are equal only if the order in which the identical elements are written is the same. All parts are false except (3).

16–2 SPECIAL SETS

Two special ideas that find extensive use are discussed here. They are the null or empty set and the concept of a subset. Some other examples of special sets are discussed in the problems.

The Empty Set

The empty (or null) set is a set with no elements in it. In symbolic form: $\{ \quad \} \equiv \varnothing.$

Examples include Mrs. Smith's portfolio, P_1, after she sells all her holdings, and the Barnesville Chamber of Commerce after B. Stone resigns. Zero is not the same idea as the null set nor is zero an element of the null set since the null set has no elements. Thus $\varnothing \neq \{0\}$.

$\sim\!\!\checkmark$: Is there more than one empty set or, alternatively, is there only one empty set (is it unique)? Answer using your intuition.

More than one _____

Unique _____

Answer. Suppose there are two different empty sets. Equal sets have the same elements. If the two sets are to differ, they must have different elements. But there are no elements in the null set, so they cannot be different. Thus the two null sets are the same and we conclude there is only one empty set; it is unique. (This type of argument is known as argument by contradiction.) If you find this argument difficult to understand, try this alternative. If one empty set has no elements, it must be the same as any other set with no elements. Thus there is only one empty set. It is unique.

Subsets

Consider the sets $S = \{1, 2, 3, 4, 5\}$, $S_1 = \{1, 2\}$, and $S_2 = \{5, 6\}$. Every element in S_1 is also in S. When this is true, we say that S_1 is a *subset of* S and write $S_1 \subseteq S$.

Let A and B be sets. If every element in A is also an element of B, then A is a subset of B. In symbolic form, $A \subseteq B$.

The set S_2 is not a subset of S since the element 6 in S_2 is not an element in S. We write $S_2 \nsubseteq S$. The notion of a subset differs from that of an element. Thus $S_1 \subseteq S$ but $S_1 \notin S$. If we define $S_3 = \{\{1, 2\}, 3\}$, then $S_1 \in S_3$; in words, S_1 is an element of S_3.

The null set is a subset of every set.

"And what sneaky trick is this that is being perpetrated on me," you say. "How can a set with no elements in it be a subset?" Well, you may accept this fact on faith or try the following friendly argument. Either $\varnothing \subseteq S$ or $\varnothing \nsubseteq S$. But if $\varnothing \nsubseteq S$, then $\varnothing$ must contain at least one element not in S. But $\varnothing$ contains no elements and hence cannot contain an element not in S. Therefore, we conclude that $\varnothing \subseteq S$. (How did you like that!)

⌢✓   :   Which of the following are true using the sets S, S_1, S_2, and S_3 defined in this subsection?

1. $S \subseteq S_1$.   True_____   False_____

2. $S \subseteq S$.   True_____   False_____

3. $2 \subseteq S$.   True_____   False_____

4. $2 \in S_3$.   True_____   False_____

5. $\emptyset \in S$.   True_____   False_____

Answers. S is not a subset of S_1 since there are elements in S that are not in S_1. Case 2 is true; every element in S is in S. For case 3, 2 is not a set, so it cannot be a subset. For case 4, the elements of S_3 are the set $\{1, 2\}$ and 3. The number 2 is not one of these. The empty set is not an element of S. It is a subset of S. Only case 2 is true.

16–3 SET OPERATIONS

It is often necessary to combine sets in various ways. This section considers some of the more important ways in which sets are combined, including the union, intersection, and difference of sets.

Set Union

The union of two or more sets is the set of all elements belonging to at least one of the sets. In symbolic form:

$$A \cup B \equiv \{x : x \in A \ or \ x \in B\}.$$

In words: "The union of the sets A and B is the set of all elements x such that x is an element of A or x is an element of B."

The set of stocks owned by Mr. and Mrs. Smith is the union of their two portfolios: $P_1 \cup P_2 = \{$Xerox, Merck, Avon$\}$.

⌢✓   :   Let $M = \{1, 2, 3\}$ and $K = \{2, 4, 6\}$. Write $M \cup K$.

Answer. $M \cup K = \{1, 2, 3, 4, 6\}$. The element 2 appears only once.

Set Intersection

The intersection of two or more sets is the set of all elements common to all the sets. In symbolic form:

$$A \cap B \equiv \{x : x \in A \ and \ x \in B\}.$$

In words: "The intersection of the sets A and B is the set of all elements x such that x is an element of A *and* x is also an element of B."

Using the sets $M = \{1, 2, 3\}$ and $K = \{2, 4, 6\}$,

$$M \cap K = \{2\}.$$

∿ : Write $P_1 \cap P_2$ and $M \cap M$. $P_1 = \{$Xerox, Merck$\}$, $P_2 = \{$Avon$\}$, and $M = \{1, 2, 3\}$.

Answer. $P_1 \cap P_2 = \varnothing$. There are no common elements. $M \cap M = M = \{1, 2, 3\}$.

The notions of set union and set intersection are illustrated in Figure 16–1 using what are called *Venn diagrams*.

FIGURE 16–1

Set Union, $A \cup B$ and Intersection, $A \cap B$, Illustrated

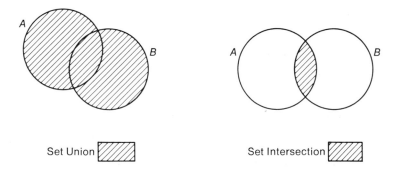

Set Difference

The difference of two sets is the set of elements in one set that are not in the other. In symbolic form:

$$A - B \equiv \{x : x \in A \ but \ x \notin B\}.$$

In words: "The set difference $A - B$ is the set of all elements x that are in A but not in B."

Using the sets M and K defined above, $M - K = \{1, 3\}$ and $K - M = \{4, 6\}$. Note that $M \quad K \neq K - M$.

If a set B is a subset of A, the set difference, $A - B$, is sometimes called the *complement* of the set B in A, and we write B' in A. In words, B' in A is the set of elements not in B but in A. When there is no possibility of confusion we write simply B'. These notions are illustrated in Figure 16–2.

FIGURE 16–2

Set Difference A - B and Set Complement Illustrated

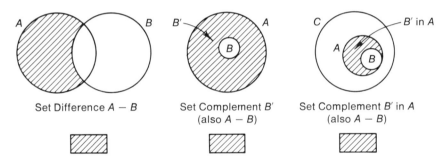

Set Difference $A - B$

Set Complement B'
(also $A - B$)

Set Complement B' in A
(also $A - B$)

Part (c) is similar to part (b) except in this case there are three sets involved, and B is a subset of both A and C. Hence it is important to specify which elements, not in B, are under consideration.

⌒ : Write answers for the following using the set definitions given earlier:

$P_1 = \{\text{Xerox, Merck}\}, P_2 = \{\text{Avon}\}, M = \{1, 2, 3,\}, K = \{2, 4, 6\}.$

1. $P_1 - P_2 =$

2. $M - M =$

3. $\varnothing - K =$

4. $P_1 - \varnothing =$

Answers. $P_1 - P_2 = P_1$ since there are no common elements. Also $P_1 - \varnothing = P_1$ since $\varnothing$ is empty. $M - M = \varnothing$, as is true of $\varnothing - K$.

16-4 FUNCTIONS

Chapter 3 dealt with the fundamental concept of a function. We were at times forced to use terminology that was undefined, such as set and domain. But since these terms have intuitive appeal, it was possible to forge ahead. Using these same terms again, we can now be more precise, if not clearer, about the important concept of a function. However, before defining a function in set terms, it is necessary to develop two additional ideas. These are the ideas of a pair and of the (Cartesian) product of two sets.

Pairs

A pair is a set consisting of two elements.

Why couldn't all definitions be this simple?

Suppose that $T = \{a, b, c\}$. Then a pair of elements taken from T would be $\{a, b\}$. Another pair would be $\{b, c\}$. It is useful at times to distinguish the order of the items selected. When this is required, we indicate the order by writing the *ordered pairs* (a, b) and (b, c). Ordered pairs can also be obtained by selecting the first element from one set and the second element from another set. Thus the ordered pairs $(a, 1)$, $(b, 2)$, and $(c, 4)$ can be obtained by drawing the first element from T and the second from $S = \{1, 2, 3, 4\}$. The concept of an ordered pair is valid even for identical elements. Thus $(1, 1)$ is a valid ordered pair where both elements come from S. This agrees with the discussion of ordered sets in Section 16-1. A pair is a set, and thus an ordered pair is an ordered set.

Consider now the set of all the ordered pairs that can be obtained by taking the first element from T and the second from S. We get the new set

$$T \times S = \{(a, 1), (b, 1), (c, 1), (a, 2), (b, 2), (c, 2), (a, 3), (b, 3), (c, 3), (a, 4),$$
$$(b, 4), (c, 4)\}.$$

This set is read as the set T "cross" S, and it is called the *Cartesian product set* of the sets T and S. It has 12 elements, each of which is an ordered pair.

Suppose we consider the Cartesian product of the set of real numbers, the set R, with itself; that is, what does $R \times R$ give? (This is another one of those rhetorical questions.) The answer is that it gives all the points in the xy plane (the plane on which we plot equations), or 2-space, as it is sometimes called. Another name for the xy plane is the Cartesian coordinate system and this is where the product-set notation gets its name.

〰️ : Is the product set $T \times S$ equal to the product set $S \times T$?

Answer. No, since the elements of $T \times S$ are $(a, 1)$, for example, while those of $S \times T$ are $(1, a)$ and these two elements are not the same. Since the ordered pairs are not the same, the two sets of ordered pairs are not the same.

Functions

A *function* is a particular set of ordered pairs constructed from two other sets. We will usually be interested in functions involving sets of numbers, but the concept is more general, as we shall see. It is best to begin with a definition.

Given two sets, A and B, and a rule that assigns to each and every element x in A a single element y in B, then this rule specifies a set of ordered pairs, f, and this set f is called a function from A into B. In symbolic form:

$f \equiv \{(x, y)$: for each and every $x \in A$, there is a unique $y \in B$ assigned to $x\}$.

For an example, let $A = \{1, 2\}$, $B = \{1, 2, 3, 4\}$, and $y \equiv f(x) = 2x$; $x \in A, y \in B$. Then the function from A into B is $\{(1, 2), (2, 4)\}$.

We now list some important points about functions. These points are then discussed at more length.

1. A function is a set (of ordered pairs). It is usually represented by a lowercase letter.

2. The rule specifies the pairs (elements) in the set. The rule, however, is not the function. This rule is often given as an equation.

3. All of the set A must be used in the matching, but not all of the set B need be used.

4. Each element in A can be used only once in the function. Elements in B can be used more than once.

Functions are defined as sets. A lowercase letter, f, is used in the definition, but either a lowercase or capital letter may be used for a function. The element y in the set B can, as we saw in Chapter 3, be written as $f(x)$; that is, $y \equiv f(x)$. The elements in the function could, then, also be written as $(x, f(x))$. Hence $f(x)$ is the element in the set B, written in general form, that is matched with x. The symbol $f(x)$ is a general symbol for the second element in each ordered pair; it is not the function. The function, which is the entire set of ordered pairs, is denoted by f.

Thus, if we use an equation $y = 2x$ as the pairing rule and allow the sets A and B to both be the real numbers, R, we can write the function f as

$$f = \{(1, 2), (0.8, 1.6), (\pi, 2\pi), \ldots\}$$

or more conveniently and precisely,

$$f = \{(x, y) : x \in R, y \in R, y \equiv f(x) = 2x\}.$$

The last form states that f is a set of ordered pairs of the form (x, y) in which both the x and y in any pair are real numbers and the y value is always twice the value selected for x. The number of such pairs is infinitely large. The latter form is more efficient and immediately specifies the function. We also see that $f(x)$ is the pairing rule and f is the function. However, if there is prior agreement on sets A and B, then the equation gives all the information about the function that is required. When not stated otherwise, it is reasonable to assume that $A = B = R$. Then the equation can stand in place of the function. [Note that every value in set R is assigned to one element in the set $B = R$ by the equation rule $y \equiv f(x) = 2x$. You might think that since $y = 2x$, set A will contain fewer numbers than B. This is not so, and you can convince yourself by trying to find a real number y in B that is not matched to a real number x in A.]

In set terminology, set A is known as the *domain* (or domain of definition) of the function f, and set B is called the *range* of the function. The process of establishing the correspondence between the sets is known as *mapping*, and the function is sometimes called *a mapping* from A into B. An equation is perhaps the most common means of specifying a function's ordered pairs, but it is not the only means. For example, the ordered pairs in the function may be simply written out, or a graph may be used.

It is important to note that every element in set A must be matched to an element in B. Hence, letting A and B be the set R of real numbers, the equation $y \equiv f(x) = 3/x$ cannot be used as the pairing rule since no element in $B = R$ is assigned to the element 0 in A. On the other hand, it is not necessary to use all of set B. Again letting $A = B = R$, the equation $y = x^2$ assigns a single value y to each and every value of x in A. But the negative values of B are not required for the matching. This is all right. Furthermore, all the positive elements in B are used twice. This is also acceptable. The elements in B can be used as often as necessary.

The elements in the set A can, however, be used only once (and each must be used once). Thus the equation $y^2 = x$ does not specify a function from $A = R$ into $B = R$. There are two reasons. First, the negative values in set A are not matched to any real numbers in set B. This is most easily seen from the graph of this function in Figure 16–3. But even if set A were rede-

FIGURE 16-3

Graph of $y^2 = x$

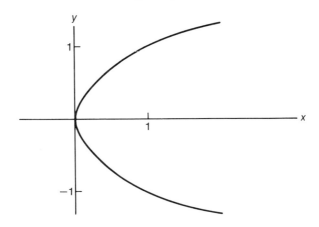

fined to exclude the negative real numbers; that is, $A = \{x : x \in R$ and $x \geq 0\}$, there is still a problem. The second reason, that two elements in A are matched to a single element in B, also prevents the rule $y^2 = x$ from specifying a valid function. The element $+1$ in A, for example, is matched to both $+1$ and -1 in set B. If, however, set B is also redefined to exclude the negative numbers, $B = \{y : y \in R$ and $y \geq 0\}$, then only the top-right quadrant of the graph in Figure 16-3 is involved, and a valid function from restricted set A into restricted set B is specified.

Sometimes graphs like the one pictured in Figure 16-3, where $A = \{x : x \in R$ and $x \geq 0\}$ and $B = R$, are called the graphs of *multivalued functions*.

It is important then to specify the domain and range sets being considered. If this is not done, we presume the set of real numbers; that is, set R is implied for both the domain and range sets.

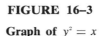 : Which of the following rules do not specify a function from $A = R$ into $B = R$, and why? ($x \in A$ and $y \in B$.)

    1. $y = 6x$ Yes_____   No, and reason_____

    2. $y = x^3$ Yes_____   No, and reason_____

    3. $y^2 - x^2 = 6$ Yes_____   No, and reason_____

    4. $y = (x - 1)/(x + 1)$ Yes_____   No, and reason_____

Answers. Cases 1 and 2 are functions. In case 3 the values of x are matched to more than one value of y. Case 3 does not specify a function.

Neither does case 4 specify a function since $-1 \in A$, but there is no element in $B = R$ matched to $x = -1$ since division by zero is not defined.

16–5 SUMMARY

This chapter is concerned with the notion of a set. A set is characterized as a well-defined collection of distinct elements. By well defined we mean that for any element it is possible to say that the element either belongs to the set or it does not belong to the set. The distinctness characteristic means that no two elements in a set are identical. Two sets are equal if they have the same elements. For ordered sets, written using parentheses rather than braces, equality requires the same ordering as well. An ordered pair is a special case of an ordered set.

The operations of combining sets (set union), finding the set of elements common to several sets (set intersection), and locating the elements in one set but not in another (set difference), are discussed and illustrated. We also discuss subsets. A set is a subset of a second set if all its elements are elements of the second set.

Finally, these ideas are used to develop the idea of a function in a more rigorous form than was done in Chapter 3. A function is defined as a set of ordered pairs. Elements from the domain are matched to elements in the range by a rule which is often an equation. The matching process must involve each and every element in the domain set being matched to a single element in the range set. If the domain and range sets are unambiguous, an equation gives all the information contained in the function; that is, it tells us each of the ordered pairs. The equation gives this information efficiently and hence is typically substituted in mathematical mumbo-jumbo for the more formal functional notation.

As Professor Spivey said in his book, *Linear Programming and the Theory of the Firm:* "The reader may now have the impression that we have proliferated definitions merely for the sport of it, getting further and further away from possible applications in the process, but it turns out that these concepts are of fundamental importance to much of pure and applied mathematics." Perhaps you already accept Professor Spivey's conclusion based on the materials you have studied. If not, time and further exposure to quantitative ideas may convert you. We have found that the basic ideas of set theory underlie many important techniques, including mathematical programming (linear programming is an example), probability theory, statistics, and critical path analysis. Probability theory, for example, is perhaps most easily grasped using the basic ideas of set theory. In short, you may visit these ideas again in your (or your children's) education.

NEW SYMBOLS

Symbol	English Translation
{ }	set
:	such that
∈	is an element of
∉	is not an element of
( )	ordered set
∅	the empty (or null) set
⊆	is a subset of (is contained in)
∪	union (set of all elements in the sets on either side of the symbol)
∩	intersection (set of all elements common to the sets on either side of the symbol)
−	difference (set of elements in set to left of symbol not in set to right of symbol)
B'	the set of elements not in B

PROBLEMS

Problems for Self-Study: 3, 9, 17, 18, 19

16–1.* Are the following true?

    a. $\{2, 4\} = \{\{2\}, \{4\}\}$

    b. $\{2, 4\} \subseteq \{\{2\}, \{4\}\}$

16–2. Suppose that $S_1 \subseteq S_2$ and $S_2 \subseteq S_1$, where S_1 and S_2 are any sets. What can you conclude?

16–3. If $S = \{x, y, z\}$ and $K = \{\{x, y\}, \{x, z\}, \{x, y, z\}\}$, indicate which of the following hold and why a statement is false.

    a. $x \in S$; $x \in K$.   *e.* $\{x, y, z\} = \{y, x, z\}$

    b. $S \in K$; $\{x\} \in S$ *f.* $S = K$

    c. $\{x, y\} \subseteq K$; $\{x, y\} \subseteq S$ *g.* $S \subseteq K$

    d. $\{\{x, y\}\} \subseteq K$ *h.* $\{\{x, y\}\} \in K$

16–4.*   *a.* $A \cup \varnothing =$

         b. $A \cap \varnothing =$

16–5.   Assuming that A, B, and C are not empty, which of the following are generally true? Venn diagrams are helpful.

    a. $A \cap (B \cup C) = (A \cap B) \cup C$

    b. $A \cap (B \cup C) = (A \cap B) \cup (A \cap C)$

    c. $C - (A \cup B) = C - [(B \cap C)]$

16–6.   Under what conditions will the following be true?

    a. $M - K = \emptyset$

    b. $M - K = M$

    c. $M - K = K$

16–7.   Determine if
$$B = (A \cap B) \cup (B - A)$$

16–8.   Given the set $\{1, 2, 3\} = A$.

    a. Form $(A \times A) \times A$.

    b. Does $(A \times A) \times A$ equal $A \times (A \times A)$?

16–9.   A salesman calls on a customer. He either makes a sale, S, or he fails, F. Write the following sets:

    a. The set of outcomes for one customer.

    b. The set of all possible outcomes for customers 1 and 2 in order.

16–10.   If the salesman in Problem 16–9 earns \$1 for every sale and nothing if he fails to make a sale:

    a. Write a set giving his possible earnings for a single customer.

    b. Write a function from the set of outcomes for a single customer to the set of earnings for a single customer.

    c. Repeat parts *a* and *b* for two customers.

16–11.   Consider the set $A = \{1, 2, 3\}$.

    a. Write the set of all subsets of A. Call this set 2^A.

    b. How many elements are there in the set 2^A?

16–12.   Define the set $A \triangle B \equiv (A \cap B') \cup (A' \cap B)$.

    a. Illustrate this set using a Venn diagram where $A \cap B \neq \emptyset$.

    b. Is $A \triangle (B \cap C) = (A \triangle B) \cap (A \triangle C)$ true?

*16–13.** The report of the inspector on a particular assembly line showed the following for 100 units reported defective in at least one or more ways.

Defect	Number of Pieces with This Defect (Piece may also have other defects)
Strength (S)	50
Flexibility (F)	20
Radius (R)	30
S and F	15
S and R	8
F and R	12
S and F and R	6

The report was returned. Why?

16–14. In a survey of consumer buying intentions conducted on 1000 families at the beginning of the year, 200 families interviewed indicated that they would purchase a new stove during the next calendar year. The other 800 said they did not intend to purchase a new stove. At the end of the year a resurvey of the 1000 families showed that of those who indicated they would purchase, 180 did so, while 200 of those who had no initial purchase intentions also bought.

 a. What proportion of families acted in accordance with their expressed intentions at the beginning of the year?

 b. Does the study suggest that if a family says it intends to purchase a stove, they usually do? Explain.

 c. Are buying intentions a good means of estimating total purchases if this study is a good example? Explain.

*16–15.** An advertising agency is provided with the following information concerning the audience for each of three magazines.

Magazine	Audience (Thousands)
M_1 only	1000
M_2 only	800
M_3 only	500
M_1 and M_2 only	160
M_1 and M_3 only	100
M_2 and M_3 only	80
M_1 and M_2 and M_3	16

How many different individuals make up the total audience of all three magazines?

16–16.* Two sets are said to be *mutually exclusive* or *disjoint* if they have no common elements. If M and K are two such sets, then how would one write their intersection?

16–17. Solve.

  a. $A \cap A' =$

  b. $(A')' =$

  c. $A \cap A =$

  d. $A \cup A =$

16–18. Let A and B be defined as the positive integers $\{1, 2, \ldots\}$ if $x \in A$, and $y \in B$ and $y = 2x$.

  a. Is a function specified from A into B?

  b. Is there an inverse function from B into A?

16–19. Define the maximum possible domain in the set of real numbers, R, such that a function is specified from the set $A = \{x\}$ into the set $B = \{y\}$ using the following rules.

  a. $y = 1/x$

  b. $y = x^5$

  c. $y = \dfrac{x - 1}{x + 1}$

16–20.* An oil wildcatter must decide whether to drill for oil at a specific location or sell his rights to that location. He may either sell immediately, or he may take seismographic recordings that yield information about the subsurface structure on the location and make his decision after examining the results. The information from the recordings is, however, not perfect. Sometimes oil is found even though the subsurface structure is unfavorable, and vice versa. Suppose the following facts are known.

  a. Sale price of drilling location (regardless of recording results) before a well is drilled: $100,000

  b. Cost of recordings if taken: $10,000

  c. Cost of drilling: $40,000

  d. Value of a producing well: $500,000

  e. Value of a dry well: $0

Set up a function from the set of possible outcomes of the wild-catters' decision into the set of real numbers so that each outcome is matched to its money value using the following symbols.

Symbol	Meaning
tr	take recordings
nr	take no recordings
fs	favorable structure
nf	structure not favorable
s	sell
d	drill
o	oil
no	no oil

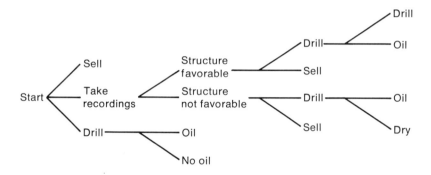

For example, if recordings are taken, the structure is unfavorable and the location is sold, the function element is ((tr, nf, s) $90,000). Write the domain set before proceeding using ordered elements as suggested in the example: e.g. (tr, nf, s).

16–21. The following sets, which describe intervals of real numbers, are in common usage (see Chapter 8) and the following simplified notation is common.

$$\text{a closed set } [a; b] \equiv \{x : x \in R; a \le x \le b; a < b \in R\};$$

$$\text{an open set } (a; b) \equiv \{x : x \in R; a < x < b; a < b \in R\};$$

$$\text{half open sets } [a; b) \equiv \{x : x \in R; a \le x < b; a < b \in R\},$$

$$(a; b] \equiv \{x : x \in R; a < x \le b; a < b \in R\}.$$

Write the following using this simplified notation; if $a < b < c < d$,

a. $(a; b) \cup \{a\} \cup \{b\}$

     b. $[a; b) \cup [b; c)$

     c. $(a; d] \cap [b; c)$

16–22.* Consider the results from flipping a coin.

     a. Write the set of outcomes for one flip using the letters H and T.

     b. Write the set of outcomes for two flips when the order is retained using the letters H and T.

     c. Write a set whose outcomes are the *number* of heads in two flips.

     d. Write the implied function from the set in part *b* to the set in part *c*.

     e. Repeat part *d* for the sets in parts *a* and *c*.

     f. If each outcome in the set in part *b* is assigned a probability number equal to $\frac{1}{4}$, write this function.

     g. Write a logical function for part *c* which matches the outcomes to the probability numbers in the set $\{\frac{1}{4}, \frac{1}{2}\}$.

16–23. Which of the following matching suggest functions. The left set is the domain.

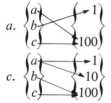 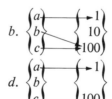

16–24.* A set function is a function whose domain is a collection (set) of sets. Suppose the following set stands for the cash receipts of a store over a 5-day week.

$$S = \{(d_1, d_2, d_3, d_4, d_5): \text{where } d_i \in R \text{ is the total cash receipts of day } i\}.$$

Describe in words the set

$$ST = \{((d_1, d_2, d_3, d_4, d_5), \sum_{i-1}^{5} d_i): d_i \in R \text{ is the total cash receipts of day } i\}.$$

16–25.* A coin is tossed twice.

     a. Using the letters H and T, write the set of outcomes keeping track of order. Call this set *S*. (It is known as a *sample space*.)

b. Write all the subsets of *S.* Each of these subsets is called an event defined over the outcome set *S.*

c. Describe each event in words.

16–26. A set *B* whose elements are the sets $B_i = (b_1, b_2, \ldots, b_k)$ is called a *partition* of a set *A* if (1) for every element $B_i \in B$, $B_i \subseteq A$, and (2) every element in *A* is an element in one but in only one of the sets B_i. Are the following partitions of the set $A = \{1, 2, 3\}$?

a. $\{\{1\}, \{2\}, \{3\}\}$

b. $\{\{1, 2\}, \{3\}\}$

c. $\{\{1, 2\}, \{1, 3\}\}$

d. $\{\{1\}, \{2\}\}$

e. $\{\{1\}, \{2, 3\}, \varnothing\}$

16–27. Consider items coming off an assembly line. They are classified as either good or defective. For two items in a row, the following possibilities exist: zero, one, or two defectives are present. Summarizing the possibilities $\{(g, g), (g, d), (d, g), (d, d)\} = B$ (*B* is called a *sample space*). Using *g* for good and *d* for defective, write out sets for the following possibilities, keeping track of order. (These possibilities are called *events*. An event is a subset of a sample space.) Each event is written as a subset of *B*. The events are:

> zero defective;
> one defective;
> only the second item was defective;
> first item defective;
> at most one defective.

16–28.* *a.* Write *B* in terms of $A \cap B$ and a complement of $(A \cap B)$.

b. Write *B* using $(A \cap B)$ and $B - A$.

c. Write *B* using A, $A - B$ and $B - A$.

16–29.* Verify the argument below by writing the hypothesis and conclusions in set terms and showing that hypotheses 1 and 2 imply the conclusion. Also show this using Venn diagrams. (If one wished to argue, where should he begin?) The hypotheses are as follows:

1. All products of the X Company have annual sales of at least $100,000.

2. No product with sales of at least $100,000 is unsuccessful.

Conclusion: No product of the X Company is unsuccessful.

16–30. A blue and a green die are each rolled once.

    a. How many separate outcomes are there in the set of outcomes if we keep track of the result of each die separately?

    b. Suppose that each of these outcomes is matched to a number equal to the total spots face up. Is a function formed? How many ordered pairs are in it?

    c. Suppose that the outcomes of rolling the two dice once are listed using the totals found in part *b*. Write the set of outcomes.

Appendix

TABLE I
Values of e^x

x	e^x	x	e^x	x	e^x	x	e^x	x	e^x	x	e^x
.00	1.0000	.50	1.6487	1.00	2.7183	1.50	4.4817	2.00	7.3891	2.50	12.182
.01	1.0101	.51	1.6653	1.01	2.7456	1.51	4.5267	2.01	7.4633	2.51	12.305
.02	1.0202	.52	1.6820	1.02	2.7732	1.52	4.5722	2.02	7.5383	2.52	12.429
.03	1.0305	.53	1.6989	1.03	2.8011	1.53	4.6182	2.03	7.6141	2.53	12.554
.04	1.0408	.54	1.7160	1.04	2.8292	1.54	4.6646	2.04	7.6906	2.54	12.680
.05	1.0513	.55	1.7333	1.05	2.8577	1.55	4.7115	2.05	7.7679	2.55	12.807
.06	1.0618	.56	1.7507	1.06	2.8864	1.56	4.7588	2.06	7.8460	2.56	12.936
.07	1.0725	.57	1.7683	1.07	2.9154	1.57	4.8066	2.07	7.9248	2.57	13.066
.08	1.0833	.58	1.7860	1.08	2.9447	1.58	4.8550	2.08	8.0045	2.58	13.197
.09	1.0942	.59	1.8040	1.09	2.9743	1.59	4.9037	2.09	8.0849	2.59	13.330
.10	1.1052	.60	1.8221	1.10	3.0042	1.60	4.9530	2.10	8.1662	2.60	13.464
.11	1.1163	.61	1.8404	1.11	3.0344	1.61	5.0028	2.11	8.2482	2.61	13.599
.12	1.1275	.62	1.8589	1.12	3.0649	1.62	5.0531	2.12	8.3311	2.62	13.736
.13	1.1388	.63	1.8776	1.13	3.0957	1.63	5.1039	2.13	8.4149	2.63	13.874
.14	1.1503	.64	1.8965	1.14	3.1268	1.64	5.1552	2.14	8.4994	2.64	14.013
.15	1.1618	.65	1.9155	1.15	3.1582	1.65	5.2070	2.15	8.5849	2.65	14.154
.16	1.1735	.66	1.9348	1.16	3.1899	1.66	5.2593	2.16	8.6711	2.66	14.296
.17	1.1853	.67	1.9542	1.17	3.2220	1.67	5.3122	2.17	8.7583	2.67	14.440
.18	1.1972	.68	1.9739	1.18	3.2544	1.68	5.3656	2.18	8.8463	2.68	14.585
.19	1.2092	.69	1.9937	1.19	3.2871	1.69	5.4195	2.19	8.9352	2.69	14.732
.20	1.2214	.70	2.0138	1.20	3.3201	1.70	5.4739	2.20	9.0250	2.70	14.880
.21	1.2337	.71	2.0340	1.21	3.3535	1.71	5.5290	2.21	9.1157	2.71	15.029
.22	1.2461	.72	2.0544	1.22	3.3872	1.72	5.5845	2.22	9.2073	2.72	15.180
.23	1.2586	.73	2.0751	1.23	3.4214	1.73	5.6407	2.23	9.2999	2.73	15.333
.24	1.2712	.74	2.0959	1.24	3.4556	1.74	5.6973	2.24	9.3933	2.74	15.487
.25	1.2840	.75	2.1170	1.25	3.4903	1.75	5.7546	2.25	9.4877	2.75	15.643
.26	1.2969	.76	2.1383	1.26	3.5254	1.76	5.8124	2.26	9.5831	2.76	15.800
.27	1.3100	.77	2.1598	1.27	3.5609	1.77	5.8709	2.27	9.6794	2.77	15.959
.28	1.3231	.78	2.1815	1.28	3.5966	1.78	5.9299	2.28	9.7767	2.78	16.119
.29	1.3364	.79	2.2034	1.29	3.6328	1.79	5.9895	2.29	9.8749	2.79	16.281
.30	1.3499	.80	2.2255	1.30	3.6693	1.80	6.0496	2.30	9.9742	2.80	16.445
.31	1.3634	.81	2.2479	1.31	3.7062	1.81	6.1104	2.31	10.074	2.81	16.610
.32	1.3771	.82	2.2705	1.32	3.7434	1.82	6.1719	2.32	10.176	2.82	16.777
.33	1.3910	.83	2.2933	1.33	3.7810	1.83	6.2339	2.33	10.278	2.83	16.945
.34	1.4049	.84	2.3164	1.34	3.8190	1.84	6.2965	2.34	10.381	2.84	17.116
.35	1.4191	.85	2.3396	1.35	3.8574	1.85	6.3598	2.35	10.486	2.85	17.288
.36	1.4333	.86	2.3632	1.36	3.8962	1.86	6.4237	2.36	10.591	2.86	17.462
.37	1.4477	.87	2.3869	1.37	3.9354	1.87	6.4883	2.37	10.697	2.87	17.637
.38	1.4623	.88	2.4109	1.38	3.9749	1.88	6.5535	2.38	10.805	2.88	17.814
.39	1.4770	.89	2.4351	1.39	4.0149	1.89	6.6194	2.39	10.913	2.89	17.993
.40	1.4918	.90	2.4596	1.40	4.0552	1.90	6.6859	2.40	11.023	2.90	18.174
.41	1.5068	.91	2.4843	1.41	4.0960	1.91	6.7531	2.41	11.134	2.91	18.357
.42	1.5220	.92	2.5093	1.42	4.1371	1.92	6.8210	2.42	11.246	2.92	18.541
.43	1.5373	.93	2.5345	1.43	4.1787	1.93	6.8895	2.43	11.359	2.93	18.728
.44	1.5527	.94	2.5600	1.44	4.2207	1.94	6.9588	2.44	11.473	2.94	18.916
.45	1.5683	.95	2.5857	1.45	4.2631	1.95	7.0287	2.45	11.588	2.95	19.106
.46	1.5841	.96	2.6117	1.46	4.3060	1.96	7.0993	2.46	11.705	2.96	19.298
.47	1.6000	.97	2.6379	1.47	4.3492	1.97	7.1707	2.47	11.822	2.97	19.492
.48	1.6161	.98	2.6645	1.48	4.3929	1.98	7.2427	2.48	11.941	2.98	19.688
.49	1.6323	.99	2.6912	1.49	4.4371	1.99	7.3155	2.49	12.061	2.99	19.886
.50	1.6487	1.00	2.7183	1.50	4.4817	2.00	7.3891	2.50	12.182	3.00	20.086

x	e^x	x	e^x	x	e^x	x	e^x	x	e^x	x	e^x
3.00	20.086	3.50	33.115	4.00	54.598	4.50	90.017	5.00	148.41	5.0	148.41
3.01	20.287	3.51	33.448	4.01	55.147	4.51	90.922	5.01	149.90	5.1	164.02
3.02	20.491	3.52	33.784	4.02	55.701	4.52	91.836	5.02	151.41	5.2	181.27
3.03	20.697	3.53	34.124	4.03	56.261	4.53	92.759	5.03	152.93	5.3	200.34
3.04	20.905	3.54	34.467	4.04	56.826	4.54	93.691	5.04	154.47	5.4	221.41
3.05	21.115	3.55	34.813	4.05	57.397	4.55	94.632	5.05	156.02	5.5	244.69
3.06	21.328	3.56	35.163	4.06	57.974	4.56	95.583	5.06	157.59	5.6	270.43
3.07	21.542	3.57	35.517	4.07	58.557	4.57	96.544	5.07	159.17	5.7	298.87
3.08	21.758	3.58	35.874	4.08	59.145	4.58	97.514	5.08	160.77	5.8	330.30
3.09	21.977	3.59	36.234	4.09	59.740	4.59	98.494	5.09	162.39	5.9	365.04
3.10	22.198	3.60	36.598	4.10	60.340	4.60	99.484	5.10	164.02	6.0	403.43
3.11	22.421	3.61	36.966	4.11	60.947	4.61	100.48	5.11	165.67	6.1	445.86
3.12	22.646	3.62	37.338	4.12	61.559	4.62	101.49	5.12	167.34	6.2	492.75
3.13	22.874	3.63	37.713	4.13	62.178	4.63	102.51	5.13	169.02	6.3	544.57
3.14	23.104	3.64	38.092	4.14	62.803	4.64	103.54	5.14	170.72	6.4	601.85
3.15	23.336	3.65	38.475	4.15	63.434	4.65	104.58	5.15	172.43	6.5	665.14
3.16	23.571	3.66	38.861	4.16	64.072	4.66	105.64	5.16	174.16	6.6	735.10
3.17	23.807	3.67	39.252	4.17	64.715	4.67	106.70	5.17	175.91	6.7	812.41
3.18	24.047	3.68	39.646	4.18	65.366	4.68	107.77	5.18	177.68	6.8	897.85
3.19	24.288	3.69	40.045	4.19	66.023	4.69	108.85	5.19	179.47	6.9	992.27
3.20	24.533	3.70	40.447	4.20	66.686	4.70	109.95	5.20	181.27	7.0	1096.6
3.21	24.779	3.71	40.854	4.21	67.357	4.71	111.05	5.21	183.09	7.1	1212.0
3.22	25.028	3.72	41.264	4.22	68.033	4.72	112.17	5.22	184.93	7.2	1339.4
3.23	25.280	3.73	41.679	4.23	68.717	4.73	113.30	5.23	186.79	7.3	1480.3
3.24	25.534	3.74	42.098	4.24	69.408	4.74	114.43	5.24	188.67	7.4	1636.0
3.25	25.790	3.75	42.521	4.25	70.105	4.75	115.58	5.25	190.57	7.5	1808.0
3.26	26.050	3.76	42.948	4.26	70.810	4.76	116.75	5.26	192.48	7.6	1998.2
3.27	26.311	3.77	43.380	4.27	71.522	4.77	117.92	5.27	194.42	7.7	2208.3
3.28	26.576	3.78	43.816	4.28	72.240	4.78	119.10	5.28	196.37	7.8	2440.6
3.29	26.843	3.79	44.256	4.29	72.966	4.79	120.30	5.29	198.34	7.9	2697.3
3.30	27.113	3.80	44.701	4.30	73.700	4.80	121.51	5.30	200.34	8.0	2981.0
3.31	27.385	3.81	45.150	3.31	74.440	4.81	122.73	5.31	202.35	8.1	3294.5
3.32	27.660	3.82	45.604	4.32	75.189	4.82	123.97	5.32	204.38	8.2	3641.0
3.33	27.938	3.83	46.063	4.33	75.944	4.83	125.21	5.33	206.44	8.3	4023.9
3.34	28.219	3.84	46.525	4.34	76.708	4.84	126.47	5.34	208.51	8.4	4447.1
3.35	28.503	3.85	46.993	4.35	77.478	4.85	127.74	5.35	210.61	8.5	4914.8
3.36	28.789	3.86	47.465	4.36	78.257	4.86	129.02	5.36	212.72	8.6	5431.7
3.37	29.079	3.87	47.942	4.37	79.044	4.87	130.32	5.37	214.86	8.7	6002.9
3.38	29.371	3.88	48.424	4.38	79.838	4.88	131.63	5.38	217.02	8.8	6634.2
3.39	29.666	3.89	48.911	4.39	80.640	4.89	132.95	5.39	219.20	8.9	7332.0
3.40	29.964	3.90	49.402	4.40	81.451	4.90	134.29	5.40	221.41	9.0	8103.1
3.41	30.265	3.91	49.899	4.41	82.269	4.91	135.64	5.41	223.63	9.1	8955.3
3.42	30.569	3.92	50.400	4.42	83.096	4.92	137.00	5.42	225.88	9.2	9897.1
3.43	30.877	3.93	50.907	4.43	83.931	4.93	138.38	5.43	228.15	9.3	10938
3.44	31.187	3.94	51.419	4.44	84.775	4.94	139.77	5.44	230.44	9.4	12088
3.45	31.500	3.95	51.935	4.45	85.627	4.95	141.17	5.45	232.76	9.5	13360
3.46	31.817	3.96	52.457	4.46	86.488	4.96	142.59	5.46	235.10	9.6	14765
3.47	32.137	3.97	52.985	4.47	87.357	4.97	144.03	5.47	237.46	9.7	16318
3.48	32.460	3.98	53.517	4.48	88.235	4.98	145.47	5.48	239.85	9.8	18034
3.49	32.786	3.99	54.055	4.49	89.121	4.99	146.94	5.49	242.26	9.9	19930
3.50	33.115	4.00	54.598	4.50	90.017	5.00	148.41	5.50	244.69	10.0	22026

From the *Handbook of Chemistry and Physics*, 48th ed. (Cleveland: The Chemical Rubber Company, 1966). Reprinted with permission.

TABLE II
Four-Place Logarithms*

N	0	1	2	3	4	5	6	7	8	9	PROPORTIONAL PARTS								
											1	2	3	4	5	6	7	8	9
10	0000	0043	0086	0128	0170	0212	0253	0294	0334	0374	†4	8	12	17	21	25	29	33	37
11	0414	0453	0492	0531	0569	0607	0645	0682	0719	0755	4	8	11	15	19	23	26	30	34
12	0792	0828	0864	0899	0934	0969	1004	1038	1072	1106	3	7	10	14	17	21	24	28	31
13	1139	1173	1206	1239	1271	1303	1335	1367	1399	1430	3	6	10	13	16	19	23	26	29
14	1461	1492	1523	1553	1584	1614	1644	1673	1703	1732	3	6	9	12	15	18	21	24	27
15	1761	1790	1818	1847	1875	1903	1931	1959	1987	2014	†3	6	8	11	14	17	20	22	25
16	2041	2068	2095	2122	2148	2175	2201	2227	2253	2279	3	5	8	11	13	16	18	21	24
17	2304	2330	2355	2380	2405	2430	2455	2480	2504	2529	2	5	7	10	12	15	17	20	22
18	2553	2577	2601	2625	2648	2672	2695	2718	2742	2765	2	5	7	9	12	14	16	19	21
19	2788	2810	2833	2856	2878	2900	2923	2945	2967	2989	2	4	7	9	11	13	16	18	20
20	3010	3032	3054	3075	3096	3118	3139	3160	3181	3201	2	4	6	8	11	13	15	17	19
21	3222	3243	3263	3284	3304	3324	3345	3365	3385	3404	2	4	6	8	10	12	14	16	18
22	3424	3444	3464	3483	3502	3522	3541	3560	3579	3598	2	4	6	8	10	12	14	15	17
23	3617	3636	3655	3674	3692	3711	3729	3747	3766	3784	2	4	6	7	9	11	13	15	17
24	3802	3820	3838	3856	3874	3892	3909	3927	3945	3962	2	4	5	7	9	11	12	14	16
25	3979	3997	4014	4031	4048	4065	4082	4099	4116	4133	2	3	5	7	9	10	12	14	15
26	4150	4166	4183	4200	4216	4232	4249	4265	4281	4298	2	3	5	7	8	10	11	13	15
27	4314	4330	4346	4362	4378	4393	4409	4425	4440	4456	2	3	5	6	8	9	11	13	14
28	4472	4487	4502	4518	4533	4548	4564	4579	4594	4609	2	3	5	6	8	9	11	12	14
29	4624	4639	4654	4669	4683	4698	4713	4728	4742	4757	1	3	4	6	7	9	10	12	13
30	4771	4786	4800	4814	4829	4834	4857	4871	4886	4900	1	3	4	6	7	9	10	11	13
31	4914	4928	4942	4955	4969	4983	4997	5011	5024	5038	1	3	4	6	7	8	10	11	12
32	5051	5065	5079	5092	5105	5119	5132	5145	5159	5172	1	3	4	5	7	8	9	11	12
33	5185	5198	5211	5224	5237	5250	5263	5276	5289	5302	1	3	4	5	6	8	9	10	12
34	5315	5328	5340	5353	5366	5378	5391	5403	5416	5428	1	3	4	5	6	8	9	10	11
35	5441	5453	5465	5478	5490	5502	5514	5527	5539	5551	1	2	4	5	6	7	9	10	11
36	5563	5575	5587	5599	5611	5623	5635	5647	5658	5670	1	2	4	5	6	7	8	10	11
37	5682	5694	5705	5717	5729	5740	5752	5763	5775	5786	1	2	3	5	6	7	8	9	10
38	5798	5809	5821	5832	5843	5855	5866	5877	5888	5899	1	2	3	5	6	7	8	9	10
39	5911	5922	5933	5944	5955	5966	5977	5988	5999	6010	1	2	3	4	5	7	8	9	10
40	6021	6031	6042	6053	6064	6075	6085	6096	6107	6117	1	2	3	4	5	6	8	9	10
41	6128	6138	6149	6160	6170	6180	6191	6201	6212	6222	1	2	3	4	5	6	7	8	9
42	6232	6243	6253	6263	6274	6284	6294	6304	6314	6325	1	2	3	4	5	6	7	8	9
43	6335	6345	6355	6365	6375	6385	6395	6405	6415	6425	1	2	3	4	5	6	7	8	9
44	6435	6444	6454	6464	6474	6484	6493	6503	6513	6522	1	2	3	4	5	6	7	8	9
45	6532	6542	6551	6561	6571	6580	6590	6599	6609	6618	1	2	3	4	5	6	7	8	9
46	6628	6637	6646	6656	6665	6675	6684	6693	6702	6712	1	2	3	4	5	6	7	7	8
47	6721	6730	6739	6749	6758	6767	6776	6785	6794	6803	1	2	3	4	5	5	6	7	8
48	6812	6821	6830	6839	6848	6857	6866	6875	6884	6893	1	2	3	4	4	5	6	7	8
49	6902	6911	6920	6928	6937	6946	6955	6964	6972	6981	1	2	3	4	4	5	6	7	8
50	6990	6998	7007	7016	7024	7033	7042	7050	7059	7067	1	2	3	3	4	5	6	7	8
51	7076	7084	7093	7101	7110	7118	7126	7135	7143	7152	1	2	3	3	4	5	6	7	8
52	7160	7168	7177	7185	7193	7202	7210	7218	7226	7235	1	2	2	3	4	5	6	7	7
53	7243	7251	7259	7267	7275	7284	7292	7300	7308	7316	1	2	2	3	4	5	6	6	7
54	7324	7332	7340	7348	7356	7364	7372	7380	7388	7396	1	2	2	3	4	5	6	6	7

N	0	1	2	3	4	5	6	7	8	9	1	2	3	4	5	6	7	8	9

N	0	1	2	3	4	5	6	7	8	9	PROPORTIONAL PARTS								
											1	2	3	4	5	6	7	8	9
55	7404	7412	7419	7427	7435	7443	7451	7459	7466	7474	1	2	2	3	4	5	5	6	7
56	7482	7490	7497	7505	7513	7520	7528	7536	7543	7551	1	2	2	3	4	5	5	6	7
57	7559	7566	7574	7582	7589	7597	7604	7612	7619	7627	1	2	2	3	4	5	5	6	7
58	7634	7642	7649	7657	7664	7672	7679	7686	7694	7701	1	1	2	3	4	4	5	6	7
59	7709	7716	7723	7731	7738	7745	7752	7760	7767	7774	1	1	2	3	4	4	5	6	7
60	7782	7789	7796	7803	7810	7818	7825	7832	7839	7846	1	1	2	3	4	4	5	6	6
61	7853	7860	7868	7875	7882	7889	7896	7903	7910	7917	1	1	2	3	4	4	5	6	6
62	7924	7931	7938	7945	7952	7959	7966	7973	7980	7987	1	1	2	3	4	5	6	6	6
63	7993	8000	8007	8014	8021	8028	8035	8041	8048	8055	1	1	2	3	3	4	5	5	6
64	8062	8069	8075	8082	8089	8096	8102	8109	8116	8122	1	1	2	3	3	4	5	5	6
65	8129	8136	8142	8149	8156	8162	8169	8176	8182	8189	1	1	2	3	3	4	5	5	6
66	8195	8202	8209	8215	8222	8228	8235	8241	8248	8254	1	1	2	3	3	4	5	5	6
67	8261	8267	8274	8280	8287	8293	8299	8306	8312	8319	1	1	2	3	3	4	5	5	6
68	8325	8331	8338	8344	8351	8357	8363	8370	8376	8382	1	1	2	3	3	4	4	5	6
69	8388	8395	8401	8407	8414	8420	8426	8432	8439	8445	1	1	2	2	3	4	4	5	6
70	8451	8457	8463	8470	8476	8482	8488	8494	8500	8506	1	1	2	2	3	4	4	5	6
71	8513	8519	8525	8531	8537	8543	8549	8555	8561	8567	1	1	2	2	3	4	4	5	5
72	8573	8579	8585	8591	8597	8603	8609	8615	8621	8627	1	1	2	2	3	4	4	5	5
73	8633	8639	8645	8651	8657	8663	8669	8675	8681	8686	1	1	2	2	3	4	4	4	5
74	8692	8698	8704	8710	8716	8722	8727	8733	8739	8745	1	1	2	2	3	4	4	5	5
75	8751	8756	8762	8768	8774	8779	8785	8791	8797	8802	1	1	2	2	3	3	4	5	5
76	8808	8814	8820	8825	8831	8837	8842	8848	8854	8859	1	1	2	2	3	3	4	5	5
77	8865	8871	8876	8882	8887	8893	8899	8904	8910	8915	1	1	2	2	3	3	4	4	5
78	8921	8927	8932	8938	8943	8949	8954	8960	8965	8971	1	1	2	2	3	3	4	4	5
79	8976	8982	8987	8993	8998	9004	9009	9015	9020	9025	1	1	2	2	3	3	4	4	5
80	9031	9036	9042	9047	9053	9058	9063	9069	9074	9079	1	1	2	2	3	3	4	4	5
81	9085	9090	9096	9101	9106	9112	9117	9122	9128	9133	1	1	2	2	3	3	4	4	5
82	9138	9143	9149	9154	9159	9165	9170	9175	9180	9186	1	1	2	2	3	3	4	4	5
83	9191	9196	9201	9206	9212	9217	9222	9227	9232	9238	1	1	2	2	3	3	4	4	5
84	9243	9248	9253	9258	9263	9269	9274	9279	9284	9289	1	1	2	2	3	3	4	4	5
85	9294	9299	9304	9309	9315	9320	9325	9330	9335	9340	1	1	2	2	3	3	4	4	5
86	9345	9350	9355	9360	9365	9370	9375	9380	9385	9390	1	1	2	2	3	3	4	4	5
87	9395	9400	9405	9410	9415	9420	9425	9430	9435	9440	0	1	1	2	2	3	3	4	4
88	9445	9450	9455	9460	9465	9469	9474	9479	9484	9489	0	1	1	2	2	3	3	4	4
89	9494	9499	9504	9509	9513	9518	9523	9528	9533	9538	0	1	1	2	2	3	3	4	4
90	9542	9547	9552	9557	9562	9566	9571	9576	9581	9586	0	1	1	2	2	3	3	4	4
91	9590	9595	9600	9605	9609	9614	9619	9624	9628	9633	0	1	1	2	2	3	3	4	4
92	9638	9643	9647	9652	9657	9661	9666	9671	9675	9680	0	1	1	2	2	3	3	4	4
93	9685	9689	9694	9699	9703	9708	9713	9717	9722	9727	0	1	1	2	2	3	3	4	4
94	9731	9736	9741	9745	9750	9754	9759	9763	9768	9773	0	1	1	2	2	3	3	4	4
95	9777	9782	9786	9791	9795	9800	9805	9809	9814	9818	0	1	1	2	2	3	3	4	4
96	9823	9827	9832	9836	9841	9845	9850	9854	9859	9863	0	1	1	2	2	3	3	4	4
97	9868	9872	9877	9881	9886	9890	9894	9899	8903	9908	0	1	1	2	2	3	3	4	4
98	9912	9917	9921	9926	9930	9934	9939	9943	9948	9952	0	1	1	2	2	3	3	4	4
99	9956	9961	9965	9969	9974	9978	9983	9987	9991	9996	0	1	1	2	2	3	3	3	4
N	0	1	2	3	4	5	6	7	8	9	1	2	3	4	5	6	7	8	9

$$* \log_e x = \ln x = [\log_e 10][\log_{10} x] = \left[\frac{1}{\log_{10} e}\right][\log_{10} x] = 2.3026 \log_{10} x$$

† Interpolation in this section of the table is inaccurate.

From *Handbook of Chemistry and Physics*, 48th ed. (Cleveland: The Chemical Rubber Company, 1966). Reprinted with permission.

Answers

CHAPTER 1

1-1.   It can be useful in each of these decision situations.

1-2.   a. variable
         b. constant

1-5.   a. $7/8 > 4/5 > 2/3 > 0 > -1/4 > -3/4 > -2$
         b. $-2/3 < -3/5 < -1/2 < 7/9 < \sqrt{1} \leqslant 1 < 4/3 \leqslant 8/6$
         c. The second term is larger.
            The first term is larger.
            Both terms are equal to zero.

1-7.   a. $3xy + 6x$ d. $yy - 1$
         b. $12xz + 4z$ e. $xz - xxy + yz - xyy$
         c. $xy + y - x - 1$ f. $axy + ax - 2azy - 2az$

1-9.   a. 10   d. 648
         b. 24   e. 42
         c. 27   f. 46,080

1-10.   a. $p = 10 + c$ d. $g \leqslant 1000$
         b. $p = c + .2c$ e. $t > 80$
         c. $f = 200 + 20s$ f. $s > I$

1-12. $.10x > 500,000 + .05x \; \forall x > 1,000,000$, where $x \equiv$ sales units.

1-13.   a. 1   d. $2\sqrt{6}$
         b. 2   e. 9
         c. 120

425

1-15.   a. Revelex
          b. No, less since dividends declined
          c. It is greater.
          d. It is greater than Revelex since $|-3 + 1| \div 2 = |-2| \div 2$
             $= 2 \div 2 = 1$. It is equal to Ezygo.

1-17.
$$(1.10)(1.15)...(1.80)75 = 75 \prod_{i=2}^{16} (1 + .05i)$$

1-20.   a. $1000 \leqslant x < 2000$ c. $1042 < x < 1050$
          b. $x = 1000$ d. Impossible

1-22.   a. $S \geqslant 50,000$ d. $50,000 < S < 68,000$
          b. $S \leqslant 65,000$ e. $53,000 \leqslant S \leqslant 65,000$
          c. $53,000 \leqslant S < 70,000$

1-24.   a. $6x_1 + 8x_2 + 4x_3 = \text{Area}$
          b. $20x_1 + 30x_2 + 40x_3 \leqslant 30,000$
          c. $.5x_1 + .65x_2 + .6x_3 = \text{Total Cost}$

1-25.   Sales of product i over the ten years will be $S_i \cdot \prod_{j=1}^{10} (1+r)^j$

So the total sales may be expressed as $\sum_{i=1}^{10} (S_i \cdot \prod_{j=1}^{10} (1+r)^j$

CHAPTER 2

2-1.   a. 27   d. 1/4096
         b. 256   e. -1024
         c. 64   f. 64

2-4.   a. $\dfrac{xz^2}{y^3}$ d. $\dfrac{x^5}{y^4}$

         b. $\dfrac{y^4}{x^2}$ e. $\dfrac{x \cdot y^6}{z^3}$

         c. $\dfrac{3x^2}{2y}$

2-5.   a. 27   d. 1/9
         b. 16   e. 5/3
         c. 1/32

2-7.   a. $x^2 + y^2 = z^2$
         b. $z = (x^2 + y^2)^{1/2}$
         c. $x = (z^2 - y^2)^{1/2}$

2-8. $P.V. = \$6000$

2-10. a. $2000 (1.05)^{10} = 3258

b. $1,500,000 (1.035)^{12} = $2,266,500$

c. $1000 \left[\dfrac{(1 + .015^{20} - 1)}{.015} \right] = $23,133$

2-11. Yes

$$P.V. = \frac{3000}{1.06} + \frac{4000}{(1.06)^2} + \frac{5000}{(1.06)^3} + \frac{4000}{(1.06)^4} + \frac{3000}{(1.06)^5}$$

P.V. = $15,998.5

2-13. The lump sum payment of $100,000.

2-15. The bond should sell for $10,000.

2-17. $$A = \frac{6}{1 - (1.005)^{-12}}$$

2-20. a. 10101   d. 1110000
       b. 111   e. 10000001
       c. 1011001

2-22. a. 11   : $9 + 8 = 17$
       b. F : $33 - 18 = 15$
       c. $C6 : 11 \cdot 18 = 198$
       d. $5 : 35 \div 7 = 5$

2-24. a. 26   c. 555
       b. 477   d. 151

CHAPTER 3

3-1.   Functions: a
       Rules for functions: e
       No functions: b (2 is matched to both 4 and 7)
       Not a rule for a function: c, d, f

3-3.   a. $12b + 18$
       b. impossible (division by zero)
       c. $-12a^2$
       d. $z^{-1} + a^4$
       e. Zero unless $az^2 = 0$
       f. $y^3 - a^4 z^2 y$

3-4. $f(x=0) = 80$ thousand; $f(x) = 4x + 80$, for $5 \leqslant x \leqslant 40$

3-7.   a. 1,000 patient hours
       b. In 20 years or by 1985

3-9.   a. $20 + 9x$
       b. $20 + 4x + 5(x-y)$, for $x - y \geqslant 0$
           $20 + 4x$, for $x - y < 0$
       c. 2 hours

3-11.   a. $100 - x$

b. $90(100-x) + 105x$

c. $90 + 0.15x$

3-13.   a. $x > \frac{1}{2}$

b. $x = \frac{1}{2}$ $y = 11\frac{3}{4}$

3-14.   a. $f(x) = 0.72x: \; x \geqslant 0$

b. $f(y) = 1.39y: \; y \geqslant 0$

3-16.   a. $R = .06I, \; 0 \leqslant I$

b. $f(x) = \begin{cases} -3 + (3/2)x : 2 \leqslant x \leqslant 6 \\ 2 + (2/3)x : 6 \leqslant x \leqslant 12 \end{cases}$

c. $V = 60{,}000 + 1{,}000s + 100(10-p)$ where $s \equiv$ no. of salesmen and $p \equiv$ the new price, $30 \leqslant s \leqslant 50$ and $7.50 \leqslant p \leqslant 12.50$

3-18.   a. $15   d. $275,000

b. $200,000   e. 40,000 (i.e., $x = 400$)

c. $1500x

3-21.   a. $y = p \cdot x$

b. $x = b/(1-p)$

3-22.   a. $c = (1+p)wL$

b. $p = \dfrac{c}{wL} - 1$

3-26.

a. $x = \dfrac{-5}{2} + \dfrac{1}{2}y$ for $0 \leqslant x \leqslant 5$ and $5 \leqslant y \leqslant 15$

b. The inverse is not defined.

c. If I is an even integer, the inverse is not defined. If I is an odd integer, the inverse is defined $x = y^{1/I}$

d. $x = \sqrt{y}$.

3-27.

a. $y = \dfrac{1}{36} \cdot x \cdot (1+a)^3$

b. $x = \dfrac{36 \cdot y}{(1+a)^3}$

3-28.   Profit, y = sales − costs

$$= p \cdot x - (4000 + 5x)$$

But $x = 10{,}000 - p$. Hence

$$y = p \cdot 10{,}000 - p^2 - 4000 - 50{,}000 + 5p$$
$$y = -p^2 + 10{,}005p - 54{,}000 \text{ for } 0 < p < 10{,}000$$

CHAPTER 4

4-2.   a. 3   d. 4

b. 0   e. 6

c. 3/2   f. 64

4-3. a. $\log_a 2 + \log_a x + \log_a y$ d. $a\log_a x$
      b. $2\log_a x + 3\log_a y - 4\log_a z$ e. $2 + 3\log_a x - \log_a 3$
      c. $\log_a(2x + y)$

4-5. a. $e^{1.75} = 5.7546$ so $x = 1.75$
      b. since x must be $< 0: e^{-x} \approx 0.02$ and $e^x = 50$ so $x \approx -3.91$
      c. $x = 63.2$
      d. $e^{9.4} = 12088$ so $'X = 9.4$
      e. $x = 479$

4-7. $\log p_n = \log p_0 + n \log (1 + r)$

4-8. a. $\log p_7 = 3.3251$
          $p_7 = \$2114$
      b. $\log p_{12} = 3.7230$
          $p_{12} = \$5284$

4-10. a. $D = 475.4$
      b. $D = 505.6$

4-13. a. Continuous compounding.
      b. Quarterly compounding.

4-14. a. Functions 2, 3, 4, 5, 6 and $x = b^y$
      b. Linear growth up to a point, then horizontal
      c. Logistic function (Function 6)

4-17. The growth pattern is exponential, but the growth rate decreases after the fourth year.

4-18. $X = 10^3 \cdot L^{.6} \cdot K^{.4}$

4-21. a. $W = 82$
      b. $W = 58$
      c. $W = 51$

4-22. a. 656
      b. 742.4
      c. 791.3

4-24. The percentage reduction is 10 percent: $a \approx 11.1 : b \approx -0.15$

CHAPTER 5

5-1. a. $T = a P^2$
      b. $I = P - T$
      c. $T = \begin{cases} a P \text{ for } P \leqslant 25,000 \\ b P \text{ for } P > 25,000 \end{cases}$
      d. $N = a J$
      e. $N = a C$

5-3. 3571 hours.

5-5.   a. $x^2 + x - 2$ d. $x^3 - 5x^2 + 2x + 8$

         b. $x^2 - 13x + 42$ e. $x^4 - 4x^3 - 8x^2 + 12x + 15$

         c. $x^3 - 3x^2 + 3x - 1$

5-7.   a. $x^4 + 3x^3 + x^2 - 3x - 2$

         b. $x^2 + x - 2$

         c. $x - 2 + \dfrac{3}{x+2}$

5-9.   a. $x = 3$ c. $x = 3/17$

         b. $x = -a$ d. $x = 0$

5-11. $S = D$ when $p = 10$

5-12.   a. $p = +5$ or $p = +15$

         b. $p = 10 \pm 5$.

5-14.   a. $x = 1, x = 2, x = 3$

         b. $x = +1, x = -1$

         c. $x = 0$ is the only real root.

5-18. $x = \sqrt{\dfrac{(p - a)}{b}}$

5-20.   14 hours.

5-22.   a. $x = \dfrac{B}{a + 2c}$

         b. 100 magazine units. Thus there are 200 television units.

5-24.   If $t \geqslant 3.3$, the output rate is greater than 95 per day.

CHAPTER 6

6-2.   a. $x = \dfrac{22}{7}, y = \dfrac{10}{7}$ c. no solution, inconsistent

         b. $x = 6, y = 4$ d. $x = y = 1$

6-3.   See answers to 6-2.

6-4.   b. $x = -2, y = 1, z = 3$

         c. no unique solution, dependence

         d. $w = 1, x = 5, y = -3, z = -2$

6-5.   a. $x = 2, y = 1$

         b. $x = 6, y = 4$

         c. $x = 3, y = 3$

6-7.   a. -2 c. 0

         b. 30   d. 0

6-8.   a. $D = -2, N_x = -8, N_y = -4; x = 4, y = 2$

         b. $D = -15, N_x = -15, N_y = -15, N_z = -15; x = y = z = 1$

         c. $D = 6, N_x = 12, N_y = 0, N_z = 0; x = 2, y = z = 0$

         d. $D = 20, N_w = 20, N_x = 40, N_y = 60, N_z = 80; w = 1, x = 2,$

            $y = 3, z = 4$

6-9.　　$a = \dfrac{25}{4}, b = \dfrac{15}{2}$

6-11.　　$a = \$75, b = \$20$

6-13.　　$a = -400, b = 10$, and $c = 30$, so $S = -400 + 10M + 30T$

6-16.　　$a = 4, b = 4$, and $c = 1$

6-17.　　$P_W = 10, P_B = 30$

6-20.　　30 gloves, 10 bats, and 15 balls

6-23.　　$a = -2000$ and $b = 0.4$, so $T = -\$2000 + 0.4 \cdot I$

CHAPTER 7

7-1.　　a. $m = 3, n = 2$; the matrix is not square, and a_{23} does not exist.

　　　　b. $m = 2, n = 2$; the matrix is square, but a_{23} does not exist.

　　　　c. $m = 3, n = 3$; the matrix is square, and $a_{23} = 7$.

　　　　d. $m = 3, n = 4$; the matrix is not square, and $a_{23} = 4$.

7-2.　　a. $D = +2$, so an inverse exists.

　　　　b. $D = +9$, so an inverse exists.

　　　　c. $D = 0$, so no inverse exists.

7-4.　　Parts b and f cannot be performed

a. $\mathbf{AB} = \begin{bmatrix} 34 & 19 \\ 2 & 7 \\ 10 & 5 \end{bmatrix}$
　　　d. $\mathbf{cb'} = \begin{bmatrix} 0 & 1 & 1 \\ 0 & 4 & 4 \\ 0 & 3 & 3 \end{bmatrix}$

c. $\mathbf{b'c} = \begin{bmatrix} 7 \end{bmatrix}$
　　　e. $\mathbf{Cc} = \begin{bmatrix} -10 \\ 3 \end{bmatrix}$

7-5.　　$\mathbf{A} = \begin{bmatrix} 6 & 4 & 5 \\ 4 & 3 & 2 \\ 4 & 4 & 3 \end{bmatrix}$　is the matrix of sales.

$\mathbf{B} = \begin{bmatrix} 8 & 8 & 8 \\ 8 & 8 & 8 \\ 8 & 8 & 8 \end{bmatrix}$　is the matrix of fixed cost shares.

$3\mathbf{A} - \mathbf{B} = \begin{bmatrix} 10 & 4 & 7 \\ 4 & 1 & -2 \\ 4 & 4 & 1 \end{bmatrix}$　is the matrix of net contributions.

They should *not* eliminate blue tricycles in region III (the combination corresponding to -2).

7-7.

a.
$$\begin{bmatrix} 3 & 1 & -7 \\ 1 & -3 & -1 \\ -1 & 1 & -2 \end{bmatrix} \begin{bmatrix} x_1 \\ x_2 \\ x_3 \end{bmatrix} = \begin{bmatrix} -14 \\ -12 \\ -2 \end{bmatrix}$$

b.
$$\begin{bmatrix} 4 & 1 & 1 \\ 2 & 3 & 1 \\ 1 & -1 & 4 \end{bmatrix} \begin{bmatrix} a \\ b \\ c \end{bmatrix} = \begin{bmatrix} 6 \\ 6 \\ 3 \end{bmatrix}$$

7-12. *a* and *b* have inverses.

a. $A = \begin{bmatrix} 1 & 2 \\ 3 & 4 \end{bmatrix}$, $A^{-1} = -\dfrac{1}{2} \begin{bmatrix} 4 & -2 \\ -3 & 1 \end{bmatrix} = \begin{bmatrix} -2 & 1 \\ 3/2 & -1/2 \end{bmatrix}$

b. $A = \begin{bmatrix} 7 & -3 \\ -4 & 6 \end{bmatrix}$, $A^{-1} = \dfrac{1}{30} \begin{bmatrix} 6 & 3 \\ 4 & 7 \end{bmatrix} = \begin{bmatrix} 6/30 & 3/30 \\ 4/30 & 7/30 \end{bmatrix}$

7-14. 49 units of *X* and 7 units of *Y*.

7-16. *a* = 5000, *b* = 30, and *d* = 75.

7-17. Both **A** and **B** have *D* = 0.

7-19. a. His estimate of the demand function is: Demand = $20 + A - 2p$
 b. The forecast is: $20 + 1(14) - 2(5) = 24$

7-21. Products A and B sell for $2, and product C sells for $3.

7-24. a. *a* = 130

b. $x = -\left(\dfrac{b}{8}\right) + \left(\dfrac{c}{4}\right)$, $y = \left(\dfrac{5b}{32}\right) - \left(\dfrac{c}{16}\right)$

CHAPTER 8

8-1. a. $14, \sqrt{2}, 1, 3/4, 0.5, -8$
 b. $14, 7, 4, 3, 2, -1$
 c. $\pi, 3, \sqrt{3}, \sqrt{2}$

8-2. *c, d, f,* and *h* are (always) correct.
 a and *b* are incorrect.
 e and *g* are conditional inequalities that hold for some *x* values; they are not correct as general statements.

8-3. *d, f,* and *g* may be incorrect; they do not follow from $x \geq 2$.
 a. Correct, by inequality preserving operation 1.
 b. Correct, by inequality preserving operation 3.
 c. Correct, by inequality preserving operation 2.
 e. Correct, by the rule for multiplying both sides of an inequality by a negative number (and inequality preserving operation 1).
 h. Correct, by inequality preserving operation 4.

8-6. a. $-2x + 6 \leqslant 0$ or $x \geqslant 3$
    b. $x + 7 > 0$ or $x > -7$
    c. $5x + 6 < 0$ or $x < -6/5$

8-8. He should invest at least \$12,500 in the 9% bond and, thus, no more than \$7,500 in the 5% bond.

8-9. a. $(x + 2)^2 \geqslant 0$, for all x values
    b. $(x + 1)(x - 1)(x - 2) > 0$ for $-1 < x < +1$ and for $x > 2$
    c. $x^2 - 1 < 0$, for $-1 < x < +1$
    d. $x^2 < 0$ never holds (for x = a real number).

8-11. Between \$20 and \$25.

8-14. The solution space is the triangular region around the intersections of $x = 15,000$, $x + y = 20,000$, and $.09x + .05y = 1500$. The three corner points are given in the answer to 8-15.

8-15. a. (i)   maximize $.09x + .05y$
        subject to $x + y \leqslant 20,000$
            $.09x + .05y \geqslant 1500$
                $x \leqslant 15,000$
                $x \geqslant 0$
                $y \geqslant 0$
        The constraints are identical for all three objectives, so only the new objective functions are given for (ii) and (iii).
      (ii)   minimize x
      (iii) minimize $x + y$
    b. The optimal solutions occur at:
      (i)   – corner point 2
      (ii)   – corner point 1
      (iii) – corner point 3
      (They are defined below.)

    c.

	x	y	*objective function (i)*
corner point 1	12,500	7500	1500
corner point 2	15,000	5000	1600
corner point 3	15,000	3000	1500

8-19.

    a. $A = \begin{bmatrix} 1 & 4 & 0 \\ 4 & 3 & 0 \\ 0 & 0 & 1 \end{bmatrix}$, $x = \begin{bmatrix} x \\ y \\ z \end{bmatrix}$, $b = \begin{bmatrix} 10 \\ 10 \\ 4 \end{bmatrix}$ and $c' = \begin{bmatrix} 1 & 2 & -1 \end{bmatrix}$

    Then: minimize $c'x$
    subject to $Ax \leqslant b$
        $x \geqslant 0$

b. $\mathbf{A} = \begin{bmatrix} 8 & 6 \\ 4 & 10 \\ 2 & 7 \end{bmatrix}$, $\mathbf{x} = \begin{bmatrix} x \\ y \end{bmatrix}$, $\mathbf{b} = \begin{bmatrix} 40 \\ 40 \\ 40 \end{bmatrix}$ and $\mathbf{c}' = [2 \ 3]$

Then: maximize $\mathbf{c}'\mathbf{x}$

subject to $\mathbf{Ax} \leqslant \mathbf{b}$

$\mathbf{x} \geqslant \mathbf{0}$

8-20.   a. minimize $0.2x + 0.5y$

subject to: $.1x + .4y \geqslant .4$

$.8x + .6y \geqslant .8$

$.1x \leqslant .1$

$x \geqslant 0$

$y \geqslant 0$

where x = amount of oats (in units of 1000 grams), and

    y = amount of $NK-34$ (in units of 1000 grams).

b. The optimal solution (cost = .52) occurs at $x = .31$ and $y = .92$.

c. The other corner points are $(x = 0, y = 1.33;$ cost = .67) and

    $(x = 1, y = .75;$ cost = .575).

8-23.   maximize $.08x_{WA} + .08x_{WB} + .05x_{PA} + .05x_{PB}$

subject to: $x_{WA} + x_{PA} \leqslant 5000$

$x_{WB} + x_{PB} \leqslant 10{,}000$

$.2x_{WA} - .8x_{WB} \geqslant 0$

$.9x_{PA} - .1x_{PB} \geqslant 0$

$x_{WA} \geqslant 0$

$x_{WB} \geqslant 0$

$x_{PA} \geqslant 0$

$x_{PB} \geqslant 0$

Inequalities 3 and 4 come from:

$$\frac{X_{WA}}{X_{WA} + X_{WB}} \geqslant .8 \ \text{(A tomatoes are 80\% of the total)}$$

$$\frac{X_{PA}}{X_{PA} + X_{PB}} \geqslant .1 \ \text{(A tomatoes are 10\% of the total)}$$

8-25.   16 TV commercials and 20 magazine advertisements

CHAPTER 9

9-2. $\lim\limits_{x \to 1} \left[\dfrac{1-x^2}{2-\sqrt{x^2+3}} \right] = 4$

9-4.   a. $+\infty$ d. 1

      b. 0   e. 1

      c. 1   f. 2.718

9-5. a. .25 or $250

b. $\displaystyle\sum_{n=1}^{5}\left(\frac{1}{2}\right)^n \approx \$969$

c. $\displaystyle\sum_{n=1}^{10}\left(\frac{1}{2}\right)^n - \sum_{n=1}^{5}\left(\frac{1}{2}\right)^n \approx \$30$

9-8. a. $\dfrac{2^{m-1}+3-t2^{m-2}}{2^m}$

b. $= 2$

9-11. a. 0   d. -1
        b. 36   e. 0
        c. 4

9-13. a. 1/2   c. 0
        b. 0   d. 1

9-15. $f(x)$ is not defined at $x = -2$ and $x = 3$.
        At $x = -2$, no limit exists.
        At $x = 3$, $\displaystyle\lim_{x\to3} f(x) = \left(\dfrac{x-2}{x+2}\right) = \dfrac{1}{5}$

9-16. a. 2
        b. 1

9-19. $A \div r$

9-21. Continuous at $x = 1$: a, b, c
        Discontinuous at $x = 1$: d

9-23. a. n
        b. a
        c. 1
        d. No, since the function is defined for only integer values of n.

9-25. Yes.
        An example is $f(x) = \dfrac{(x-2)^2}{x-2}$.

9-27. $y = 6$

9-29. a. The limit does not exist.
        b. 20
        c. 1,000,000
        d. 1,000,000

9-31. $y = 0$

9-33. $\dfrac{(x)^n}{n!}$
        $e^{0.5} = 1.648$
        $e \approx 2.667$

CHAPTER 10

10-2.   Each of these statements gives a rate of change
         a. The rate of change of distance in miles with respect to time in hours
             is 30.
         b. The rate of change of velocity in miles per hour with respect to dis-
             tance in feet is .1; i.e., $(10 - 0) \div 100$.
         c. The rate of change of total reported flu cases with respect to time
             in weeks is 1000.
         d. The rate of change in the number of new cases of flu reported per
             week with respect to time in weeks is zero.

10-3.   a. $r = 30$ $r \equiv$ rate of change in distance in miles with respect
                                to time.
         b. $r = .1$ $r \equiv$ rate of change in velocity in miles per hour with
                                respect to distance in feet.
         c. $r = 1000$ $r \equiv$ rate of change in total reported cases of Asian
                                flu with respect to time in weeks.
         d. $r = 0$ $r \equiv$ rate of change in the number of new cases of
                                Asian flu reported per week.

10-5.   b

10-7.   a. 1000   d. 1100
         b. 1100   e. $S = 18{,}000 + 1100t$
         c. 1000 $\dfrac{dS}{dt} = 1100.$

10-9.   a. slope at $x = -1$ is 3   b. slope at $x = 1$ is 1/2
             slope at $x = 2$ is 12   slope at $x = 4$ is 1/4

10-11.   a. 3.42   c. 3.0
         b. 3.1   d. slope = 3

10-12.   Yes. The derivative of $f(x) = 3x$ is $3 = f'(x)$. The derivative of $f'(x) = 3$
         is 0 using the definition $f'(x) = \lim\limits_{\Delta x \to 0} \left[\dfrac{f(x+\Delta x) - f(x)}{\Delta x} \right]$

10-15.   a. $f''(x) = -12$ c. $f''(x) = 6x$
         b. $f''(x) = 2$ d. $f''(x) = 14$

10-17.   a. 42
         b. 42

10-20.   a. Yes
         b. Yes
         c. No
         d. Yes, since the slope of $f(x)$ is the same on both sides of $x = 1$.

10-22.   a. No.
         b. No. To make it so, let $f(x) = x^2 - 1$ for all x.

10-25. $na_n x^{n-1}$

CHAPTER 11

11-1.   a. $f'(x) = 15x^2, f''(x) = 30x$
      b. $f'(x) = -x^{-2}, f''(x) = 2x^{-3}$
      c. $f'(x) = 24x^5, f''(x) = 120x^4$
      d. $f'(x) = a, f''(x) = 0$
      e. $f'(x) = -abx^{-a-1}, f''(x) = a(a+1)bx^{-a-2}$
      f. $f'(x) = (4a-1)x^{4a-2}, f''(x) = (4a-1)(4a-2)x^{4a-3}$

11-2.   a. $f'(x) = 6 + 6x, f''(x) = 6$
      b. $f'(x) = -x^{-2} + 4x^{-3}, f''(x) = 2x^{-3} - 12x^{-4}$
      c. $f'(x) = 8.1x^2, f''(x) = 16.2x$
      d. $f'(x) = (7/2)x^{5/2} + 7x; f''(x) = (35/4)x^{3/2} + 7$
      e. $f'(x) = a(bx^{b-1} - bx^{-b-1}), f''(x) = ab(b-1)x^{b-2} + (b+1)x^{-b-2})$
      f. $f'(x) = 3x^2 + 6x + 3, f''(x) = 6x + 6$

11-3.   a. $4x^3 + 3x^2$
      b. $(a+b-c)x^{a+b-c-1}$
      c. $-56dx^{-5}$
      d. $-3x^2 + 50x + 26$
      e. $4y + 5$
      f. $bcx^{b-1} + arx^{d-1} + (b+r)x^{b+r-1}$

11-4.   a. $\dfrac{x^2 - 2x}{(x-1)^2}$ d. $\dfrac{a^2 bx^{b-1}}{(a+x^b)^2}$

      b. $\dfrac{-x^2 + 2x}{x^4}$ e. 0

      c. $\dfrac{-1}{(x-2)^2}$ f. $\dfrac{z^2 - 6z + 7}{(z-3)^2}$

11-6.   a. $20(x^2 + 3x - 1)^{19}(2x + 3)$
      b. $-1/2(x^2 + 4x)^{-3/2}(2x+4)$
      c. $3[(y+12)(7y^2-3)]^2(21y^2+168y-3)$
      d. $2/3(7z^6+4z^4+20z^3+6)^{-1/3}(42z^5+16z^3+60z^2)$
      e. $7/6\dfrac{(x^2+3x-2)^{1/6}}{x^2-9} \cdot \dfrac{(-3x^2-14x-27)}{(x^2-9)^2}$

11-11.   a. $\dfrac{2}{x}$

      b. $\dfrac{2x}{x^2} \log_3 e$

      c. $\log_{10} e$

      d. $\dfrac{2x+4}{x^2+4x-7}$

      e. $\dfrac{2x \log_{10} e}{(x^2+1)\ln(x^2+1)}$

11-13.   137.2

11-15. a. 9

   b. 38 million

11-17. a. ≈ 13.5

   b. ≈ 8.5

   c. ≈ 14.1

11-19. 755

11-21. The derivative should be taken with respect to x.

$$\frac{ds}{dx} = \frac{-(ab^x)\ln b}{[k + ab^x]^2}$$

11-23. $\dfrac{20}{9\pi}$

11-25. $\dfrac{dy}{dx} = \dfrac{5 - 2x}{3y^2 - 4}$

11-27. a. 14

   b. 186

CHAPTER 12

12-1. a. At $x = +1$ there is a relative minimum, and at $x = -3$ there is a relative maximum.

   b. At $x = -2$ there is a relative minimum.

12-2. a. At $x = 0$ there is a relative minimum, and at $x = +2$ there is a relative maximum.

   b. At $x = +\sqrt{3/2}$ there is a relative minimum, and at $x = -\sqrt{3/2}$ there is a relative maximum.

12-3. a. The global min is: $f(1/4) = -1/8$.
   The global max is: $f(10) = 190$.

   b. The global max is $f(2) = -1$.
   There is no global min.

   c. The global max is: $f(4) = +7$.
   The global min is: $f(0) = -5$.

12-5. $f(x) = x(x + 2)(x - 2)$, so $f(x) = 0$ at $x = -2, x = 0$ and $x = +2$.
   $f'(x) = 0$ at $x = +2/\sqrt{3}$ and $x = -2/\sqrt{3}$
   $f''(x) = 6x$ so $x = +2/\sqrt{3}$ implies a minimum and $x = -2/\sqrt{3}$ implies a maximum.
   The critical points are: $-2, -2/\sqrt{3}, 2/\sqrt{3}$ and 2.
   The global maximum is: $f(x) = \sqrt{3}\,(16/9)$ at $x = -2/\sqrt{3}$.
   The global minimum is: $f(x) = -\sqrt{3}\,(16/9)$ at $x = 2/\sqrt{3}$.

12-7. 15

12-9. 8 3/4; 8

12-10. He should order 400 units.
   The constraint causes a loss of $900 per year!

12-12. 5

12-14. a. 4.13
      b. 5

12-19. $100\sqrt{6}$ is a *minimum* not a maximum. It is not possible to solve this problem using differential calculus. The solution is to make the stadium as long as possible.

12-22. a. $x = y = 0$, and we have a minumum, since $f(x, y)$ increases as x and y depart from zero.
      b. $x = y = 0$, but we have neither a maximum nor a minimum.

12-25. $p = 20, A = 8\ 1/2$, and the new profit will be lower.

CHAPTER 13

13-2.   a. 3.5   d. 0.245
      b. 1.0   e. 0.085
      c. 0.33

13-3.   The answers are approximately the same as in 13-2.

13-4.
      a. $F(x) = \dfrac{ax^2}{2b} + c$

      b. $F(x) = \dfrac{x^3}{6} - \dfrac{x^2}{2} + c$

      c. $G(y) = -\dfrac{1}{3}(a - y)^3 + c$

      d. $F(x) = \dfrac{x}{x + 1} + c$

          or

          $F(x) = \dfrac{-1}{x + 1} + c$

      (The second answer differs from the first only by the constant $-1 = \dfrac{-(x + 1)}{x + 1}$.)

13-6.   a. $17/12 = 1.416$
      b. 1
      c. $\dfrac{7}{4} = 1.75$

13-8.   a. 3.5   d. $\dfrac{1}{4}$
      b. 1
      c. $\dfrac{1}{3}$ e. $\dfrac{1}{12}$

13-10. 8

13-11. 15

13-12. a. For $t > a/b$, sales will be negative.

b. $\frac{1}{6}(\frac{a^3}{b^2})$

c. 166 2/3

13-16. a. 86

b. 85 1/3

13-20. a. $e^x + c$

b. $\frac{a}{b}e^{bx} + c$

13-21.

a. $\frac{S_0}{a}(e^a - 1)$

b. \$1,105,000

13-24. \$133

CHAPTER 14

14-1.

a. $\frac{2}{5}(4\sqrt{2}) + \frac{1}{2}(4)$

b. $\frac{1}{5} + \frac{3}{8}$

c. $(-x^{-2} - x^4) + c$

14-3. a. 6875   b. 27

14-5.

a. $c = 0$ and $f(x) = \frac{3}{2}x^2 + 4x^3$

b. $f(x) = \frac{7}{2}x^2 + \frac{x^5}{5}$ and both constants are zero.

c. $\frac{x^2}{2} + \frac{x^3}{6} + \frac{x^6}{30}$, and both constants are zero.

14-7. a. 28 1/8 $- 12 \log_4 e$

b. $1/2\, e^{2x} + x + x^{-1} - \log_e x + c$

14-10. $a(\log_e a - 1) = 1$.   By trial and error, $a \approx 3.6$ years.

14-12. \$27,328.

14-13.

a. $\frac{1}{8}e^{4x} + c$

b. $\frac{1}{\log_e 2}(2^b - 2^a)$

c. $e^{x+2} + \frac{x^3}{3} + c$

14-15. Total destruction = total area sprayed, and
Rate of destruction = a, the rate of spray.
Thus:

$$20{,}000 + \int_0^T 1000e^{2t}dt = aT \text{ and}$$

$$1{,}000e^{2t} = a$$

b. By trial and error; we have 2 equations and 2 unknowns, a and T. The solution in the chapter, $T = 1.34$ and $a = 20{,}000$ was close.

14-17.
a. $\dfrac{dN}{dt} = K(P - N)$

b. $N(t) = P - e^{-Kt-c}$, where c is some constant determined from the initial value of N.

14-19.
a. $\dfrac{3}{2}\, e^{(x^2+4)} + c$

b. $\dfrac{2}{9}\,(16\sqrt{2} - 1)$

c. $\dfrac{1}{b(d+1)}\,(a + bx)^{d+1} + c$

14-20.
a. $\dfrac{x(x+2)^3}{2} - \dfrac{(x+2)^4}{12} + c$

b. $x^2 e^x - 2xe^x + 2e^x + c$ (The formula for integration by parts must be applied twice.)

14-23.
a. $a = 2$ or $a = -4$.

b. $b = 20/13$.

c. There are many pairs of values that will work. For example, if we set $a = 0$, then $b = \sqrt{8}$.

CHAPTER 15

15-1.
a. They should choose Investment B since its value exceeds both B's cost and the value of A.

b. namely Investment A.

15-3.
a. To get total sales of 10 (in thousands), a must be $\geqslant 3$. Thus a < 3 will make them abort.

b. $5\dfrac{1}{4}$.

15-4.
a. \$5,474,000

b. \$7,880,000

c. \$10,000,000.

15-6.
a. Investment B

b. Investment A

c. It is impossible to tell without having a discount rate.

15-7.
a. Investment A is preferred.

b. Yes, but it depends on what is done in A in year 6.

15-8. a, b, d, e, f, g, are probability density functions. c and h are not, c because of negative value of $f(x)$, h because it integrates to $\dfrac{1}{24}$.

15-12.
    a. $\dfrac{2}{3}$ d. $\dfrac{1}{2}$

    b. $\dfrac{2}{3}$ e. 0

15-14.   1/2

15-19. $S(t) = e^{a + bt + \frac{c}{2} t^2}$

15-20.   a. $a = 0, b = 1$ and $c = 0$, so $S(t) = e^t$.
           b. $S(t) = e^t = 20$ when $t = 3$.

15-22.
    a. $A = \dfrac{a}{b}$

    b. $A = \dfrac{a}{b}$

    c. $A = \dfrac{ac - 1}{bc}$

15-23.   a. $S(A) = 4 \log_e A + 5$.
           b. Profit as a function of $A = f(A) = p[4 \log_e A + 5] - A$.
           c. $\dfrac{df}{dA} = \dfrac{4p}{A} - 1 = 0$ when $A = 4p$.

CHAPTER 16

16-2.   They are the same set: $S_1 \equiv S_2$.

16-3.   a, b, c, f, g, h are false
           d, e   are true

16-6.   a. $M \subseteq K$ (example: $M = K$)
           b. $M \cap K = \emptyset$ (example: $K = \emptyset$)
           c. Both K and M are the empty set.

16-9.   a. $\{S, F\}$
           b. $\{(S, S), (S, F), (F, S), (F, F)\}$

16-10.   a. $\{1, 0\}$
           b. $\{(S, 1), (F, 0)\}$
           c. $\{2, 1, 0\}$
              $\{((S, S), 2), ((S, F), 1), ((F, S), 1), ((F, F), 0)\}$

16-11.   a. $2^A = \{\{1\}, \{2\}, \{3\}, \{1, 2\}, \{1, 3\}, \{2\ 3\}, A, \emptyset\}$
           b. There are 8.

16-14.   a. 78 percent
           b. Yes. Ninety percent of those with buying intentions did so.
           c. No. $200 \div (180+200)$ or over 50 percent of all purchases were made by those who had no intention to buy. Unless this ratio is stable, such studies would give poor forecasts of total sales.

16-17. a. ∅   c. A
       b. A   d. A

16-18. a. Yes
       b. No

16-19. a. $A = \{x: x \in R, x \neq 0\}$
       b. $A = \{x: x \in R\}$
       c. $A = \{x: x \in R, x \neq -1\}$

16-21. a. $[a; b]$
       b. $[a; c)$
       c. $[b; c)$

16-23. The matchings in parts a and b suggest functions.

16-26. Only parts a, b and e are partitions.

16-27. *Event*
       No. defective

       zero $\{(g,g)\}$
       one $\{(g,d), (d,g)\}$
       second only $\{(g,d)\}$
       first $\{(d,g), (d,d)\}$
       at most one $\{(g,g), (d,g), (g,d)\}$

16-30. a. There would be 36 outcomes.
       b. Yes. It has 36 elements.
       c. $\{1, 2, 3, ..., 12\}$

Index